wish History and Culture

by *Aron Rodrigue and Steven J. Zipperstein*

Stanford Studies in J

EDITI

Sephardism

Spanish Jewish History and the Modern Literary Imagination

Edited by Yael Halevi-Wise

STANFORD UNIVERSITY PRESS

STANFORD, CALIFORNIA

Stanford University Press
Stanford, California

This book has been published with the assistance of the Canadian Social Sciences and Humanities Research Council.

Printed in the United States of America on acid-free, archival-quality paper

Library of Congress Cataloging-in-Publication Data

Sephardism : Spanish Jewish history and the modern literary imagination / edited by Yael Halevi-Wise.

pages cm.–(Stanford studies in Jewish history and culture)

Includes bibliographical references and index.

ISBN 978-0-8047-7746-9 (cloth : alk. paper)

1. Sephardim in literature. 2. Jews, Spanish, in literature. 3. Literature, Modern–History and criticism. I. Halevi-Wise, Yael, 1965- editor of compilation. II. Series: Stanford studies in Jewish history and culture.

PN56.3.S47S48 2012

809'.9335846004924–dc23 2011049959

Typeset by Bruce Lundquist in 10.5/14 Galliard

To Dani,
without whom all this would not have been possible,

To Tali, Stevie, Ari, and Yoni,
without whom it wouldn't have been worth undertaking,

To my mother and father,
whose differences illuminate my understanding of cultures,

And to each of the wonderful friends and collaborators
assembled around these pages,

Above all, to Michael Ragussis (z"l),
who left us, much too early, with a profound intellectual
legacy we are still trying to fathom.

Contents

Contributors

Edna Aizenberg, professor emerita of Hispanic literature at Marymount Manhattan College, has played an instrumental role in the development of Latin American Jewish Studies and the idea of literary sephardism. Her books include *The Aleph Weaver: Biblical, Kabbalistic and Judaic Elements in Borges* (1984), *Parricide on the Pampa? A New Study and Translation of Gerchunoff's Los gauchos judios* (2000), *Books and Bombs in Buenos Aires: Borges, Gerchunoff, and Argentine-Jewish Writing* (2002), and *Contemporary Sephardic Identity in the Americas*, co-edited with Margalit Bejarano (2012).

Stacy N. Beckwith, associate professor of Hebrew and director of Judaic Studies at Carleton College, is the editor of *Charting Memory: Recalling Medieval Spain* (2000). She teaches and lectures widely on portrayals of national history and collective memory in Israeli and Spanish literature, has published on Spanish cinema and religious perspectives in Spanish Jewish fiction, and is currently working on a study of Sephardic themes in modern Spanish literature.

Yael Halevi-Wise, associate professor of English and Jewish Studies at McGill University, is the author of *Interactive Fictions: Scenes of Storytelling in the Novel* (2003) and of many articles on English, Spanish, Latin American, and Hebrew literary history, which have appeared in journals such as *The Dickensian*, *Hispania*, *Jewish Quarterly Review*, and *Prooftexts*. A background in theory of the novel and comparative literature led to her current interest in uses of history among literary works from different periods and national contexts.

Diana R. Hallman, associate professor of musicology at the University of Kentucky, is the author of *Opera, Liberalism, and Antisemitism in Nineteenth-Century France: The Politics of Halévy's "La Juive"* (2007). Her research interests center on French grand opera and nineteenth-century cultural history, as well as the history of American concert life. She is now completing a new book on the turn-of-the-century Austrian-American pianist Fannie Bloomfield Zeisler.

Bernard Horn is professor of English at Framingham State University and author of *Facing the Fires: Conversations with A. B. Yehoshua* (1997). In addition to this foremost critical biography on this Israeli author, he has published journal articles on Yehoshua, as well as on the Hebrew Bible, Herman Melville, and Norman Mailer in *Symposium*, *American Quarterly*, *Shofar*, and other journals. His collection of poems *Our Daily Words* (2010) was named a "Must Read" by the 2011 Massachusetts Book Awards and won the Old Seventy Creek Press Poetry Award.

Dalia Kandiyoti, associate professor of English at the College of Staten Island, City University of New York, is the author of *Migrant Sites: America, Place, and Diaspora Literatures* (2009). She specializes in Diaspora literatures of the Americas, including Latina/o and Jewish writing, contemporary Sephardic literature, and gender studies. Her articles in journals such as *MELUS* and *Modern Fiction Studies* have brought together studies of Latina/o, Latin American, and North American fiction.

The late *Michael Ragussis* was professor of English at Georgetown University. His books *Acts of Naming: The Family Plot in Fiction* (1986), *Figures of Conversion: "The Jewish Question" and England's National Identity* (1995), and *Theatrical Nation: Jews and Other Outlandish Englishmen in Georgian Britain* (2010) have changed the way we interpret the role of minority cultures in British literature. This volume could not have been undertaken without his groundbreaking analysis of ethnicity, religion, and gender in British literature and culture.

Judith Roumani, an independent scholar of comparative literature, editor of the online journal *Sephardic Horizons* (http://sephardichorizons.org), and translator, is the author of *Albert Memmi* (1987). Her essays have appeared in the *Canadian Review of Studies in Nationalism*, *Peamim*,

Philological Quarterly, *Prooftexts*, and *La Lettre Sépharade*, among other journals. Her translation of Renzo De Felice's *Ebrei in un paese arabo (1835–1970)* has been published as *Jews in an Arab Land: Libya, 1835–1970* (1985).

Ismar Schorsch, former chancellor of the Jewish Theological Seminary and Rabbi Herman Abramovitz Professor of Jewish History, has been a leading figure in the study of modern German Jewish history. In that context, he is best known for the essays collected in *From Text to Context: The Turn to History in Modern Judaism* (1994), *Jewish Reactions to German Anti-Semitism, 1870–1914* (1972), and his edited translation, *Heinrich Graetz: The Structure of Jewish History, and Other Essays* (1975). He is currently interested in the interdisciplinary nature of oriental studies in the nineteenth century.

Efraim Sicher, professor of English and comparative literature at Ben-Gurion University of the Negev, is the author of numerous books and articles on Russian, Jewish, and British literature, including *Jews in Russian Literature After the October Revolution* (1995), *Rereading the City/Rereading Dickens* (2003), and *The Holocaust Novel* (2005). He has published widely on modern Jewish culture, dystopia, and nineteenth-century realism. His book *Under Postcolonial Eyes: Figuring the "jew" in Contemporary British Writing* (with Linda Weinhouse) is due out in 2012.

Jonathan Skolnik, assistant professor of German at the University of Massachusetts, Amherst, has published studies on German Jewish cultural history including "Heine and Haggadah: History, Narration, and Tradition in the Age of Wissenschaft des Judentums" (2003), "Writing Jewish History in the Margins of the Weimar Classics: Minority Culture and National Identity in Germany, 1837–1873" (2000), and "Kaddish for Spinoza: Memory and Modernity in Heine and Celan" (1999). He is currently completing a book on the German Jewish historical novel.

Preface

My scholarly interest in sephardism began with a very personal connection when my mother gave me a copy of Rosa Nissán's *Novia que te vea*, and my friend Ileana Lubetzky wondered if I would enjoy this quaint account of growing up as a Ladino speaker in modern Mexico. I too, had grown up in Mexico, though speaking Hebrew rather than Ladino. At one point, however, my Ladino-speaking grandmother came to visit us from Jerusalem, and to our amazement we saw that she could communicate more comfortably with indigenous merchants in the marketplace than with our modern Castilian-speaking friends. This was because her language, like theirs, contained antiquated expressions dating from the time of the conquistadors and the expulsion of the Jews from Spain.

This was my personal eye-opening encounter with Sephardic history, for, in Haifa, where I was born, I had been surrounded by Hungarian-speaking grandparents who had lived through the Holocaust; within my own immediate family, a hodgepodge of languages and cultures reigned; and even around my Sephardic grandparents, Hebrew was the dominant language. Under such conditions, one tends to see the world comparatively—that is, in relation to *other* places, epochs, and peoples. Therefore, as soon as I tasted Nissán's new cultural mixtures, I began to wonder if other Latin American writers had found similar inspiration in Sephardic history and traditions? It turned out that they had, and Latin American sephardism was already an incipient scholarly field led by Edna Aizenberg. So then I began to wonder if other writers *beyond* Latin America had been drawn to examine themselves in relation to Spain's Jews? This book answers such questions, offering not a conventional history of Sepharad but rather a probe into how Sephardic history has been imagined by writers from many different national, ethnic, and religious backgrounds from the nineteenth century to the present.

Unmooring itself from questions of Sephardic identity, this comparative cross-cultural approach to Sephardic history leads us to examine how others identify *themselves* in relation to conflicting ideas about the Sephardic experience. Hence sephardism is defined here as a politicized literary metaphor used by Jewish and gentile novelists, poets, and dramatists from Germany, England, France, the Americas, Israel, and even India to explore their own preoccupations with modern national identity. But why did so many writers and intellectuals from such varied cultural environments choose the multifaceted and conflicted Judeo-Spanish experience to express concerns about minorities and dissidents in modern nations? To what extent does sephardism overlap with orientalism, hispanism, medievalism, and other politicized discourses that grew out of the clash between authoritarian, progressive, and romantic ideologies during the age of modern revolutions? As I began to unravel the impact of Sephardic history on the development of modern genres and modern nationalisms, I came to understand how deeply it has affected personal and collective matters shaping our world to this day.

Detectivesque is the best way to describe the labor that went into assembling the twelve case studies offered in this volume. From locating examples of sephardism in different national traditions to hunting for scholars who could situate these examples within a historical, political, and aesthetic context, I found myself groping for missing pieces of a puzzle that gradually cohered into a picture whose diverse parts relate to one another. Three essays in particular—Ismar Schorsch's "The Myth of Sephardic Supremacy in Nineteenth-Century Germany," Michael Ragussis's "Writing Spanish History in Nineteenth-Century Britain," and Edna Aizenberg's "Sephardim and Neo-Sephardim in Latin American Literature," originally published in completely different contexts and without any knowledge of one another—function as the cornerstones of our volume. They were distributed among all new contributors to establish a common vocabulary, and are gathered here for the first time under the umbrella of sephardism, now complemented by new articles exploring the scope and implications of sephardism as a politicized literary phenomenon.

The principal aim of this book is to offer a conceptual foundation for understanding the phenomenon of sephardism, based on a series of case studies that can be expanded in the future. I believe we cover the leading examples of this phenomenon in Europe, Asia, and the Americas, including several languages and literary traditions. Two more case studies that I had hoped to include and consider necessary, but that unfortunately did not materialize for practical reasons, are an essay on eastern European Yiddish sephardism and another on Ottoman Ladino sephardism. Although both take their cues from German and English sephardism, they each adapt scenes of inquisitorial trials and Sephardic luminaries to reflect their own changing attitudes toward history and modernization throughout the nineteenth century and until the eve of the Holocaust. I am grateful to Joel Berkowitz and Julia Phillips Cohen for sharing these insights with me.

An exceptional aspect of this book has been the high degree of collaboration among its contributors. Over the past ten years, we met at conference panels and roundtables, where together with genuinely supportive audiences, we tried to chart a new approach to Sephardic Studies in ways that rechannel ethnic history into an analysis of how medieval and early modern Iberian history has served as a template and catalyst for the development of literary forms and political ideologies that helped create the modern world. If I occasionally adopt a plural voice in introducing this volume, it is to convey the sense of close collaboration which has accompanied this project all along.

This is a very welcome opportunity to mention the early encouragement of Debbie Castillo, Michael Ragussis (z"l), Aron Rodrigue, and Jonathan Sarna. With uncommon generosity, Darrell Lockhart sent me a working bibliography when I first became interested in the topic. The warm spirit of collegiality that I found at McGill, Cornell, and the Hebrew University enriched this work in ways that cannot be itemized. And this warmth and friendship extends also to meetings with members of the Association of Jewish Studies, LAJSA (Latin American Jewish Studies Association), and the Modern Languages Association's Sephardic Studies Group—among whom Edna Aizenberg, Jonathan Schorsch, Monique Balbuena, and Johann Sadock come especially to mind. For sending me to the needed references, sharing ideas, and generally "being there" as colleagues and friends, I would especially like to thank Stacy Beckwith, Bernie Horn, Dalia Kandiyoti, and Leor Halevi. During its last stages of preparation, the manuscript benefited from valuable feedback from Richard Kagan, Carlos Fraenkel, and above all the anonymous reader for Stanford University Press, whose exceptional care and intelligent advice were much appreciated by all of us. The degree of professionalism at this press has been outstanding at every stage of the book's production.

Claudio Palomares, Louise Larlee, Greg Ellerman, and Hadji Bakara—former graduate students at McGill—worked on this project as research assistants, translators, and editors. Adam Blander did all of the above, functioning as my editorial right hand during the last stages of production; and Brett Hooton—so often and judiciously—lent his invaluable stylistic advice, making the process of assembling this volume significantly easier and also more fun. Finally, it is my pleasant duty to thank the following granting agencies for supporting this project: the Social Science and Humanities Research Council of Canada, the Fonds québecois de la recherché sur la société et la culture, the Memorial Foundation of Jewish Culture, and a Lady Davis Fellowship administered by the Hebrew University, all of which enabled the implementation of a project that could be conducted only through a genuinely comparative and collaborative endeavor.

Y. Halevi-Wise
Montreal, 2011

Sephardism

Introduction: Through the Prism of Sepharad

Modern Nationalism, Literary History, and the Impact of the Sephardic Experience

Yael Halevi-Wise

In 2001, the Spanish novelist Antonio Muñoz Molina published a volume of loosely bound historical vignettes entitled *Sepharad*—a somewhat misleading title, considering that its narratives about communists and Nazis, Holocaust survivors, and unemployed Spaniards ostensibly have little to do with the actual history of Spain's Jews. Although the Sephardic experience occupies a small percentage of Muñoz Molina's book, Sepharad as a concept nonetheless hovers over all its historical junctures, binding them together.

This collection of essays about the history of Spain's Jews likewise focuses on Sepharad from a distance, obliquely, as a prism through which we examine different ways in which creative authors use the history and heritage of Spain's Jews to discuss their own national preoccupations at times of heightened political consciousness. With growing intensity from the end of the eighteenth century onwards, writers with completely different viewpoints from Germany, England, Latin America, North Africa, and even India found in Spain's roller-coaster history a useful metaphor, remarkably well suited to reimagining the image and political status of minorities in competing national agendas.[1] As is generally known, in 1492, the Catholic monarchs Ferdinand and Isabella asserted themselves against eight centuries of Muslim rule in the Iberian Peninsula by establishing a policy of religious homogeneity that unraveled a multicultural balance of power—known as *convivencia*, or cohabitation—which, despite significant caveats, yielded many positive results for all three of the cultures involved, Christians, Muslims, and Jews.[2] The cataclysmic experience of Spain's Jews, who, after enjoying several centuries of (relatively) stable existence in Iberia, were caught up in a hysterical period of mass conversions and inquisitions, followed by a dramatic expulsion, has struck writers from completely different backgrounds—whether Sephardic or Ashknazic, Jewish or gentile—as a useful model for considering their own national and religious reconfigurations.

Although we approach the Sephardic experience obliquely—paying attention to how it has been strategically selected and even willfully misrepresented in interesting ways by writers from different backgrounds in a variety of times and places—our collection nevertheless remains grounded in the specific history and heritage of Spain's Jews and conversos.[3] It thus differs from Muñoz Molina's attitude to Sepharad as a universal symbol of deracination and exile, so that from our point of view, Muñoz Molina's perspective becomes one possible variation of a phenomenon whose roots go back to the Enlightenment's attempts to reevaluate common attitudes to religion, ethnic minorities, and absolute forms of government.

Historical romances, which placed cultural identities in a comparative and historicized perspective, became the principal vehicles for the kind of politically engaged representations of Sepharad discussed in these pages. Primarily novelists, but also librettists, poets, and dramaturges, in the aftermath of the French Revolution and the Napoleonic Wars became increasingly interested in showing how social systems that had reigned in the past could be reconfigured in relation to new attitudes toward the rights and responsibilities of states and individuals in modern polities. In this context, the cataclysmic experience of Spain's Jews at the end of the Middle Ages, turned into a model—occasionally even a gimmick—found to be especially good to think about when mulling over the birth and characteristics of modern nations.[4]

By the end of the eighteenth century, the clash between Enlightenment values and theocratic absolutism led to political platforms increasingly conceived not as God-given but rather as freely chosen according to rational principles. The status of all minorities, and notably that of Jews, then turned into an issue of widespread concern to writers, philosophers, and statesmen who sought to reconfigure a medieval society of orders into pluralistic nations governed according to modern ideas of progress. How to treat the Jews "rationally" became a major bone of contention at this time.[5] And in an attempt to reevaluate old patterns of social relations between Jews and gentiles, the history of

Sepharad stood out as a particularly useful trope. Liberal intellectuals writing in the wake of the French Revolution regarded the theocratic absolutism that Spain chose at the end of the fifteenth century as a stark counterexample to the doctrine of religious tolerance that they were promoting. Spain and Portugal under the shadow of the Inquisition thus became a popular background for assessing different conceptions of sudden alienation, religious persecution, and split identity, projected into dramatic scenes of ruptured harmony, expulsion, inquisitorial trials, and marranism. To illustrate sephardism's literary and political characteristics, this introductory essay surveys such dramatic scenarios in the context of the Enlightenment's attitudes to despotism, and especially in the context of the cultural discourses that began to emerge from a counterclash between Enlightenment and romantic ideologies. This conflict between progressive and pluralistic agendas continues to generate tensions within liberal Western ideologies to this day.

Before launching into this historical survey, however, it is important to underscore in view of the current academic focus of Sephardic Studies, that until recently, the kind of sephardism examined here was found less in writings by Sephardim than in historical novels by Ashkenazi and gentile authors with no biographical links to Sepharad. Genealogical connections to Spain are therefore irrelevant to this study, except in those instances where Sephardic writers such as A. B. Yehoshua or Yehuda Burla deliberately use Sephardic history or their Sephardic heritage to promote cultural visions linked to their own ethnic backgrounds.

Discussions of actual Sephardic identity and its expedient appropriation are, of course, integral to most essays in this volume, as for example in Bernard Horn's analysis of Yehoshua's sephardism and Stacy Beckwith's assessment of Burla's modern Zionist Sephardic position. Yet even Horn's analysis of Sephardic elements in A. B. Yehoshua's novels positions this prominent Israeli author *away* from any narrow allegiance to his Sephardic ethnicity and stresses instead that Yehoshua's sephardism functions as an imaginative conceptual platform from which he promotes conversations across cultural barriers in ways that insist on sympathy for, and also from, other ethnicities, religions, and nations.

In our current cultural environment, it is rather to be expected that Sephardim would write historical sagas about their own "lineage"—and they do. The above-mentioned chapters attest to many such examples.

However, this volume as a whole stresses an *unlikely* fascination with the history and heritage of Spain's Jews among writers from a wild variety of backgrounds: For why in the world should a Scotsman like Walter Scott or a British Indian fabulist with a fatwa on his head like Salman Rushdie concern themselves with Sephardic history? And why should the historical problems of Spain's conversos bother Homero Aridjis, a Mexican poet of Greek background, whose personal lineage bears no ostensible relationship to Sepharad? Here we are therefore less intrigued by the ethnic identity of Sephardim themselves than by the agendas of writers from diverse faiths, ethnicities, and national backgrounds who deliberately use the theme of Sepharad as a metaphor—as Edna Aizenberg has put it succinctly—through which to express ongoing preoccupations with political diversity in a variety of environments.

To define the scope of this project, we must therefore distinguish between sephardism as an expression of Sephardic ethnic identity and sephardism as a wider vehicle for representations of modern nationalism and postnationalism. In "Disappearing Origins: Sephardic Autobiography Today" (2007), Jonathan Schorsch confronts this issue head-on by confining his analysis of representations of Sephardic history to memoirs and autobiographical novels "by Jews who are not Ashkenazic"—an entirely justified choice in this case, given the extensive multilingual and international scope of this material alone.[6] George Zucker similarly decided to focus on Sephardim as an ethnic group in *Sephardic Identity: Essays on a Vanishing Jewish Culture* (2005).[7] However, if we deliberately move beyond Sephardic identity to consider the impact of Sephardic history on a variety of ethnic, religious, and national identities, how does our approach remain engaged with the sociology, folklore, and history of Sephardim and Mizrahim? For one thing, any comparative discussion of sephardism must rest on the bedrock of such research on Sepharad and Sephardim in order to anchor itself in a concrete knowledge of their history and heritage.[8] It can in turn enrich Sephardic Studies by demonstrating that Sepharad occupies a far more central position within Western culture than has generally been realized. That the Sephardic experience exerted considerable impact on literary history, modern nationalism, and the general development of modernity is something that scholars of Jewish Studies have increasingly acknowledged.[9] Yet only a wider awareness of sephardism as a politicized literary metaphor can carry this awareness over to fields that intersect with Jewish Studies by showing that changing political epistemologies were negotiated in the modern imagination through a widespread interest, and occasionally even an obsession with Jews in general, and with Sephardic history in particular.

So how have creative writers imagined the Sephardic experience? What political and literary pressures have prompted their representations? What are they reacting against? To put it schematically: what exactly has been told, by whom, to whom, when, and where? To begin answering these questions—or at least give them some conceptual foundation and bibliographic coordinates—we offer twelve case studies of sephardism as a politicized literary phenomenon in key examples ranging from Germany, France, and England in the nineteenth-century to Latin America, North America, North Africa, and Asia in the twentieth- and twenty-first centuries. We approach sephardism as a form of literary expression that functions politically during heightened moments of historical consciousness in diverse national contexts. To keep our volume focused, we privilege historical fiction and drama over other forms of cultural expression such as historiography, folklore, or film, but this focus in not monolithic. We open, for instance, with Ismar Schorsch's identification of a German Jewish obsession with Sepharad among four interrelated venues of cultural expression: historical fiction, architecture, historiography, and liturgy.

The truth is that categorizations of all kinds tend to crumble when approached through the prism of sepharad: one religion folds into another, national boundaries are brushed aside in favor of supranational alliances, ethnic history intertwines with political history, and any series of historical events involving the Inquisition or the expulsion functions like a ready-made plot in a medieval setting. Sephardism is hence perfectly positioned to reconfigure conventional markers of identity by unsettling them through historical counterpoints: if Spain at the end of the Middle Ages tried to abolish religious pluralism, British novelists in the middle of the nineteenth century could use Sepharad either to promote ethnic diversity or to prove its undesirability; while a Marrano's identity could stand for treacherous falsity in one novel, in another it could symbolize a positive badge of steadfastness pushed to the point of martyrdom or a sign of persistent multiculturalism in the face of persecution. And recent cases of sephardism written from a postcolonial perspective enjoin us to altogether reconsider categories of ethnic identity and national politics. For example, the U.S. Latina novels that Dalia Kandiyoti analyzes blend Latin-American folklore into a North American platform of pluralism in ways that render obsolete traditional differences between Jews, Catholics, Hispanics, and Native Americans by historicizing them all through a Sephardic matrix.

Since sephardism functions as a politicized literary discourse, to trace its literary history is to dwell at least to some extent on the political histories of its different manifestations. This intimate link between literature and politics is illustrated most poignantly in two of our main examples—one from Victorian England in the middle of the nineteenth century and the other from Argentina after the fall of the military junta in 1983. The first example relates to Benjamin Disraeli, a convert from Judaism who became Queen Victoria's favorite prime minister; the second involves Marcos Aguinis, a patriotic Argentinean neurosurgeon, psychoanalyst, political analyst, and prize-winning novelist, who from the platform of his Jewish background has written extensively about Argentina's prospects as a democratic nation. Within their entirely different national and personal contexts, Disraeli and Aguinis participated vigorously in the most important political reconfigurations of their countries, while simultaneously writing best-selling novels depicting the history of the Jews of Spain and its colonies as a cultural model, against which their own societies were invited to reinterpret themselves.

As Michael Ragussis demonstrates, Disraeli's public image was intimately linked to Sephardic history, not only because he felt proud of his Sephardic heritage and "imbedded stories of Jewish persecution and flight under the Inquisition in an extremely popular series of novels," but also because he himself was eventually subjected "to the charge of crypto-Judaism."[10] Sephardic heritage remained a badge of distinction for Disraeli, which he hoped would help make the public admire him, though the public was often ambivalent.

Marcos Aguinis likewise linked Sephardic history to his country's democratization process. After serving as secretary of culture, he published a highly acclaimed historical novel, *La gesta del marrano* (1991), which details the operations of the Inquisition in colonial Latin America as a way of bringing Latin Americans to realize that their current difficulties with democracy and pluralism are in part ingrained in the continent's cultural heritage, as Edna Aizenberg shows in this volume.

Whether it seeks to promote nationalism, or to unhinge it, as in the postmodern and postcolonial cases examined by Dalia Kandiyoti and Efraim Sicher, sephardism tends to operate in the junctures between political systems. Its heroes and heroines are usually on the move, crossing borders. In fact, among the creators of sephardism, we find many figures of in-betweenness, such as the octoroon playwright Victor Séjour, who traveled from Louisiana to Paris in the nineteenth century to stage a play about Spanish conversos, or intellectuals from around the Mediterranean who immigrated to Paris during the second half of the twentieth century, rekindling the buzz about marranism, as Judith Roumani shows regarding the idea of Sepharad among overlapping generations of francophone Jewish writers.

Spain's roller-coaster history at the end of the Middle Ages offers a malleable model that adapts itself quite conveniently to the various interests and levels of historical awareness of different authors. But when we assess discrepancies between historical data on Sepharad and these literary representations, we must also take into account that historians themselves have sometimes been ideologically tendentious, and that writers of fiction have sometimes tried to correct this. In *The Vale of Cedars* (1850), for example, Grace Aguilar sought to correct an influential account of the Spanish Inquisition written by John Stockdale, who systematically occluded the fact that throughout its four hundred years of operation, the Spanish Inquisition's primary targets had been descendants of Jews. Stockdale's history had been written to reinforce the Protestant character of the British nation at a time when Catholics and Jews were hoping for enfranchisement. Stockdale, as Michael Ragussis shows, preferred to keep both of these groups out of his nation, and so, in writing about the Inquisition, he tried to set Anglicans against Catholics without enfranchising Jews.

A stranger divergence from historical data occurs in Heinrich Heine's misrepresentation of Isaac Abarbanel, generally considered to be an icon of Jewish steadfastness at the time of the expulsion of the Jews from Spain. Heine, however, turned him into a wishy-washy "nephew" who has little in common with the historical Abarbanel. As Jonathan Skolnik explains, Heine's view of Abarbanel did not derive just from the poet's own intimate experience with assimilation and conversion: it also reflects an unfortunate scarcity of historical data at a time when Heine's peers in the Verein für Cultur und Wissenschaft der Juden (Society for Jewish Culture and Science) were just beginning to assemble the body of scholarship that later became the basis for modern scholarship on Jewish topics. Skolnik's essay thus reveals that one *can* learn history from Heine's unfinished historical novel *Der Rabbi von Bacherach* (*The Rabbi of Bacherach*) (1824–40), but in this case it is primarily the history of Heine's dilemmas in their contemporary context rather than Sephardic history per se.

On the other hand, many works of literary sephardism do offer accurate representations of the Sephardic experience in ways that both complement and enhance reliable historiographic sources. Homero Aridjis's description of the conversionist mobs of 1391 and Marcos Aguinis's portrayal of the Inquisition's inner mechanisms especially come to mind in this respect. Yet even in the hands of the most scrupulous and knowledgeable historical novelists, who spend months poring over archival material, all portrayals of Sephardic history are necessarily selective because of the aesthetic and structural conventions of literary plots and the extraordinary length and diversity of the Sephardic experience. Elena Romero's complaint that Ladino publications on Spanish topics dwell disproportionately on expulsion and inquisition, rather than on Sephardic luminaries or on Spain as a country in its own right,[11] makes sense when we keep in mind that the full spectrum of the Sephardic experience really does span periods of *convivencia* as well as inquisition, and that even the impressive creative output of Jews, Muslims, and Christians before the expulsion pales in comparison to the Golden Age of Spanish literature that followed the expulsion, in which converso authors and translators played a significant role both within Spain and abroad.

Sepharad Among the -isms

Sephardism as a politicized literary device belongs to a family of cultural discourses that from the end of the eighteenth century, and with renewed intensity in our own times, has tended to compare historical periods, ethnicities, and nations with an eye to reassessing ideas about national reform and progress. Like its cousins medievalism, hispanism, and orientalism, the discourse of sephardism grew out of a tension between the Enlightenment's desire to reexamine all that had been thought in the past, and romanticism's distrust of the Enlightenment's idea of progress, which it sought to soften and even bypass by noting commonalities among different cultures and historical periods. One point of contact between the Enlightenment's call for change and romanticism's penchant for mythologization plays itself out in their mutual fascination with the Middle Ages as a counterpoint to modernity and progress.

As Howard Bloch and Stephen Nichols stress in *Medievalism and the Modernist Temper* (1996), "modernism was the hidden agenda of medieval studies. . . . The modern was a way of distinguishing between what was current and what was old or ancient . . . 'les anciens contre les modernes.'" An ostensible obsession with history thus operated "in the service of the present"—whether the present was perceived as already superior or in need of urgent repair.[12] Within literary history, sephardism's kinship with medievalism becomes particularly apparent in the Gothic novel. Often set in Spain or the Mediterranean, and regularly featuring Jews, though rarely in a positive light, the Gothic novel favored descriptions of inquisitorial dungeons and torture chambers, depicted as a threat against which modern forms of authority were implicitly compared.[13]

Sephardism of course intersects widely with orientalism as well, for both these discourses stereotype members of another race, faith, or ethnicity as a means of defining the self by comparison. Edward Said famously defined this type of rhetoric as a Western strategy for coming to terms with the Orient by aggressively misrepresenting Arab and Muslim cultures in order to dominate them.[14] Dovetailing with such politicized attempts to mythologize "the Arab," sephardism likewise sets out to assess and reconfigure "the Jew," whether s/he is conceived as an exotic Oriental hailing from another time and place or as an integral but nonetheless estranged participant in the development of Western culture.[15] However, sephardism is not only a type of orientalism: it is also a generator and catalyst for modern notions of the Orient. In *History: Remembered, Recovered, Invented* (1987), Bernard Lewis notes that the nineteenth century's rediscovery of Al-Andalus emerged from a wider "cult of Spain, which formed an important component of the romantic movement."[16] Muslim and Jewish historians then united to minimize the negative aspects of Muslim rule in the Iberian Peninsula, stressing instead its periods of successful multiculturalism. This idealization of Islamic tolerance (which, in this volume, Ismar Schorsch discusses in relation to a broader German Jewish complex of Sephardic supremacy), was fostered particularly by nineteenth-century German Jewish scholars, "who used it as a stick with which to beat their Christian neighbours."[17]

But among the politicized literary discourses that emerged in the nineteenth century, hispanism is no doubt sephardism's closest relative. One might even say that sephardism is a branch of hispanism, since representations of Jews or conversos in medieval or early modern Spanish settings appear whenever there is a larger interest in Spanish history, but the reverse does not necessarily follow. Thus, Alberto Gerchunoff's appropriation of a Sephardic heritage for himself and his peers in 1910, within the framework of Argentina's centennial celebration of its independence from Spain, corresponds to a general period of Latin American rapprochement with the mother country after a century of wariness.[18] In contrast, sephardism had an unusually low profile in France, although hispanism flourished there throughout the nineteenth century.[19] Victor Hugo's *Notre-Dame de Paris* (1831)—that delectable historical novel about Paris in the Middle Ages, better known as *The Hunchback of Notre Dame*—places an inquisitorial trial at the center of its plot, as does Walter Scott's influential *Ivanhoe*. However, Hugo replaces *Ivanhoe*'s Jewess with a gypsy named Esmeralda; through her he activates both the "black" and "white" legends associated with Spain—an inquisitorial torture chamber and an eroticized flamenco-dancing gypsy with a Spanish name. Thus, an orientalized hispanism undoubtedly operates here, but since Hugo makes no reference to a Jewish subject, there is no sephardism.

Notwithstanding this last example, hispanism, medievalism, judaism, and orientalism were frequently intertwined in the cultural imaginations of nineteenth-century intellectuals, as demonstrated in the following remark by a Harvard professor of modern languages who, upon travelling to Spain in 1878, found it to be "as *primitive* in some ways as the books of *Moses* and as *oriental*."[20] The broadened definition of hispanism proposed by Richard Kagan—not only a "study of the language, literature, and history of Spain by foreigners," but also an analysis of "studies in Spanish art, music, and folklore"[21]—dovetails with George Zucker's definition of Sephardic Studies as an academic endeavor that has been pursued for centuries, but has only recently been recognized as an academic field of inquiry: "The field, like the Sephardim themselves, refuses to be bound by limits set by outsiders—in this case disciplinary limits. The inherently interdisciplinary nature of Sephardic Studies . . . [ranges] from historical and sociological studies through Sephardic philosophy, language, literature, and the performing arts."[22]

William Prescott's famous remark in 1837 that "English writers have done more for the illustration of Spanish history than for that of any other, except their own," which opens Michael Ragussis's study of Victorian representations of the Inquisition (in this volume), can be best understood in relation to a nineteenth-century ideology in which sephardism and hispanism vitally intersected.[23] Both these cultural discourses, along with medievalism and orientalism, emerged from the romantic movement's desire to *reconsider* the Enlightenment's revision of the past as a counterpoint to the present. Whereas for some writers, Spain symbolized religious fanaticism, a preindustrial resistance to modernity, and an opposition to progress, for others—particularly in Germany, looking toward Spain in opposition to France—"Spain was becoming the country of romantic yearning . . . [there was a] reversal of traditional attitudes towards Spain . . . motivated by a desire to seek an alternative to the cultural and literary values propagated by the enlightenment."[24] Even today, subtle differences within *liberal* Western ideologies continue to unfold through this tension between the Enlightenment's notion of progress and romanticism's idealization of cultural differences; the Jews' status sits uncomfortably in the midst of this crux.

The literary representation of cultural and historical differences that emerged from this tension—widely disseminated, as we shall shortly see, through Walter Scott's historical romances—took the shape of sephardism, hispanism, orientalism, and medievalism, with a growing crescendo toward the middle of the nineteenth century. Like orientalism, sephardism sets up a horizontal comparison between two or more cultures, but like medievalism or a historicized hispanism, it also goes "down into history" (as Judith Roumani puts it), to construct a "vertical" comparison between cultures in different epochs.

From its beginnings, no matter whether it took the form of warning scenes of persecution or idealized visions of *convivencia*, sephardism tended to examine the consequences of political change at a time when change had become expected and possible in an age of revolutions. In this sense, sephardism participates in what Susannah Heschel calls "Jewish Studies as Counterhistory": an expanded and refined awareness of ideological positions not only within Judaism but also within all the cultural positions with which Judaism intersects. As Heschel notes, Jewish scholars have been investigating and criticizing the construction of Judaism and its politics for over a century, but have yet to develop a concerted response to a "master narrative of Western history, which is rooted in traditions of Christian religious supremacy."[25] By positioning representations of Judaism among intersecting representations of orientalism, hispanism, and medievalism, we can identify recurrent attitudes toward Jews and Jewish history in Western culture, and in this manner contribute to the counterhistorical enterprise that Heschel advocates.

Seminal projects such as Garb and Nochlin's *The Jew in the Text* (1995); Cheyette and Marcus's *Modernity, Culture and 'the Jew'* (1998); Galchinsky, Biale, and Heschel's *Insider/Outsider (1998)*; and Sander Gilman's many volumes on self-constructions and representations of Jews have established a critical set of parameters through which to discuss the complicated attitudes that have shaped representations of Jews and Judaism in Western culture.[26] With the advantage of being relatively more focused on a single, albeit complex, historical paradigm, this volume similarly brings forward the multivalanced cultural perspectives of creative writers who have emphasized different aspects of Spanish Jewish history to express their particular visions of national identity and progress. Thus, issues that are vital for understanding evolving Western ideologies of multicultural legitimacy and national identity can be productively observed across sephardism's thematic and political spectrum. This is especially true regarding representations of conversos or Marranos, for if Jews in general "occupy a position of ambivalence and ambiguity that functions as a kind of counterhistory to the multicultural account of the West," as Heschel underscores,[27] then the alleged dynamism of the Marrano—one of sephardism's main constructs, discussed later in some detail—typifies this conceptual ambiguity by functioning as a sign of persistent multiculturalism within all sorts of competing national particularisms in the modern world.

Charting Sephardism's Literary and Political History

If we chart the most prominent cases of sephardism between 1800 and 2010 by their dates and places of publication, we notice two principal clusters (see figure on next page).

The first cluster occurs in England and Germany during the first half of the nineteenth century, and the second globally toward the last two decades of the twentieth century. In between, Alberto Gerchunoff and his neo-Sephardic Argentinean friends remind us of the physical transition between Europe and colonial environments, into which Old World literary and ideological models were imported. North African francophone writers similarly draw our attention to a converse movement of postcolonial subjects toward Europe. And the interruption of publications in Yiddish and Ladino in large centers of Jewish life such as Warsaw and Salonika marks the obliteration of these communities during the Holocaust.

With mounting insistence toward the middle of the nineteenth century, sephardism took the shape of historical romances responding to the new possibilities of political change made possible by an age of revolutions. Even more than the Dutch Republic's informal doctrine of tolerance during the seventeenth century, or the United States Constitution of 1787, the French Revolution's legislation of freedom of thought and civic equality at the end of the eighteenth century struck intellectuals across Europe and Latin America as an antithesis to the religious and political totalitarianism Spain had legislated at the end of the fifteenth century—and, as demonstrated by Prescott's remark, intellectuals in the United States likewise conceived of their own modernizing values in opposition to Spain. Whether they viewed these revolutionary developments with admiration or horror, writers across Europe and the Americas felt impelled to examine their own political identities and national prospects in light of modern possibilities of political reform, social liberalism, and religious emancipation. This imaginative impulse redoubled during the liberal revolutions of 1848 known as the Spring of Nations, when so many revolutionary groups around Europe tried to abolish absolutist regimes. The first wave of historical romances, operas, plays, and epic poems featuring the history of Sepharad took shape in this heady climate of political ferment and ideological transition.

	1800	1810	1820	1830	1840	1850	1860	1870	1880	1890	1900	1910	1920	1930	1940	1950	1960	1970	1980	1990	2000	2010
France	•						•											•		•		
England			•	•	•	•	•															
Germany			•	•	•	•	•															
E. Europe									•					•								
Turkey									•											•		
Argentina												•	•							•		
Brazil																			•			
Mexico																		•	•			•
N. Africa													•					•	•			
Israel																•			•	•	•	
Spain																		•			•	•
USA				•																•	•	•
India																				•		

Figure 1. Sephardism in Modern World Literature

NOTE: This figure marks significant examples of sephardism in modern world literature, many of which are explored at length in this book. A comprehensive list of titles, dates, and places of publication appears in the selected bibliography.

The second wave of sephardism occurred globally—though it emerged most innovatively from postcolonial environments—during what we may call an Autumn of Nations shaped by new attitudes toward the expression of ethnic identities frustrated with democratic and pluralistic platforms judged as still incompletely or erroneously achieved. We can point to the French Revolution in 1789 as the main cultural milestone to which sephardism reacted in the nineteenth century; the 1992 quincentennial commemorations of Columbus's discovery of America, concomitantly with the fall of Granada and the expulsion of the Jews from Spain, can be similarly identified as the central cultural event around which sephardism rallied at the end of the twentieth century. Widespread commemorations of that first meeting between Europe and America, and the renewed attention paid to Spain's multicultural heritage, generated at the end of the twentieth century what one scholar called "an ocean of print."[28] Also situated conspicuously at the end of a millennium, the 1992 quincentennial facilitated a period of heightened cultural introspection during which intellectuals and political activists called for greater pluralism and democratization in ways that question and challenge the political configurations of European and American nationalism over a century and a half earlier.

But if from the point of view of sephardism's political history, it is crucial to recognize the cultural resonance of 1789 as an antithesis to 1492, both in regard to the rise of historical fiction in general and the flourishing of sephardism in particular, then from the narrower point of view of sephardism's literary history, it is equally crucial to acknowledge the impact exerted by Walter Scott's *Ivanhoe* (1820) on the popularization of a historicized attitude toward national development via the new medium of the historical novel.[29] In fact, as soon as *Ivanhoe* made its appearance, it was translated and disseminated throughout Europe and the Americas to unflagging appeal over the course of a century.[30] As Michael Ragussis notes, it not only became the basis for England's vision of its own medieval past, but through countless imitations and adaptations, was also the primary literary model for historicized depictions of ethnic, racial, and religious cultural relations within many other nations emerging or reconfiguring themselves anew at this time.[31] Perhaps more than any other single literary artifact, *Ivanhoe*'s implicit romantic criticism of its own era's presumption of historical progress cohered and popularized a modernizing sense of historical consciousness that had been brewing in the Western world since the Enlightenment.

What Will Future Ages Think?

As Michael Ragussis explains in detail, *Ivanhoe* overturned a "conventional model of national identity based on racial homogeneity, with a countermodel in which the [medieval] intermixture between Saxons and Normans becomes the basis of cultural diversity and national identity in England."[32] Walter Scott furthermore reminded his readers that Saxons and Normans were not the only protagonists of England's medieval history; Jews, expelled in 1290 and gradually tolerated again from the time of Oliver Cromwell in the seventeenth century, were also a part of England's cultural identity. Without explicitly mentioning the expulsion of 1290, Scott hinges his plot on the plight of a Jewish maiden, Rebecca, whom the reader—according to the conventions of romance—expects will marry the hero, so that they can live happily ever after in Merry England. Yet, instead, she leaves the land of Albion for Al Andalus's shores after nearly being burned at the stake for witchcraft.

By deliberately circumventing the conventional ending of romances, Scott drives home the point that English identity "was founded in racial expulsion as well as inclusion." He thereby rewrites English history as Anglo-Jewish history, setting up an introspective comparison between nations: for in choosing Muslim Spain over Christian England, Rebecca declares that "less cruel are the cruelties of the Moors unto the race of Jacob than the cruelties of the Nazarenes of England."[33] This famous remark of Rebecca's initiated an entire line of historical romances that traced a comparative history of religious persecutions in England and Spain: a critical tool that became useful not only for constructing English identity in relation to other European national identities, as Ragussis shows, but also for constructing a modern sense of historical consciousness suited to imaginative reconfigurations of national identity according to pluralistic, democratic, and secularized approaches to the status of minorities, as each chapter in this book demonstrates in a different way.

Scott hints that *if* England had once reconfigured itself into a homogeneous type of nation, it could just as well reconfigure itself again into another, more pluralistic type; or perhaps he merely shows that there are limits to how pluralistic a nation can be. At any rate, this Scotsman reminded his English readers that they had to face their own history of intolerance, prodding them to reconsider their pride in thinking about themselves as a progressive nation, and furthermore prompting comparisons not only between medieval England and Muslim Spain (and thus implicitly between Catholic Spain and Protestant England), but also between France, which had emancipated its Jews in 1790-91, and England, which by 1819 definitely had not.[34] Thus in *Ivanhoe,* the Templar's exasperated plea to dissuade his medieval contemporaries from burning Rebecca at the stake encapsulates Scott's plea to assess one's values in the present both in light of the past and in view of the future: "Will future ages believe that such stupid bigotry ever existed?" the Templar asks in his medieval setting.[35] Through the medium of historical romance, Scott imprinted this sense of historical perspectivism upon his contemporaries and on the generations that followed.

As many of the essays assembled here make clear, nineteenth-century sephardism exhibits a persistent indebtedness to *Ivanhoe*. Among historical novels written today, the debt to Scott no longer operates as directly, though new experiments with historical fiction still reconfigure narrative conventions established via Scott's model.[36] In the following chapters, we deal at length with several postmodern historical novels, such as Salman Rushdie's *The Moor's Last Sigh* (1996), Kathleen Alcalá's *Spirits of the Ordinary* (1997), and Moacyr Scliar's *The Strange Nation of Rafael Mendes* (1983), all of which mix new genres and cultural perspectives into the historical novel's conventional form, but still, like *Ivanhoe*, rely on Spanish Jewish history as a rehabilitative counterpoint for the construction of hybrid identities in a multicultural environment. This dimension was not obvious to György Lukács when he outlined the characteristics of the historical novel according to Scott's model, but it is a dimension we must now take into consideration when we examine the history of this genre.

One additional point that needs to be made here about Scott's representation of Jews in *Ivanhoe*—a point crucial for understanding the wider context of sephardism's literary history—is Scott's own indebtedness to *The Merchant of Venice*. Shakespeare's play in fact mediated *most* representations of Jews in literary works from the romantic era to the beginning of the twentieth century; in some instances, as in Rushdie's *The Moor's Last Sigh*, it continues to operate as a direct cultural subtext for literary representations of Jews until today.[37] But although, on its own, Shakespeare's tragicomedy does not function as an example of sephardism (because it does not deal specifically with Sephardic history even when one notes that Venetian Jews were usually of Sephardic extraction),[38] the pervasiveness of its plot scheme—which portrays a moral and material rivalry between Jews and Christians, and the dilemma of a Jewish maiden torn between allegiance to her father and attraction to a Christian suitor—undoubtedly precedes *Ivanhoe* among the most influential antecedents to modern literary sephardism.

Antecedents and Precursors: A Brief Literary History

A bird's-eye view of sephardism draws our attention, as mentioned, to two main clusters congregating around 1848 and 1992, both of which are high points in the development of the historical novel.[39] The literary history of sephardism as a politicized metaphor begins much earlier, though, far before the publication of *Ivanhoe* in 1820, or the extensive influence exerted by *The Merchant of Venice* on romantic representations of Jews. Sephardism may have flourished in England and Germany during the Spring of Nations in the middle of the nineteenth century, but its seeds were planted over a century earlier, especially in the Netherlands and France during the Enlightenment. One can also make a strong case for locating the origins of sephardism in the Iberian Peninsula itself, both in literature composed during the medieval period under Islamic dominance and in the baroque period under Catholic rule, as discussed further below.

From where, then, should we actually begin to tell the story of literary sephardism? Should we start with the dichotomy voiced by the medieval Andalusian poet Yehuda Halevi, who felt such a contradiction between his heart in the East (Jerusalem) and his body in the West (Sepharad) that he undertook the perilous journey eastward, as Stacy Beckwith describes in this volume by analyzing how Yehuda Burla, an Israeli writer from the 1950s, reimagines Halevi's journey in a modern Zionist context?[40] We could also point to premodern instances of sephardism in elegies written to memorialize Jews massacred in Spain during the conversionist hysteria of 1391.[41] Moving on to early modern England, one finds the rather gruesome example of Christopher Marlowe's *The Jew of Malta* (1590), where the Jew Barabas gets boiled alive in a cauldron in the context of a martial conflict between Spain and the Ottoman Empire. Unlike *The Merchant of Venice*, Marlowe's play engages explicitly with both Spain and Jews in a manner that situates his English audience within a competitive forum that includes Spaniards, Jews, and Turks. Central features of Marlowe's and Shakespeare's plays—as well as of *The Jewess of Toledo* (1617) by the Spanish dramaturge Lope de Vega—would be later ironized and joined together in Eugène Scribe and Fromental Halévy's opera *La Juive* (1835), as Diana Hallman observes in this volume.[42] As already noted, moreover, *The Merchant of Venice* (ca. 1596), which was likely conceived as a response to Marlowe,[43] has functioned as the most common subtext for general representations of Jewish subjects since the romantic era.

Among plays and novels by seventeenth-century converso authors who made their way to the Netherlands, one finds further precursors to modern literary sephardism in rebuttals and adaptations of anti-Semitic works by Spanish authors such as Francisco de Quevedo and Lope de Vega.[44] This importation of Spain's Golden Age literature deep into Europe contributed to the creation of a Dutch Republic of Letters, whose insistence on rationality fostered enlightenment values throughout Europe and the Americas.[45] It is in this vein that Rebecca Goldstein's *Betraying Spinoza* (2006), which I discuss in the postscript to this volume, can be said to grow out of modernizing seeds scattered across the world as a result of Spain's reconfiguration at the end of the Middle Ages.[46]

Indeed, from a literary historical perspective, sephardism's most vital roots come from the rich body of literature invented in Spain itself by both New and Old Christians during the two centuries that followed the cataclysmic events of 1492. One could even argue, as some scholars have done, that latent ethnic strife in Spain during the sixteenth and seventeenth centuries led to the development of the modern novel as an expression of an irreconcilable tension between individuals and society. I am thinking especially of the first picaresque novels that cast the converso's plight into the fictional confession of an orphan narrator, who explains how he became a criminal in order to survive in a cruel, hypocritical environment. As I show in a chapter devoted to the picaresque novel, late twentieth-century Latin American authors have now begun to historicize the picaresque genre to exhume from it the converso's predicament. Yet in so doing, they actually turn the history of the novel inside out: for here we have an instance of postmodern Latin American novelists reconfiguring the medieval picaresque according to modern literary techniques such as psychological realism and historical romance, in order to depict an ethnic conflict that contributed to the invention of the picaresque itself at the very beginning of the novel's development as a genre.[47] From this perspective, the role played by Spanish Jewish history in shaping genres such as the picaresque and the historical novel may affect the way we henceforth think about the historical development of the novel as a genre.

But probably the most powerful antecedents of sephardism as a politicized literary discourse can be traced to the persistent condemnation of the Inquisition by the French philosophes. Here we must keep in mind, though, that when the philosophes were writing in the middle of the eighteenth century, the Spanish and Portuguese Inquisition was still going strong, so that Montesquieu's comment on an auto-da-fé in *De l'esprit des lois* (1748) is actually a reaction to current events in Lisbon. Voltaire and the marquis d'Argens, who was instrumental in explaining the philosophes' positions to a wider audience, repeatedly wrote about the Inquisition in relation to Jews, Protestants, and Catholic dissidents.[48] Spanish authors were also occasionally able to disseminate in France narratives about the Inquisition—though not necessarily with any Jewish dimension—as in *Cornelia Bororquia, or the Victim of the Inquisition* (1801), attributed to the Spaniard Luiz Gutiérrez, which was reprinted in its French translation throughout the nineteenth century. Among antecedents to sephardism in the writings of the philosophes, one might also include Isaac de Pinto's defense of his Sephardic heritage in *Apologie des Juifs* (1762), drafted in response to Voltaire's diatribes against Jews.[49] But most relevant from a literary point of view is an episode in Voltaire's own *Candide* (1759), where Candide kills a Jew and a Portuguese inquisitor who are blackmailing each other to share Candide's beloved Cunegonde as their sex slave and maid. Voltaire's inquisitor appears here as a figure of injustice and venality who deserves no place in "the best of all possible worlds," and much the same can be said about Voltaire's Jew. Moreover, it is quite interesting to compare Voltaire's attitude to romance in *Candide* with Walter Scott's historicization of English nationalism in *Ivanhoe*: while Scott circumvents the expected romance between his Jewish heroine and his Saxon hero, perhaps in order to preserve their religious integrity, Candide and Cunegonde's affair perseveres under such preposterous conditions that Voltaire's reader is enjoined to dismiss the romantic ideal altogether on both a personal and national level.

French Sephardism in a Comparative Context

In researching the literary history of modern sephardism, I have been struck by how interconnected its early manifestations were, so that an innovative work originating in London or Madrid could pass through a revolving door in Amsterdam or Edinburgh, only to acquire new contours in Paris or Berlin.[50] Although each reconfiguration of literary models was affected by the personal attitudes of the translators, editors, or rewriters through whose hands it passed, the ideological and artistic changes to which every master text was subjected in its various cultural centers also responded to forceful national particularities in each of the cultural centers where these masterworks were being read and translated.

Throughout Europe and the Americas, writers of sephardism continuously reacted to the same masterworks, recycling and adjusting them in different ways—from the picaresque *Lazarillo of Tormes* and the Jewess of Toledo legend to Shakespeare's *Merchant of Venice* and Scott's *Ivanhoe*. Although these precursors and antecedents to modern literary sephardism passed through France, and although ideologically France's emancipation of the Jews gave modern literary sephardism its main impetus, it is nonetheless curious that while sephardism flourished so conspicuously in nineteenth-century England and Germany, it did not take root to the same extent in France.

The relative absence of sephardism in nineteenth-century France may be a paradoxical result of emancipation itself. As Michael Brenner points out, French Jews "received their equality early and subsequently had to prove that they were worthy of it, while German Jews were promised equality as the ultimate reward for their successful integration and acculturation into German society."[51] French Jews and their supporters might have judged, then, that it was better to avoid dredging up any sensitive issues related to the history of Jews in Catholics lands;[52] they might have preferred to avoid stirring the pot in the manner in which it did eventually get stirred during the Dreyfus affair at the end of that century.[53]

Addressing what I perceive as a relative absence of French sephardism in the nineteenth century is therefore one more way of thinking about the tensions that have shaped competing ethnic and religious identities in modern Europe.[54] One gradually realizes that modern national agendas were filtered through the prism of Sepharad at least twice: *first*, through the history and heritage of Spain's Jews, and *then* through the impact exerted by the French Revolution and Napoleonic Wars on different European particularities, as they tried to adjust to growing tensions between revolutionary and conservative forces within France itself and in other countries reacting to events in France. Like Germany and England, nineteenth-century France had its fair share of hispanism, medievalism, and orientalism; and it likewise generated plenty of artistic stereotypes of Jews, such as those that Tamar Garb and Linda Nochlin feature in *The Jew in the Text* (1995).[55] Yet nineteenth-century French authors rarely linked these four mythologizations of the Other into the discourse of sephardism as occurs so extensively elsewhere. Curiously, sephardism seems to have been rather suppressed in the nation to which Spain's negative treatment of the Jews was implicitly compared.

This is not to say that sephardism as a modern literary phenomenon did not exist in nineteenth-century France. But it tended to derive from a foreign source, such as Jacques Cazotte's and P.-E. Chevalier's translations and adaptations of Spanish versions of the Jewess of Toledo legend.[56] Another extraordinary example is a play by Victor Séjour, the wealthy son of a free octoroon businessman from francophone Louisiana, who in 1844 staged *Diégarias* or *The Jew of Seville* to considerable acclaim in Paris.[57] Though this play is not particularly sympathetic to the converso's predicament, I would maintain that its original measure of sephardism emerges from the author's own racial in-betweenness, grafted onto the

New Christian's ambiguous situation in Spain. When by the 1860s sephardism began to wane in England and Germany, the newly established French Jewish press woke up to the idea of publishing essays and literary narratives dealing with Jewish themes, including novellas about Sephardic history, such as David Schornstein's "Les Marannos, chronique espagnol" (1862). But even this late appearance of sephardism in historical fiction originally written and published in France still tended to import episodes from German and English sources, without necessarily readjusting them to deal profoundly with issues faced by Jews and other minorities in France itself. As Maurice Samuels observes of Schornstein's "Les Marannos, chronique espagnol," its crypto-Jewish characters "convert outwardly but risk life and limb to practice Judaism in secret and eventually sacrifice their high position in Spain for religious liberty."[58] This may have served to shore up French Jewish identity against the temptation to blend into France's dominant Christian culture, but it hardly demonstrates an original reconfiguration of national history, politics, and literary forms, via the prism of Sepharad, that we have found elsewhere in the nineteenth century.

It is quite likely that further research will overturn my assessment of nineteenth-century French sephardism. The twentieth-century profile of this phenomenon, as Judith Roumani demonstrates in her chapter on colonial and postcolonial francophone sephardism, is already richer and more complicated. However, while sephardism flourished among German and English authors in the 1840s—even while Heinrich Heine sat in Paris churning out images of German sephardism for an avid German readership—contemporary politicization of Spanish Jewish history seem to be conspicuously absent in France, as far as I've been able to ascertain, despite extensive interconnections between French and other European literatures. Moreover, as we saw earlier regarding Victor Hugo's relationship to Scott's *Ivanhoe*, French writers were reconfiguring German, Spanish, and especially English sephardism into a discourse that partakes of medievalism, orientalism, hispanism, and even politicized representations of Jews, but deliberately avoids yoking these perspectives together.

An example that proves this point is Fromental Halévy and Eugène Scribe's celebrated opera *La Juive*, which premiered in Paris in 1835, during Louis-Philippe's July Monarchy, and has been on every tenor's repertoire since. *La Juive* was written in collaboration between an established Catholic librettist, Scribe, and a young Sephardic composer, Halévy (with the assistance of the latter's brother Léon, who later became a respected historian and dramatist in his own right).[59] As Diana Hallman recounts in her chapter for this volume, the opera's original setting had been Goa, the capital of Portugal's dominions in India, where the Inquisition operated with particular fierceness against converted Jews, Muslims, and Hindus. Early on during the opera's composition, however, a German medieval setting was selected instead, one about which Voltaire had written extensively in reference to the trial of Jan Hus, a medieval Christian dissenter burned alive during the Council of Constance. Moreover, the opera's working title, "Rachel, ou l'auto-da-fé," with its strong hispanist and sephardist connotations, was changed to the more neutral *La Juive*. As Hallman explains, "Scribe's final choice of title, with its Orientalist inflection, actually returns to a variant of 'la belle juive,' his idea in an early plot outline . . . His conspicuous use of 'juive' . . . while calling attention to the romantic Jewish character, veers away from the anticlericalism baldly suggested [by the originally planned title]." Indeed, the censors sent to preview the opera not only approved it but were sincerely pleased that the costumes were "historical rather than contemporary," and they were likewise satisfied that all "Catholic ceremonies . . . religious figures, and emblems were presented with dignity and solemnity."[60] At any rate, the production did not offend the official censors, who, despite the diminished power of the Church in the early July Monarchy, were still sensitive to Catholic imagery on stage.

If *La Juive*'s initial title and setting had been retained, we would have had a clear instance of sephardism here. Instead, we are confronted with a measure of self-censored sephardism in the context of the July Monarchy, which though it ratified freedoms of thought and religion legislated by the Revolution, also established a stronger balance between the Catholic Church and the liberal bourgeoisie. As it is, *La Juive* rewrites the highly anti-Semitic Jewess of Toledo legend and engages in innovative ways with many of sephardism's other literary antecedents—*The Jew of Malta*, *The Merchant of Venice*, *Ivanhoe*—yet any potential sephardism arising from these sources was actively minimized.

The relative absence of an indigenous sephardism in the country whose emancipation of the Jews inspired so much sephardism elsewhere strikes one as less surprising when we consider the numerous claims—by Elaine Marks, Hélène Cixous, Shmuel Trigano, and Jacques Derrida—that Jewish identity in France has always been a "Marrano" identity, in the sense that although everything was granted to the Jews as individuals, modern liberalism was deemed incompatible with a continued allegiance to their ancient national identity, so that any such allegiance had to be diverted or kept under wraps.[61] This attitude changed in the course of the twentieth century with the arrival of francophone Jewish immigrants from around the Mediterranean and North Africa, whose Jewish identity had been more traditional. It is only at this point, as Judith Roumani notes, that one begins to find increasing references to Sephardic themes, for instance, in the novels of Albert Cohen and Albert Bensoussan. In anticipation of the quincentennial commemorations of the Spanish expulsion of the Jews, several historical novels set in Spain were published by French and francophone authors that fully exhibit the kind of politicized representations of Sephardic history traced here. A particularly intriguing case is *Le chemin de l'exil* (1992) by Didier Nebot, who melds Sephardic history with contemporary Middle Eastern affairs in a manner that invites the reader to consider current relations between Jews and Muslims through an idealized contrast between Jews who lived under Muslim dominance and Jews who lived under Catholic rule. Set in inquisitorial Spain, Nebot's novel ends with a converso's escape to Algeria, where the protagonist, David, responds "Shalom" to a young Muslim's "Salam alaikum."[62]

In *The Roots of Romanticism*, Isaiah Berlin contends that after the Napoleonic Wars, it became fairly clear that the French Revolution had been a failure in the sense that "the majority of Frenchmen were not free or equal and not particularly fraternal." Although the Revolution had promised "a perfect solution to human ills" based on a doctrine of peaceful universalism and unimpeded rational progress, it did not go the way its proponents had hoped, and this in many quarters produced an opposite effect to that intended.[63] Nonetheless, for religious minorities in France and elsewhere, at least some of the Revolution's achievements were clearly a definite improvement over the medieval value system that it had set out to replace—in particular, the legal emancipation of Protestants and Jews signaled a clear move away from the institutionalized religious homogeneity that Spain had endorsed so dramatically in 1492.

Responding to this complex framework of modernization and disappointed expectations, sephardism participates in an ongoing reassessment of the goals and achievements of modern nationalism, using new literary forms and political platforms to reconsider and readjust cultural attitudes to religion, the Middle Ages, and the Orient.

Convivencia, Inquisition, Marranism

To round out this survey of sephardism in modern literature, I would like to illuminate in further detail how sephardism actually uses history with reference to the two main political systems that inform the Sephardic paradigm: on the one hand, the ethnic and religious pluralism known as *convivencia*, associated with certain periods of Islamic rule and the multicultural court of Alfonso X, and on the other hand, expulsion and inquisition associated with Catholic homogeneity in Iberia and its colonies. German Jewish literature during the nineteenth century (described by Ismar Schorsch and Jonathan Skolnik in this volume), as well as Israeli and U.S. Latina sephardism during the second half of the twentieth century (as in Bernard Horn's and Dalia Kandiyoti's examples) tend to emphasize and call for *ethnic and religious coexistence*, while the Inquisition looms large in English literature of the nineteenth century (as in Ragussis's examples), as well as in Latin American sephardism after the Holocaust (as in Marcos Aguinis's *La gesta del marrano*, discussed by Edna Aizenberg, and in the historicized picaresque novels I examine). Nevertheless—and this is an important caveat—even when one facet of the Sephardic experience is emphasized, others are usually implied either through an assumption of the reader's wider knowledge of the Sephardic experience or through plot patterns indicating that *convivencia* eventually disintegrated into conversion, expulsion, and inquisition: a classical order/disorder/order plot scheme that more often than not defers the final achievement of harmony to an indefinite point in the future.

Alberto Gerchunoff's *Los gauchos judíos* (1910), among the most enthusiastic celebrations of a new potential age of *convivencia* in the New World, proffers positive and negative assessments of the Sephardic experience side by side. Already in its first chapter, during an afternoon chat among Ashkenazi immigrants to Argentina, Gerchunoff's narrator notes that "the rabbi from Tolna sang the praises of Spain," upon which another community leader immediately retorts: "I have never been able to mention the name of Spain without blood welling up in my eyes . . . for having tortured our brethren and burned our priests." But the prospects for Jews in Catholic environments such as Argentina's is further complicated here by the presence of a fourth historical vortex, Zion, ironically reinterpreted in reference to Latin America via the Sephardic paradigm: "when Rabbi Zadock Kahn informed me about the immigration to Argentina, I forgot the return to Zion in the midst of my joy, and remembered the words of Yehuda Halevi: Zion is wherever peace and happiness reign. We'll all go to Argentina."[64]

When I first began to investigate sephardism, it seemed to me that its main examples were polarized according to ("negative") warning plots emphasizing persecution and ("positive") celebratory plots emphasizing *convivencia*: a best of times followed by a worse of times—unlike *A Tale of Two Cities*' famous opening line, where Dickens describes the era of the French Revolution as *simultaneously* the best and worst of times. Upon closer examination, however, it now seems to me that sephardism rarely celebrates multiculturalism naïvely; and that its accounts of persecution are likewise tempered by scenes of love affairs and friendship between religions and ethnicities in ways that preserve the conventions of historical romance, whether the romance ends happily ever after or not.

Shuttling between gradations of *convivencia* and expulsion, across the gamut of themes associated with sephardism as a politicized literary discourse, we continually encounter the figure of the Marrano. The ambiguity and doubleness that characterize the Marrano's New Christian condition—whether s/he is presented as a crypto-Jew or not—lend themselves to different, and even opposed, ideological interpretations across the cultural contexts in which sephardism occurs. Thus, marranism can be portrayed as a threat lurking under the surface of a homogeneous political system: a sabotaging element that must be ferreted and stamped out. Or as a warped form of bicultural coexistence: a survival strategy enabling individuals from rejected cultures to participate in political systems that brook no multiculturalism. I doubt whether any literary work portrays the paradoxical irony inherent in the term itself—that bizarre association of swine with Jews biblically proscribed from having anything to do with pork and pigs—more poignantly than *Zithers Hanging from the Trees* (1974) by the Spanish dramaturge Antonio Gala, whose New Christian lead melds so grotesquely with a pig butchered on stage that she seems to be "reborn" out of its carcass as she emerges clutching its entrails. As Stacy Beckwith argues, this scene draws the Spanish notion of the Marrano back to its Germanic medieval roots in the *Judensau* motif of anti-Semitic drawings and engravings of a sow being suckled and touched obscenely by Jewish men and children.

The stressful vigilance New Christians had to maintain in order to avoid being accused of marranism, whether or not they were crypto-Jews, explodes sometimes into unambiguous declarations of identity, as in Grace Aguilar's *The Vale of Cedars* (1850), where the heroine announces that she is a Jew in order to invalidate incriminating testimony against a Catholic Englishman who loves her. With this declaration, Marie seals her fate—the novel's subtitle is *The Martyr*—in a move calculated to dissociate the crypto-Jew's plight from negative connotations of disloyalty to Christianity in the minds of Aguilar's British readers. But the opposite perspective, as Michael Ragussis shows, had been presented earlier in Edward Bulwer-Lytton's *Leila; or, The Siege of Granada* (1838), where the Marrano is an amoral double agent. The figure of the Marrano, still waiting to be fully explored through cultural studies, appears to be a pliable trope that portrays paradoxical images of identity vis-à-vis cultural groups that demand unambiguous or uniform allegiances.[65]

Even when the plots of sephardism do not focus specifically on crypto-Jewish or converso figures, they often hinge on dramatic moments of historical change. For instance, Salman Rushdie's expansively named Moor, son of a Christian mother and a Jewish father, travels across space and time, as Efraim Sicher indicates, to witness King Boabdil's loss of Granada to Catholic Spain, all the while reflecting on India's own complex history of multiculturalism. Indeed, Spain's last Muslim ruler, Boabdil, frequently appears within English sephardism's repertoire as a tragic emblem of transition: his kingdom is mentioned anachronistically in Scott's *Ivanhoe* as the goal of Rebecca's search for a safe destination and it appears prominently in Bulwer's *Leila* as well. However, interestingly enough, Muslim Spain does not appear as frequently as one would expect among the German Jewish works to which Ismar Schorsch attributes a "myth of Sephardic supremacy," even though they promoted a tolerant cosmopolitan image of Sepharad under Islamic rule, in contrast with the treatment of Jews in Christian dominions.

Instead, Isaac Abarbanel, the leader of the expelled Jews, occupies a prominent position as a tragic figure of transition in German Jewish sephardism and its close adaptations within the Yiddish and Ladino-speaking world. Abarbanel appears in many novels and plays fruitlessly pleading with the Catholic king and queen to repeal their edict of expulsion, and then majestically leading the Jews into the unknown when his plea fails. However, as mentioned earlier in relation to Jonathan Skolnik's work on Abarbanel, Heine portrays him as a heroic-pathetic figure, who, much like Rushdie's Moor, brings to mind Don Quixote's quest to recreate a chivalric ideal in the modern age.

While the figure of the Marrano provides a suggestive crux around which complex notions of national and religious identity can be explored, and although "the period of the inquisition and expulsion with its dark cellars and priests wrapped in robes and mitres, bearing crosses and icons" offers excellent material for historical novels and dramas,[66] literary representations of Judeo-Spanish history also present opportunities to discuss the brighter side of the Sephardic experience: the political conditions that had once nurtured a multicultural civilization in the Iberian Peninsula. As Reyes Coll-Tellechea asks: "How did Jews, Muslims, and Christians coexist in the Iberian Peninsula? What conditions and actions made coexistence possible? What conditions and actions were necessary to produce the sophisticated advances in all areas of knowledge, culture, and art that characterized Jewish, Muslim, and Christian Iberia? How were those life conditions reached? How did the leaders of those communities interact? How did the common men and women interact?"[67]

Historical romances rarely illuminate the actual, day-to-day life of the different ethnicities and religious groups around which the Sephardic experience coalesced—for this we must turn to historiography proper, which is less constrained than historical fiction by the aesthetic and structural demands of characterization and plot (*pace* Hayden White).[68] As a scholar of narrative fiction, I cannot stress enough how important it is to cultivate awareness of the generic conventions that creative authors choose to follow or breach. But while keeping in mind its aesthetic and generic constraints, a study of literary sephardism can provide a framework for approaching questions such as those that Coll-Tellechea poses. It would then lead us to a reinvigorated appreciation of literature's complexity and a nuanced awareness of how history has been filtered and refashioned by many minds in different environments. This is a process that notes positive continuities between historical periods, as well as "ruptures, breaches, breaks"—as Yosef Yerushalmi aptly observed, for "not everything of value that existed before a break was either salvaged or metamorphosed, but was lost, and . . . some of what fell by the wayside can become, through our retrieval, meaningful to us."[69]

As counterhistory to the status quo, sephardism sets up comparisons between historical periods and national identities anchored in the political preoccupations of the present, where the role of Jews and Jewish history is legitimized or delegitimized according to changing attitudes towards coexistence between nations or within them. "Why drag dead Jews out of the closet?" a publisher once asked Homero Aridjis when he presented his historical picaresque novel *1492: Vida y tiempos de Juan Cabezón de Castilla*.[70] The answer has been given often enough—because those who ignore the past are condemned to repeat it—yet this answer turns out to be insufficient. From the point of view of world history, it is sobering, even frightening, to realize that until the eve of the Holocaust, Jewish writers in Germany kept staging and publishing accounts of Sepharad, less now as a model for emulation than as a warning about the imminent destruction of their civilization.[71] To what avail? Their awareness of the Sephardic experience demonstrates that merely knowing the past does not help to avoid a repetition or recrudescence of past misfortunes: the road to *convivencia* cannot be paved just with knowledge of the past; the problem is rather who knows the past, and what they do with this awareness.

Never Again?

"For all of one's justified mistrust of historical parallelism," Yosef Yerushalmi writes, "it is hard to escape the feeling that the Jewish people after the Holocaust stands today at a juncture not without analogy to that of the generations following the cataclysm of the Spanish Expulsion." The expulsion, he explains, generated an unprecedented surge of historiographic interest among Jewish scholars who were then devoted primarily to the study of scripture.[72] As we shall see in the following chapters, the events surrounding the year 1492 also generated new literary genres, such as the picaresque novel, and new philosophical positions, such as Spinoza's appeal for a universalized nonpartisan rational thought. "As a result of emancipation in the diaspora and national sovereignty in Israel," Yerushalmi continues, "Jews have fully re-entered the mainstream of history, and yet their perception [and the perception of others, I would add] of how they got there and where they are is most often more mythical than real. Myth and memory condition action."[73]

I mentioned earlier that initially I had thought that sephardism polarizes Sephardic history either into idealizations of *convivencia* or scenes of persecution, but upon closer examination I found a more nuanced representation of the Sephardic experience. I surmised, as well, that sephardism in the second half of the twentieth century would be filtered through the prism of the Holocaust, registering perhaps a new sense of urgency in scenes of *convivencia* and warnings against persecution. Upon closer examination, I was again surprised to find that although the Holocaust may indeed loom large in the awareness of readers and writers of literary sephardism after 1945, there is no measurable difference in the tone, themes, or attitudes of sephardism before and after the Holocaust, even in cases where the latter is mentioned explicitly.[74]

Sephardism after the Holocaust continues to deal with problems of identity politics and international reconfiguration, just as it did in the age of revolutions. But if at the time of the Spring of Nations, in the middle of the nineteenth century, sephardism tended to filter Spanish Jewish history through a modernizing ideology of rational progress, then nowadays, in the Autumn of Nations, Spanish Jewish history gets filtered rather through a continuing frustration with sometimes incompatible ideals of pluralism and progress, viewed both horizontally (across cultures) and vertically ("down into history"), according to new political concerns with postcolonialism and globalization. The spirit of multiculturalism and globalization that was partly conceived in response to the disastrous nationalistic goals of two world wars has given sephardism a new thematic and structural coloration that endorses connections between Jews, conversos, and gentiles over a long, transnational historical span. Such a reconfigured sense of solidarity beyond national borders (sometimes over and above historical realities) is celebrated in postmodern and postcolonial works of sephardism, such as those that Efraim Sicher and Dalia Kandiyoti examine, where an old/new network of historical and political connections to Sepharad is expansively reimagined.

Ultimately, the core problem that our case studies keep uncovering is an ongoing battle over status and self-definition among different national, ethnic, and religious groups intertwined with each other in the kind of competitive dynamics that Liah Greenfeld documents in *Nationalism: Five Roads to Modernity* (1992).[75] Sephardism helps to articulate this thorny problem of competing national, ethnic, and religious particularisms by allowing us to observe a set of historicized attitudes about the images and status of Jews in Western culture. However, to trace a literary and political history of sephardism is not only to uncover latent competitions among different combinations of cultures; it is also to identify the impact that the Sephardic experience has had on the formation of the most pliable and modern of literary genres, namely, the novel, and to acknowledge at the same time the role played by the Sephardic experience in the development of a modern political philosophy based on rational thought and the rights of individuals within a civic polity. To examine modern literature through the prism of Sepharad is to realize that the Sephardic experience has played a far more important role in modern literary and political history than has been generally acknowledged. Thus sephardism's thematic and ideological patterns continue to touch keenly on core matters of personal and collective identity shaping our world.

Part I *The Problem of National Particularism in German, English, and French Literature on the Jews of Spain*

One The Myth of Sephardic Supremacy in Nineteenth-Century Germany

Ismar Schorsch

With the advent of emancipation in Central Europe, German-speaking Jewry gradually unhinged itself from the house of Ashkenazic Judaism. Inclusion in the body politic sundered a religious unity born of common patrimony. Historians have tended to focus on the institutional expressions of this rupture—the repudiation of the educational system, the mode of worship, and the rabbinic leadership intrinsic to Ashkenazic Judaism—with special emphasis on the Western tastes and values that propelled the transformation of all areas of Jewish life. What has been singularly overlooked is the simultaneous quest for a Jewish paradigm that would ground institutional rebellion in Jewish soil. With surprising speed, German Jews came to cultivate a lively bias for the religious legacy of Sephardic Jewry forged centuries before on the Iberian Peninsula. Without this bias, they would have cut loose from Judaism altogether. The embrace of what had previously hovered on the liminal level of Ashkenazic consciousness enabled them to redefine their identity in a Jewish mode. The critique of Ashkenazic Judaism was leveled from the vantage point of a usable past. During the next two centuries, modern Jewish history would replay this dialectic of rebellion and renewal by recourse to the periphery of group consciousness, but not beyond, with some degree of regularity. Counterhistory fed both the impulse for rejuvenation and the desire for continuity.

As construed by Ashkenazic intellectuals, the Sephardic image facilitated a religious posture marked by cultural openness, philosophic thinking, and an appreciation for the aesthetic. Like many a historical myth, it evoked a partial glimpse of a bygone age determined and colored by social need. Eventually, as we shall see, the Sephardic mystique came to operate in four distinct areas of Jewish life in nineteenth-century

Germany—liturgy, synagogue architecture, literature, and scholarship. The romance with Spain offers yet another perspective on the degree to which German Jewry distanced itself from its eastern European origins.

*

The multifaceted interaction between Sephardic and Ashkenazic Judaism in the centuries following the Spanish expulsion has yet to be studied comprehensively. Still there is little doubt that beyond the worldwide influence of Lurianic Kabbalah, the religious culture of Spanish Jewry held little allure for a self-sufficient and self-confident Ashkenazic Judaism in its age of spiritual ascendancy. Ashkenazic religious leadership in the second half of the sixteenth century began to turn its back on the rich rationalistic legacy of Spain—its biblical exegesis, grammatical research, and philosophic enterprise.[1] Typical of the growing assertiveness was the public attack delivered in 1559 by the chief rabbinic figure of Poznań in the synagogue on the sabbath before Passover, in which he defended the Talmud as the sole and infallible source of all knowledge required by Jews and depicted the burning of the Talmud in Rome in 1553 by order of the papacy as an expression of divine displeasure at the publication of Maimonides' *Guide of the Perplexed* in Venice two years before.[2] Similarly the Prague polymath David Gans in his historical chronicle *Zemah David* (The Shoot of David) of 1592 betrayed an unmistakable sense of Ashkenazic superiority by dryly juxtaposing the Sephardic tendency to convert in times of persecution with the supposed Ashkenazic resolve to embrace martyrdom.[3]

Throughout this period of cultural estrangement, however, there are traces of self-criticism within Ashkenazic Judaism inspired by Sephardic example. The fascination with Spain that came to characterize the German Jewish scene of the nineteenth century was a discontinuity with its historical roots. The criticism is most often directed at the insular, ungraded, and adult-oriented educational system of the Ashkenazic world. While it is not clear whether the educational reforms of Jehuda Löw ben Bezalel (better known as the Maharal of Prague) in the sixteenth century were inspired by a Spanish model, the comments and proposals made by Shabbatai Sheftel Horowitz, Shabbatai Bass, and Zevi Hirsch Ashkenazi in the following two centuries were certainly informed by direct contact with the Sephardic Diaspora.[4]

Bass, who was born in 1641 in Poland and educated in Prague, spent five years in the quickening ambience of Amsterdam's Sephardic community, completing his Sefer *Sifte yeshenim* (The Lips of the Sleeping), the first bibliography of Hebraica prepared by a Jew, in 1680. The significance of this work, for our purpose, goes well beyond his praise in the introduction of the graded and efficient Sephardic educational system he came to admire in Amsterdam. As an instrument of scholarship, the bibliography, with its 2,200 titles, provided the Hebrew reader with a sense that Jewish literary creativity transcended the writing of legal codes, commentaries, and *responsa*. With autodidacts in mind, Bass stressed in his introduction the centrality of method and system in the mastery of any discipline. The ability to arrive at reliable conclusions, and not the mechanical assimilation of factual knowledge, was the mark of the true scholar.[5]

No less unusual for his time was Zevi Ashkenazi, the devout yet worldly father of Jacob Emden. Known by the Sephardic title *Hakham* (sage), Ashkenazi was born in Moravia in 1660, educated in Salonika, and for the rest of his life moved easily between the Ashkenazic and Sephardic orbits. His intellectual horizons, though, were distinctly Sephardic, and he possessed a good command of European languages, secular learning, Jewish philosophy, and Hebrew grammar, all of which made him a lifelong critic of the educational curriculum that prevailed in Central Europe.[6]

That same critique was substantially amplified in the middle of the eighteenth century by Isaac Wetzlar, a native of Lower Saxony and successful merchant with a solid rabbinic education, in his unpublished Yiddish ethical tract "Liebes Brief." Whatever else his use of Yiddish may have betokened, it signaled a desire to deliver his indictment of Ashkenazic society to the largest possible audience. Wetzlar was discomfited by gentile ridicule of Judaism, angered by the low quality of lay and rabbinic leadership, and envious of the orderliness and emphases of the Sephardic educational system. He extolled the study of Jewish philosophy, the decorum of the Sephardic synagogue, and its willingness to employ Spanish or Portuguese in communal worship. Consciousness of Sephardic practice, nurtured by at least one visit to Hamburg, with its still bustling Sephardic community, and perhaps elsewhere, had sensitized Wetzlar to shortcomings in his own Jewish world.[7] In fact, as the autobiography of Glückel of Hameln illustrates, frequent travel by Ashkenazic merchants and entrepreneurs to the emporiums of Amsterdam and Hamburg and to international fairs in this age of mercantilism constituted an infectious source of exposure to the contrasting religious style of the Sephardic Diaspora.[8] In sum, then, it is possible to identify an unbroken if modest tradition of Ashkenazic self-criticism informed by a selective admiration for Spanish Judaism long before the emergence of a veritable Sephardic mystique in the last quarter of the eighteenth century.

The full-blown cultural critique of the *Haskalah* (German Jewry's ephemeral Hebraic version of the European Enlightenment) drew much of its validation, if not inspiration, directly from Spain. The advocacy of secular education; the curbing of talmudic exclusivity and the resumption of studies in Hebrew grammar, biblical exegesis, and Jewish philosophy; and the search for historical exemplars led to a quick rediscovery of Spanish models and achievements. Given the deep Ashkenazic aversion to any serious study of the Bible, Moses Mendelsohn's extensive Hebrew commentary on the Pentateuch was no less of a revolutionary break than his German translation, and it relied heavily on the grammatical and exegetical spadework of Spanish forerunners. The combined result of commentary and translation at least partially warranted Heine's arresting comparison of Mendelsohn to Luther by virtue of their common endeavor to restore the centrality of the biblical text to their respective religious cultures.[9]

A quintessential expression of the *Haskalah*'s repudiation of Poland for Spain may be found in a withering satire by Aaron Wolfsohn, a teacher in the modern Jewish school of Breslau (now Wrocław) and one of the editors of the movement's ailing Hebrew periodical *Hame'asef*. Serialized in its pages during 1794–95, "Siha be-eretz ha-Hayim" (A Conversation in Paradise) takes place in the heavenly abode on the day of Mendelsohn's death. Prior to Mendelsohn's arrival, we are treated to a delicious exchange between a reluctant Maimonides and an uncouth Polish rabbi, whose two-year residence on a lower level of paradise has improved his Hebrew enough to discourse with the Sephardic sage. The rabbi is overjoyed at the chance to display his immense knowledge of Maimonides' twelfth-century codification of all Jewish law to the author himself. After much badgering, Maimonides unhappily agrees to test his learning, but when he begins by asking whether God might be corporeal—a subject on which Maimonides' own rationalistic view had already given rise to bitter controversy—his Polish tormentor protests that he never wasted his time studying trivia, but only matters of import: the laws governing sacrifices, family purity, and financial affairs. In regard to the realm of theology, he firmly believed that lightning was created to punish the wicked and personally warded it off by placing salt on the four corners of his table and opening the book of Genesis.

When Mendelsohn finally arrives on the scene, he is affectionately embraced as an equal by a weary and perturbed Maimonides. In response to his urgent inquiry as to the reasons for the benighted condition of Ashkenazic Jews, Mendelsohn offers three: oppression, which brought them to despise gentile learning; the absence of legal consensus; and an abstruse and casuistic mode of learning. Wolfsohn concludes his satirical foray by having Moses himself come out to welcome Mendelsohn to paradise, thereby uniting in symbolic religious accord the three towering Moses figures of Jewish history. The scene graphically exemplified the deeper meaning of the *Haskalah*'s famous bon mot that "from Moses to Moses there was no one like Moses." Collapsing the Moses of Egypt and Moses Mendelsohn, the Moses of Dessau, into the Moses of Córdoba rendered the philosophic strain of Spanish Judaism both pristine and normative.[10]

A modicum of personal experience helped to fuel this flight of historical imagination. At one point, Wolfsohn has Mendelsohn confess that it was only his discovery of Maimonides' *Guide* that extracted him from the ignorance and confusion of the talmudic world, and indeed the *Guide* served as the great intellectual emancipator for an entire generation of autodidacts, as Isaak Euchel stressed in his 1788 biography of Mendelsohn.[11] It provided their first taste of secular knowledge and remained a model for a rational exposition of Judaism. There was nothing exceptional about the pious Jews of the city of Poznań forbidding the itinerant Salomon Maimon, whose very name testifies to his indebtedness to Maimonides, to introduce their children to the *Guide*.[12] If, in fact, the *Haskalah* is unthinkable without the *Guide*, then its republication in 1742 in Jessnitz, just a few miles from Dessau, after a hiatus of nearly two centuries, amounted to a major breach in the intellectual defenses of Ashkenazic society. The glaring lack of even a single introductory rabbinic approbation underscores the official hostility to the venture, though Mendelsohn's own teacher of Talmud, David Fränkel, seems covertly to have favored it. Without question, however, the new edition of the *Guide*, with several commentaries and a glossary of foreign words, opened up a road for many an inquiring mind that would eventually terminate in the alluring vistas of the Enlightenment.[13]

Political considerations tended to reinforce the cultural attraction to Spain. The far more privileged, prosperous, and assimilated Sephardic Jews of Amsterdam, London, and Bordeaux served as the cutting edge of the campaign for emancipation. The respected Amsterdam philosophe Isaac de Pinto had defended his co-religionists against Voltaire's scurrilous article on the Jews in 1762, chiding the latter for his blanket indictment of all Jews, which entirely ignored the vast economic, social, and cultural differences between Ashkenazim and Sephardim, implying that the latter by virtue of their noteworthy accomplishments enjoyed a greater claim to admission into the body politic than their oppressed brethren.[14] And, indeed, the resistance in revolutionary circles in 1790 to emancipating the Sephardic Jews of Bordeaux and southern France proved much less severe than that which forced a delay of yet another twenty months in granting emancipation to the larger number of far more alien Ashkenazim in Alsace and Lorraine.[15]

The import of events in France was not lost on young German Jewish intellectuals engaged in their own struggle for equality, and they often cast their argument in de Pinto's terms. Thus, for example, Eduard Gans, the staunch and acute young Hegelian president of the ephemeral Verein für Cultur und Wissenschaft der Juden (Society for Jewish Culture and Science), submitted a lengthy petition to the Prussian government in the spring of 1820 seeking official approval for the name and activities of his society. To enforce his contention that Judaism posed no threat to meeting the demands of good citizenship, Gans pointed to the enduring record of Spanish Jewry:

> These Jews, resembling all others both physically and mentally, but granted equality with Muslims by the Arabs, proceeded to plumb in concert all the known sciences of the day. . . . And they employed (in their writings) not Hebrew but Arabic. Indeed, those Jews expelled

> from this land to France, Holland, Italy, and England, to the detriment of Spanish economic life, and their still living progeny have never formed the contrast to Christian society so striking in the other family of Jews, kept intentionally apart. They are marked by less discrepancy in morality, purer speech, greater order in the synagogue, and in fact better taste.[16]

But a few years later the more prosaic Isaak Markus Jost, who had distanced himself from the messianic fervor of the Verein für Cultur und Wissenschaft and who bore little affection for his own Ashkenazic culture, wrote in a late chapter of his multivolume *Geschichte der Israeliten* that Spanish and German Jews, for all their agreement in matters of religion, "constitute practically distinct national groups" (*verschiedene Völkerstämme*).[17]

Napoleon's willingness in 1806 to reopen the issue within France of whether adherents of Judaism were even capable of citizenship augmented Sephardic prestige still further. His famous twelve questions and the rhetoric of his officials imposed a far-reaching distinction on Judaism that would become basic to the protracted emancipation debate in Central Europe. As formulated by the Sanhedrin in February 1807 in the preamble to its nine-point doctrinal and halakhic pronouncement, that distinction divided the provisions of Jewish law into two kinds—religious provisions, which are eternal, and political ones obtained only for the period of Jewish statehood. In his invaluable transactions of the preceding Assembly of Notables, Diogene Tama, the secretary of the deputy from Bouches du Rhône, astutely linked this novel distinction in a general way to the figures of Don Isaac Abravanel and Maimonides. The former, he contended,

> establishes a judicious distinction between things essentially connected with religious dogmas, and those which have reference only to points of civil morals, which last are always susceptible of changes and modifications, according to the civil and political state of those whose happiness they have in view.[18]

Not only were Sephardic Jews more worldly, then, but their conception of Judaism met the political needs of the modern age. This highly imprecise, essentially alien, but immensely useful distinction unveiled a powerful means for friend and foe alike to strip Judaism of any rite, restriction, or institution that was perceived to jeopardize the goal of integration.[19]

To consolidate this historical overview, we might say that the movements for *Haskalah* and emancipation had fanned a spark into a fire. A restricted tradition of self-criticism with a distinguished genealogy was about to erupt into a broad social force that would permeate the major expressions of an emergent Jewish subculture. A changing political context had ignited a growing rebellion against Polish Judaism, while the need for continuity and legitimacy begged for a new cultural paradigm.

⁕

The rapid diffusion of the Spanish mystique is attested to by its appearance in four distinct areas of Jewish culture in nineteenth-century Germany. The impulsion was not passed along from one cultural element to the other, but instead derived from a common source that simultaneously penetrated into the domains of liturgy, synagogue architecture, literature, and scholarship. The shift toward Spain was not gradual or sequential but sudden and ubiquitous.

Since with emancipation, the synagogue emerged for a time as the dominant area of Jewish expression, it should come as no surprise to discover that the Spanish bias affected both its liturgy and architecture. Already, Naftali Herz Wessely, whose admiration for the Sephardim of Amsterdam was born of personal experience, had contended in the fourth and final letter of his *Words of Peace and Truth* that the Sephardic pronunciation of Hebrew was grammatically preferable to the manner in which the Ashkenazim rendered it.[20] A generation later, the teachers and preachers who pioneered the development of a German rite adopted the Sephardic pronunciation for their "German synagogue."[21] Not a point of halakhic contention, the switch could be defended by Eliezer Liebermann in terms of grammatical propriety and by Moses Konitz of Ofen (Buda) in terms of demography—more than seven-eighths of the Jewish world prayed in the Hebrew of the Sephardim![22] But the ultimate motivation of this unnatural and self-conscious appropriation of Sephardic Hebrew was the desire to distinguish the sound of the sacred tongue from that of Yiddish, which these alienated Ashkenazic intellectuals regarded as a non-language that epitomized the abysmal state of Jewish culture.[23]

No less symptomatic of that degradation for them was the condition of the traditional German liturgy for festivals (the *Mahzor*), thickly overlaid with impenetrable Hebrew poems (*piyyutim*) composed by medieval sages and with mystical interpolations from the realm of Lurianic Kabbalah. At the turn of the century, its state of disrepair had prompted Wolf Heidenheim—the founder of a famous Jewish publishing house in the Frankfurt suburb of Rödelheim, and one of the most anomalous and understudied figures of the German *Haskalah*—to undertake a new, nine-volume edition of the German *Mahzor* with the semblance of a critical text, a lucid German translation (in Hebrew characters) and an expansive Hebrew commentary. Working entirely alone, Heidenheim hoped to rid the Hebrew text of innumerable corruptions, to illuminate the difficult vocabulary and abstruse allusions of the *piyyutim*, and to drive out of circulation the egregious older German translations that were available at the time. The edition bespoke a heroic effort by an open-minded scholar, singularly free of any affinity for Spain, to restore and defend the religious grandeur of his own Ashkenazic liturgical tradition. Heidenheim regarded the rhyme and meter of Sephardic *piyyutim* as alien to Hebrew literature, which to his mind had always accorded priority to content over form. Accordingly, his commentary focused on the sources, grammar, and meaning of his texts and not on their literary quality. Overall, the project was clearly analogous to and perhaps even inspired by Mendelsohn's edition of the Pentateuch. Nevertheless, its import was more mixed. Whereas the religious tastes of the age militated against the retention of large chunks of *piyyutim* in the synagogue, Heidenheim's signal accomplishment would place all future students of the subject in his debt.[24]

In 1841 a second edition of the prayer book of the Hamburg Temple, the most enduring and influential of the early "German synagogues," ignited a second broad controversy that betrayed yet another aspect of the preference for Spain within the synagogue. In addition to its transliteration of Hebrew according to the Sephardic pronunciation, which obviously still prevailed in the temple, the prayer book comprised a parsimonious selection of *piyyutim* drawn entirely from the Sephardic orbit.[25] Among other features, that rejection of native *piyyutim*, familiar and sacred to German Jews, for the utterly strange, though perhaps superior, products of the Spanish synagogue also drew the ire of Zacharias

Frankel of Dresden, whose differences with the Reform camp were beginning to crystallize. His espousal of liturgical continuity and familiarity over poetic quality indeed challenged the very operating principle if not underlying motive of the Hamburg circle and their allies.[26] Without the embrace of Sephardic culture, the rebellion against Ashkenaz was hardly possible. In their defenses of the Hamburg Temple's prayer book, Gotthold Salomon and Abraham Geiger, representing the old and new generations of Reform rabbinic leadership, both asserted the grammatical, literary, and philosophical superiority of Spanish religious poetry. The Ashkenazim were deemed inferior in all three respects, and their poets were labeled "baroque in their extreme and [their] language barbaric and monstrous."[27] Furthermore, Salomon protested his synagogue's living connection to the Sephardic tradition. The selection of *piyyutim* was neither academic nor arbitrary. "At the founding of our temple," he writes, "our association counted quite a few respected Portuguese families among its most enthusiastic supporters."[28]

Basic to this preference for Spanish *piyyutim* was a general conception of what separated the liturgical creativity of medieval Sephardim and Ashkenazim first enunciated by Shlomo Yehudah Rapoport in 1827. His subsequent fame as one of the founders of the academic study of Judaism, despite his unassimilated origins in eastern Galicia, made his early observation a stock stereotype of the age. Rapoport claimed that "the religious poetry of the Sephardim was an instrument of communication between the soul and its Maker, whereas that of the Ashkenazim linked the nation of Israel and its God."[29] The distinction served to endow Spanish Jewry with a sense of individualism. Its public worship did not muffle the anguish of the individual beneath the oppressive fate of the community, but rather facilitated the expression of his personal pain directly to God. Such immediacy not only lent a special intimacy to Spanish *piyyutim*, it also helped to blunt the frequent charge of dual loyalty.

The same year (1842) that the controversy over the Hamburg Temple prayer book reverberated through Central Europe, Leopold Dukes published a modest German introduction to the study of medieval Hebrew poetry, which elegantly elaborated and justified the substitution of a few choice specimens of Sephardic *piyyutim* in the synagogue for the entire Ashkenazic liturgical corpus. A native of Pressburg (now Bratislava) and a product of its famous yeshiva, Dukes was a scholarly autodidact who led an impoverished existence in Germany scouring archives for manuscripts pertaining to medieval Hebrew literature. His *Zur Kenntnis der neuhebräischen religiösen Poesie* (Toward an Understanding of Neo-Hebraic Religious Poetry) deepened the stereotypes. The unattractiveness of Ashkenazic religious poetry, Dukes concluded, was a function of social context. Totally excluded from Christian society, the Jews of northern France and Germany vegetated intellectually on a meager diet of rabbinic texts. The ungrammatical, unedifying, and artless nature of their poetry was a mirror image of the curriculum on which they were nurtured. The human dimension of either Jew or Christian was denied a means of universal expression. In contrast, the open atmosphere and secular arena that existed in Muslim Spain enriched its Jews with the chance to cultivate a thirst for knowledge as a source of truth and an appreciation for language as an instrument of power and beauty. Its poetry, consequently, is meticulously crafted, echoes universal themes, and laments national calamities with the gentleness of a lover. Historical research had been enlisted to shift cultural paradigms.[30]

The external façade of the synagogue likewise bore the impress of the Sephardic bias. Emancipation, although incomplete, permitted German Jews for the first time to discard the inconspicuous, nondescript, and often unofficial status of their houses of worship. The magnificent edifices constructed in the course of the nineteenth century gave resounding public testimony to their confidence in the durability of emancipation and their pride in their religious distinctiveness. But the freedom to build synagogues posed a serious architectural challenge: no conscious tradition existed of what might constitute the most appropriate style for a Jewish sanctuary. The insecurity of medieval Jewish life had impeded the formation of such a tradition. After several decades of experimentation, Christian architects and Jewish communal boards arrived at a consensus that synagogues ought to be built in what became known as the Moorish style, and in the 1850s and 1860s, imposing Moorish-style synagogues rose to grace the rapidly expanding Jewish communities of Leipzig, Frankfurt, Cologne, Mainz, Budapest, Vienna, and Berlin. Not till the end of the century, according to the leading scholar of this fascinating, long-neglected subject, did the rising tide of anti-Semitism in Germany induce communities to opt for an architectural style that lowered their public profile.

In his seminal work *Synagogen in Deutschland*, Harold Hammer-Schenk suggests that the acceptance of a Moorish design, based largely on the mosques of North Africa and the Alhambra and not on any knowledge of the few medieval synagogues left in Spain, rested on two factors. The first was the conviction of historians that Arabic architecture, though distinctly inferior to Gothic, clearly foreshadowed later developments in Europe and therefore accorded perfectly with the prevailing gentile perception of the relationship between Judaism and Christianity. Since Gothic was held to be quintessentially Christian, the synagogue was assigned a style that symbolized both its chronological and qualitative position in the history of religion. Moreover, and this was the second factor, Moorish architecture seemed to harmonize with the course of Jewish history by highlighting the oriental origins of the Jew, although, as Hammer-Schenk realized, Jews in the process of Westernization were scarcely pleased at being reminded of their "primitive" ancestry. Consequently, the theory falls short of explaining the phenomenon. Communal boards, which always made the final decision over what style to employ, irrespective of the architect, were unlikely to choose one that accentuated both the inferiority and orientalism of Judaism.[31]

My own view, given the burden of this essay, should be clear. The appeal of Moorish architecture for the emancipated synagogue derived from its Spanish connection. It answered the need for a distinctive style precisely because it dovetailed so completely with the overriding Spanish bias of German Jewry. There was nothing oriental about the Arabs; without them Greek philosophy would never have reached the West. One was fully entitled to draw on the inspiration of Spain to renovate both the interior and the exterior of the synagogue. What more powerful symbol of the rupture with Ashkenazic culture than to build synagogues in the spirit of Spain!

*

The Sephardic mystique, however, extended well beyond the confines of the synagogue. It also played a formative role in the nascent field of Jewish belles lettres—an underutilized source of insight for social and intellectual historians of German Jewry—comprising works by writers born as Jews who used fiction or poetry either to air a problematic relationship to Judaism or to mediate it positively. What stands out is the degree to which writers of both types turned for their material to the Sephardic experience, which obliged them with equal bounty as a font of pride or self-criticism.

Heine's frequent recourse to that font is well known and has prompted one astute scholar to speak of his "Marrano pose." The designation is meant to capture not only his lifelong fascination with Spain, but also his recurring identification with the fate of unwilling converts left no choice by a society bent on complete religious conformity. Heine was not beyond intimating a Spanish provenance for some of his own ancestors.[32] But the metaphor is also misleading, for Heine, the most celebrated and defiant convert of the century, never concealed his Jewish patrimony from his readership, and his oeuvre is saturated with Jewish themes, animadversions, and memories. A figure of unique talent and complexity, Heine's preference for Spain is nevertheless typical.

In Heine's *Der Rabbi von Bacherach*, to cite but one example, the bias manifests itself in a paradoxical way. Begun before his conversion, while he was still a member of the Verein für Cultur, this truncated novella represented the first effort by a German to mediate the religious beauty and historical pathos of Judaism through fiction. Heine's romantic nature protested the evisceration of both by the Hegelian scalpel of Gans, the Verein's chief conceptual surgeon. With the few Christian resources put at his disposal by Leopold Zunz, Heine struggled to convey that Judaism was a living organism, subject to abuse and capable of feeling pain, and not a set of heartless abstractions.

As the first chapter of *Der Rabbi von Bacherach* shows, it was not the worldly Judaism of Spain but the besieged and unyielding Judaism of Germany that Heine intended to evoke. His choice was consistent with a remarkably sympathetic portrait of present-day Polish Jewry that he had published in 1823, just one year earlier, wherein he praised its spiritual wholeness and unconflicted character.[33] And yet the Spanish penchant could not be held at bay. Heine introduced into the story of Rabbi Abraham the utterly unhistorical fact of a medieval German rabbinical student spending some seven years of study in Spain. The asceticism of Ashkenazic Judaism is softened by the self-indulgence of the

Sephardim, and one is tempted to explain Rabbi Abraham's subsequent flight with Sarah, his wife, from their crowded seder table, just prior to a charge of ritual murder—an act so contrary to the Ashkenazic ethos of martyrdom but fully in tune with the surging spirit of individualism—as a consequence of the Spanish sojourn. Whatever the great descriptive merits of this chapter—which was probably the only one finished by the time of Heine's conversion in 1825—it still embodied the self-conflict he had set out to transcend.[34]

Sephardic subject matter remained a staple of the early Jewish historical novel. No one contributed more to this genre than Ludwig Philippson, perhaps the most adept popular mediator of Judaism in nineteenth-century Germany, who along with his brother Phöbus, a talented writer and physician, produced numerous historical novels meant to inspire respect and sympathy for Judaism. The drama usually unfolds at high speed on a familiar international stage; Jews are awash in persecution but abound in virtue, and the courtship of a gentile paragon never manages to overcome the religious loyalty of an exquisite Jewish damsel. The ingredients for this formula, as in *Die Marannen* (1843), *Hispania und Jerusalem* (1843), and *Jakob Tirado* (1867), are often drawn from the stockpile of Sephardic history. Its massive appeal is epitomized in a memorable scene in *Die Marannen*, which is set in Granada in 1492 after the final defeat of the last Arab stronghold on the Iberian Peninsula. Don Isaac Abravanel appears before Ferdinand and Isabella to avert the immediate consequence of victory, the pending expulsion of Spanish Jewry. His argument is threefold: The Jews have lived in Spain since the destruction of Jerusalem's First Temple, longer than in any other country of Europe. They have cultivated the arts and sciences, which ennoble the human spirit. And they have never demeaned themselves by lapsing into petty trade or moneylending. "In the entire realm there is not a single grandee, hidalgo, or burger who is indebted to a Jew," Philippson writes. If indeed Abravanel's words have a ring of contemporaneity to them, it is because the entire German Jewish perception of Spanish Jewry was such a mix of present need and past reality.[35]

In Berthold Auerbach's first novel, a fictionalized life of Spinoza published in 1837, the myth is extended to Amsterdam, as it is in Philippson's *Jakob Tirado*, and facilitates the reappropriation of Spinoza for Jewish history.[36] The book is the work of a young freethinker who has but recently abandoned the idea of devoting his life to the rabbinate, and it certainly is a brief for the supremacy of reason and the freedom of the individual. But for all his alienation from the theology and group primacy of Judaism, Auerbach portrays Spinoza as a reincarnation of Maimonides. As the young Spinoza is about to cross the intellectual threshold separating Judaism from the rest of humankind, the narrator exclaims: "Did not Maimonides already teach that the pious of all religions attain eternal salvation?"[37] The implicit universalism of Sephardic rationalism is about to be rendered explicit. Despite the evident break, on a deeper level, the secular messianism imputed by Auerbach to Spinoza seems but a step along the cultural continuum from Córdoba to Amsterdam. Spinoza became the cultural hero of German Jews, not only because they read him selectively, but also because he seemed to sum up the loftiest ideas of the Sephardic tradition.[38]

The fourth and final area pervaded by the Spanish bias is German Jewry's greatest and most enduring cultural achievement—the science of Judaism (*Wissenschaft des Judentums*). Its relationship to that bias was dialectic: while historical research certainly did not set off the Spanish siren, its ready submission worked to enrich and enhance its resonance. The course of modern Jewish scholarship cannot be understood apart from the Spanish mystique, and in fact, no other area of modern Jewish culture remained under its sway as long. The purpose of our present discussion is merely to adumbrate its development and to show its consonance with the broader cultural scene.

Historical thinking in modern Judaism was nurtured on a Spanish diet. The most cogent proof of this is the fact that the first two subfields to emerge—medieval Jewish philosophy and poetry—consisted primarily of texts produced by Spanish authors. Both foci represent an unforced extension of the *Haskalah*'s prior interest in the philosophy of Maimonides and the revival of Hebrew poetry. By the 1840s, the pages of the weekly *Literaturblatt des Orients*, for a decade the most fecund forum of Jewish scholarly exchange in Central Europe, teemed with texts and studies of Jewish cultural creativity under Islam.[39] There was nothing fortuitous about the rash of German translations and paraphrases of the ethical and philosophic works of the likes of Bahya ibn

Pakuda (1836), Maimonides (1838, 1839), Joseph Albo (1844), Saadia (1845), and Halevi (1853), often without benefit of manuscripts or in some cases the Arabic original.[40] The recovery of the medieval rationalist tradition rejected by Ashkenazic Judaism addressed internal and external religious and political needs.[41] Yet despite the impulse of extraneous concerns, the subfield of Jewish philosophy early on—thanks to the heroic scholarship of Salomon Munk, a Prussian expatriate in Paris—could boast of two of the crowning achievements of nineteenth-century Jewish Wissenschaft: the identification of Salomon ibn Gabirol as the unexpected author of a major eleventh-century Neoplatonic work, the *Fons vitae (Mekor Hayim)*, which till Munk was held to be the treatise of a non-Jewish philosopher (1846), and the publication and translation into French of the Arabic original of Maimonides' *Guide* (1856–66).[42] Decades of spadework emboldened Munk to declare exactly what his Jewish audience yearned to hear: "Jews unquestionably shared with Arabs the distinction of having preserved and disseminated the science of philosophy during the centuries of barbarism, thereby exercising a civilizing influence on Europe for a long time."[43]

The early flowering of the study of medieval Hebrew poetry was also indebted to Spanish soil. Scholarship fleshed out intuition. In this case, the first serious work devoted to the history of Hebrew poetry did not come from a Jewish scholar but rather from a conservative young Lutheran academic at the University of Leipzig by the name of Franz Delitzsch, who was destined to become the greatest Christian Hebraist of the century. A modest study, but of immense sweep and lavish empathy, Delitzsch's *Zur Geschichte der jüdischen Poesie* unfurled a vision of an unbroken tradition of Hebrew poetry from the close of the Hebrew canon down to the *Haskalah*. It thus constituted a worthy sequel in subject and spirit to Herder's renowned analysis of biblical poetry published a half-century before.[44] Its relevance to our immediate concern is Delitzsch's clear Spanish bias, which he either absorbed from Julius Fürst, his Hebrew mentor, or arrived at on his own. Indeed, his value-laden nomenclature strengthened the preference. He was the first scholar to bestow on specific periods of Spanish Jewish poetry such glowing rubrics as "the golden age" (940–1040), "the silver age" (1040–1140), and "the age of roses among the thorns" (1140–1240?), and thereby to forge a literary classification that would long govern the field and even discolor the picture of the political and social context.[45] By way of contrast, he depicted the later medieval poetry of German Jews with all the animus of a typically alienated Ashkenazic intellectual:

> Without civic freedom, without secure domicile, facing an ignorant, fanatical papal and monastic world, excluded from all public, useful activity and forced into the most menial and mindless occupations, Jews of the German Empire vegetated within the halakha's four ells and talmudic study halls and took refuge in the secret and mystical recesses of the Kabbalah. . . . Thus the Jewish literature of the time, in comparison with that across the Pyrenees . . . bears the character of dark seclusion, of sorrowful and esoteric impenetrability, of tasteless and artless literary style and structure.[46]

A few years after the appearance of Delitzsch's book, the Sephardic mystique evoked a full-fledged study of the religious poetry of Spanish Jewry. Its author was Michael Sachs, a trained philologist and gifted translator, who in 1844 had been chosen to become the first modern rabbinic leader of the burgeoning Jewish community in Berlin. More pertinent, he was an eloquent romantic completely at odds with the self-criticism and religious program of the radical Reform movement, which was gaining strength in Germany. To confound the low self-esteem on which the movement was predicated, he sought to unveil and celebrate for a German audience some of the finest religious expressions of the Jewish spirit, a search that quite naturally took him to Spain. And, as might be expected, his book of translations and exposition opened with a splendid German rendition of Ibn Gabirol's *Keter malkhut* (Royal Crown), whose poetic depiction of the cosmos from a religious perspective is a gem of Jewish universalism.[47]

Ironically, Sachs's monument to the religious creativity of Spanish Jewry owed much to an Italian romantic who battled for a lifetime against the very bias the book epitomized. In his letters to Sachs, Samuel David Luzzatto chided his slightly younger German colleague, with whom he generously shared his trove of manuscripts and incomparable knowledge of Hebrew, for avoiding the religious legacy of German Jewry. He disputed the alleged distinction by Shlomo Yehudah Rapoport between the poetry of Ashkenaz and Sepharad that informed Sachs's principle of selection. In the face of the still vast number of unpublished poems from both geographic sectors, the generalization simply did not hold:

> And after what God has brought into my hands of these poems, it seems to me that the Sephardim composed more "national songs" than the Ashkenazim. Moreover, I've noticed that a sense of Israel's superiority, a love for its national concerns, a hatred of its enemies, a national enthusiasm, and even fanaticism are no less evident in the poems of Sepharad than Ashkenaz. . . . For in truth, what can a creature say to his Creator if he avoids every expression of nationality and individuality? Philosophy and poetry are adversaries, and if we remove from the realm of poetry the spirit of zeal and hatred, then "who could endure its coldness?"[48]

But Sachs persisted in his plan to minimize the parochial and pointedly omitted from the book all the specimens of Sephardic nationalism that Luzzatto had sent him.[49] Yet in the end, despite the reservations that Luzzatto aired in a generally favorable review when the book appeared, he warmly appreciated Sachs's religious conservatism: "Far be it for me to raise my sword against you," he wrote toward the end of the review, "for you are an ornament for Judaism, and I shall always hope that if for now our hearts are not alike, someday they will unite."[50]

The power of Sachs's achievement did, however, touch the heart of the ailing Heine en route to his "mattress grave." Without that book, Heine, reduced now to the state of "a poor Jew sick unto death, an emaciated image of wretchedness, an unhappy man," would never have written his epic poem "Jehuda ben Halevi."[51] In his notes to the poem, he quotes Sachs verbatim, and even in its unfinished form, it gives the appearance of a poetic version of Sachs's Sephardic galaxy. But Heine's hero is the poem's namesake, and in one memorable passage on Halevi's unique talent, the two identities merge completely: "The extraordinary poet graced by God sins neither in prose nor poetry. Responsible to God alone, he may be killed by the people, but they can never pass judgment on him."[52] Sachs had provided Heine with the inspiration he had lacked years before when he began his *Rabbi of Bacherach*—a work of Jewish history that uplifted as well as informed.

Scholarship, like literature, soon moved to embellish the Sephardic mystique by appropriating the Diaspora created after the expulsion from Spain. The link was effected in 1859 by Moritz Meyer Kayserling in a study of the vernacular poetry of Sephardic exiles that may, in fact, have been intended as a complement to Sachs's initiative. Born in Hanover in 1829, and the son-in-law of Ludwig Philippson, Kayserling eventually became the liberal rabbi of Budapest and his generation's leading Jewish scholar of Sephardic Jewry. In this early work, boldly entitled *Sephardim: Romanische Poesien der Juden in Spanien*, and cast in a rather militantly Jewish tone, Kayserling exults in the contributions of Sephardic literati, mainly in Amsterdam, to Spanish and Portuguese literature of the early modern period. The group portrait he crafts highlights the very traits that would resonate with a readership of Jews justifying emancipation to themselves and others. Persecution had not destroyed the aristocratic bearing, the cultural loyalty, the linguistic purity, and the alliance of religion with secular learning that had distinguished Spanish Jewry. Retention of an unadulterated language became a measure of character and culture, and worldliness tempered religious fanaticism. Without restraint or refinement, Kayserling dared to assert that the Spanish and Portuguese Jews

> were the first who united in themselves religion and science, maintaining both in equal measure. Their religious behavior was always so pure, so free of all hypocrisy, forever remaining one and the same, far removed from all incursions of vapid rationalizing, because it emerged united with science, which in turn kept it from ever losing its way. We must constantly acknowledge the benefit that wherever Spanish and Portuguese Jews settled, they spread culture, knowledge, and solid learning.[53]

The relevance of this cultural paradigm is not only blatant, but precludes any possible appreciation of the "anomalous" history of Sephardic mysticism.

Nevertheless, the historical canvas had been significantly broadened. Kayserling inaugurated the scholarly study of the Sephardic legacy in Amsterdam; he demonstrated the validity of a definition of Jewish literature that went beyond works by Jews in Hebrew; and finally he drew a number of inventive parallels between Mendelsohn and Menasseh ben Israel that solidified the Sephardic affinity for the Dessau sage by tracing it through Amsterdam. But the study of Sephardim in Amsterdam could not break out of the conceptual grid created by the dominant periodization of the Wissenschaft circle. Mendelsohn's persona and achievement signaled the "renaissance" of Judaism in the modern period; its "dark ages" had not set in until the extinction of Judaism in Spain. A chronological sequence is given a causal nexus: the triumph of rampant rabbinism in Poland in the sixteenth century is made a consequence of the destruction of Spanish Jewry in the fifteenth century. And it is only with Mendelsohn's spiritualization of Judaism that the synthesis once forged in Spain is restored. Thus the Sephardic bias shapes the need to order the seamless continuum of Jewish history into meaningful and manageable structural units, and the resulting periodization long defied the accumulation of conflicting evidence.

An early and unsophisticated, but therefore instructive, example of this periodization is to be found in the 1820 *Vorlesungen über die neuere Geschichte der Juden* by Salomon Löwisohn (Shlomo Levisohn), which Zunz dismissed with cryptic sarcasm three years later.[54] Löwisohn, who died at the age of thirty-two in 1821, was a transitional figure—a Prague *Maskil* (i.e, a proponent of internal rejuvenation) who came to Vienna in 1815 to work as a Hebrew editor in the press of Anton Schmid, and a talented Hebrew poet with more than a passing interest in Jewish history. His German tract is little more than a collection of aperçus on some of the more noteworthy figures of Jewish history in the Diaspora, usually selected from the Islamic or Sephardic orbit, and relies far too heavily on evidence culled from Latin chroniclers and Christian bibliographers. Of interest here is that while modern Jewish scholarship would soon repudiate his methodological naïveté, it would remain largely subservient to his periodization. Despite the attainments of the Sephardim in Amsterdam, and Löwisohn extols their famous synagogue as the most beautiful Jewish sanctuary since the Second Temple, he declares that the Spanish expulsion ushered in the most benighted period in Jewish history. As the Enlightenment advanced in the Christian world, Jewry sank beneath the pall of Polish Judaism—its mounting burden of commandments and commentaries, its suffocating talmudism, its proliferating superstitions, and its antagonism to morality and secular learning—not to be redeemed until "that marvelous man [*Wundermann*], chosen by fate for a higher calling, until Mendelsohn came and effected that stunning revolution in the inner life of Israel, whose healing and glorious results are still not in full view."[55]

After three decades of critical research, the same periodization is still one of the few points in common between works as dissimilar as Ludwig Philippson's popular public lectures in 1847 on *Die Entwickelung der religiösen Idee im Judenthume, Christenthume und Islam* and Moritz Steinschneider's massively erudite encyclopedia essay of 1850 on *Jüdische Literatur*. Adversaries rather than colleagues, both men nevertheless treated the Spanish expulsion as a cultural watershed. For all that Steinschneider knew of the cultural productivity of Jews during the three centuries before his own, his uniformly harsh assessment of the quality of its diverse expressions concurred with the far less learned opinion offered by Philippson: "Longer than among the Arabs and Christians, a scientific impulse survived among the Jews till into the fifteenth century. Amid widespread persecutions, specifically the expulsion from Spain, it was extinguished."[56]

The import of this passage is that the demarcation is cultural. Not the loss of life or the trauma of suffering but the disappearance of a distinctive religious style is what blankets the next age in "darkness." The uniqueness of Sephardic Judaism on which this periodization rests is most evident when we look for its point of emergence, and by 1850 the cultural historians of the Wissenschaft movement—Zunz, Sachs, and Steinschneider, in particular—had built a strong case for placing the start of the period that ended with the collapse of Judaism on the Iberian Peninsula back in the eighth century. The triumph of Islam had brought the major centers of Jewish life within the ambience of a dynamic society in cultural ferment.[57] The confrontation between an unreflective, text-based, and inward-looking Judaism and a self-confident Islamic civilization fertilized by the legacy of Greece resulted in a transformation of Jewish thought patterns and modes of expression. The flowering of Jewish learning under Islam diminished the independent study of halakha, thereby increasing popular reliance on the *geonim* (the heads of the rabbinic academies in Baghdad), and turned the undifferentiated and intuitive corpus of midrash (the vast literature of rabbinic exegesis of the Bible) into distinct and critical disciplines.[58] According to Steinschneider, whose historical survey of Jewish literature is predicated on this periodization, "midrash and Haggadah were the emanation of the national spirit through the prevailing method of oral transmission. With the Arab-Greek culture, the spirit of the individual comes to the fore. Only now do writers, authors, and distinct disciplines actually arise."[59] What is more, Steinschneider was prepared to call this sustained leavening of rabbinic Judaism by the world of Islam Sephardic Judaism, after its dominant representatives—Spanish Jewry (*Sefarad* being the Hebrew term for Spain).[60] But in this instance, the metonymy is not just a figure of speech: it is the sanctification of an ideal type that is more symbol than substance. The Sephardic bias had rendered Spanish Jewry synonymous with an era of Jewish history that shamed the religious fanaticism and cultural narrowness of medieval Christendom. To see that era as ended by the Christian-inspired expulsion from Spain only confirmed the truth of the periodization.[61]

What should be equally evident by now is that the ultimate power and appeal of the Sephardic mystique in the age of emancipation derived from its Greek core.[62] In 1847, Luzzatto had admonished Steinschneider, at the outset of his scholarly career, not "to glorify and flaunt those Jews whose being was not truly Jewish but Greek or Arabic."[63] But the temptation was reinforced by need. Islamic civilization had fertilized Judaism with the philosophy and science of the Hellenic world, and that link was vital to the process of Westernizing Judaism in the nineteenth century. The Sephardic mystique not only provided emancipated Jews with a source of pride and an instrument of rebellion, but also enabled them to recover a classical heritage in common with German culture. On one level, it was the Jewish equivalent of what one historian has called "the tyranny of Greece over Germany."[64] If our analysis has proven anything, it is that a literate German Jew was as likely to venerate the Sephardim as a Wilhelm von Humboldt the Greeks:

> Our study of Greek history is therefore a matter quite different from our other historical studies. For us, the Greeks step out of the circle of history. . . . Knowledge of the Greeks is not merely pleasant, useful or necessary for us—no, in the Greeks alone we find the ideal of that which we ourselves should like to be and produce.[65]

Substitute the word "Sephardim" for "Greeks" and the tribute could have come from any number of the people discussed in this chapter.

But on a deeper level, the resemblance rested on identity, for in Spain, Islamic culture as conduit infused Judaism with a large dose of Greek rationalism. In 1841, at the end of a majestic survey of Jewish contributions to geographical literature, Zunz elaborated on the Greek role in Jewish history. "Three times did Jews encounter the Hellenic spirit, the emancipator of nations." Besides the experience of his own day and the confrontation in the Greco-Roman world, Zunz spoke of the encounter under Islam:

> When in the eighth century, the victorious Arabs were subdued by the books of the conquered, Syrian and Arabic authors introduced for a second time Greek knowledge among the Jews of Muslim countries: astronomy, philosophy, medicine, and by degrees geography. German and French Jews, in contrast, partook of the darkness of the Middle Ages, although they still retained advantages over the Christians, not only by virtue of a more ancient cultivation, but also by the gradual introduction and influence of the Hebrew-Arabic literature.[66]

Paradoxically, contact with Islam had made Judaism part of the Western world.

Two Writing Spanish History in Nineteenth-Century Britain

The Inquisition and "the Secret Race"

Michael Ragussis

Writing in 1837, prominent American historian William Prescott remarked that "English writers have done more for the illustration of Spanish history than . . . any other, except their own."[1] In the following pages I wish to explain the ideological uses to which Spanish history was put in England, focusing on how one era in particular, the period of the Inquisition, became a charged subject, especially for Victorian writers of historical romance. The forced conversion of masses of Jews, the famous edict expelling them in 1492, and the Inquisition's persecution of crypto-Jews made fifteenth-century Spain an object of fascination for nineteenth-century England, where the Evangelical drive to convert the Jews and the parliamentary debates over Jewish emancipation had put "the Jewish question" at the center of England's national agenda. Moreover, as England attempted to define the origins of the nation-state as a way of articulating its own national identity, the history of Spain provided a dangerous model—dangerous, at least, for England's Jews, for by locating the origins of modern Spain in the conquest of Muslim Granada and the banishment of the Jews, nineteenth-century historians and novelists alike began to use fifteenth-century Spain as a paradigm for the birth of a nation based in racial and religious homogeneity.

It is of course well known that after the immense public success of Walter Scott's historical romances, the writing of history began to be taken up by writers of romance. Prescott himself applauded the contributions that romance could make to historical study, remarking that Scott "had given new value to romance by building it on history, and new charms to history by embellishing it with the graces of romance."[2] But Victorian historical romance owed more than a general debt to Scott. The specific literary model behind Victorian romance's focus on the role of the Jews in medieval Spain was *Ivanhoe*'s depiction of Jewish persecution in medieval England. By depicting the persecution of the Jews at a critical moment in history—the founding of the English nation-state—*Ivanhoe* located "the Jewish question" at the heart of English national identity.

In the first half of this essay, I examine a group of historical romances written between the 1830s and the 1860s that reveal the ways in which representations of "the Jewish question" set in fifteenth-century Spain became a means of exploring urgent issues of national identity perceived as racial difference in Victorian England. Focused on a daughter's duty to her father and her fatherland, and the threat of her conversion, these romances define the role of women in the construction of the modern nation-state. The literary trope of the converted Jewish daughter, descended from such texts as Marlowe's *The Jew of Malta* and Shakespeare's *The Merchant of Venice*, was reinvented in countless now-forgotten nineteenth-century novels during the Evangelical revival's immensely influential drive to convert the Jews.[3] When writers of historical romance situated the converted Jewish daughter at the founding moment of Christian Spain, she became a sign of the ideology that required Jews to be converted before they could become full-fledged English citizens. In the second half of this essay I turn to the way in which the story of the Inquisition was reinscribed in the 1870s, both in the culture of England at large and in the novels of Anthony Trollope and George Eliot in particular. At this point the drama of the converted Jew was staged in England, not in the misty pages of historical romance, but in the daily events of the life of the nation. All eyes were fixed on the premiership of Benjamin Disraeli, during what became a crisis in English national identity, when it was jibed that an "Oriental dictator" ruled England.

The historical romances I examine—*Leila; or, The Siege of Granada* (1838) by Edward Bulwer-Lytton; *The Vale of Cedars; or, The Martyr* (1850) by Grace Aguilar, an English Jew; and *The Spanish Gypsy* (1868) by George Eliot—can be seen as a direct response, even a sequel, to *Ivanhoe*. Rebecca's stinging critique of England at the end of *Ivanhoe* and her justification of her impending flight to Spain invited Scott's successors in historical romance to take up "the Jewish question" in medieval Spain. Scott's extraordinary anachronism—Rebecca, in late twelfth-century England, plans her protection under a king (Boabdil of Granada) who reigned in late fifteenth-century Spain—opened the way for these sequels to undercut Scott's contrast between intolerant England and tolerant Spain, for by the late fifteenth century, the relative peace and prosperity that the Jews had enjoyed under the Moors was about to end in a kind of recapitulation of Anglo-Jewish history: the expulsion of the Jews that had occurred in 1290 in England was repeated in 1492 in Spain. In short, the persecution of the Jews that dominated fifteenth-century Spain, including the forced conversion of masses of Spanish Jews and the eventual institution of the Inquisition, provided sufficient historical material to challenge Rebecca's choice of Spain over England. In this light, these historical romances can be read within a larger field of nineteenth-century English discourse in which different national identities are defined, usually through a more or less explicit contrast—in this case, between Protestant England and Catholic Spain.

Each of these historical romances is set in Spain in the final decades of the fifteenth century in the midst of the extraordinary political upheavals out of which the modern nation-state would develop. As in *Ivanhoe*, the birth of a nation is represented as occurring in an environment of extreme racial conflict, amid the politics of religious conversion and racial annihilation. In *Ivanhoe*, intermarriage between Saxon and Norman (after generations of conflict), and the impending exile of the Jews (after the failure of many attempts at converting them), signals the birth of modern England. A similar pattern emerged in Spanish history in 1492 when the Spaniards conquered the Moors at Granada, and the Catholic monarchs Ferdinand and Isabella banished the Jews (after the failure of periodic attempts at converting them). In both nations, at both epochs, then, the Jews made up the third "racial" group in what was essentially a battle between two other, more powerful groups seeking control of a land on the verge of modern nationhood. In this way, late fifteenth-century Spain replicated the conditions of late twelfth-century England represented in *Ivanhoe*.

But whereas Scott's novel stresses the ultimate union of the Saxons and Normans and identifies the expulsion of the Jews as a blot on English history, his successors frequently used Spanish history to proclaim racial exclusivity as the basis for the nation-state. Prescott's immensely popular history of Spain, for example, which Eliot read as part of her research for *The Spanish Gypsy*, was based on a crucial revision of Scott's views. Prescott disqualified the parallelisms which Scott set between a racialized model of Saxon and Norman conflict and Spain's clash between the "Oriental" (Moor) and the "European" (Spaniard). Rejecting Scott's model of interracial blending as a foundation for modern nations, Prescott argued that in Spain

> the Oriental and the European [were] for eight centuries brought into contact with one another, yet, though brought into contact, too different in blood, laws, and religion ever to coalesce. Unlike the Saxons and Normans, who, sprung from a common stock, with a common faith, were gradually blended into one people, in Spain, the conflicting elements could never mingle.[4]

Spanish history was thus used by Prescott to establish the category of "race" as an insuperable barrier between different peoples, and to define national identity on the basis of racial and religious homogeneity.

While Prescott's justification of the Spanish conquest and eradication of the Moors allowed him, during his own nation's ongoing debate over "the Indian question," to defend (if only indirectly) the extermination of entire Native American populations, the writing of Spanish history in England had its own ideological goals. For example, John Stockdale's highly influential *History of the Inquisitions* (1810), one of the source texts to which writers of Victorian romance turned, did not hide the urgent political ends it served, namely, to undermine Catholic emancipation, which Stockdale saw as threatening the English national character. At a time when "the important question [about] the claims of the Roman Catholics to equal political rights with Protestants" was being "forced upon the Parliament," Stockdale felt the necessity of laying before Protestant Britain the horrors of papal power, as displayed in the various inquisitions of Spain, Portugal, Venice, and Rome. In this context, Stockdale writes a "history" that misrepresents the historic origins of the Inquisition in Jewish persecution. Stockdale periodically writes "Moor" when "Jew" would be historically correct, as in his assignment of the origins of the Spanish Inquisition to Torquemada's attempt to protect Christianity from the heretical influences of the Moors. After all, Stockdale's goal was to defeat "what is insidiously termed Catholic Emancipation," and insofar as Catholic emancipation might have opened the door to removing similar civil and political disabilities from which the Jews themselves suffered, he managed to write a history that was anti-Catholic without being pro-Jewish—that is, a history that inflamed Protestant Britain against Catholic fanaticism while refusing to stir British sympathies for the Jewish martyrs of the Inquisition. Such a history of the Inquisition was intended to keep the English national character secure from Catholic *and* Jewish influence.[5]

This double goal was already evident in the Gothic novel, an immensely popular source of ideas about the Inquisition for English readers. In *The Monk* (1796), for example, Matthew Lewis anatomized "monastic cruelty" in Catholic Spain at the same time that he represented the Jew not as a victim of the Inquisition but as a ghostly figure from legend, part of the machinery of Gothic horror, "doomed to inspire all who look on me with terror and detestation."[6] In the character of the Wandering Jew, Lewis managed to construct a figure of fantastic homelessness, while making reference neither to the real diaspora that Spanish Jews suffered after 1492 nor to the real persecutions Jews suffered under the Inquisition. So, in the writing of both history and fiction, representations of the Inquisition in England typically served the purpose of attacking Catholicism, while neglecting and even obfuscating the history of Jewish persecution.

Daughter and Father(land): The Ideology of Conquest and Conversion

The central character in each of the three historical romances I wish to explore here is a daughter who undergoes a dramatic and painful confrontation with her father, who pleads with her in the manner that Scott's Cedric pleads with his two symbolic daughters, Rowena and Ulrica, to uphold their Saxon heritage. In the politics of nineteenth-century European nationalism, women's central trial is represented as the trial of national, religious, or racial loyalty—a paradigm originating in Scott's portraits of Rowena, Ulrica, and Rebecca in *Ivanhoe*. Filial loyalty in all these texts is the pretext for racial loyalty; the heroine is not simply the daughter of the father but the daughter of the race. Unlike the heroic Rebecca, the "daughter of Zion" who decides without any counsel from her father to "tear this folly from my heart, though every fibre bleed as I rend it away,"[7] the daughters in *Ivanhoe*'s sequels I discuss here—Bulwer-Lytton's *Leila*, Aguilar's *Vale of Cedars*, and Eliot's *Spanish Gypsy*—must be persuaded by the father to give up a love that threatens "the God of your fathers." In all three of these romances, the father prohibits intermarriage, making the novel's focus a battle between father and lover over the possession of the young heroine. The real object of this battle is the propagation and extinction of different, even warring, religions and races: in each text the survival of a minority population is threatened through a daughter's conversion, or what amounts to the same thing, her intermarriage. The relationship in these texts between father and daughter, then, can be formulated in the following way: the threat of racial extinction is represented through the pairing of a widowed father, without further means of procreating his race, and a sole daughter in danger of becoming, through conversion or intermarriage, a tool in the procreation of the enemy race. Hence the daughter's pure instrumentality in these tales; she serves the critical function of propagating the race and preserving the racial name. For this reason, these texts revise the conventional marriage plot that ends when the lover supersedes the father, becomes the husband, and changes the heroine's name to his own; in the racial plot, the father reemerges at a critical moment in order to reestablish the heroine's racial identity and thereby to preclude the successful completion of the marriage plot.

The double title of Bulwer-Lytton's novel, *Leila; or, The Siege of Granada*, instructs us in the way in which these historical romances focus on a double storyline: the domestic story of the daughter and the public story of the nation. So in *Leila*, while we follow the Jewish father's complicated switching of allegiances between Christian and Moor, in what eventually becomes the famous siege of Granada, we also follow the Jewish family plot—namely, Almamen's attempt to guard his daughter Leila's Jewish heritage. In other words, the larger historical plot involving the battle for political power among three races in fifteenth-century Spain is paralleled in the domestic plot in which both Christian and Moor threaten the Jewish family. In fact, I argue that the parallel plots spell the complete Christianization of Spain, one by battle and the other by conversion, for the conquest of Granada, in which Muslim Spain is finally put to rout, is echoed in the conquest of the Jewish daughter.

Leila's plot of conversion begins in the following way. While successfully secreting his daughter from her Moorish lover, Almamen inadvertently delivers her into the hands of the Christian monarchs and Leila is subjected to the procedures of conversion by the queen's intermediary, Donna Inez. The depiction of a Christian woman trying to convert a Jewish woman becomes a set piece in nineteenth-century historical romance, recalling the climactic moment in *Ivanhoe* when Rowena offers Rebecca the means of conversion. As in Scott's novel, the Jewish maiden in *Leila*, as well as in *The Vale of Cedars*, is asked to unveil herself, at which point the Christian woman in power takes pity on her and prescribes the procedures of conversion to act on "the yielding softness of our sex."[8]

Donna Inez's specialty is "by gentle means to make the conversions which force was impotent to effect," and Leila is commanded to "listen with ductile senses to her gentle ministry." But even such a gentle ministry—this proselytization of woman by woman—proceeds as a parallel to the siege of Granada that is the novel's public and masculine plot: "Donna Inez sought rather to undermine than to storm the mental fortress she hoped to man with spiritual allies." The strategies of proselytism are exposed as an arsenal of weapons that Donna Inez uses to undermine "the belief upon which she waged war" (*Leila*, 87, 82, 87). In this way, the conquest of Muslim Granada runs parallel to the conversion of the Jewish daughter; each is part of a cooperative effort in the birth of the new Catholic Spain.

During a brief reunion with Almamen in a striking tableau, daughter and father are represented as extreme antitheses, both fantasies of the Christian ideology of conversion—the daughter the symbol of easy conversion, the father the symbol of the "stubborn race": "And so passed the hours of that night; and the father and the child—the meek convert, the revengeful fanatic—were under the same roof" (*Leila*, 110, 109). This tableau, with its images of male intransigence and female docility, pinpoints the roles of father and daughter in these racial plots. Almamen succeeds in winning Leila back, so that the convert, converted back again, yields in the presence of patriarchal power: "Father, wheresoever thou goest, I will wend with thee." Leila, variously named "Jewess," "Christian," and "deist," is the unending object of conversion, and therefore is most appropriately named in the address that takes away her proper name and names her by her function in the plot: "Thou, my sweet convert" (113, 88–90, 107).

The highly symbolic function of the Jewish daughter in the clash among three races and religions in fifteenth-century Spain has its final demonstration in our last view of Leila, surrounded by the three male characters who claim her: Almamen, her Jewish (biological) father; Torquemada, the Catholic (spiritual) father; and Muza, her Muslim lover. The characters meet at the altar of a convent in which Leila is about to take her vows as a nun. While Muza hopes to revise this setting according to the conventions of the happy climax of comedy, the father turns the potential marriage altar into the altar of sacrifice, realizing the full extent of patriarchal power in the act of filicide: "thrice the blade of the Hebrew had passed through that innocent breast; thrice was it reddened with that virgin blood. Leila fell in the arms of her lover," her virgin blood spilled at the sacred altar before she can marry either the mortal or the eternal bridegroom. The battle over Leila ends when she is no longer able to perform her regenerative function as the "daughter of the great Hebrew race," a function explained to her by her father earlier in the novel: "If thou perish, if thou art lost to us, thou, the last daughter of the house of Issachar, then the haughtiest family of God's great people is extinct. . . . I look to thee and thy seed for . . . regeneration" (*Leila*, 160, 20, 114). In killing his daughter, Almamen reenacts what he sees as her death through conversion, so that the converted Jewish daughter functions in *Leila* as a sign both of the birth of the Spanish nation and the extinction of the Jewish race in Spain.

Bulwer-Lytton ends his novel by pressing the analogy between the conversion of Leila (the domestic plot) and the conquest of Boabdil (the national plot) as cooperative events in the Christianization of Spain (or the extinction of Jew and Muslim): "While in this obscure and remote convent progressed the history of an individual, we are summoned back to witness the crowning fate of an expiring dynasty." After the conquest of Granada during the final departure of the last monarch of the Moorish dynasty, Leila's conversion is recalled when Queen Isabel seeks to make the military conquest of the Moors complete by turning it into a religious conquest: "May we not hint at the blessed possibility of conversion?" (144, 174). But already Boabdil recognizes the ways in which this "blessed possibility" has become the accomplished fact of political power. He sees the silver cross of Spain atop the watchtower of the Alhambra and hears the chant of "Te Deum." Conquest and conversion have already become inseparable.

Finally, the climactic moments of the double plot of *Leila* are given over to parental charges of unfulfilled filial duty. Almamen reproaches Leila for failing to preserve the house of Issachar, and Boabdil's mother reproaches him for failing to preserve the Moorish dynasty. The nature of the mother's stinging reproach makes us see the conjunction between conversion and conquest in a new light. The feminine ductility responsible for Leila's conversion also seems responsible for Boabdil's conquest; his mother chides him: "Ay, weep like a woman over what thou couldst not defend like a man!" (175). The "converted" (Jewish daughter) and the "conquered" (Moorish son) function under the sign of the feminine in *Leila*. What Spanish history teaches us, then, is a lesson, not simply in Catholic intolerance, but in the birth of the modern nation-state through the twin successes of religious conversion and racial extinction.

In its focus on the docility of "woman's heart" (89), Bulwer-Lytton's *Leila* keeps in place the conventional ideology of the convertibility of the Jewish daughter descended from such texts as *The Jew of Malta* and *The Merchant of Venice*. In fact, Bulwer-Lytton uses the figure of the feminine to represent both the conversion of the Jews and the conquest of the Moors as decisive moments in the development of Spain as a nation. By contrast, Grace Aguilar's *The Vale of Cedars; or, The Martyr* depicts "the female heart" as peculiarly strong and resilient—so strong that Jewish survival depends on it.[9] So while Bulwer-Lytton, through the figure of conversion, represents the erasure of minority cultures in the development of the racially and religiously homogeneous nation-state, Aguilar depicts the survival of Judaic culture in fifteenth-century Spain through her heroine's inconvertibility. For Marie epitomizes Jewish steadfastness, not the stubbornness that underlies the anti-Semitic stereotype of the "stiff-necked race," but "the martyr strength, for which she unceasingly prayed, to give up all if called upon for her God" (*Vale of Cedars*, 190, 187). In this way Marie, the martyr of Aguilar's title, recalls Scott's Rebecca, who redefines for the Templar "the heart of woman":

> Thou knowest not the heart of woman . . . not in thy fiercest battles hast thou displayed more of thy vaunted courage than has been shown by woman when called upon to suffer by affection or duty . . . when

> we enter those fatal lists, thou to fight and I to suffer, I feel the strong assurance within me that my courage shall mount higher than thine. (*Ivanhoe*, 443)

In these variations on the weakness and strength of "the heart of woman," historical romance in the nineteenth century explores woman's role in the erasure and preservation of religious and racial identity.

The Vale of Cedars is organized around a series of trials that test Marie's capacity to withstand the attempt to rewrite her Jewish identity. Marie's first "trial" comes when, having revealed her secret Judaism to Arthur Stanley, an English Catholic exile living in Spain, she sacrifices her love for him on the grounds of her religion: "There is a love, a duty stronger than that I bear to thee. I would resign all else, but not my father's God." We already hear the paternal interdiction of this intermarriage sounded in the name of Marie's God, "my father's God." Having discovered that her father has already planned a marriage for her with her cousin Ferdinand Morales, another secret Jew, Marie announces to her father, "Oh, my father, do what thou wilt, command me as thou wilt—I am henceforth wholly thine." This vow suggests the way in which the daughter is wed to the father, and thereby functions in the father's plan to propagate the race through her, so that the wedding between Morales and Marie soon turns into a scene of lovemaking between father and daughter: "She threw herself upon his bosom, and covered his cheek with kisses" (*Vale of Cedars*, 9, 10, 27, 34).

When Morales is murdered and Stanley is framed and falsely accused of the murder, the trials of Marie are temporarily interrupted by the legal trial of Stanley. Asked to give evidence of a heated argument that she witnessed between her husband and Stanley, Marie subverts the trial in an extraordinary act of self-sacrifice that, for the Jew in Christian Spain, amounts to no more than an act of self-naming: "My evidence is valueless. I belong to that race whose word is never taken as witness, for or against, in a court of justice. I cannot take the oath required, for I deny the faith in which it is administered. I am a JEWESS!" (*Vale of Cedars*, 122). In *Ivanhoe* the Jewish heroine on trial is saved by the English champion, Ivanhoe; but in *Vale of Cedars*, in a powerful revision of Scott's novel, the English hero on trial is saved by the Jewish heroine. Moreover, this reversal occurs through a potent reminder of the contemporary English debate over requiring Jews to take the same kind of oath that Marie refuses.[10] The fullest irony of this scene, then, depends on the Victorian reader's recognition that the civil disabilities from which the Jews suffer in contemporary Protestant England can be traced to what England typically viewed as the barbaric intolerance of fifteenth-century Catholic Spain. In short, the scene subtly unravels that contrast with Spain on which English national identity often depended.

Once the public recognition of Marie's Jewish identity occurs, the novel turns to an exploration of the institutional means by which the Spanish community attempts to convert Marie. Under the aegis of the Inquisition, Marie undergoes a trial that is no more than a pretext for rape. The Inquisitor insists that Marie sacrifice her body to his lust and her soul to his religion; raping Marie and converting her become part of a single desire, a single mission. Like Rebecca at the mercy of the Templar, Marie defends herself with a threat of suicide that temporarily staves off her pursuer. The torture that the Inquisitor subsequently inflicts on Marie's body functions at once as the substitute for his passion and the instrument of his proselytism. In this way the ideology of conversion once again merges with an ideology of the feminine; the ductility that makes woman the perfect candidate for conversion is equal to what is seen as her sexual weakness, her sexual submissiveness, her sexual usefulness.

Finally rescued from the prisons of the Inquisition, Marie falls into the hands of Queen Isabella, who now begins the third and last of Marie's trials. Isabella initiates the procedure of "gentle conversion," pointing out the error of Marie's faith but sympathizing with her sex: "Unbeliever though she be, offspring of a race which every true Catholic must hold in abhorrence, she is yet a *woman*" (*Vale of Cedars*, 131). The gentle conversion that the queen plans, like that devised by Bulwer-Lytton's Isabel in *Leila*, is a specifically feminine effort bent on protecting the Jewish heroine from the severity of the fanatical monks. Nonetheless, in a reprise of Rebecca's words, Marie rejects the womanly offer of conversion: Rebecca tells Rowena, "I may not change the faith of my fathers like a garment unsuited to the climate in which I seek to dwell" (*Ivanhoe*, 518), and Marie tells Isabella, "My creed . . . is no garment we may wear and cast off at pleasure." After a brief period of "banishment," Marie dies (*Vale of Cedars*, 196, 201).

Although the Jewish heroine dies in both *Leila* and *Vale of Cedars*, Aguilar never hints at the theme of racial extinction that preoccupies Bulwer. Insofar as Marie is "preserved from the crime [of] apostasy," Aguilar's novel focuses on the means by which the continuity of Jewish belief was secured in fifteenth-century Spain, often at the cost of martyrdom. Moreover, Aguilar's narrative stance in the novel is a powerful way of asserting the survival of Jewish belief. I refer here to those moments when Aguilar deliberately punctures the stance of the anonymous and neutral third-person narrator, to name herself both as a woman and as a Jew (*Vale of Cedars*, 214, 51, 144). Both acts of self-naming become narrative gestures that respond to the question of the survival of Jewish identity, addressing especially what had become the chief stereotype of apostasy, the converted Jewish woman. The narrator's identity as a Jew in nineteenth-century England becomes a special form of testimony to all those ancestors (including Aguilar's own Sephardic forebears) "whose children still survive" ("History of the Jews," 309). In further naming herself a Jewish *woman*, the narrator realizes her authority on the nature of the Jewish woman's heart—a topic too often represented by writers (like Bulwer) at once non-Jewish and male, and too often used for conversionist ends. Aguilar sought to critique the conversionist claim that the particular iconography and ideology of Christianity were especially suited to the female heart,[11] as Bulwer-Lytton's novel suggests in its picture of the pale and long-suffering Jewish heroine: "The sufferings of the Messiah, His sublime purity, His meek forgiveness, spoke to her woman's heart" (*Leila*, 89). Marie's inconvertibility, then, her discovery of dignity and purpose in living as a Jew, becomes the cornerstone of a historical commentary on why and how the Jewish woman played a role in preserving that Judaic heritage of which the author herself is the latest preserver. And when Aguilar, in her addresses to her reader, unveils her own identity as a Jewish woman, she represents for her contemporary audience what Marie herself desired: the full disclosure of Jewish identity, without reprisal; the full authenticity of the Jewish woman's word, even as evidence of the legitimacy of Jewish history and Jewish belief.

In such a context the narrator's own interested position becomes less a sign of narrative intrusion than a testimony to the continuity of Jewish belief in nineteenth-century England. After all, according to the narrator of *Daniel Deronda*, in Victorian England the Christian majority doubted the power and even the existence of Jewish belief, regarding "Judaism as a sort of eccentric fossilised form" rather than "something still throbbing in human lives, still making for them the only conceivable vesture of the world." For this reason the historicization of the Jewish question in *Vale of Cedars* is supplemented by the acknowledgment of the narrator's present belief. Without such an acknowledgment, Scott's medievalism might lead the nineteenth-century reader to view the Jew as no more than a historic relic, an exotic of another time and place. Eliot represents this danger in *Daniel Deronda* when the Meyricks view Mirah entirely in the light of Rebecca and seem to tolerate Judaism only as a condition of medieval romance: they "found the Jewish faith less reconcilable with their wishes in her [Mirah's] case than in that of Scott's Rebecca."[12] Similarly, Aguilar complains that of the Jew's "modern history so little is generally known, that the word *Jew* is associated only with biblical and ancient recollections."[13] For this reason *Vale of Cedars* represents both its heroine (of fifteenth-century Spain) and its narrator (of nineteenth-century England) as participants in the continuous development and preservation of Judaism.

In moving from a representation of the individual secret Jew in Bulwer-Lytton's novel to "the secret race" in Aguilar's novel, we see the critical importance of Aguilar's project for Victorian culture: the historicization of the mystified (and ahistorical) figure of the masked Jew, whether an amoral double agent in Bulwer-Lytton's novel or an amoral social climber in Trollope's novels of the 1870s, that is, the Jew who keeps his race secret in order to invade and to subvert Christian culture. First of all, Aguilar overturns on historical grounds the charge of Jewish hypocrisy, the latest libel against the Jews: "to accuse the secret Jews of Spain of hypocrisy, of departing from the pure ordinances of their religion, because *compelled* to simulate Catholicism, is taking indeed but a one-handed, short-sighted view" (*Vale of Cedars*, 22, 145). Moreover, in depicting the complicated strategies of duplicity that "the secret race" developed in order to survive, Aguilar conceives of the large population of crypto-Jews of Spain and Portugal as a specific social group living in specific historical conditions with customs and behavior designed to meet particular—and deadly—historical exigencies.

But even more pointed reasons stand behind the attempt by Aguilar and the Anglo-Jewish community in general to record the history of the Catholic persecution of the Jews during the Inquisition. First, this history was used as a defense against the renewed drive to convert the Jews in England, a drive reminiscent of Spanish Catholic proselytism. In *The Inquisition and Judaism* (1845), for example, Moses Mocatta used his translation of a conversionist sermon delivered by a Catholic archbishop at an auto-da-fé in Portugal in order to historicize the ideology of conversion, to situate it within a setting of persecution, and to decry its institutionalization in contemporary Britain: "In many parts of the Old and New World, but more especially in Great Britain, the conversion of the Jews has become an organized system."[14] Second, the history of Jewish persecution in Catholic Spain was used in an attempt to remove what in Aguilar's eyes was "the last relic of religious intolerance," namely, "the disabilities under which the Jews of Great Britain labour" ("History of the Jews," 272). It was not unusual during the Jewish emancipation debates that went on for thirty years for Protestants and Jews to align themselves in an anti-Catholic position: "Both Christians and Jews were apt to claim that biblical Judaism was the fount of primitive Christianity—corruption and persecution had been introduced into the Church together by the Popes, and only dispelled at the Reformation."[15] In this context the Anglo-Jewish community's complete unveiling of Jewish persecution under the Catholic Inquisition can be seen as an indirect argument for Jewish emancipation in a nation that had passed the Catholic Relief Act in 1829 but still failed at midcentury to grant Jews similar relief.

Aguilar's depiction of her Jewish heroines' *amor patriae*, even in the midst of persecution, functioned as an indirect critique of the anti-emancipation argument that the Jews would always constitute a (foreign) nation within a nation, as opposed to being loyal citizens of England. One may wonder "what secret feeling it was which thus bound [the Spanish Jews] to a country where, acknowledged or discovered, Judaism was death." Nonetheless, Aguilar's stories record "that feeling of *amor patriae*, . . . an emotion experienced in various degrees by every nation, but by the Jew in Spain with a strength and intensity equalled by none and understood but by a Jew."[16] And it is on the basis of such historical knowledge that the Jewish writer hints to the English nation that the English Jew is capable of a similar "love of fatherland" ("History of the Jews," 260). In this light, Jewish steadfastness, traditionally seen as the obstacle to conversion, is reimagined as the hallmark of the loyal (Jewish) citizen of England. Finally, if the banishment of the Jews signaled the founding of the intolerant nation-state of Catholic Spain, the full enfranchisement of the Jews was to mark the tolerance of Protestant England, the ultimate goal of the Anglo-Jewish community's attempt to record the history of the Inquisition in Spain for Victorian readers.

Like Marie in *Vale of Cedars*, Fedalma in Eliot's *The Spanish Gypsy* is a portrait of the heroism of the female heart that takes the form of a daughter's sacrifice to father and fatherland. The entire project of *Spanish Gypsy* was framed from the beginning by an attempt to understand in what ways the genre of tragedy could function as a category of the feminine—that is, as a representation of a specifically female action:

> A young maiden, believing herself to be on the eve of the chief event of her life—marriage—about to share in the ordinary lot of womanhood, full of young hope, has suddenly announced to her that she is chosen to fulfill a great destiny, entailing a terribly different experience from that of ordinary womanhood. She is chosen, not by any momentary arbitrariness, but as a result of foregoing hereditary conditions: she obeys.[17]

Eliot's example of the Annunciation invites us to see the mortal father transformed into a kind of god for whom the daughter functions as the obedient handmaid or sacrificial victim. So whereas in Bulwer-Lytton's and Aguilar's novels the daughter is sacrificed to what she names as the God of her fathers, in *The Spanish Gypsy* the daughter is sacrificed to the father as God. Hence Fedalma "knelt, / Clinging with piety and awed resolve / Beside this altar of her father's life," where she obediently sacrifices her own life while taking the pledge of worship: "He trusted me, and I will keep his trust: / My life shall be its temple. I will plant / His sacred hope within the sanctuary / And die its priestess."[18]

While Eliot defined the function of "hereditary conditions" in tragic plots in a variety of ways, more and more she came to mean *racial* conditions:

> A story simply of a jealous husband is elevated into a most pathetic tragedy by the hereditary conditions of Othello's lot, which give him a subjective ground for distrust. . . . A woman, say, finds herself on the earth with an inherited organization; she may be lame, she may inherit

a disease, or what is tantamount to a disease; she may be a negress, or have other marks of race repulsive in the community where she is born. (*George Eliot*, 3: 33–34)

Once the concept of race became the medium through which Eliot would realize the tragic circumstances of her own version of the Annunciation, fifteenth-century Spain seemed the inevitable choice for the "set of historical and local conditions" that would embody her idea:

> My reflections brought me nothing that would serve me except that moment in Spanish history when the struggle with the Moors was attaining its climax, and when there was the gypsy race present under such conditions as would enable me to get my heroine and the hereditary claim on her among the gypsies. I required the opposition of race to give the need for renouncing the expectation of marriage. (*George Eliot*, 3: 31)

In choosing fifteenth-century Spain, Eliot chose what had become for the nineteenth century a kind of historical laboratory in which experiments on the question of race could be performed.[19]

At the center of Eliot's text is the question of the heroine's identity, or how she is to be racially and religiously named and claimed. Fedalma is raised a Christian, rumored to be a Jew, dressed as a Moor at one point, and claimed by Zarca as a Gypsy. Zarca, the chief of the Zíncali and the father of Fedalma, explains that she was stolen from him by a band of Spaniards when she was a young child. In requiring that she not marry Silva, her Spanish lover, the father asks his daughter to sacrifice herself to the name of the father, or the name of race, and thereby to exchange her individual identity for her corporate identity: "Fedalma dies / In leaving Silva: all that lives henceforth / Is the poor Zíncala," the Spanish Gypsy of the title. Zarca explains that as the sole offspring of her widowed father, she is the "Chief woman of her tribe," and that after his death she will be the tribe's leader. So in prohibiting the marriage with Silva, the father offers his daughter a different kind of marriage, and Fedalma accepts: "I will wed / The curse that blights my people, . . . / Father, now I go / To wed my people's lot" (*Spanish Gypsy*, 138, 239, 137, 138). The conventional marriage plot is reconfigured here as the means by which the daughter serves her father as the bride of his people. Intermarriage with the racial other is cancelled in a figure: marriage with the entire body of one's own race.

In the daughter's self-sacrifice, the central ideology of the text is upheld, voiced most powerfully in the father's scathing denunciation of intermarriage and conversion:

Such love is common: I have seen it oft—
Seen many women rend the sacred ties
That bind them in high fellowship with men,
Making them mothers of a people's virtue:
Seen them so levelled to a handsome steed
That yesterday was Moorish property,
To-day is Christian—wears new-fashioned gear,
Neighs to new feeders, and will prance alike
Under all banners, so the banner be
A master's who caresses. Such light change
You call conversion; but we Zíncali call
Conversion infamy. (*Spanish Gypsy*, 239)

In recording the procedures by which women of a minority race or religion are absorbed by men of the more powerful group, Zarca adds conversion to the crimes of rapine and murder by which the systematic genocide of a people proceeds. And Eliot, however she might sympathize with the tragic loss and suffering of her title character, upholds the paternal critique of conversion.

Eliot uses the specific example of the "hurry to convert the Jews" in fifteenth-century Spain to ground historically what often appears to be her text's exaggerated horror of apostasy. While the main characters of *Spanish Gypsy* are Catholics and Gypsies, it is in her depiction of a converted Jew (Lorenzo) and a practicing Jew (Sephardo) that Eliot attempts to provide the historical basis for her study of Inquisitorial Spain.

Even Eliot's portrait of her Gypsy heroine takes as its model the better-known example of the converted Jewish woman; while Silva points to Fedalma's baptism, Father Isidor protests, "Ay, as a thousand Jewesses, who yet / Are brides of Satan." But Eliot fails to represent the historical complexities of the issue of conversion in Spain; instead, she is quick to make an example of the Jews to advance her argument against conversion. This results in making the converted Jew no more than the kind of opportunist Zarca warns Fedalma of becoming—the man or woman who would convert to "win the prize of renegades": "Thus baptism seemed to him [Lorenzo] a merry game / Not tried before, all sacraments a mode / Of doing homage for one's property, / And all religions a queer human whim / Or else a vice, according to degrees." Because Eliot focuses on the converted Jew who easily quits his Judaism to assume a new religion for self-advantage, as in the case of the "fat-handed" Lorenzo, her Jewish convert never seems to be the product of the fierce religious intolerance and racism that periodically erupted in Spain in the pogroms of the late fourteenth and fifteenth centuries, in which large masses of the Jewish population were converted on threat of death (*Spanish Gypsy*, 27, 69, 123, 11–12, 11). Instead, Eliot's portrait of the converted Jew seems to function as an indictment of Jewish hypocrisy and opportunism. In the end, Eliot's depiction of the converted Jew is one-sided, neglecting both those conversos who converted out of genuine conviction to worship devoutly and sincerely as Catholics and those crypto-Jews who converted to Catholicism (sometimes on the threat of death) while secretly practicing Judaism. In *Spanish Gypsy*, then, we have a late development in the historiography of the Spanish Inquisition in England: an anti-Catholic attack aimed at the intolerance of the Inquisition that nonetheless represents the Jewish convert as hypocrite and opportunist, a figure reborn in the pages of Trollope's novels and in the anti-Semitic attacks aimed at English converts like Disraeli.

The Secret Jew in England

The story of crypto-Judaism in Spain and Portugal did not remain safely bound between the covers of antique romance. It became the focus of a crisis in English public life when an especially prominent public figure not only claimed this Sephardic heritage for himself, not only imbedded stories of Jewish persecution and flight under the Inquisition in an extremely popular series of novels, but was finally himself subjected to the charge of crypto-Judaism. I mean, of course, Benjamin Disraeli, who was elected to the House of Commons in 1837 on his fifth attempt and who remained a significant political force from the 1840s through the 1870s. His political career reached its zenith during his years as prime minister (1874–80), when "the attention of Britain and, for much of the time, Europe, too, was centred upon Disraeli."[20]

During Disraeli's premiership, Anthony Trollope produced a series of novels whose anti-Semitism was unprecedented in the nineteenth century, and George Eliot wrote the work that has become the most celebrated philo-Semitic novel written in England. This extreme antithesis in the representation of Jewish identity indicates the pitch "the Jewish question" reached in these years. In the following pages I wish to explain the way in which, during the years of Disraeli's public prominence, the idea of "the secret race" became the ideological center of representations of Jewish identity in English politics and English letters.

Until now, I have described the idea of "the secret race" as essentially historical, of another time and another place, a subject taken up most popularly between the covers of historical romance, though of course not without its relevance to questions of racial and religious difference in Victorian England. Disraeli became the catalyst for the popular reemergence of the idea of "the secret race" in the 1870s and its use as the center of anti-Semitic representations for two reasons. First, there was the fact of Disraeli's Jewish ancestry and his conversion at a young age, a conversion that made possible his entrance into Parliament when the entrance of practicing Jews was barred. This conversion, if represented in any way as suspect, was capable of making Disraeli look like an English variation on the Spanish converso who (opportunistically, according to the stereotype) converted outwardly to Christianity but remained at heart, and often in practice, a Jew. Second, there was the fact of Disraeli's consistent championing of Hebraic culture in his writings and his support in Parliament—against his own party's position—of Jewish emancipation.

In 1849, Disraeli published a memoir of his father, Isaac D'Israeli, prefaced to the fourteenth edition of the latter's *Curiosities of Literature*, a work that would be issued in many more editions during the second half of the nineteenth century. In the memoir, the story of the Inquisition, so often popularized as historical romance, became the family history of a member of Parliament. Such events as the persecution of the Jews by Torquemada, their expulsion from Spain, and their flight to Holland and England are all framed by the following family narrative: "My grandfather, who became an English Denizen in 1748, was an Italian descendant from one of those Hebrew families, whom the Inquisition forced to emigrate from the Spanish Peninsula at the end of the fifteenth century."[21] In claiming this specific heritage, Disraeli became the most prominent living example of the link between the crypto-Jews of fifteenth-century

Spain and the (converted) Jews of Victorian England. While Disraeli saw this heritage as linking him to a heroic and martyred past, his critics would eventually use it to claim that he was a crypto-Jew.

Five years before publishing this memoir, Disraeli had already represented the Spanish persecution of the Jews and their eventual flight to England in *Coningsby* (1844), the first novel of his political trilogy on the condition-of-England question. There the material on the Inquisition and the crypto-Jews is largely compressed into a single chapter (book 4, chapter 10) and takes the form of the family history of the central Jewish character, who is nonetheless defined as "an Englishman, and taught from his cradle to be proud of being an Englishman."[22] In other words, as in the case of the memoir, a representation of the historical conditions of crypto-Judaism functions within the family history of an English citizen. This is the clearest way in which Disraeli began to rewrite a significant portion of English history as Anglo-Jewish history and to make a place for his own Jewish ancestry in contemporary English culture.

The main thrust of the history of crypto-Judaism in *Coningsby* is of course a story of prejudice and persecution. But central to Coningsby's reeducation is the idea of the Englishman's kinship with the Jew, which the English aristocrat learns at the feet of his symbolic father-mentor, Sidonia:

> You must study physiology, my dear child. Pure races of Caucasus may be persecuted, but they cannot be despised, except by the brutal ignorance of some mongrel breed, that brandishes fagots and howls extermination, but is itself exterminated without persecution, by that irresistible law of Nature which is fatal to curs.
>
> But I come also from Caucasus, said Coningsby. (273)

This role reversal in which the Jew proudly announces his superior racial makeup and his heritage as a Caucasian and the English nobleman almost timidly seeks to find his niche in the same racial category is a richly ironic and jarring moment in the history of Anglo-Jewish relations. If race began to be inscribed as the key to history in Scott's *Ivanhoe* and the historical romances that followed it, *Coningsby* was certainly the first novel to conceive of history as the record of Jewish racial superiority.

Sidonia's role throughout the novel is to critique the Eurocentric, and especially the Teutonic, conventions of racial superiority. This leads to a brilliant maneuver, namely, finding the most ancient basis of English life not in Teutonism but in Hebraism. Hence for Disraeli to write as an English Jew offers no contradiction whatsoever. Disraeli's project is merely to recall his English fellow citizens to those traditions more ancient than the Anglo-Saxon—an idea that, after Disraeli, became sufficiently plausible to allow Matthew Arnold to establish (and to criticize) Hebraism as the basis of English life in *Culture and Anarchy* (1869) and even to use his own name as evidence of such an idea: "why, my very name expresses that peculiar Semitico-Saxon mixture which makes the typical Englishman."[23]

Sidonia's critique begins at his first meeting with Coningsby. When Coningsby describes cleanliness as "an inheritance from our Saxon fathers" and claims that "the northern nations have a greater sense of cleanliness, of propriety, of what we call comfort," Sidonia answers, "By no means. The East is the land of the Bath. Moses and Mahomet made cleanliness religion" (*Coningsby*, 142). This is only the beginning of a series of legacies that the European owed to the Asian, the Englishman to the Jew, in what becomes a radical reevaluation of the system of indebtedness that previous writers had worked out, such as the following formula created by Disraeli's father in *Vaurien* (1797): for example, "the Christian should be generous and the Jew grateful."[24] The conventional picture of the Jew's debt to England, as in the example of Ivanhoe's deliverance of Rebecca from the fires of her Inquisition-like trial in *Ivanhoe*, is overturned by Disraeli, who claims that all of Europe, but especially England, depends on the ancient legal and ethical traditions of the Jews, an idea most prominently expressed in *Tancred* (1847), the third novel of his trilogy: "The life and property of England are protected by the laws of Sinai. . . . And yet [the English] persecute the Jews, and hold up to odium the race to whom they are indebted for the sublime legislation which alleviates the inevitable lot of the labouring multitude!" Disraeli, then, reconceives the idea of the indebtedness of the Jew, and his strategy for doing so is to intertwine the very heart of English political institutions—the subject of his political trilogy—with the ancient institutions of the Jew: "Vast as the obligations of the whole human family are to the Hebrew race, there is no portion of the modern populations so much indebted to them as the British people."[25] Disraeli does not try to negotiate a place in England for the Jew as outsider but instead, in a bold move, makes English national identity depend on Hebraic culture.

Disraeli's famous trilogy came back to haunt him in the 1870s when it was used to attack his ministry during the Eastern crisis and to divide Jewish and English interests instead of seeing them as intertwined. The Eastern question, quiet for a number of years after the Crimean War, erupted again in English politics in the summer of 1875 when rebellion against Turkish rule spread in the Balkans. English popular sentiment began to swing away from Turkey and toward Russia, especially when the problem of Turkey-in-Europe began to be viewed as the victimization of Christian subjects by an "Oriental" people.[26]

T. P. O'Connor's *Lord Beaconsfield* (1877) is an example of the kind of anti-Semitic attack against Disraeli that became fairly common during this period. In an introduction written some years after the first edition, O'Connor formulates the un-English identity of Disraeli by contrasting him to Lord Derby, who possessed "a character essentially English": "The somewhat commonplace Englishman, with notions of duty to his country, a horror of bloodshed, the fears of an avenging conscience, had no chance in times of perilous and fateful resolves against the brilliant, callous, self-adoring Oriental." A physiological contrast seals the difference: "the robust and massive frame of the Englishman" is contrasted with "the thin, light, though lithe, frame of the Oriental." O'Connor claims that Disraeli's Eastern policy represents "the triumph, not of England, not of an English policy, not of an Englishman," but "the triumph of Judea, a Jewish policy, a Jew." For "as a Jew he is a kinsman of the Turk, and . . . as a Jew, he feels bound to make common cause with the Turk against the Christian." O'Connor bemoans the way in which his fellow citizens have fallen "under the spell of our Oriental dictator": "the Hebrew Premier had indeed reduced the Gentiles to an abyssal depth of degradation." Finally, it is Disraeli's novels (especially *Coningsby* and *Tancred*), quoted profusely by O'Connor, that convict the prime minister: "People who will persist in thinking that it was an English policy can only be those who have not read Lord Beaconsfield's works, or who, having read, have not intelligence to interpret them."[27]

The Eastern crisis crystallized the anti-Semitism that had shadowed Disraeli's career from the beginning and threatened his attempt to reveal Hebrew culture as the basis of English life and to prove in his public career that a person of Jewish ancestry could lead England. Finally, the Eastern crisis created the political climate in which Disraeli's opponents could make the charge of crypto-Judaism. When Gladstone, Disraeli's old political opponent, came out of semiretirement to crusade against the "savage" Turks, he characterized Disraeli in the following way: "What he hates is Christian liberty."[28] Like O'Connor, Gladstone and the duke of Argyll claimed that Disraeli's policy was Jewish rather than English, though Disraeli's modern biographers have agreed that his pro-Turkish, anti-Russian position had been the traditional English policy on the Eastern question for many years.[29] The duke of Argyll believed that "Disraeli may be willing to risk his government for his Judaic feeling," and Gladstone told the duke, "I have a strong suspicion that Dizzy's crypto-Judaism has had to do with his policy."[30] In short, the Eastern crisis proved, according to his detractors, that Disraeli was "the secret Jew" par excellence. Disraeli's novels provided the surest source of evidence: having entered the fray, Gladstone went off to read *Tancred* to bolster his charges against Disraeli.[31]

We begin to see the way in which the phenomenon of Iberian crypto-Judaism became fraught for the nineteenth-century English Jew: the history of the persecution and martyrdom of the Jews during the Inquisition, which the Anglo-Jewish community was at pains to record, could be overturned through the stereotype of "the secret Jew," masked, subversive, and prodigiously powerful. After all, Disraeli himself had recorded the way in which many crypto-Jews had reached the highest positions in the Church and the state in Spain and Portugal.[32] In *Codlingsby* (1847), a parody of Disraeli's *Coningsby*, William Makepeace Thackeray seizes on the theme of crypto-Judaism: "His Majesty is one of *us* . . . ; so is the Pope of Rome," Rafael Mendoza (loosely based on Disraeli's Sidonia) whispers to Lord Codlingsby. Benjamin Disraeli, member of Parliament, himself a convert from Judaism, is hereby viewed as the author of a fantastic dream of power, the power of crypto-Judaism. We find in *Codlingsby* the central ideological construction of Jewish identity in Victorian England: "half the Hebrew's life is a disguise."[33]

This idea reached its apogee in the 1870s when Trollope, with Disraeli as his most prominent model, represented the Jewish infiltration of English culture in such novels as *The Eustace Diamonds* (1873) and *Phineas Redux* (1874), climaxing in *The Way We Live Now* (1875), and *The Prime Minister* (1876). *The Way We Live Now* began appearing in monthly installments in 1874 during the same month that Disraeli became prime minister, and it contained pointed references to Disraeli as the leader of the Conservative Party, and a fictional plot in which the career of the vulgar but immensely successful financier Melmotte, thought to be a Jew, is capped by his election to Parliament as a Conservative member. George Eliot was reading these monthly installments in the summer of 1874 while she was completing the opening chapters of *Daniel Deronda*.[34] For this reason it is possible to see Eliot's novel as a reaction, not simply to Disraeli, but to the way in which her friend Trollope was recording his own version of Jewish identity, particularly as he imagined it enacted in the daily activities of the prime minister. This chain of interlocking political and literary events climaxes in 1876, when Disraeli is named earl of Beaconsfield by the queen and when *Daniel Deronda* and *The Prime Minister* are published in book form, Trollope's title making most patent his growing obsession with the real prime minister.

The chief feature of the Jewish plots that Trollope creates in his novels of the 1870s is the secret identity of the characters thought to be Jewish. In these novels, it is "said," "supposed," and "suspected" of persons—Madame Max Goesler, Mr. Emilius, Mr. Alf, Augustus Melmotte, Ferdinand Lopez—that they are Jewish, for in this world there is no Jewish badge, and Jewish origins are hidden, suppressed; that is, Jewish identity is a secret identity in need of ferreting out. In such a world the tragic effects of the Jewish diaspora are reimagined as no more than the process of Jewish infiltration and subversion, as in Lady Pomona Longestaffe's paranoiac version of biblical history: "An accursed race . . . expelled from Paradise. . . . Scattered about all over the world, so that nobody knows who anybody is."[35] With the social, economic, and political barriers to Jewish achievement removed, Trollope's fiction concentrates on the assimilated Jew, the converted Jew, the Jew with pretensions to being an Englishman, a gentleman, and finally a member of Parliament. Trollope's attack on such figures demonstrates in England the ultimate dilemma of the conversionist plot of Christian culture. The final attack of this culture is aimed not at the stereotypical "stiff-necked Jew" who cannot be penetrated by Christianity but at the Jew who does in fact convert and thereby gains access to the highest echelons of Christian society. In this way Victorian England faced its own version of Spain and Portugal's converso problem, namely, how to cut short the Jews' success in entering the hegemonic culture once they had converted and assimilated.

The Prime Minister, with its suspected Jew descended from a Portuguese father, is the clearest example of Trollope's use of the idea of "the secret Jew." Ferdinand Lopez's origins are unclear, but at one point in the novel he is made to confess his identity with the prototype of the Jew in England, as if proving both his racial origins and his moral degeneracy: "I'm like Shylock, you know."[36] Critics have noted that Lopez is named after the historical personage that is often seen as the catalyst for Shakespeare's *The Merchant of Venice*.[37] I wish to use this historical connection in a special way, as additional evidence for seeing Lopez as part of the developing ideological construction of "the secret Jew" in Victorian England in the 1870s, with special reference to Disraeli.

Roderigo Lopez, a Portuguese New Christian who was deeply involved in the crypto-Jewish community of London, became medical attendant to Elizabeth in 1586, and was arrested in 1593 and executed in 1594 for plotting to poison the queen,[38] a case history that could be read as a kind of parable of the life and death of the secret Jew who subversively turns on the society that he has infiltrated and exploited. In returning to the historical Lopez for the name of his character, Trollope returns to the historical urgency to which Shakespeare responded, the Jewish threat to English society. This threat, whether in Elizabethan or Victorian England, is personified in the secret Jew whose family origins can be traced to the Iberian Peninsula, a pertinent reminder of the origins of the man who served as actual prime minister when *The Prime Minister* appeared. In publishing this novel during Disraeli's premiership, Trollope yielded to a kind of social and political fantasy: he makes Lopez, the man who runs for but fails to win a seat in Parliament, the epitome of the opportunism and moral bankruptcy of "the secret Jew," while making his fictitious prime minister, Plantagenet Palliser, a paragon of virtue and "the truest nobleman in all England" (1: 168). In short, Trollope rewrites contemporary British politics, unseating Disraeli and replacing him with the perfect English nobleman.[39]

Trollope similarly disables Lopez in the novel's domestic plot, but only after the English heroine makes the mistake of marrying him, of failing to see the difference between "such an English gentleman as Arthur Fletcher on one side, and . . . this Portuguese Jew on the other." By the end, however, the novel returns to the formula of those racial fatherland-daughter plots I have already examined, where the values of the father and the fatherland are reinstated over the claims of the interloping, or racially other, young lover. Father and daughter are realigned against the outsider, as Lopez himself confesses: "she clung to her father instead of clinging to her husband." But whereas in the texts we have already examined, it was a minority race—Jew or Gypsy—that was protected in the racial plot, in *The Prime Minister* it is the daughter of the hegemonic community, of English Protestant culture, who stands in need of protection and who is required to uphold her father's religion and race. Trollope makes clear that the protection of the daughter functions as a kind of metonymy for the protection of the nation; while "no one really thought that the Prussians and French combined would invade our shores and devastate our fields, and plunder London, and carry our daughters away into captivity" (1:124; 2:170, 148), Trollope represents another kind of invasion, the Jewish invasion of the English nation, signaled most clearly in the Jew's stealing the English daughter in marriage.

Before the daughter can be finally "taken back into the flock," Trollope must find a means of eradicating the Jewish husband from the plot. If in a text like *The Merchant of Venice*, conversion is imagined as the means by which Jewish identity can be erased, in Trollope's novels conversion is seen as the Jew's passport into Christian society, that is, as the legitimization of the Jew's invasion of English culture. In fact, in novels like *The Eustace Diamonds* and *The Prime Minister*, the Jew is no longer the moneylender on the sidelines of the marriage plot but the suitor for the heiress's hand, precisely because he is converted and "disguised" as an English Protestant. In Trollope's novels, then, the conversion of Shylock, the goal of "the Jewish plot" in *The Merchant of Venice*, comes back to haunt English culture. So a more desperate means of erasing the Jew is imagined by Trollope: suicide, a kind of murder about which the Christian community can feel guiltless because the murderer and the victim are one, and no Christian hand is raised against the Jew. Lopez's suicide, like Melmotte's in *The Way We Live Now*, is based in a kind of Christian fantasy: unable to sustain his masquerade as an English Protestant gentleman, the Jew, the "self-made" man, whose whole life has been given over to self-invention and self-promotion, ends his life in an act of self-destruction. In *The Prime Minister*, the so-called natural order returns only when the Jew kills himself and the heroine can marry her English gentleman, that is, when "the fair skin and bold eyes and uncertain words of an English gentleman" triumph over "the swarthy colour and false grimace and glib tongue of some inferior Latin race" (2: 368; 1: 1, 132). Trollope has managed to stage the paranoiac fantasy of the English male, his fear of the interloping Jew, as if it were a story in which nothing short of English national identity were at stake.

For all the differences between *The Prime Minister* and *Daniel Deronda*, Jewish identity is shrouded in secrecy, deception, and disguise in both, for as I have claimed, "the secret Jew" is as much the ideological center of Eliot's world as Trollope's. But while the secret Jew in Trollope's novels manipulates the secret of his origins and thereby functions as a conniver, an interloper in English life, even a subtle and successful criminal, the secret Jew in *Daniel Deronda* is victimized by, even held hostage to, the secrecy of his Jewish origins. Thus Eliot begins the radical deconstruction of the ideology of "the secret Jew," for Deronda is the secret Jew who has been prohibited from knowing his racial origins and robbed of his cultural inheritance.

Eliot stages the revelation of Deronda's Jewish ancestry against the backdrop of a famous historical tableau from the time of the Spanish Inquisition. Deronda's mother summons him to a meeting in Genoa, where he meditates on the specific Jewish history of this setting even before finding out that he is a Jew:

> Among the thoughts that most filled his mind while his boat was pushing about within view of the grand harbour was that of the multitudinous Spanish Jews centuries ago driven destitute from their Spanish homes, suffered to land from the crowded ships only for brief rest on this grand quay of Genoa, overspreading it with a pall of famine and plague—dying mothers with dying children at their breasts—fathers and sons agaze at each other's haggardness, like groups from a hundred Hunger-towers turned out beneath the midday sun. (*Deronda*, 682)

In the opening pages of Book 7, "The Mother and the Son," Deronda reflects on the history of the Spanish Jews, as if he has read Henry Hart Milman's or Prescott's famous histories in the course of his reeducation (as, of course, Eliot herself had)[40]—indeed, as if a page from the well-known histories were running through his mind:

> No one . . . could behold the sufferings of the Jewish exiles unmoved. A great many perished of hunger, especially those of tender years. Mothers,

> with scarcely strength to support themselves, carried their famished infants in their arms, and died with them. Many fell victims to the cold, others to intense thirst, while the unaccustomed distresses incident to a sea-voyage aggravated their maladies. . . . One might have taken them for spectres, so emaciated were they, so cadaverous in their aspect, and with eyes so sunken; they differed in nothing from the dead, except in the power of motion, which indeed they scarcely retained.[41]

So here in *Daniel Deronda* we encounter another example of the way in which the history of the Inquisition and the subsequent banishment and diaspora of the Iberian Jews reenter the literature of England. Even the man who serves as Deronda's mentor, a kind of symbolic father, is represented through the story of the Jewish martyrs of the Inquisition when Deronda finds Mordecai, impoverished and sickly, with no outlet for his vision, as "in some past prison of the Inquisition" (437)—as if the story of Inquisitorial oppression continues, in its own way, in Victorian England.

The prelude to Daniel's acceptance of the inheritance of the Jew, then, comes with a return to the critical moment of Spanish history, and Jewish history, for England. My argument has been based in part on recognizing the way in which the work of English Jews in the 1840s attempted to restore to the nineteenth-century Anglo-Jewish community its historical origins in the Iberian diaspora. But more than this, the critical moment in Victorian England's consciousness of Jewish identity occurred with the publication of Disraeli's memoir, in which he claimed the martyred and heroic history of the Inquisition for himself and his family. And here, in *Daniel Deronda*, Eliot maps onto the story of her hero the genealogy of the current prime minister. We discover, in the course of the mother's tale, that Deronda has the same lineage as Disraeli; both are descended, not only from English and Italian Jews, but from Iberian Jews persecuted and banished in the late fifteenth century. And like Disraeli, Deronda is fond of emphasizing one particular strand of this lineage: "And it is not only that I am a Jew . . . but I come of a strain that has ardently maintained the fellowship of our race—a line of Spanish Jews that has borne many students and men of practical power" (*Deronda*, 817). I think it is no accident, then, that one can hear the echo of "Disraeli" in "Deronda."

Eliot had already told a version of the life stories of Disraeli and Deronda, in a highly compressed and symbolic form, in *Romola* (1862). I am referring to that strange interlude when the heroine flees from her home in Florence and floats suicidally in a boat on the sea until she awakens the next morning to hear the piercing cry of an infant from the nearby shore. In searching for the child, Romola experiences firsthand what Deronda, at the beginning of "The Mother and the Son," imaginatively reconstructs from his reading. When Romola discovers a group of dead bodies surrounding the crying infant, she meets the victims of the Iberian Inquisition and banishment, once again represented in the manner of Milman and Prescott:

> The strongly marked type of race in their features, and their peculiar garb, made her conjecture that they were Spanish or Portuguese Jews, who had perhaps been put ashore and abandoned there by rapacious sailors, to whom their property remained as a prey. Such things were happening continually to Jews compelled to abandon their homes by the Inquisition.[42]

Eliot uses this historical tableau as the scene of rebirth for Romola. Aimless, exhausted by her past life, in search of death, Romola finds a new life in the deliverance of this Jewish child. The rescue of the Jewish child from death, then, functions as a kind of revival of consciousness, even as a catalyst for action, for the title characters in both *Romola* and *Daniel Deronda*. Romola is a female version of a figure we meet time and again in the English novel, even in Deronda as the rescuer of Mirah: "the champion of the Jews."[43] In fact, Eliot represents the latest and most explicit stage in the development of this topos: the regeneration of (English) consciousness through the deliverance of the persecuted Jew.

Romola's discovery and rescue of the orphaned Jewish child is rewritten in *Daniel Deronda* in a way that marks the development of Eliot's consciousness of Jewish identity. At first, the scene in *Romola* seems merely to be copied in *Daniel Deronda*; Deronda, after a dreamy boat ride like Romola's, rescues Mirah, and eventually finds new purpose in his life because of this rescue. But whereas Deronda's rescue of Mirah becomes, as the plot unfolds, also the rescue of her Jewish family and heritage (and Deronda's own as well), the rescue of the Jewish child in *Romola* ends in conversion: "the Hebrew baby was a tottering tumbling Christian, Benedetto by name, having been baptised." Conversion is the means by which the Christian community assimilates "the queer little black Benedetto,"[44] the quintessential outsider who seems to bear a kind of double racial marking (like Trollope's Ferdinand Lopez, "a black Portuguese nameless Jew" [*Prime Minister*, 1: 146]). In the character of Daniel Deronda, Eliot returns to the Hebrew baby raised as a Christian with no knowledge of his Jewish origins, but in the later novel, she ultimately returns this child to the Jewish heritage that was lost when he was absorbed by the Christian community.

The story of the baptized Hebrew baby in *Romola* may encode the story not only of Daniel Deronda but also of Benjamin Disraeli, who himself recalled the setting of the Inquisition to tell his own family history, for the Christianized Benedetto in some sense recalls the Christianized Benjamin Disraeli: the Jewish child baptized in order to be assimilated and, finally, to enjoy all the rights and privileges of the hegemonic Christian community. Perhaps Queen Victoria half sensed this meaning when she presented Disraeli with a copy of the 1880 edition of *Romola*.[45] The queen of course must have viewed the conversion of the Hebrew baby with enthusiastic approval—after all, a similar event had delivered her beloved prime minister to her. But it is precisely from this perspective that the story of the hero in *Daniel Deronda* flows athwart the mainstream of history—the history of Inquisitorial Spain and the history of Victorian England—for instead of simply recording the Christianization of the Jew, it sets about to re-Judaize the Christian, to return him to the Jewish origins that the events of history have so often required that he abandon.[46] In this way *Daniel Deronda* critiques not only the scene of conversion associated with the period of the Inquisition but also the social and political conditions in Victorian England that required the current prime minister's conversion.

But Eliot aims her critique also at the Jew who yields to such social pressures and converts out of self-advantage. For however much Eliot sympathizes with the suffering that Deronda's mother describes as her Jewish experience, Eliot nonetheless makes the story of Leonora a critique of the Jew who converts out of ambition and opportunism. Eliot attempts to win our approval of this critique by making the story of Leonora's apostasy and eventual conversion the story of the abandonment of her child. Eliot encourages our condemnation of Leonora by setting her story against the historical backdrop of the heroic Jewish mother in the time of the Inquisition. For when Eliot reinscribes the historical tableau of the banished Iberian Jews in *Daniel Deronda*, she returns to a picture of the heroic Jewish mother clinging to her dead infant, a portrait that has a profoundly ironic effect as a prelude to the story of "The Mother and the Son." Deronda, in his recollection of this tableau, recalls "dying mothers with dying children at their breasts," but the story he is about to hear from his own mother is very different. Deronda's mother is the Jewish mother who abandoned her son, even the mother who is seen as squelching his life, in some sense murdering him. Daniel is, then, the dead Jewish baby of the historical tableau, with a difference: he is killed not by persecution and famine but by a form of symbolic infanticide. He is the Jewish child Leonora symbolically murders when she puts out the report that he is dead and when she gives him away to be remade as an English Christian; he is the child his mother "willed to annihilate." In this light we see the peculiar pathos of Eliot's use of the historical backdrop of the banished Iberian Jews as a prelude to recording Deronda's family history. Deronda was banished by no national edict, but by maternal interdiction. In his meeting with his mother, Deronda accuses her: "You renounced me—you still banish me—as a son" (727).

Unlike Aguilar's Marie and Eliot's own Fedalma, then, Leonora is the daughter who rejects the God of her fathers: "Before I married the second time I was baptised; I made myself like the people I lived among." Eliot's representation of Leonora's story in *Daniel Deronda* becomes an anatomy of the modern conditions of Jewish self-hatred: "rid myself of the Jewish tatters and gibberish that makes people nudge each other at sight of us, as if we were tattooed under our clothes" (*Deronda*, 698).[47] It is a story that Eliot could have learned from Disraeli's memoir, where the phenomenon of Jewish self-hatred is subtly analyzed in terms that anticipate the story of Leonora. Disraeli describes his beautiful and vain grandmother, who

> imbibed that dislike for her race which the vain are too apt to adopt when they find that they are born to public contempt. The indignant feeling that should be reserved for the persecutor, in the mortification of their disturbed sensibility, is too often visited on the victim; and the cause of annoyance is recognized not in the ignorant malevolence of the powerful, but in the conscientious conviction of the innocent sufferer.[48]

The phenomenon of Jewish self-hatred and its corollary, the impetus to assimilate and convert, is the modern context for understanding the family stories of both Disraeli and Deronda (including the conversions they underwent as children), even though these sons, one real and the other fictitious, are quick to emphasize the more heroic history of persecution and martyrdom that stands behind them.

With the conventional plot of the converted Jewish daughter occupying only a subsidiary position in the novel, the plot of the converted Jewish son becomes central in *Daniel Deronda*, as well as in Trollope's novels, because it was precisely such a plot that was enacted on the stage of English public life in the career of Disraeli. In this light I wish to read the ending of *Daniel Deronda* as a kind of fantasy that rewrites the life of Disraeli. During the period in which Disraeli, a converted Jew, was the leader of Protestant England—that is, of his adopted people—Eliot produced a novel in which her hero, also a converted Jew, decides to leave England to become the leader of his ancestral people. Deronda explains to Mordecai:

> Since I began to read and know, I have always longed for some ideal task, in which I might feel myself the heart and brain of a multitude—some social captainship, which would come to me as a duty, and not be striven for as a personal prize. You have raised the image of such a task for me—to bind our race together. (819–20)

As a fantasy based on the life of England's prime minister in 1876, the plot functions symbolically to liberate Disraeli to do what his critics accused him of doing under cover of being the leader of Protestant England, that is, to represent his own ancestral people, to seek their best interest. Such a plot depends on Eliot's refocusing of the history of crypto-Judaism in a way that will ultimately undercut the paranoiac view of "the secret race." Hence her decision to focus on the moment in which the secret Jew, escaped from the dangers of persecution, confesses his identity. So the history of those martyred crypto-Jews who ultimately confess their Jewish identity becomes the model for Deronda's own story, as well as a kind of paradigm by which he understands and admires Mirah, his future wife: "she seemed to Deronda a personification of that spirit which impelled men after a long inheritance of professed Catholicism to leave wealth and high place, and risk their lives in flight, that they might join their own people and say, "I am a Jew" (*Deronda*, 819–20,426).

Eliot's legitimation of the idea of the Jewish leader (whether Disraeli or Deronda) working openly toward the liberation of his oppressed people is made possible in *Daniel Deronda* by the complete legitimation of the claims of Jewish identity, that is, by acknowledging the need for a Jewish state. Unlike "the secret Jew" that Disraeli's critics paranoically constructed—the Hebrew premier who worked secretly to support Jewish interests (and thereby to undermine the English nation)—Deronda works openly for the establishment of a Jewish state. Hence Deronda's decision to journey to Palestine to fulfill Mordecai's wish "to found a new Jewish polity." In Mordecai's words, "then our race shall have an organic centre, a heart and brain, to watch and guide and execute; the outraged Jew shall have a defence in the court of nations, as the outraged Englishman or American" (*Deronda*, 594, 595). In this way, at the end of *Daniel Deronda*, Daniel steps outside the predominant configuration of Jewish identity in English discourse. Not only does his story challenge the predominant ideology of Jewish conversion, but at the end of the novel the central Jewish characters, Daniel and Mirah, no longer serve the purpose of helping to define the English national character; they work instead toward the construction of their own national identity.

In the course of the nineteenth century, then, the story of the birth of a nation shifted from medieval England and Spain, in the pages of historical romance, to Palestine, a new center of nationalist activity at the end of *Daniel Deronda*. An anticipation of such a shift was sounded in Rebecca's half-articulated desire in *Ivanhoe*: "I had wellnigh said . . . my country, but, alas! we have no country" (422). Rebecca invites the English public, who celebrate their own national origins while reading *Ivanhoe*, to recall the lack of national identity suffered not simply by the medieval Jew but by the modern Jew as well. And in the 1870s, while Trollope was preoccupied with the invasion of the nation, transforming Scott's Norman Conquest into the Jewish conquest of England, Eliot was imagining the birth of a nation by returning to *Ivanhoe* in her own way: unlike Isaac and Rebecca's journey in search of asylum in another land (from which the Jews would be banished in the diaspora of 1492), Deronda's journey is meant to preclude, once and for all, the Jews' homeless wandering, their dependence on a nation not their own.

Three "Rachel, ou l'Auto-da-fé"

Representations of Jews and the Inquisition in the French Grand Opera *La Juive* (1835)

Diana R. Hallman

In the initial plans for the 1835 French grand opera *La Juive* by the librettist Eugène Scribe and the composer Fromental Halévy, the Inquisition and its relationship to Jewish persecution figured prominently. In Scribe's notebook "Quelques idées des pièces," a sketch headed "La belle juive opera" roughly outlines five acts about a forbidden liaison between a beautiful Jewess and a non-Jewish man whom she later discovers to be married. Using the solitary term "l'autodafe" for the fifth act, the librettist makes clear that this will be the central dramatic idea for the opera's denouement and the Jewess's fate.[1] He accentuated the term even more strongly in the title of another synopsis for the opera, "Rachel, ou l'auto-da-fé," although by the time of this later draft, the opera's setting had changed (as noted in several accounts) from Goa, the capital of Portuguese India, where the Inquisition had been established in 1560, to Constance (Konstanz), the German city that hosted the Council of Constance of 1414–18.[2] Despite this shift to a famous ecumenical convocation of the Catholic Church, allusions to the Portuguese (or Spanish) Inquisition remained in its metaphorical proximity to the Council—which burned at the stake the religious "heretics" Jan Hus (1372/73–1415) and Jerome of Prague (1365–1416)—and as a symbol of the despotism of the ancien régime with which the Church was closely linked. Scribe's early thoughts about the Inquisition and his ultimate choice of the Council of Constance for the opera's setting, in conjunction with the persecution of the beautiful Jewess (and her Jewish father, a character added as the libretto developed), lay at the ideological foundation of this Enlightenment-tinged, politically charged historical opera.

In the following discussion, I shall explore the significance of the Inquisition as alluded to in the opera's genesis and as symbolically linked to the Council of Constance, the intersection of literary and social stereotypes in the construction of the principal Jewish characters, Rachel and her father Eléazar, and the depicted oppression of Jews on the stage during the early July Monarchy in France of the 1830s. The representation of well-established literary tropes reinforces, and sometimes subverts, the symbolism of the Jews as the alienated and oppressed Other, but their characterization remains clearly tied to the use of the auto-da-fé as an emblem of authoritarian oppression and medieval power. From early to late stages of this historical opera's development, up to and even shortly after its premiere on 23 February 1835 at the Académie royale de musique (i.e., the Paris Opéra), the construction and modifications of setting, character, and plot point to ideas and values that are weighted with sociopolitical implications. Within the French milieu, this reinterpretation of Jewish stereotypes and the Inquisition metaphor resonates with central historical questions and contested values of the nation, in its contradictory paths toward and away from a republic of individual citizens, and in its expanding legal acceptance of Jews as part of its citizenry.

In the history of the late eighteenth and nineteenth centuries, the "emancipation" of Jews in France in 1791 became forever linked with the French Revolution and establishment of the First Republic, and with Enlightenment ideals that fueled these cataclysmic events. In successive decades, the acknowledgment and treatment of Jewish citizens fluctuated within changing regimes. During the Empire, the Grand Sanhédrin convened by Napoleon in 1807 and the Consistoire central de Paris and seven regional Consistoires established in 1808 helped to ensure Jewish civil rights, acting as forces of acculturation through the governmental administration of Jewish congregations and communities. A return to a strongly allied Church and state during the Restoration monarchies, particularly the regime of Charles X, took France farther away from republican values with laws such as the Anti-Sacrilege Act of 1825 that prohibited blasphemy and sacrilege, as defined by Catholicism. With the 1830 July Revolution and the advent of the constitutional monarchy of the "Citizen-King" Louis-Philippe came renewed promises of a nation more fully embracing of civil liberties and improved status for its Jewish and other non-Catholic citizens—to the dismay of oppositional factions that continued to favor the dominance of the aristocracy and hereditary rights, along with the cultural authority of the Catholic Church and faith, and to think of Jews as foreign or alien to French society. Within Jewish communities themselves, attitudes ranged from those of reform-minded individuals who supported Jewish acculturation, or even assimilation through conversion and full acceptance of French values and mores, to the beliefs of Orthodox Jews who continued to view the "Jewish nation" as a separate entity within the country.

With political principles and ideals being reassessed under the July Monarchy, after France's recent emergence from the authoritarianism of Charles X's neo–ancien régime, the staging of the opera *La Juive* highlighted central concerns pertinent to the reframing of national identity. Scribe's dramatic use of a condemning Church tribunal of the early fifteenth century in conjunction with the presentation of a beautiful Jewess and her "fanatical" Jewish father, a Jewish seder, and Jewish-Christian confrontation, touched on polemical questions about the French past of authoritarian monarchies and clerical power and its relation to a French present built on a renewal of the republican values of individual freedom. By focusing on characters that symbolized "heretics" oppressed by the Church and state of the past, Scribe and his collaborators also broached the "Jewish question" concerning these relatively new citizens of France: the question (or questions) surrounding Jewish acculturation or assimilation versus Jewish separatism, as well as tolerance or intolerance by the French government, Church, and populace. With such politicized metaphors and contemporaneous meanings, *La Juive* can be clearly aligned with Sir Walter Scott's *Ivanhoe* (1820), a master text that Michael Ragussis places at the center of an international debate about "the relation between national identity and alien populations," as Jews had long been regarded throughout Europe. According to Ragussis, *Ivanhoe* functions as an exploration of "the relationship between Jewish persecution and the incipient birth of English national unity in the twelfth century."[3]

Ivanhoe, in fact, served as one of the sources of the opera's libretto. Although Scribe clearly built his portrayals of Eléazar and Rachel on the stereotyped pair of the benevolent, beautiful Jewess and her vengeful, avaricious, Christian-hating father found in Shakespeare's *The Merchant of Venice* and Christopher Marlowe's *The Jew of Malta*, he also borrowed character and plot elements from *Ivanhoe* (which itself reinterpreted the

Shylock-Jessica pairing in the characters Isaac and Rebecca), as well as Gotthold Ephraim Lessing's *Nathan der Weise* (Nathan the Wise; 1779).[4] As suggested in Scribe's initial title and skeletal ideas, he may have also constructed basic elements of character and identity on the famous legend of the love between the Jewess of Toledo and the Spanish king Alphonso VIII, which he could have known through several representations, including P.-E. Chevalier's melodrama, *Rachel, ou la belle juive* (1803).[5] Scribe's clear turn to Shakespeare's play paralleled and even anticipated that of nineteenth-century British authors, who drew from *Merchant* so consistently that Ragussis deems it the "ur-text of the representation of Jewish identity in England"—but his use of Shakespeare and Scott also synchronized with the waves of French enthusiasm for both authors.[6] Admiration for Shakespeare's works peaked in the 1820s and 1830s with the appearance of new French editions, a brilliant season of performances by an English troupe at the Odéon and Théâtre-Français in 1827, and informed tributes by Stendhal, Hugo, and other French romantic writers. From 1826 to 1830, *Ivanhoe* became one of the most popular novels in France, appearing in ten editions,[7] and inspiring the pasticcio *Ivanhoé*, set to music of Giaochino Rossini and arranged by Antonio Pacini for the Odéon in 1826. As a well-read author and man of the theater, Scribe clearly would have felt the public impact of both works.

Scribe's fleshing out of Rachel's character, beyond the stock identity of a beautiful daughter of a Shylockian father, appears most indebted to Scott's characterization of Rebecca. Through this modeling, in part, Rachel moves beyond her representation as a generic *juive* to that of a Jewess who carries hints of a Sephardic identity. These allusions resonate with fundamental character elements found in Chevalier's treatment of the Raquel-Alphonso legend, and become more vivid through the depiction of an "oriental"—or orientalist—Rachel in costumes designed for *La Juive*'s first production at the Paris Opéra. Not only do the orientalist references coincide with Sephardic allusions, but the orientalist/Sephardic aspects of Rachel's characterization blend with suggestions of her assimilation into Christian society, by virtue of birth and behavior, in contrast to her vengeful, recalcitrant father, who remains more fully separate from it. As I consider the contemporary significance of the work by focusing on the symbolism of its Inquisition metaphor and Jewish characters, I shall also confront the possibility that the "Sephardic mystique" so influential in European literature later in the century had already touched this French opera of 1835.

⁎

La Juive underwent numerous transformations, not all of them traceable or easily explicable, in over two years of genesis between Scribe's initial sketches and its staging at the Paris Opéra. Some changes undoubtedly originated with the librettist himself, but others may have been determined by Fromental Halévy as he set Scribe's words to music, or even by his brother Léon Halévy, who claims to have played a large role in revising the libretto (with Scribe's allowance and approval) as he sat at his brother's side.[8] Although Scribe, a prolific dramatist and librettist, is often described as more opportunistic and pragmatic than political,[9] he nonetheless produced a number of works with political content in the late 1820s and 1830s, including the *comédie-vaudeville Le moulin de Javelle* and the dramas *Avant, pendant et après* (1828), *Bertrand et Raton, ou, L'art de conspirer* (1833), *L'ambitieux* (1834), *La camaradérie* (1837), and *Les Indépendants* (1837). Identifying himself as liberal, he seemingly leaned more toward Louis-Philippe's ideal of *juste milieu* (happy medium) liberalism than the Halévys, who were both drawn to the progressive liberalism espoused by the followers of Comte Henri de Saint-Simon (1760–1825), with Léon becoming a leading disciple and articulator of Saint-Simonian thought.[10] As sons of the talmudic scholar and Hebraic poet Élie Halévy, who co-founded the first Jewish journal in France, *L'Israélite français* (1817–19), which sought to remind French "Israélites" of their dual loyalty to Jewish tradition and to the country that had given them citizenship, both Fromental and Léon were interested in the "Jewish question" in regards to French society and their own lives.[11] Both sons exhibited allegiance to their Jewish heritage in varying degrees. Fromental wrote compositions for the synagogue, and Léon published two early Jewish histories that echoed his father's Enlightenment-inspired beliefs in Jewish "regeneration" within French culture, but also sharply criticized the "clerical party" for its encouragement of apostasy, threats to Jewish political rights, and efforts to exclude Jews from public employment.[12] In the 1820s and 1830s, the brothers became well integrated into French élite culture through their education and participation in leading French institutions, although not without difficulties. Despite differences of heritage and experience, the Halévys and Scribe shared many of the ideals associated with the "Generation of 1820," including an opposition to the retrogressive monarchies of the Restoration, an admiration for Enlightenment thought, and a belief in the basic liberal principles fought for in the July Revolution and embodied in the early July Monarchy.[13]

Although I shall not deeply explore biographical or ideological links to the opera's creators in this chapter, the librettist and composer and libretto contributors are important in our consideration of the developments and meanings of *La Juive*. Moreover, other individuals or groups that frequently influenced an opera's development in the nineteenth century included administrative figures, general directors, stage directors, choreographers, conductors, performers, censorship bodies, the press, and even audiences themselves. One person who played an important role in the production of *La Juive* was Louis Véron, *directeur-entrepreneur* of the Paris Opéra where it premiered. As the first director of this prestigious theater to operate with partial, rather than full, government subsidy and one unrestricted by a censorship body during the years of his directorship, from 1831 to 1835, Véron had the power to approve works with only seemingly minimal oversight. He would write later in his memoirs that he had intended to appeal to the "victorious bourgeoisie" of the July Revolution of 1830 with new large-scale operas that would be driven by "the grand passions of the human heart and powerful historical interests."[14] Although theatrical censorship had been prohibited by the Charter of 1830, Véron was obliged to report to the Commission de Surveillance, a government-appointed, non-censorship of administrators, who worked under the authority of the minister of the interior, the comte de Montalivet. Véron, the Commission, and the minister undoubtedly affected the representation of the opera's subject, directly or indirectly, but in this discussion I focus chiefly on Scribe as initial developer of the libretto, with references to his central collaborator, Fromental Halévy.

Most likely Scribe first sketched the term "l'auto-da-fé" in late 1832 or early 1833, based on dating that appears within a notebook where he outlined his thoughts about "la belle juive."[15] Whether he was modeling his thin scenario on a particular source at this point is unknown, but clearly he was thinking of the Inquisition, and of the history of Jewish persecution at the hands of the Inquisition, although—effective dramatist and librettist that he was—he suggested a forbidden love affair rather than lack of conversion as the main motive for the Jewess's fate. As he expanded his ideas, adding Rachel's father Eléazar as a principal character, for example, his literary models became more evident, and he considered making Rachel's conversion the opera's denouement, following a well-trodden literary path.[16] Ultimately, however, he retained his first idea of the Jewess being put to death by *some* kind of Inquisition or other Church body.

As evident from his draft scenario and middle-stage versions of the libretto, Scribe not only tried to work out the solution of conversion but chose another common literary method of distinguishing the Jewish heroine from her father: he made her Christian by blood. By representing Rachel as the biological daughter of Cardinal Brogni and the adopted daughter of Eléazar, Scribe followed a number of literary precedents, including those in *The Merchant of Venice* and *Nathan der Weise*. Salerio questions Shylock's paternity in *Merchant of Venice* 3.1.34–36: "There is more difference between thy flesh and hers than between jet and ivory; more between your bloods than there is between red wine and Rhenish."[17] A few scenes later (3.5.9–10), the clown Launcelot raises doubt in an exchange with Jessica: "Marry, you may partly hope that your father got you not—that you are not the Jew's daughter." Going beyond such allusions, Scribe's opted to make Rachel's birth identity definitively Christian and to use the revelation of this identity as an important plot device, not only following more closely the portrayal of Recha in *Nathan der Weise* but also relating to operatic conventions of disguise and recognition. In *La Juive*, as in *Nathan*, the revelations of the Jewess's Christian birth occur at the end of the drama.

Scribe's drafting of Rachel's conversion, which he and his collaborators would reject well before the opera's 1835 premiere, went through several versions, as revealed in the draft scenario and other manuscript sources of the libretto. In the scenario, Scribe sketched out Rachel's conversion through baptism as a symbolic return to her true Christian roots after her discovery that Brogni is her biological father: "'Ah, God of the Christians, receive the lost child returning to your bosom,' Rachel cries, overcome and falling to her knees—soft, religious hymn. Solemn and heavenly song that ends the work. [T]he holy water of baptism purifies her brow."[18]

He worked out two other versions in libretto fragments: in one, at the beginning of act 5, Brogni himself reveals to Rachel that he is her true father, prompting her to condemn Eléazar as her deceiver;[19] in another, in act 4, scene 6, Eléazar tells Brogni of her birth identity, with Rachel overhearing.[20] In both versions, at the end of act 5 (scene 3), as Eléazar and Rachel await death, Brogni realizes the hypocrisy of executing heretics at the Council's opening and offers clemency and conversion to both, but only Rachel accepts:

O celeste lumière! Qui brille & qui m'éclaire De ses feux radieux! Bénissez moi, mon père, Et qu'à votre prière Pour moi s'ouvrent les cieux!	O heavenly light! That glows and shines on me With its radiant flames! Bless me, my father And at your prayer May the skies open for me.[21]

Rachel then kneels before Brogni, who blesses her, as banners are lowered and a "celestial harmony" is heard; Eléazar looks at her in anger as he moves away, shortly before the curtain falls.[22]

Although Scribe, perhaps encouraged by the composer and other collaborators, reverted to his original plan of having Rachel put to death, he retained an offer of conversion, but ultimately has her reject it.[23] In the opera's finale, act 5, scene 4, Rachel chooses death and martyrdom over baptism, remaining devoted to her adoptive father and to the Jewish faith in which she was raised:

ELÉAZAR	
Ils veulent sur ton front verser, l'eau du baptême Le veulent-tu, mon enfant?	On your brow they want to pour baptismal water, Is that what you want, my child?
RACHEL	
Qui? Moi! Chrétienne? Moi! La flame étincelle, Venez!	Who? Me! A Christian? Me! The flames sparkle! Come on!
ELÉAZAR	
Leur Dieu t'appelle!	Their God calls you!
RACHEL	
Et le nôtre m'attend! C'est le ciel qui m'inspire, Je choisis le trépas!	And ours awaits me! I am inspired by heaven, I choose death!

Oui, courons au martyre,	Yes, let us hurry to our martyrdom,
Dieu nous ouvre ses bras!	God opens His arms to us![24]

With this ending, Rachel's Jewish identity is clearer and stronger than in earlier stages of the work. However, the duality in her religious (and social) portrayal remains in the opera through the heritage implied by her birth, and through suggestions of her receptiveness to Brogni, evident when she joins in a warm response to the cardinal's gesture of reconciliation in act I, no. 2 (*Si la rigueur*). As she awaits her death in act 5, she again bonds with Christians as she sings a phrase with women of the chorus, "Unissons nos prières / Vers le Dieu de nos pères" (Let us join in prayer to the God of our fathers). Also signifying her duality is the paternal protection exhibited by both Eléazar and Brogni; although Brogni's protective impulses are less evident in the staged opera, a noteworthy vestige survives in a "duettino" with Rachel in act 4, in which Brogni sings of "a secret voice" in his soul telling him to defend her and then promises, "Je veillerai sur vous" ("I will watch over you"); in recitative preceding his duet with Eléazar, he laments Rachel's fate, "Mourir, mourir si jeune" ("to die, to die so young").[25] One aria planned for Eléazar, "O fille chérie," also uses the verb *veiller* to signal his guardianship in the phrase, "Je veille ici pour te bénir" ("I watch over you here to bless you").[26] With the omission of this number, Eléazar's most extended, sincere expression of fatherly love comes in his heartfelt aria ending act 4, "Rachel, quand du Seigneur," in which he reveals his inner struggle between his desire to save his daughter—this time through his conversion—and his vengeance-laden loyalty to his faith.

The claim of paternity and the claim over Rachel's soul figure strongly in the opposition between Eléazar and Brogni and in the overall Jewish-Christian conflict that permeates the work. Although the paternal opposition is somewhat mitigated in later stages of the opera's genesis, it nonetheless intensifies the religious animosity between the characters that is both doctrinal and personal: prior to Brogni's years as cardinal, when he was magistrate of Rome, he had banned Eléazar from the city and had caused his sons to be burned at the stake. The loss of Eléazar's children is somewhat matched by Brogni's assumed loss of his baby daughter in a fire, but Eléazar's rescue of her from the burning house—a plot element that may have been drawn from Lessing's *Nathan der Weise*—gives the Jewish jeweler a personal power over the cardinal; his withholding of Rachel's identity until the moment of her execution heightens his revenge, because it inverts Brogni's inquisitorial injustice and throws it back upon himself. To his horror, as the cardinal pleads with Eléazar to reveal the identity of his daughter before he is put to death, the condemned man points to Rachel and exclaims the words, "La voilà!" as she is thrown into a vat of boiling oil.

Scribe's binding of his story of Jewish persecution and Jewish-Christian opposition in an Inquisition-like setting with an engagement of topical political concerns certainly promised to meet grand opera's (and Véron's) criteria of a work built on "grand passions" and "powerful historical interests." This adaptation of the Council as the Church authority that condemns the Jews (in place of the real-life pre-Protestant figures Jan Hus and Jerome of Prague) moves away from historical precision; but Scribe's substitution of one institution linked to the abusive power of Church and state for another (and of one set of "heretics" for another) does not diminish his basic symbolic intent. However, his choices, as suggested above, place his libretto within a large body of nineteenth-century literature and drama that link Jewish representation to questions of national, religious, and racial identity.

Whether in his initial focus on the Portuguese Inquisition, Scribe considered drawing attention to the historical treatment of Sephardic Jews in particular is uncertain. Like other early-nineteenth-century French citizens, he may have heard or read tales of eighteenth-century autos-da-fé in Portugal, which had burned over a hundred Marranos at the stake, setting off Jewish emigrations to France and other countries and stimulating discussions of the "Jewish question."[27] What is more certain is that Scribe was well aware of the symbolic implications that the Inquisition carried in the eighteenth century and that continued to reverberate in the early nineteenth century, as the discourses on religious fanaticism and oppression framed by Voltaire and other Enlightenment thinkers were widely read in France (e.g., six editions of Voltaire's complete works appeared in 1825 alone, and more by 1830) and were echoed by liberal writers of his generation. Among Voltaire's repeated attacks on the Inquisition are his statements made in a chapter devoted to the subject in *Essai sur les moeurs et l'esprit des nations*, in which he speaks sharply of Inquisition tribunals exemplifying the human debasement that can occur "when superstitious ignorance is armed with power."[28] In describing autos-da-fé as "public sacrifices," he writes of the condemned being led to a public square by a procession of monks and brotherhoods, and notes sardonically, "they sing, they say mass, and they kill people."[29] Although this account or other commentary by Voltaire may not have been used as a direct source for Scribe's libretto, the philosopher's views seem to provide an ideological subtext to his ideas. Adding merit to this supposition is the fact that Scribe drew from Voltaire's writings for other dramas: he adapted Voltaire's *Scythes* for his melodrama *Koulikan* and used Voltaire's *Essai sur les moeurs* as a source for his libretto of Meyerbeer's *Le Prophète*, which he began in 1836. Moreover, a critic in the ultraroyalist, clerical paper *La Gazette de France* found the basis clear, referring to *La Juive* after its premiere as a "truly little masterpiece of the Voltairean genre."[30] In another Enlightenment treatment of the Inquisition metaphor, Montesquieu presented a "reprimand to the Inquisitors of Spain and Portugal" through a poignant account of the burning at the stake of a young Jewess in Lisbon.[31]

During the Restoration, particularly under the reign of Charles X, the re-empowering of Church authority resulted in such actions as the prosecutions of the papers *Le Courrier français* and *Le Constitutionnel* for their attacks on religion, clerical refusal of burial to liberals or Jansenists, and a proposal to institute a law that would result in the death penalty for sacrilege. In this political context, liberal writers reconsidered the historical implications of the Inquisition.[32] Some even feared its return, as Étienne-Léon de Lamothe-Langon warned in the introduction to his *Histoire de l'Inquisition en France* (1829).[33] Although Lamothe-Langon refers to the Portuguese and Spanish Inquisitions, he is intent on recounting the details of "a dreadful history written in strokes of blood" in France itself, which he claims had remained hidden from his generation and had to be told in order to counteract "the torrent of hypocritical fanaticism that inundates us from all parts, and the inclination to return to the errors of our fathers," as suggested by the recurring "éloge" to the Inquisition that he noticed.[34]

Within the July Monarchy, debates about religious and political intolerance would again bring forward the Inquisition as a central emblem of religious and political absolutism, which liberal minds saw as a continuing threat to French society. In his arguments supporting the 1831 law of the *culte israélite* that mandated treating Judaism as a state religion by extending government stipends to rabbis, Ministre de l'Instruction publique et des cultes Joseph Mérilhou, who had served on the defense counsel for the sacrilege trial of *Le Courrier français*, cautioned that an enlightened France must not retain the "rust of the Middle Ages." No doubt in his reference to the Middle Ages, Mérilhou was considering France's expulsion of Jews in 1394 and likely the medieval vestiges present in contemporary acts of religious intolerance under Charles X, including the attacks on *Le Courrier français*, which he had defended. In a speech to the legislature, he demanded: "Let us erase these distinctions that exist between our neighbors, let us erase these last vestiges of an oppression that must never be reborn, and let us ensure that in France there are only French citizens, rather than *religionnaires* divided by their religion."[35] Mérilhou's contrast of Christian medievalism with an enlightened republic that abhorred religious intolerance resonates with the grappling over the "Jewish question" that emerged in public discourse, as well as literary constructions of nationhood outside of France.

Close to the time of the premiere of *La Juive*, an exchange in the columns of the short-lived republican paper *Le Réformateur* and the pro-Church periodical *L'Univers religieux, politique, scientifique et littéraire* epitomizes the oppositions within French debates about religious, social, and political intolerance. In an unsigned article of 15 February 1835 in *Le Réformateur*, the author contrasts republican ideals of rational thought, respect for varied beliefs, and religious freedom with the intolerance of the Church, again recalling the auto-da-fé:

> [The Church] threatens and anathematizes, it dooms books to the Index and authors to the hell of excommunication; it opens the gates of hell to the souls of dissidents; it closes the doors of its temples to their mortal remains, it hoards overhead the arsenal of punishments its faith promises it in the other world, and when it can seize the scepter here below, it does not wait for the hereafter to take revenge on the recalcitrant; *the Inquisition becomes its tribunal, the auto-da-fé, its scaffold* [my emphasis]. . . . We ask you: if the Church were to ascend the throne again tomorrow, would it use other means of propaganda and repression? Well, republican opinion dares to flatter itself with a totally different kind of tolerance; it seeks liberty for itself *and* for you.[36]

L'Univers religieux countered by claiming that "[t]he sciences, letters, philosophy, all doctrines, all systems, all religions, all beliefs, all opinions, including republican opinion itself, ARE GUILTY OF INTOLERANCE."[37] Furthermore, it emphasized that the Church itself was guilty only of the practice of "dogmatic or spiritual intolerance," but not of the violence of the Inquisition, which it claimed was primarily a political institution.[38]

A few years before Scribe began work on the libretto of *La Juive*, he had jotted down his own aversions to the Inquisition during a visit to the Palais des Papes in Avignon. In a travel journal of 1827, he described the rooms in which the tribunal's proceedings took place, including the "preparatory room," where the Inquisitors went "to invoke the Holy Spirit or, rather, the devil that inspires them," and the "torture chamber."[39] In another journal of the previous year, during a visit to Constance and the scene of the Council, he gave details of the heresy trial and execution of the Bohemian religious reformer Jan Hus, making note of the stone block on which Hus kneeled during the Council's sentencing and the chair that bore him to the stake.[40] Scribe's final choice to use the Council as the opera's setting may have been motivated by these firsthand recollections of the medieval despotism that took place in German lands, but he may also have been aware of the post-Napoleonic "revival of medievalism" in the German states,[41] and sensed that the Council would in fact serve as an equally powerful—and perhaps equally immediate—reminder of European despotism as the Portuguese Inquisition.

Scribe's thoughts about the Inquisition and Council of Constance were undoubtedly more than just the reflections a tourist, for the staged oppression of the Jews in *La Juive* tapped into the renewed significance of the Inquisition in contemporary discourse. This discourse was reflected not only in historical and journalistic writings and political exchanges, but also in novels such as Victor Hugo's *Notre-Dame de Paris*, published in 1831, close in time to the librettist's early work on *La Juive*.[42]

Even after Scribe shifted his initial setting from Goa to Constance, he retained the idea of the *bûcher* (stake), as is evident from the retention of the title "Rachel, ou l'auto-da-fé" on Scribe's draft scenario, as well as other Inquisition references in administrative correspondence of the Paris Opéra.[43] The president of the Commission de Surveillance, the duc de Choiseul, wrote to the minister of the interior on 23 May 1834 that he had finally been apprised of the subject of the opera in progress, which he refers to as "L'Auto-da-fé": "it seems that this *inquisition* subject will bring to the stage a *cardinal*, the Grand Inquisitor and his retinue, etc."[44] Choiseul's focus on the Inquisition and the featuring of Church figures hints at nervous concern, which does not seem to have abated as the opera developed further during the rehearsal period and in the weeks heading to production in February 1835 (after several delays of its premiere). On 3 February, the minister reflected similar concerns when he wrote to question Choiseul about the religious subject and its staging, asking that a new libretto manuscript incorporating the changes made during rehearsals be sent to him.[45] Even after Véron submitted the requested manuscript—less than two weeks prior to the anticipated premiere—the minister hesitated to authorize performances without seeing the opera's mise-en-scène and advised Choiseul that Commission members should attend the final rehearsals. Ultimately, as revealed in a report to the minister advocating authorization for performance, the Commission did not express uneasiness about the use of an Inquisition-like subject, the depiction of the cardinal's condemnation of the Jews, or the Jewish-Christian confrontations in the opera. Rather, it was primarily concerned that Catholic ceremonies, religious figures, and religious emblems be treated in a dignified, solemn manner, as the report indicated that they were, and was relieved that the costumes of the cardinal and other clergy were historical, rather than contemporary.[46]

These documents reveal that the Commission, though not a strictly censoring body, retained the authority to request changes and even prevent performances, although the oversight was rather loose and tolerant, as compared to years in which preventive censorship was in place. An experienced dramatist and librettist, Scribe had spent most of his career working under Restoration censorship prior to the early July Monarchy's "years of liberty."[47] Thus in the case of his modifications to the title and setting of *La Juive*, the downplaying of the more immediately accessible Portuguese Inquisition and change of the title "L'Auto-da-fé" could very well have been self-censoring gestures made after he became aware of the initial discomfort of Choiseul and the minister of the interior. Whether Scribe truly feared that the Commission might not authorize the opera's performance, or whether he avoided the Portuguese connection because of predicted sensitivity to a history closer to the French populace in time and place, cannot be determined conclusively. The latter speculation seems questionable, however, in the face of the likely resonance of the medieval German setting, as well as his choice of St. Bartholomew's Eve of 1572 as setting for Meyerbeer's *Les Huguenots*, which he created for the Paris Opéra in 1836. Set during an incendiary event in French history when thousands of Huguenots were massacred by Catholics in Paris, Scribe's libretto confronted themes of religious-political intolerance built on a controversial historical subject. Moreover, despite the renewal of Opéra censorship, he later did use the Portuguese Inquisition in his libretto for Gaetano Donizetti's *Dom Sébastien, roi de Portugal* (1843), based on Foucher's play *Dom Sébastien de Portugal* (1838).

The highlighting of Jewish oppression at the heart of *La Juive* retells the historical plight of Jews, in contrast to their more recent social and political acceptance in France following the groundbreaking declaration of their civil rights in 1791. This important change of legal status did not guarantee an unproblematic social integration, however, and the portrayal of Eléazar as an avaricious jeweler as well as a *fanatique*, as described by the composer himself and by several journalists,[48] alludes to biased views and stereotypes, and even to Voltairean prejudices, that remained pertinent within the nineteenth-century milieu. However, the loving, compassionate aspects of Eléazar's character, as revealed in his actions toward or on behalf of his daughter, soften the harsher aspects of the Shylock model, and, along with the portrayal of a benevolent Rachel, reinterpret Jewish stereotypes in ways that parallel the sociopolitical reconsiderations of the Jewish presence in France that had been occurring for several decades.

From the outset of the opera, Eléazar is ostracized by Christian celebrants as a heretic and a pariah whose work on the opening feast day of the Council is deemed sacrilegious and worthy of death by the provost of Constance, Ruggiero. The maltreatment of the Jews continues, although the cardinal temporarily quells the anger of Ruggiero and the Christian celebrants; after Brogni enters and realizes that he knows Eléazar from Rome, he calls for clemency and reconciliation. Later in act 1, in a scene adapted from *Ivanhoe*, Eléazar and Rachel are shunned as they search for a seat to await the entrance of the Council's entourage, similar to the manner in which Rebecca and Isaac are repulsed with invectives as they look for a seat at the tournament in chapter 7 of the novel. Although scores published by Maurice Schlesinger close to the time of the 1835 performances largely omit this scene, Scribe's 1835 published libretto includes a recurring chant of "C'est un Juif! c'est un Juif!" ("He's a Jew!" "He's a Jew!"), along with such remarks as "N'approche pas! Ton souffle impur / Doit porter malheur, j'en suis sûr!" ("Don't come near! Your unclean breath / Must carry misfortune, I am sure of it!").[49] In the confrontation in the act 1 finale that does appear in the Schlesinger scores, Ruggiero reminds the crowd of Jesus's chasing the vendors from the Temple when he sees Eléazar and Rachel on the Church steps, and sets off the townspeople's cries for "these Hebrews, these accursed ones" to be plunged into the lake. Jewish-Christian interactions continue in the following acts, within both private and public spheres. In the intimacy of Eléazar's home in act 2, Rachel's lover, disguised as a Jewish painter, participates in the family seder, but furtively throws his piece of unleavened bread to the floor, arousing Rachel's doubts; when she confronts him later, he admits his deception and true identity as a Christian, unleashing her full anger in the duet "Lorsqu'à toi je me suis donnée" (act 2, no. 11). She decries her dishonor before her father and "a vengeful God," and the inevitable sentence of death that their forbidden relationship will bring, but after he persuades her to flee with him, she relents. Eléazar unexpectedly bursts in to foil her Jessica-like escape and curses Léopold for his betrayal in attempting to abduct his daughter, and then for his deception in hiding his Christianity; momentarily, Eléazar turns from anger when Rachel tearfully invokes his love and pleads for his pardon and blessing for the couple's betrothal. But Léopold's shout of "Jamais!" at the suggestion of marriage, instigates Eléazar's full malediction that ends act 2, and anticipates the publicly heightened events of act 3 in the gardens of the royal palace. When Rachel discovers that her lover Samuel is in actuality the prince and the husband of Eudoxie, she denounces him and admits their illicit (and illegal) affair. This exposure sets off Brogni's more consequential malediction (bolstered by the chorus of courtiers singing "Sur eux anathème"), which then leads to sentences of death for Eléazar, Rachel, and Léopold, although the prince is pardoned through Rachel's intercession in act 4.

The Council's sentence of death for Eléazar and Rachel as social and religious pariahs, as well as the enactment of Rachel's shocking execution, made visceral the realities of an intolerant authoritarian past, including the historical expulsion of Jews from France, Spain, and Portugal and the forced conversions and death sentences imposed by various Inquisitions. Such representation symbolically juxtaposed the harsh, intolerant treatment of past centuries with the comparatively tolerant political present, as France continued to move along its revolutionary path toward religious and political freedom for individual citizens. Although the characterization of Eléazar retained unsympathetic elements of Shylock, his deep love for Rachel and his acceptance of the Christian Léopold as her betrothed mitigate the stereotype; fundamentally, he is portrayed as a victim of the Council, along with Rachel. As both accept martyrdom at the opera's conclusion, and hold onto their faith and Jewish identity, Eléazar and Rachel could be viewed as icons of the postemancipation French citizenry: in the distant past, in the world of the Inquisition or Council—and perhaps in the more immediate past of Charles X's Restoration—their religious and cultural differences would not have been tolerated, but in the world of the July Monarchy, they were individuals who would not be denied "liberté, fraternité, et égalité."

In the opera's meshing of historical reality with literary stereotypes and tropes, however, it is Rachel who becomes the clearest representative of the formerly alien citizen, one who embodies assimilationist ideals in her stronger affiliations with Christian society (though her links to her biological father, Cardinal Brogni, and her lover, the disguised Christian prince Léopold, are hidden in much of the opera). Whereas Eléazar reveals his vengeful feeling toward Christians at key moments, refuses Brogni's gesture of reconciliation in act 1, and never lets go of his hatred of this authoritarian figure who has banned him from Rome in the opera's prehistory, Rachel responds warmly to the cardinal's appeal, as described above, and shows that her humanitarian concern extends to both Jews and Christians. Despite her discoveries of Léopold's deceptions, in act 4, Rachel accepts the blame for their illicit, inter-religious affair, leading to Léopold's pardon by the Council. Rachel's dual identity and her pro-Christian actions could be interpreted as a willingness to assimilate or at least soften her separatist identity, although her compliance is more overt in Scribe's initial drafting of her actual conversion. But the retention of her somewhat mixed identity suggests that she, as the more acquiescent, and easily dominated female, represents the Jew who would be more acceptable within French society than the Shylock-inspired Eléazar, who refuses to forget and forgive past persecutions, clings tightly to religious difference, and remains separate from Christian culture. However, with Rachel's final act of defiance (in her refusal to convert), her martyrdom, along with Eléazar's, simultaneously signifies the oppression that the European/French Jew had endured as "heretic" and "alien," while also evoking for French audiences the contrasting political realities of their era, with the return of promises of religious freedom in the 1830 *Charte*, the dropping of Catholicism as the sole religion of state, and the expanded acceptance of Jews in French institutions.

One aspect of Rachel's characterization—the suggestion of an orientalist or Sephardic identity—also distinguishes her from Eléazar's portrayal, further complicating her blended Christian-Jewish identity and enhancing traits that made her attractive, and even fascinating, to French audiences. One wonders whether this distinction could have possibly embodied perceived differences between Sephardic and Ashkenazi Jews in the French context, and differences in their acceptance within French society—although more research is needed in order to support this hypothesis. Ismar Schorsch has noted that France's emancipation of Sephardic Jews of Bordeaux met with less resistance than that of Alsatian Ashkenazi. Furthermore, Schorsch points out that the Sephardic concepts of Judaism fit well within the postemancipation political world, holding sway, for example, in formulations of the Napoleonic Sanhédrin that distinguished between religious doctrine and civil laws or morals.[50]

The allusions to Rachel's Sephardic identity align with Sir Walter Scott's portrayal of Rebecca in *Ivanhoe*, along with the blended religious-social identities and the general feminine traits of kindness, courage, compassion, and a sacrificial, compliant nature that the two characters share. As mentioned above, Rachel forgives Léopold for his deceptions and even takes full blame for their affair in order that his life be spared; in a similar manner, Rebecca pardons the Templar, Bois-Guilbert: "But I do forgive thee, Bois-Guilbert, though the author of my early death" (chapter 39). Both are also represented as beautiful, desirable, exotic women who fit the literary stereotype of "la belle juive" that intersects with nineteenth-century orientalist depictions. According to Edgar Rosenberg, the paradigm of "la belle juive" was set through the character of Jessica in *The Merchant of Venice*, and later evolved into an exotic prostitute in nineteenth-century French literature, as represented by Esther in Balzac's *Splendeurs et misères des courtisanes*.[51] Lucette Czyba links the type to "la femme orientale," including "l'esclave orientale,"[52] and this exotic object of fantasy can certainly be sensed in Victor Hugo's 1835 poem "Sultane favorite" in *Les Orientales*, which idolizes the "adored Jewess" for her dark-toned beauty gilded "with a ray of sun."

The merging of the stereotype of "la belle juive" with the image of a Sephardic courtesan is evident in P.-E. Chevalier's *Rachel, ou la belle juive*, a Parisian melodrama of 1803 based on the legend of the love of Alfonso VIII of Castile for the Jewess Raquel, which, as mentioned above, may have informed Scribe's basic portrayal and naming of Rachel. Although I have not yet found a clear reference to the legend or to Chevalier's play among Scribe's papers, the title of his early thumbnail sketch, "La belle juive," raises the possibility that the librettist knew of the work and perhaps drew his early heading and other basic elements from it, or possibly from other works with similar titles (such as Jacques Cazotte's novella).[53] Chevalier's Rachel is similar to Scribe's Rachel in its archetypal foundations: in alliance with other models mentioned above, she is the adopted daughter of the Jew Ruben, as alluded to in Ruben's statement to Mathan that he had been "charged with caring for Rachel in childhood" (act 1, scene 1).[54] Moreover, she is the lover of a royal figure (Alfonso VIII) who leads a Christian kingdom and who is revered for his conquests, as is Léopold, prince and conqueror of the Hussites in *La Juive*. She is also a courtesan, the king's "favorite," an identity that Rachel assumes, at least temporarily, in the opera. Beyond these basic elements, however, the ambitious, power-loving character of Chevalier's Rachel bears little resemblance to the modest, sacrificial Jewess of the opera.

In Chevalier's melodrama both Ruben and Rachel become advisers to the king at his court, with Rachel's desire to usurp and retain power foiling Ruben's more surreptitious, or diplomatic, plans to win and sustain special treatment and protection for the Jews of Castile.[55] As she gains control over the king's will, and the Castilian people are levied a tax from which the Jews of the region are exempt, old retainers of the king who have been banned from court begin to plot her death. Fernand, a faithful follower and magistrate of Toledo, prevents her assassination, but persuades the king to respond to the people's wish and ban Rachel, Ruben, and other Jews from court. Unable to resist Rachel's charms and seeming love for him, the king rescinds his decision. However, as Rachel grasps for more power, he realizes her treacherous desires and condemns her in the penultimate scene of the play. Instead of death, however, which occurs in other treatments of the legend, the king orders his soldiers to remove both Rachel and Ruben, to "be cast into an eternal dungeon" (act 3, scene 7). Unlike the condemnation and death of *La Juive*'s Rachel, who is more clearly portrayed as an oppressed victim and martyr unwilling to give up her Jewish faith, the condemnation of Chevalier's Rachel is made to appear as her just reward, with the king announcing the moral of the story in the final scene: "What a lesson for me: unfortunate are princes when they are captivated by their passions and surrounded by treacherous courtesans" (act 3, scene 8). In this work, Rachel is not portrayed as the compassionate foil to a vengeful father, but as the more despicable and blameworthy character of the father-daughter pair, with Ruben's complicity. Despite certain resemblances of characterization, Chevalier's Jewish representations and plot carry very different implications than those of *La Juive*. Rather than Scribe's (and Halévy's) cautionary tale about the errors of religious, social, and political intolerance, Chevalier's *Rachel, ou la belle juive* warns against the embracing of Jews within a society, particularly at its center of power, by casting Rachel and Ruben as calculating and, ultimately, treasonous figures, similar to the portrayal of the Jewess of Toledo legend in the Spanish sources.[56]

However, the image of the courtesan in Chevalier's Rachel clearly correlates with one aspect of Rachel's portrayal in *La Juive*, particularly in opening scenes of act 3, where she is cast more obviously in an orientalist, and possibly Sephardic, light. In the initial three scenes performed, but omitted after the opera's premiere, Rachel disguises herself as a "slave" in order to gain passage at Léopold's court, first through Princess Eudoxie, appearing as "une pauvre fille inconnue, étrangère" ("a poor unknown, foreign girl") and requesting that Eudoxie admit her as a slave: "Parmi vos nombreuses esclaves / Daignez pour aujourd'hui m'admettre!" ("As one of your many slaves, deign to accept me for today!")[57] In scene 5, following choruses and the ballet, when Rachel is summoned by Léopold with the words, "Esclave! À boire!!" ("Slave! Bring me a drink!!"), she emerges from a group of women, seemingly a harem of slaves or courtesans, to serve him.

This image is certainly orientalist, and made more so by the exoticism of her costuming, particularly the turbans and scarves that accessorized her two costumes designed by Paul Lormier for the 1835 production.[58] The "turbaned and caftaned" Rebecca of *Ivanhoe* may have in fact served as a model, in her appearance in "a sort of Eastern dress" highlighted by a turban of yellow silk, leading Ivanhoe to mistake her initially for an Arabic woman (chapter 7). Such ambiguity of representation (and, likely, the contemporary perception of such representation) was not uncommon at the time, and Lormier could have used any number of models, for the turbaned Oriental permeated French romantic art, literature, and ballet in the early nineteenth century.[59] The costumes include similar orientalist—and possibly Sephardic—features as found in Eugène Delacroix's now-famous paintings set in Jewish and Arabic communities of North Africa, which signify the beginnings of France's colonial presence, as well as its fascinations with exotic cultures. In these paintings, Delacroix seemingly recreated the authentic dress that he found during his excursions in Morocco and Algiers, but he may have combined a painter's symbolic play with ethnographic exactitude. In a 1832 painting of a Jewess, for example, *Jeune femme juive assise*, he uses yellow as the predominant color in her dress, and paints a gold headscarf for another seated Jewish woman, *Étude de femme juive assise*.[60] Yellow was also the fabric color chosen for the main part of Rachel's first-act costume, as shown in a watercolor by Eugène du Faget illustrating Lormier's design, but yellow becomes gold in a portrait of Cornélie Falcon, the first Rachel, painted in the same costume by Grévedon in 1837.[61] Atop the yellow (or gold) dress are a tight bodice and overdress of blue and white, with a white turban, scarf, full sleeves ornamented with gold tassels, and a sash tied at the waist, ending with gold braided tassels.[62] Her second costume, a flowing blue silk caftan embellished with purple velvet and gold, may have been used for the second act in the interior of Eléazar's home, as well as for the third act, befitting her guise as "slave" in the palace of Eudoxie and Léopold.[63] An 1835 portrait of Falcon by A. Colin seemingly depicts her in this costume, resting her elbow on a table in a boudoir filled with oriental symbols: an oud propped to one side on a cushioned seat, an oil lamp emitting smoke (perhaps incense), an ornate pitcher, rich curtains, and a barred window that evokes the interior of a seraglio. Her headscarf in the portrait strongly resembles those depicted by Delacroix in *Femmes d'Alger dans l'appartement* (1834); it appears more loosely folded than the turban of the act 1 costume, and flows to her shoulder.[64] Moreover, the flowing sleeves closely match those found in his 1832 watercolor of a Jewish mother and daughter, *La femme d'Abraham Benchimol et une de leurs filles*.

Other elements of stage and action, some realized and others not, further point to orientalist, and perhaps Sephardic, evocations. A sketch for a stage set of the interior of Eléazar's house planned by Cicéri for act 2 features arabesque design and an arched doorway, which, if retained, offered an "oriental" aura that encompassed Eléazar as well as Rachel, and the groups of Jews included in the seder scene of act 2.[65] The first set for act 3, before cuts were made after the premiere, represented the interior of a tent, "with furniture and accessories," and may very well have depicted the seraglio-like interior shown in Colin's painting.[66] The *divertissement* of act 3 also evoked an orientalist aura in its ballet featuring knights errants, a Saracen magician, and "infidels in turbans" who guard a fortress and refuse to surrender it, before its metamorphosis into a "gothic edifice" from which "hostesses" emerge to dance for the emperor's entertainment—as described by a review of 25 February 1835 in *Le Figaro*.[67] Although detached from the plot of the opera, this ballet further embodied cultural stereotypes and representations of the domination of the alien Other through the transformation of female figures.

Despite the lack of overt references to Spain or Portugal in *La Juive* as it was first performed at the Paris Opéra, the auto-da-fé remained at the center of the drama, serving as a metaphor for authoritarian despotism and intolerance and as a link to a heavily politicized discourse that intersected with sephardism. The opera's use of Jewish characters to articulate questions of national identity recalled France's own medieval banishment of the Jews, but also evoked more immediately the contrast to the nation's progressive role as the first European "emancipator" of the Jews. In its portrayals of Rachel and Eléazar, inspired by several literary ur-texts of Jewish representation, this opera appropriated Sephardic inflections that were more clearly present in those literary models, from possible skeletal links to the Spanish Jewess of Toledo legend to deeper connections with *The Merchant of Venice* and *Ivanhoe*. Even though what Ismar Schorsch calls the "Sephardic mystique" is not as fully evident here as in *La Juive*'s literary models, this historical French grand opera offers a parallel to the kind of sephardism activated by Scott's historical novel, not only in its reinterpretation of the Shylock-Jessica pairing of Isaac and Rebecca, but also in its casting of Eléazar and Rachel as political symbols and representatives of a minority, alien population. Whereas this operatic treatment of the "Jewish question" may appear to be an anachronism within the context of the July Monarchy, when over forty years had passed since the country had granted Jews the rights of citizenship, in actuality it demonstrates a timely reconsideration of the question in the wake of the absolutist actions of Charles X, which had set off a second revolution in 1830 and ushered in the monarchy of Louis-Philippe. Although the political crisis had passed, fears of governmental repression, Church power, and the abrogation of individual rights and freedoms lingered; moreover, as reflected in the political debate surrounding the 1831 law of the *culte israélite*, the integration of Jewish citizens into French society continued to be a contested reality. In response to an ongoing discourse that resounded with themes and metaphors broached in *La Juive*, Scribe and his collaborators clearly believed that an exploration of the "Jewish question" within a staged medieval world at the Paris Opéra was not an anachronism but a topical cautionary tale that served "powerful historical interests," reminding French audiences of the revolutionary, republican ideals of the nation.

Four The Strange Career of the Abarbanels from Heine to the Holocaust

Jonathan Skolnik

In June 1937, the Jewish Museum in Berlin organized an exhibition in honor of Don Isaak Abarbanel's five hundredth birthday.[1] The exhibition catalog listed old and rare publications by this Bible scholar, statesman, and financier for Portuguese and Spanish kings.[2] Fifteenth- and sixteenth-century paintings, medallions, and other collector's items were shown, including pieces borrowed from museums and collections abroad. At first glance, it is astonishing that such an exhibition took place in Berlin under the Nazi regime, as German Jews who wished to emigrate struggled to find a country that would take them in. In view of the imminent catastrophe, it is astounding that the life of a Sephardic court Jew who died in the sixteenth century could attract such attention. Don Isaak Abarbanel was indeed a figure with rich historical symbolic value for German Jews: supposedly a descendant of King David, he was a religious and political authority and an adviser to the court of King Ferdinand and Queen Isabella. His commentaries on the Torah and the Haggadah revived faith in messianic hopes. In 1492, as the Jews were forced to leave Spain, Abarbanel wielded his influence on behalf of his fellow believers, and when his efforts proved powerless in the face of the Inquisition, he led his people into exile.[3] Moreover, in stark contrast to the opposite choice made by his influential friend Abraham Senior, Abarbanel refused to submit to conversionist intimidation and thus became a symbol of unwavering adherence to Judaism.

In 1937, on the occasion of the Abarbanel quincentennial, several studies dedicated to this Iberian scholar and statesman were published. Numerous works made reference to the historical analogy between the dilemma facing the Jews in Nazi Germany and the Inquisition and expulsion from Iberia.[4] In one study, Rabbi Abraham Joshua Heschel (1907–

72) noted the sense of foreboding evoked by the Abarbanel anniversary, remarking that "the shimmer of autumn glows around Abarbanel"; he "served states from which he had to flee, acquired wealth that was confiscated," and his appeal to King Ferdinand was a tragic failure.[5] But the desperate Spanish Jews could not see, according to Heschel, that their exile simultaneously meant freedom from a role in the murderous enterprise of Spanish colonialism, which turned out to be an unexpected blessing. Heschel's interpretation of Abarbanel's legacy was a message to German Jewish readers regarding the vicious nature of the Nazi regime and its aims. The parallel with the Sephardic past was meant to warn German Jews of the coming persecution and to strengthen their resolve to flee.

About a century earlier, Heinrich Heine was also responding to a crisis occasioned by anti-Semitism when, in 1840, he published a novel fragment entitled *Der Rabbi von Bacherach* (*The Rabbi of Bacherach*). The 1840 blood libel and pogrom in Damascus—and the disappointing reactions of European powers—had given new relevance to Heine's fictional narrative about an accusation of ritual murder in fifteenth-century Germany. This motivated Heine to continue working on a novel he had begun and abandoned in the 1820s.[6] In a newly added third chapter, Rabbi Abraham—Heine's eponymous protagonist—and his wife Sara now meet in the Frankfurt ghetto a figure by the name of "Don Isaak Abarbanel." The latter identifies himself (ahistorically) as a convert from Judaism, and a supposed "nephew" of the great rabbi of the same name.

Surprisingly, Heine's *Rabbi of Bacherach* is mentioned neither in the 1937 Berlin exhibition catalog nor in contemporary discussions of this exhibition in German Jewish newspapers.[7] In a letter to the curator of the Berlin exhibition, the art historian Rahel Wischnitzer (1885–1989), the German Jewish historian Sigmund Seeligmann (1873–1940) wondered why it did not to take into account the modern interest in Abarbanel's work.[8] But perhaps the associations with German Jewish images of Abarbanel and their resonance with the contemporary situation were so obvious that it was thought unnecessary to mention them.

Heine's fictional Abarbanel stands at the beginning of a long German Jewish tradition for, during the hundred years that passed from emancipation to exile and ultimately mass murder, German Jewish writers returned again and again to the figure of Don Isaak Abarbanel.[9] Writers of historical fiction such as Heinrich Heine, Phöbus Phillipson

(1807–70), Hermann Reckendorf (1825–75), Alfred Nossig (1864–1943), Hermann Kesten (1900–1996), and Leo Perutz (1882–1957) employed fictionalized Abarbanel figures, and used them as reference points for various, and often widely differing, ideological positions: assimilation, Zionism, religious liberalism, orthodoxy. They projected conflicting notions of modern Jewish identity onto a Jew of the fifteenth century and articulated countless contemporary concerns in the guise of this historical figure. While Heine's Abarbanel novel is well known to scholars and readers, the works of Kesten and Perutz, who completed their German-language novels in exile, have received less attention. The other authors—Phillipson, Reckendorf, Nossig—have for the most part been ignored by German literary history, since they wrote exclusively for Jewish readers. Even Lion Feuchtwanger's 1907 study of Heine's novel refers to these Jewish writers only in a disapproving aside.[10] To what extent are these other literary Abarbanels comparable to Heine's fictional Don Isaak? And what new tones do we hear in Heine's *Rabbi of Bacherach* when we consider the later Abarbanel figures of German Jewish literature? The following analysis explores the extent to which these subsequent literary depictions of Don Isaak Abarbanel shed light on various facets of Heine's own very condensed and nuanced portrait.

When he commenced work on *Der Rabbi von Bacherach*, Heine intended it as a contribution to the project of the Verein für Cultur und Wissenschaft der Juden (Society for Jewish Culture and Science), the first systematic attempt to write Jewish history in a modern scholarly way, detached from the Christian theological paradigm. The fact that Heine could not call upon Jewish sources in his research on the historical background of German and Spanish Jews in the fifteenth century demonstrates the novelty of a modern *Wissenschaft des Judentums* and the magnitude of the task the Verein faced.[11] It has been pointed out many times that Heine's Don Isaak is not identical with the historical figure, and that Heine made up much in his unfinished novel. But while the modern historians of *Wissenschaft des Judentums* sought to demystify Jewish history, for Heine as a historical novelist, invention and myth were no disadvantage. On the one hand, Heine's novel is a modern historical myth that complements the demystifying project of an objective, scholarly modern Jewish historiography. On the other hand, historiography is rarely free of ideology, and the undertones with which Heine depicts his Abarbanel are indeed related to the worldview of the first generation of modern Jewish historians.[12] The founders of the Verein für Cultur und Wissenschaft der Juden saw a useful precedent in Sephardic Judaism, a cultivated and enlightened contrast to the purportedly pedantic, degraded, and "unhealthy" Ashkenazim who could function as ammunition for the enemies of emancipation. Heine's Don Isaak seems to have been constructed in view of these prejudices. In contrast to the ghetto Jews, Heine's Abarbanel stands out; his nobility is already apparent to the beautiful Sara from afar. However, Heine's Abarbanel goes far beyond the image required by a Sephardic model that could inspire a modern "purified" Judaism: Heine's hero is an apostate, a self-declared heathen.

Many commentators see in Heine's Don Isaak a self-portrait in fictionalized form. The genesis of this novel fragment is understood by these interpreters as proof of Heine's increasingly problematic relationship to Judaism; they therefore suggest that he changed and ultimately abandoned this project because of his own changing attitudes toward religion. In their view, Heine's previous plans to include not an Isaak but a Jehudah Abarbanel—"a young Spanish Jew, who was at heart a Jew, yet had himself baptized out of the impetuousness that luxury affords"—were superseded in the 1840 version by an even more distanced account of the historical Abarbanel figure.[13] Indeed, Heine's own baptism and the fact that the fictional Don Isaak is identified as the "nephew" of an important figure in the Jewish community, speak in favor of a biographical interpretation.

However, to equate Heine's position with Don Isaak's in the third chapter would be to overlook the satirical aspects of Heine's portrait.[14] Like Don Quixote, whose language he evokes, Heine's Don Isaak is both heroic and pitiable and seeks to revive knightly values in a disenchanted modern world. Nevertheless, in contrast to Rabbi Abraham and to the Jews of the Frankfurt ghetto, Heine's Abarbanel is in no way a singularly "positive" representative of a worldly modern Jewish identity. Heine's ability to establish contrasts between the "backward" premodern Jew and the progressive Jew, for the sole purpose of reversing these categories later, becomes clear in his book *On Poland*, where he writes: "in spite of the barbaric fur hat, that covers his head, and the even more barbaric ideas, that fill the same, I hold the Polish Jew in far higher esteem than many a German Jew, who carries his Bolivar on his head and his Jean Paul in his head" (DHA, 6: 62). Here, it is the purportedly "progressive" Jew who becomes the target of Heine's irony. Therefore, it would be premature to infer that the apostasy of Don Isaak Abarbanel's in Heine's *Rabbi of Bacherach* is privileged by its narrator.[15]

In preparation for his *Rabbi of Bacherach*, Heine searched for sources and discovered some information about Don Isaak and several other members of the Abarbanel family. Looking at Heine's notes, however, one cannot say with certainty which elements of the Abarbanel saga attracted his attention. Was it the kinship with King David or was it the crossing of boundaries between the Jewish and non-Jewish world? Heine notes that at the end of his life, Isaak Abarbanel regretted that he had dedicated himself to worldly concerns earlier in his career. Isaak's son Jehudah (the Neoplatonic philosopher whose works appear in Alonso Quijana's library in *Don Quixote*) was, on the other hand, the most famous example of an Abarbanel who strayed from a traditional Jewish path and then returned to it. In his fragment, Heine therefore condenses numerous historical characteristics and legends associated with the Abarbanels into one barely developed literary figure. Filled with ambivalence and tension, Heine's Abarbanel simultaneously evokes the idea of exile and messianic hope; successful integration through education and baptism forced through persecution; assimilation and a heroic Jewish world beyond the ghetto.

These tensions, which remain unresolved in Heine's fragment, had been explored more fully by Phöbus Phillipson in *Die Marannen* (1837).[16] First published as a serial novella in the influential German Jewish periodical *Allgemeine Zeitung des Judentums*, Phillipson's narrative reached the public three years earlier than Heine's *Rabbi of Bacherach*. Phillipson's story begins with the siege of Granada in the year 1492, and the center of attention is a young Jewish girl named Dinah, who loses her family and comes under the protection of Isaak Abarbanel, portrayed here as a benevolent father figure. There is no evidence that Heine read Phillipson's work, but Heine's Don Isaak would surely have found a kindred spirit in Phillipson's Jehudah Abarbanel, though not in that character's father: "Relentless earnest studies in the sacred canon of his nation, extensive world experience acquainted the father only with the serious side of life, [but] Jehudah was more familiar with the sweet sounds of Spanish poetry and with the blossoming literature of the people."[17]

Phillipson's *Marannen* is a parable of the prodigal son. The stunningly beautiful Dinah rejects a Christian suitor and instead brings Jehudah back to the faith of his fathers. Thus the Jewish people are saved, and the father figure Isaak Abarbanel presides over the perseverance of the Jewish family and religion so they are not lost to apostasy. Although it is difficult to imagine Heine's *Rabbi of Bacherach* with as happy an ending as Phillipson's story, it is not impossible, even if the path to return for Heine's Don Isaak would be much longer. As it is, both Phillipson's Jehudah and Heine's Don Isaak reach the realization that the Hebrews and "Nazarenes" are equally foreign to them. Yet while Phillipson's Isaak and Jehudah Abarbanel are fully developed characters, Heine's Don Isaak remains a "nephew"—far removed from the role of loyal son (as in Phillipson's story), who will someday be a father himself, to both his children and his people.

If Phillipson's historical novella uses Jewish history as a moral example to preach to an implicit Jewish reader about the importance of the transmission of Jewish culture, Isaak Abarbanel's plea to Ferdinand and Isabella in *Die Marannen* has a different mission. Were the text to presuppose two implied readers—one Jewish and another non-Jewish—then that non-Jewish reader would be in the position of Spanish monarchs. With Phöbus Phillipson's help, Don Isaak's historical speech becomes a liberal political parable for the present, an argument against the still incomplete emancipation of Jews. Phillipson's novella broadly uses Jewish history to argue the importance of the transmission of Jewish culture, but Isaak Abarbanel's plea to Ferdinand and Isabella in *Die Marannen* states the liberal political case for fully emancipating Jews in the Europe of 1837: "We are not strangers in a foreign country, we are sons of Spain. . . . The Spanish Jew, my king, detests the lowly practice of usury."[18] Phillipson's Abarbanel argues that an expulsion of Jews would be detrimental to Spanish prosperity and, ultimately, to the Catholic religion as well. He offers to sacrifice all his wealth in order to finance Columbus's expedition. He falls on his knees and cries out that the Jews would give everything for Spain's glory if only they were permitted to stay. Ferdinand and Isabella are deeply moved, but Torquemada intervenes and Abarbanel is forsaken. Abarbanel's plea evokes empathy. Hence, Phillipson's story attempts to demonstrate to both Jewish and Christian readers that despite their leading separate familial and religious lives, a common ground could be found in resistance to reactionary forces.

Would it be possible to enlist Heine's Abarbanel in such a struggle? He curses and slanders the Jewish religion but draws a line at the mockery of the Jewish people: "Sennora . . . you misunderstood me . . . but by God, no mockery, no mockery of Israel" (DHA, 5: 140). Whoever seeks a clear answer from Heine to the Jewish question in *The Rabbi of Bacherach* will be disappointed. Heine's position is perhaps not as extreme as that of Karl Marx, who demands nothing less than the total elimination from society of a Judaism understood only as exploitation and deception, or as prophetic as that of Moses Hess, who could imagine a just social order that continues to include the Jews as Jews. Nevertheless, it is certain that his Abarbanel is much more radical than Phillipson's, because he embodies a more profound form of religious criticism.

In Hermann Reckendorf's five-volume historical novel, *Die Geheimnisse der Juden* (*The Secrets of the Jews*, 1856–57), the story of the Abarbanels unfolds in epic dimensions. Reckendorf recounts the drama of Jewish history through fictional testaments in which descendants of King David tell their stories from the destruction of the Second Temple to the age of Moses Mendelsohn.[19] Reckendorf was a teacher of Hebrew and Arabic in Heidelberg and translated the Koran into Hebrew. He was the father of the Orientalist Hermann Reckendorf (1863–1923). The stories of Don Isaak and his son Jehudah play a significant role in Reckendorf's novel, but their purpose is situated in a larger context. Here the portrayal of the expulsion of Jews from Spain, as well as Jehudah's rebellion and reconciliation, occurs in the final—most critical—part of the novel. Reckendorf makes his message to the Jewish reader clear in a postscript:

> Did you ever consider . . . that your ancestors once forged a path over steep cliffs and the deepest precipices, residing in damp and dark caves, prepared to be attacked at any moment, in order to bear witness in their way to the God of their fathers?—Dear brother in faith! You are like the pilgrim of the fable, wrapped in his coat; the coat that you are wrapped in is your fatherly faith, which should be your constant companion on your earthy pilgrimage. The storms of persecution and the sun of humanity seem to have wagered with one another on who

> would first succeed in removing your coat. . . . I hope that the latter does not succeed in what the former could not accomplish.[20]

In Reckendorf's *Geheimnisse*, the Abarbanel family's troubles have the purpose of urging the reader not to give up religious tradition under any circumstance. Jewish history is a continuing saga of threat and resistance, martyrdom and survival, for which the story of the Abarbanels becomes a symbol.

Reckendorf's reluctance to continue the story of the Abarbanels beyond Moses Mendelsohn's time also shows his understanding of the implications of modernity for the Jews, for his plea for tradition proceeds from a very limited conception of Jewish history beyond the Enlightenment. According to Reckendorf, the world subdivides into states that are either sufficiently enlightened to permit their Jewish citizens a free life as traditional Jews or that continue to behave barbarically. Nevertheless, *Geheimnisse* contains a revolutionary countercurrent—an additional conception of history implied by Reckendorf. For whoever clings to the belief that the Messiah will emerge from the House of David will experience the five-volume historical novel, to use Walter Benjamin's terms, as one that is not filled with "empty homogeneous time" but rather with "now time"—the potential saving entrance of the Messiah.[21] One can never say with certainty whether the mystical layers of meaning implicit in the figure of Don Isaak were also evident to Heine, who was interested in religious-political movements like Saint-Simonism. Nevertheless, the messianic connotations associated with the figure of Abarbanel can raise anew questions about the relationship between politics, Judaism, and history in Heine's thought.

Reckendorf's novel also illustrates a conventional German Jewish perspective on Abarbanel that was common in the nineteenth century. For both the liberal Phöbus Phillipson and the orthodox Hermann Reckendorf, Isaak Abarbanel represents a model of erudition that embodies a modern spirit within the boundaries of tradition. In Reckendorf's novel, Isaak Abarbanel appears as a forerunner of *Haskalah*, the Jewish Enlightenment movement: "My favorite studies were pure exegetical research in the Holy Scriptures; I did not attach special importance to the talmudic interpretations. But I also pursued other sciences, especially logic and mathematics, with great enthusiasm."[22]

A nineteenth-century German Jewish reader would have recognized in this Abarbanel a conservative *maskil* (enlightened man), an advocate of harmony between enlightenment and religion. Heine's *Rabbi of Bacherach* stands in sharp contrast to this. In Heine's work, the German rabbi Abraham, who has studied in Spain, represents "progressive" religious trends. Heine's Abarbanel in turn abandons all connections to Judaism save for Jewish cuisine. Yet even though Heine's Abarbanel can be interpreted as a representative of a modern Jewish identity that departs from traditional Judaism, he is far from being an uncritically positive figure. The satirical aspects of Heine's portrait are thus an anticipation of caricatures of superficially modernized "inauthentic" *maskilim* in the later literature of the Jewish Enlightenment.[23]

Alfred Nossig's 1906 play *Abarbanel: Das Drama eines Volkes* emphasizes the knightly, heroic qualities that are found in the Heine figure.[24] Nossig was a statistician as well as a sculptor and writer. Born in Lemberg (L'viv) in 1864, he advocated Jewish-Polish assimilation before becoming a Zionist, but later broke with Zionism to advocate non-Zionist Jewish colonization projects. He was assassinated by the Jewish underground in the Warsaw ghetto in 1943 for allegedly collaborating with the Germans. He wrote his Abarbanel play during his Zionist phase.

Nossig's Abarbanel resembles an idealized turn-of-the-century Zionist of the Theodor Herzl or Max Nordau kind: he has "the upright, proud posture of Spanish noblemen" and "only his two-pointed black beard gives any indication of his Jewishness."[25] Set in Spain in 1492, the play begins with a scene that recalls Captain Dreyfus's predicament in late nineteenth-century Paris. While Spanish generals and ministers are celebrating their victory over the Moors, the conversation turns to "the inner enemy"—the Jew. "Spain was Spanish," says one. "Today it belongs to the Jews."[26] Abarbanel's enemies accuse him of having sent secret messages to the Moorish king's Jewish doctor during the siege of Granada.

The affair turns Abarbanel into a proto-Zionist. He is eventually restored to favor, but King Ferdinand realizes that it was a mistake to fill prominent posts with Jews. The focus of the drama is not in an eloquent speech aimed at persuading the Spaniards to recognize the Jews as their countrymen, as in Phillipson's novella, but Abarbanel's warning against the illusion that Jews will ever be accepted in Spain. This, and his dream of an immediate return to Zion, bring him the enmity of both the "liberal" and the "orthodox" Jews. In Nossig's drama, though, Abarbanel succeeds in winning the hearts and minds of the youth for his vision, and the journey into exile turns into a heroic exodus, leaving no ambiguity as to prospects for the future. Heine's 1840 fragment and Nossig's 1906 drama are in their different ways both literary responses to modern anti-Semitism.

In Phöbus Phillipson's 1837 novella, an entire chapter is dedicated to Abarbanel's apologia for the Spanish Jews. The passionate, well-planned rhetoric with which Phillipson's Don Isaak attempts to establish the Jews' right to co-exist with Catholics in their common Spanish birthplace precedes the "enlightenment work" of the Centralverein deutscher Staatsbürger jüdischen Glaubens (Central Association of German Citizens of Jewish Faith), which fought unceasingly against anti-Semitic slander in imperial and Weimar Germany. Ninety-nine years after the publication of Phillipson's *Die Marranen*, efforts such as Abarbanel's petition would be irrevocably doomed to failure in Germany.

In 1936, the writer and dramatist Hermann Kesten found himself in Amsterdam, a refugee from Nazi Germany. There, he wrote a historical novel entitled *Sieg der Dämonen: Ferdinand und Isabella*, in which we find yet another version of Abarbanel's plea to the king and the queen:

> "Abarbanel," he calls, "were you always a banker?"
> "I started out as a scholar, Majesty."
> Disappointed, Ferdinand asked: "Are you at least still a Jew? Or already baptized, too?"
> "Majesty," Abarbanel replied mockingly, "Spain needs Jews."
> "Why?" asked Ferdinand.
> "Without us, our countrymen might get the idea that their misfortune is not the fault of the Jews, but rather of the kings."
> "Our countrymen, Jew?"
> "I am a Spaniard," Don Isaak replied proudly, "since the age of Romans. We Abarbanels remember well when there weren't yet any Christians. The Jewish cemeteries are the oldest in Spain."
> "You Jews are so old?" said Ferdinand. "And nobody finished you off?"[27]

In contrast to Phillipson's accommodating, apologistic Abarbanel, Kesten's shows his fury. In so doing, Kesten's Abarbanel laconically employs the arguments of German Jewish liberals in the 1930s, although he knows that they serve to comfort Jews rather than to persuade anti-Semites. He is convinced that dictators cannot manage without scapegoats for long—and perhaps hopes that a return will be possible some day. This scene, however, is the sole appearance of Abarbanel in Kesten's novel. The reader hears no more of the statesman and scholar after he goes into exile.

Not so in Rabbi Abraham Heschel's 1937 Abarbanel study, mentioned at the beginning of this essay. In the library of the Leo Baeck Institute in New York, there is a handwritten dedication in a copy of Heschel's Abarbanel study, which more than anything else demonstrates the continued significance of this historical figure for German-speaking Jews:

> "Your nobility should not look back but forwards! Your honor is not given to you by where you come from but by where you are going!" In this way, grandchildren will become ancestors! And so, the descendant of the great scholar Abarbanel strives in the upbringing of herself and her children.
> Berlin 1938: Regine Marcus, whose mother still bore the name Abarbanel

Regine Marcus's dedication illuminates the purpose that these fictional Abarbanels served for German Jews during the course of more than a century. They were not historical monuments frozen in time, but rather pointed to the present and into the future. These fictional pasts were themselves part of a historical process, because their message was not one of contentedness and pride in a noble past, but of courage and honesty toward the future, an appeal to their descendants to see themselves, not as the last generation, but as the next generation.

The name "Regine Marcus" is found multiple times in lists of Berlin Jews deported to concentration camps. Was one of them the author of the dedication quoted above? Numerous individuals who still bore the name Abarbanel (or Abarbanell as her family spelled it) are listed there as well. But the destruction of European Jewish life and Jewish culture also meant the death of the fictional Abarbanels. Perhaps this fact makes the epilogue to Leo Perutz's 1953 novel, *Nachts unter der steinernen Brücke* (*By Night Under the Stone Bridge*), especially significant.[28] In this epilogue, the narrator is revealed to be Perutz's teacher in turn-of-the century Prague. The narrator tells the young Perutz about the famous lost treasure of the sixteenth-century financier Mordechai Meisel (an ancestor of the narrator's). After its loss, Meisel distributes his remaining property, a book collection, among his relatives; and an ancestor of the narrator's inherits four books by Don Isaak Abarbanel. These, too, are lost over the years. Then the narrator turns to the recently "sanitized" Prague ghetto and points out the sites of all the buildings that no longer exist. Thus, Perutz writes not about Abravanel, but about loss: after the Holocaust, the figure of Abarbanel is thus associated with the experience of irretrievable loss. After 1945, there are no more German-language Abarbanel stories.[29]

⁂

The reader of Heine's *Rabbi of Bacherach* last sees Don Isaak on his way to enjoy a meal in an eatery in the Frankfurt ghetto in 1489. The expulsion of the Jews from Spain—the biggest catastrophe since the destruction of the Temple—still lies ahead. Three years later, the apostate Abarbanel will suffer the same fate as Rabbi Abraham: that of a refugee for whom the return to his home country could mean death. The persecution of the Jews has forged a shared common destiny that not even apostates can escape—this is the view of history that lies at the core of Heine's novel.

How would the story have turned out if Heine had finished his novel? Would he have united the renegade with the bastion of faith, as in Phillipson's novella? During his life, Heine decided to cling to these contradictions. Could Heine's Abarbanel lead his people heroically to freedom, safety, and self-determination, as in Nossig's drama? In contrast to the Ashkenazim of the German ghetto, Heine's Don Isaak is armed. Or should Heine's Abarbanel secure his honor with determination and disappear into exile, like Kesten's Abarbanel? In Heine's eyes, Isaak Abarbanel was always associated with the idea of exile; a reference to Abarbanel in Heine's *Ideen. Das Buch Le Grand* places him in a long list of historical figures who had to flee (DHA, 6: 204).

Heine's fragment begins with a seder evening, where the door is opened to greet the prophet Elijah, who is to announce the Messiah; to show non-Jews that no children are slaughtered here; and to castigate those who do not observe the commandments, in particular the seventh commandment: "You shall not kill!" Heine's fragment opens the door, so to speak, for the Jewish historical novel, a product of modern times, which makes it possible for later generations to continue writing Jewish history, now as a part of world history, with all of the meanings associated with this rite of door opening: hope, apology, admonishment. With that, *The Rabbi of Bacherach* opens the door for numerous historical possibilities including, alas, the very worst.

Part II *Jews and Hispanics Meet Again: Latin American Revisions of Judeo-Spanish Relations*

Five Sephardim and Neo-Sephardim in Latin American Literature

Edna Aizenberg

To the memory of Günter Böhm

Reality/Mythology/Neo-Sephardism

What relevance does the metaphor of Sepharad have in contemporary Latin America? I say "metaphor," because more than a real place, Sepharad is an imaginary construct that recalls villainies and dreams. The Sephardic metaphor has nurtured Latin American Jewish literary discourse from its very beginnings, and like all archetypes it has related past and present in an incessant process of recreation.

As a way of entering this metaphor, I begin with three interrelated facets: Sephardic reality, Sephardic mythology, and the knotty quandary of neo-sephardism. I then move on to a prominent case study that illustrates the complexities of literary sephardism. I use the phrase "Sephardic reality" to refer to the fact that since colonial times and down to our own days there have been Sephardim in Latin America creating literature in Spanish. The earliest Jewish settlers and the earliest Jewish writers were Sephardim; in the period between discovery and independence, they were members of the Marrano diaspora who emigrated to Spain's New World dependencies; immediately after independence, they were Sephardim of Caribbean, usually Curaçaoan, stock who were among the founders of modern Latin American Jewry. Their numbers were small—because the Jewish communities they lived in were small—and, for reasons ranging from newness in the environment to lack of talent, their production was not necessarily of the first order. But they were there, part of the literary fabric of Latin America.

In sixteenth-century Mexico, we have the figure of Luis de Carvajal, a Spanish-born Crypto-Jew who was martyred by the Inquisition. Carvajal, the author of prayers, religious poetry, a memoir, and other works, was probably the earliest of the Sephardic writers.[1] He was followed, three centuries later when the independent South American republics abolished the Inquisition and made it possible for Jews to live openly, by such authors as Abraham Zaharia López-Penha (Colombia) and Elías David Curiel (Venezuela). Both were poets of Sephardic-Curaçaoan descent who were quite likely the first aboveboard Jews to make a contribution to Hispanic American letters.[2]

In their wake came other writers of Judeo-Hispanic lineage; for example, in the Dominican Republic, another López-Penha with roots in Curaçao, Haim Horacio López-Penha, a novelist active in the 1930s and 1940s; and, again in Venezuela, Isaac Chocrón.[3] Chocrón, a product of the newest wave of Sephardic immigration to Latin America—from North Africa and the Middle East—is a leading contemporary dramatist, having achieved stature both in his country and abroad. Talents such as Ricardo Halac, Marcos Ricardo Barnatán, Reina Roffé, and Ana María Shua in Argentina, Teresa Porzecanski in Uruguay, Miriam Moscona and Rosa Nissán in Mexico, and again in Venezuela, Sonia Chocrón, have added their names to the roster of Latin American Sephardic authors of Asian and African origin.

There are other contemporary names: the Argentine Humberto Costantini, from an Italian Sephardic family, and the Mexicans Angelina Muñiz-Huberman, whose return to her ancestral roots brings us back to the Iberian and Crypto-Jewish sources of sephardism, and Jacobo Sefamí, novelist and scholar of the Latin American Sephardic heritage.

Like all realities, the Sephardic literary reality in Latin America is multifaceted and contradictory. It has room for both a Carvajal, who makes his beleaguered Jewish faith the very core of his writing, and a Curiel, whose poems in the then-fashionable *modernista* style deal mainly with the pleasures of the flesh and the bottle as an escape from the angst of provincial life. It likewise includes Haim Horacio López-Penha, a freethinking Mason from the small, intermarried Dominican Sephardic community, who defends Jews and Judaism during the Nazi period in his novel *Senda de revelación* (1936; Path of Revelation), and Chocrón, an author with a much stronger Sephardic background, who paints a scathing portrait of Sephardic family life in his play *Animales feroces* (1963; Ferocious Animals). It embraces Rosa Nissán, whose autobiographical bildungsroman *Novia que te vea* (1992; May I See You a

Bride), followed by a sequel, *Hisho que te nazca* (1996; May You Give Birth to a Son), rings so much with the sounds of the spoken and sung Ladino of the author's childhood in Mexico City's Sephardic immigrant community that she provides a glossary,[4] and Marcos Ricardo Barnatán, for whom the legacy of Sepharad is bookish and Borgesian, gesturing toward the intellectual, mystical traditions of the Kabbalah and the midrash.[5]

Writings by Latin American Sephardim are as varied as the authors' divergent inclinations, life experiences, and historical circumstances. There is even variation within the same writer, with Chocrón, for instance, taking a more positive attitude toward his Sephardic inheritance in the epistolary novel *Rómpase en caso de incendio* (1975; Break in Case of Fire) and the play *Escrito y sellado* (1993; Signed and Sealed). The novel chronicles the journey of self-discovery of a Venezuelan Sephardi named Daniel Benabel, a journey that takes him back to the Sephardic sources—Spain and North Africa. In the work, Chocrón touches on a particularly significant aspect of Sephardic reality in Latin America: the phenomenon of *resefardización*,[6] or the renewed integration of Sephardim into a wider Hispanic context.

We might expect Jews marked by Hispanic culture and character (the description is Mair José Benardete's) to adapt easily to an Iberian setting; to find that their Jewish and general cultures complement each other and even mesh, despite religious and other differences. This seems true in Chocrón's case. Speaking through his protagonist, Benabel, Chocrón indicates that his Sephardic identity forms part of the same Spanish-Moorish complex as his Venezuelan identity. "You're forgetting that I'm a Sephardic Jew," Benabel writes to an American friend, "so African, so Spanish, and so Venezuelan that the *Yiddish* from Brooklyn [the Ashkenazim] would consider me a heretic" [Olvidas que soy judío sefardita: tan africano, tan español y tan venezolano que los *yiddish* de Brooklyn me considerarian hereje].[7]

Chocrón's Curaçaoan forerunners also found their at-homeness in Latin American culture facilitated by their sephardism. Abraham Z. López-Penha was born in Curaçao and only settled in Barranquilla, Colombia, as an adult. Yet the fact that, like most of the Sephardim on the Dutch island, he was fluent in Spanish and familiar with the Hispanic ethos undoubtedly smoothed the way for his rapid entry into the literary circles of fin de siècle South America. As for the Dominican Haim Horacio López-Penha and the Venezuelan Curiel, they were members of communities where sephardism had been such an effective tool of assimilation that their very survival as Jews was threatened. López-Penha's Judaism, though a meritorious ancestral heritage, blends in easily with his Dominican identity. (His novel, set in Germany, where he studied, tells of the love between Gretchen, a German girl of Jewish descent, and Enrique, a Dominican student.) Curiel's alienation is as much, if not more, that of an artist from an uncomprehending milieu rather than that of a Jew from his Hispano-Catholic surroundings—although that dimension is not absent.

So despite their diversity, Sephardic authors in Latin America share the benefits of a Hispanic patrimony on which to draw in the process of acculturation to Spanish America. What about the Ashkenazim, the Jews of non-Hispanic extraction? Ashkenazic Jews and Ashkenazic authors far outnumber their Sephardic brethren in the region. Although the first Jewish immigrants to Latin America were Sephardim, by the beginning of the twentieth century the influx of Russian and eastern European Jews not only increased the numbers but also changed the face of Latin American Jewry. Today probably 80 to 85 percent of some 550,000 Jews living south of the border are Ashkenazim. For them, feeling at home in Latin America did not come painlessly or naturally. Most arrived in the New World speaking Yiddish, with traditions and an outlook developed in a German-Slavic environment. There was nothing in their experience to connect them to the unfamiliar Iberian *ambiente*.

Or perhaps there was. Couldn't the *rusos*, as the Russian and Polish Ashkenazic immigrants were popularly called, use the Sephardic heritage to link Judaism and Hispanism? Couldn't they create a Sephardic mythology for themselves—and a myth *is* a story of origins that gives meaning to the present—in which they too were cast as sons of Sepharad, part of an old Hispanic heritage that allowed them to blend easily into the new one? Indeed they could. And that is exactly what some of the outstanding first-generation Ashkenazic intellectuals in Latin America did.

The most notable example is the patriarch of Argentine Jewish letters, Alberto Gerchunoff. Despite the strangeness of the pampas confronting his Russian-born, Yiddish-speaking newcomers in his book

Los gauchos judíos (1910; The Jewish Gauchos), Don Alberto had argued that the newcomers *do* have a legacy that anchors them in Latin American soil: the legacy of noble, truly Hispanic eras when Jews lived peacefully under the protection of the kings of Castile.[8] His carefully crafted Sephardic mythology was two-directional: he wanted to give the Ashkenazic immigrants a sense of belonging but, just as important, to convince their non-Jewish neighbors that they indeed belonged. These efforts, which could not, single-handedly, bridge the real gap between the Ashkenazim and Sephardim, and between eastern European Jews and Hispanic Christians, nonetheless had resonance among both Jews and non-Jews. The Argentine critic Francisco Luis Bernárdez, writing of Gerchunoff, picks up on his mythology and comments: "Being Jewish, he had much of the Spaniard in him."[9] Carlos M. Grünberg, another distinguished Ashkenazic intellectual of Gerchunoff's generation, sounds much the same theme in a memorial sonnet dedicated to his co-author and friend:

Somos, Alberto, la sección hispana de los nabíes
y de los rabíes,
que dobla en sus ladinos otros íes
la unicidad jerosolimitana.
Somos la cuadradura castellana del círculo judío, Sinaíes
en buen romance, toras sefardíes,
salmos y trenos a la toledana.
Tu has sido nuestro sumo sacerdote . . .

[We are, Alberto, the Hispanic section
Of the prophets and the rabbis,
Intoning Jerusalem's oneness
In deep Ladino cadences.
We are the Castilian squaring
Of the Jewish circle, sons of Sinai
To put it plainly, Sephardic Torah scrolls,
Psalms and lamentations in the Toledan style.
You have been our high priest . . .][10]

The poem, which celebrates Gerchunoff's proposition that Jewish life and creativity in Latin America are but a continuation of the Jewish experience "in the Toledan style"—Toledo was the capital of Jewish Spain—

displays Grünberg's own studied brand of sephardism: the references to the Judeo-Hispanic heritage and, even more, the Sephardized, medievalized style allusive of the epoch most associated with Hispano-Judaism.

Grünberg's homage abounds in words like *nabíes*, *rabíes*, *ladino*, *almenar*, *taled* (prophets, rabbis, Judeo-Spanish, candelabrum, prayer shawl), all of old Spanish or Judeo-Hispanic stock. Grünberg's most famous work, the poetic collection *Mester de judería* (1940; Poems of Jewry), with Jorge Luis Borges's fervid introduction,[11] is so full of such vocabulary that he includes a glossary in which he points out which Hispano-Hebraic words have been accepted by the Royal Spanish Academy of the Language, arbiter of idiomatic respectability. Only three years earlier, writing as fascism and falangism spread over Europe, Grünberg had berated Ramón Menéndez Pidal, Spain's most prominent linguist, for ignoring Hebrew as a hoary constituent element of Spanish, providing a long list of venerable Spanish words of Hebraic origin—from *desmazalado*, luckless, to *pismón*, song or hymn, in "Hebraísmos y criptohebraísmos en el romance peninsular y americano" (1937; Hebraisms and Crypto-Hebraisms in Peninsular and American Spanish).[12]

Mester de judería follows the same linguistic line, its very title a conscious throwback to the *juderías*, the Jewish quarters of Sepharad, and to the two poetic modes of medieval Spain: *mester de juglaría*, the style of the minstrels, and *mester de clerecía*, the style of the learned poets. Some of the poems skillfully evoke the *clerecía* form with its monorhymed quatrains; Sem Tob de Carrión, Jewish Spain's major Spanish-language poet, wrote his masterful *Proverbios morales* (c.1350; Moral Proverbs) in *clerecía*.

Borges, ever sensitive to literature as rewriting and to the relation of literary precursors and successors, penetratingly understands Grünberg's creation of Sem Tob as his poetic forefather. Like Rabí don Sem Tob, who composed lucid verse in the wordy and troubled fourteenth century, says Borges, Grünberg fashions crystalline yet delicately impassioned lyrics in the mid-twentieth-century *tiempo de lobos*, the Hitler time of the wolf; his poems declare the honor and the pain of being Jewish in the perverse, unimaginable world of 1940. "Limpidity is a habit of Israel," Borges concludes, not without creating Sem Tob as his own ancestor by alluding to his own likely Judeo-Portuguese ancestry through the maternal Acevedos.[13]

Along with Gerchunoff, Grünberg saw the Sephardic door as the most appropriate way to enter Latin American culture and as a bulwark against xenophobes and fascists who wanted to deny a deep Jewish connection to Latin America. Does that make them neo-Sephardim? Mair José Benardete claims to have invented this neologism, and that would be entirely in character, since he and fellow travelers like Henry Besso saw Latin America as a sort of Promised Land for a renewal of Judeo-Spanish culture.[14]

There, not only would Sephardim be re-Sephardized, Ashkenazim would be neo-Sephardized, losing their Yiddish cultural baggage and taking on the quality of Hispanic Jews. By Benardete's definition, Gerchunoff and Grünberg *are* neo-Sephardim, all the more so because of their deliberate and enthusiastic adoption of the Sephardic heritage as an accculturative tool. But are all Jewish intellectuals in Latin America neo-Sephardim? They do write in Spanish and do reflect a Judeo-Hispanic symbiosis in their works, but most do not use the Sephardic entranceway to Latin American culture and do not feel that they are keepers of a Sephardic flame or continuers of an interrupted Sephardic tradition.[15]

Native-born Ashkenazic writers, whatever their angst about belonging, speak as Latin Americans and have no need to look for other Hispanic links. If that is so, can they be considered neo-Sephardim? Should the label be selectively reserved for writers like Juan Gelman, the distinguished poet who composed verse in Ladino in *dibaxu* (1994; Beneath) and "recomposed" poems by medieval Golden Age Judeo-Spanish greats in *com/posiciones* (1986);[16] Antonio Elio Brailovsky, whose novel *Identidad* (1980) deals with a Judeo-Hispanic El Dorado; Alicia Dujove Ortiz, who constructs a fictional genealogy around the Khazars made famous by Yehuda Halevi (*El árbol de la gitana*, 1997; The Gypsy's Tree); Marcos Aguinis, nourished again and again by a literary Sepharad; Gabriela Avigur-Rotem, who creates a kind of neo-Ladino in her Hebrew-Spanish novel *Motsart lo haya yehudi* (1992; Mozart Was Not a Jew); or Alicia Freilich, author of *Colombina descubierta* (1991; Colombina Discovered), in which Columbus is transmuted into Bina Colom, a woman explorer of Judeo-Hispanic roots?

What about, on the Luso-Iberian, Portuguese-language side, the renowned Brazilian-Jewish author Moacyr Scliar, who has explored the Judeo-Portuguese legacy of Sepharad, most prominently in his fabulistic novel *A estranha naçao de Rafael Mendes* (1983; The Strange Nation of Rafael Mendes)?[17]

Unlike their predecessors, and critical of the latter's maneuvering to be accepted, the newer writers underline the mythology of Sepharad as a means to deflate the exclusionary nationalism that forms part of the legacy bequeathed by the Spanish lion to its American cubs. That is why there is such an emphasis on the Inquisition and its replays in Aguinis and Brailovsky and Freilich. These intellectuals use literary sephardism as a bridge *from* the Latin American *toward* the Jewish, reversing the direction traveled by their forerunners. For the new generations, sephardism serves as an instrument to reconnect with submerged or fragmented Jewish identities: the sweet syllables of Ladino in collections like *dibaxu* transport Gelman from his Latin American exile (he had to flee Argentina during the last dictatorship) to an older Sephardic diaspora, while Dujovne Ortiz, another writer banished from dictatorial Argentina, finds Khazar-Crypto-Jewish nomadism to be an apt metaphor for her persecuted, wandering family tree. Sephardic hybridity, along with pastiche, carnivalization, and decanonization, becomes a way to sap sedentary definitions of citizenship and nation.[18]

But the question remains: Are all Latin American-Jewish writers neo-Sephardim? Ashkenazim as well as Sephardim have questioned the whole idea of neo-sephardism. Moshe Attías, an Israeli educator and participant in the First Symposium on Sephardic Studies held in Madrid in 1964, stated flatly in his *ladinos otros íes*: "No se puede dicir que hay 'neo-sefaradismo': el sefaradismo es una idea histórica y no puedemos hacer sefardim muevos" (You cannot say that there is such a thing as "neo-sephardism": sephardism is a historical idea, and we cannot create new Sephardim).[19] Benardete reported enormous resistance to the term on the part of Spanish-speaking Ashkenazic Jews.[20]

Leon Pérez, whose study on sephardism in Latin America I mentioned earlier, attempts to explain such opposition. He observes that for Jews, a sense of identity is closely tied up with the past, with the cultural types—Ashkenazim, Sephardim—forged in the course of Jewish history. Therefore, says Pérez, Jews reject what they see as a usurpation of consecrated notions or names. Recognizing that, he does not slap a fixed, completed label—"neo-Sephardim"—on the Ashkenazim of Latin America, but rather proposes a process, which he calls *sefardización secundaria*.[21] This secondary Sephardization is not a two-way dialogue between Ashkenazim and the Spanish American matrix society but a three-way conversation among Ashkenazim, Sephardim, and Latin America's already immigrant, already multiple cultures. Out of this threefold exchange, Pérez argues, there will emerge a new "Sephardic cultural type," the neo-Sephardi.

For Pérez, neo-Sephardim are not the present-day Spanish-speaking Ashkenazic Jews but the future Jewish inhabitants and creators of Iberian America, who may be of any single or mixed Jewish stock but whose continuous and living intercourse with Hispanic civilization will, as time goes on, result in a neo-Sephardic ethos and a neo-Sephardic literature.

While it may be convenient or flattering to speak of all Jewish writers in Latin America as neo-Sephardim, I prefer Perez's model for its fluidity, its openness to mixture and the vagaries of history. As of now, *ya que neviim no somos*, even if we are not prophets, as the Ladino proverb reminds us, both Ashkenazim and Sephardim can take pride in the Sephardic reality in Latin American letters, in its productive and provocative Sephardic mythology, and in the possibility of the emergence of a truly neo-Sephardic culture—provided that the internal and external forces that threaten Jewish life in Latin America allow such a culture to flourish.

Marcos Aguinis: Inquisitorial Dungeons and Literary Sephardism

I would like to further examine one of Sepharad's recreations, the novel by Marcos Aguinis entitled *La gesta del marrano* (1991; The Epic of the Marrano), which is based on the true story of the Chilean-Argentine Sephardic martyr, Dr. Francisco Maldonado da Silva. Aguinis both realizes and transgresses the inheritance of his literary precursors, who inaugurated Jewish writing in the South and first gave fictional expression to the Sephardic metaphor.

As I have outlined, a significant group of Ashkenazic authors—Gerchunoff, Grünberg, and Samuel Glusberg (a.k.a Enrique Espinoza, a homage to Heinrich Heine and Baruch Spinoza)—turned sephardism into a primordial element in their new cultural discourse, with Don Alberto leading the way. On the opening pages of his canonical book,

Gerchunoff remembers conversations in his snowy Russian shtetl about the hoped-for migration to the agricultural colonies of the pampas. One rabbi praises Spain, its climate, and the era in which the People of Israel lived on Spanish soil. Another religious leader, the Dayan Yehuda Anakroi, reacts violently:

> May it perish and turn into dust! I have never been able to recall . . . the name of Spain without blood welling up in my eyes and hate filling my heart. May God . . . turn it into an everlasting pyre for having tortured our brethren and burned our priests. In Spain, Jews stopped tilling the earth. . . . That's why when I . . . [heard] about the immigration to Argentina . . . I remembered the phrase from Yehuda Halevi: Zion is wherever peace and happiness reign. We'll all go to Argentina and go back to working the land.[22]

Gerchunoff closes the heated exchange with this coda: "Thus spoke Rabbi Yehudah Anakroi, last representative of those great rabbis who illuminated the communities of Spain and Portugal with their wisdom" (23).

I have quoted this suggestive passage in its entirety to demonstrate the subtle and skillful imaging of Sepharad, with Gerchunoff directing the conversation to suit his interests. The exchange opens with the praise of Spain. Even though the Dayan cites the horrors of the Inquisition and the *herem*, or ban, placed on Spain after it expelled the Jews, his energetic condemnation is softened by words attributed to Yehuda Halevi, one of the glories of Sepharad, and these words are used to justify immigration to a new, happy Hispanic land. Moreover, the Dayan's thoughts, obviously expressed in Yiddish, are identified as the pronouncements of a Sephardic sage; elsewhere, Gerchunoff had indicated that the Dayan was an Ashkenazic *hasid*, an ecstatic pietist from the Russian Jewish villages.

Gerchunoff ignores historical reality by selecting and molding the material to achieve his amalgamating aim; his literary cohorts did much the same. As their metaphoric sephardism came under criticism in ensuing decades, one younger Jewish Argentinian writer termed it an "apologetic strategy to gain legitimacy."

For this author, the writings of Gerchunoff's era

> did not determine the course of history, as beautiful and effective as they might have seemed. Jews . . . were not able to harmonize easily

> with the new land. There were anti-Semitic movements, many expressions of self-hatred, conflicts. The Holocaust and the creation of Israel gave rise to significant readjustments, as did the course of events in Argentina.[23]

In other words, there was a need to question and readjust a Sephardic model that for all its legerdemain could not mask the dark zones of Sephardic, Jewish, and Latin American history. Gerchunoff and his coreligionists gradually became aware of this need, but the modernization of the initial model was the task of later generations. And they would have to struggle mightily with the weight of the archetype.

Marcos Aguinis is one of the modernizers; I have cited his thoughts from an essay significantly entitled "De la legitimación apologética a la crítica reparadora" (From Legitimizing Apologetics to Corrective Criticism). Aguinis, well-known author, human rights activist, and former secretary for cultural affairs in the Alfonsin government—the first democratically elected after the years of Argentine dictatorship—writes fully aware of his place within a Jewish Argentinian literary tradition. He underlines its sephardism because his own entry into literature was through the very Sephardic door opened by Gerchunoff and others.

His first literary efforts were biographies of the great personalities of the Spanish Golden Age: Yehuda Halevi, Ibn Gabirol, and, above all, Maimonides, known as the Rambam. Aguinis published two long essays on the Rambam, intrigued in part by the fact that both he and the Sephardic sage were physicians and authors born in cities named Córdoba. It is not strange, then, that Maimonides reappears in the novel *La gesta del marrano*. The protagonist's father, also a physician, administers Maimonides's medical oath to his son in secret, defying the vigilance of the Inquisition.[24] Francisco Maldonado da Silva is a sort of Argentinian Maimonides—Jew, writer, doctor, a native of Córdoba. A literary character cannot be reduced to a single inspiration, but Maimonides is important in the construction of Maldonado da Silva. What is more, the various recreations of the figure of Maimonides in Aguinis's writings can help us trace the changes in the metaphor of Sepharad.

According to Aguinis himself, his first Rambam, in *Maimónides, un sabio de avanzada* (1963; Maimonides, a Pioneering Intellectual), grew out of the same need that his predecessors felt to "legitimize Jewishness through apologetics and to justify the Jewish contribution to Spain's greatness as an indirect means of justifying the Jewish presence in Argentina."[25] The book underlines the Rambam's love for his native Hispanic land, his deep devotion to Scripture, his ethical values, solidarity, and love of learning—all topics that Gerchunoff had emphasized. Aguinis quotes Don Alberto directly and writes with a distinctly Gerchunoffian tone.

The Rambam's Hispanicism is still operative in Aguinis's second Maimonidean text, *Maimónides, sacerdote de los oprimidos* (Maimonides, Minister to the Oppressed), but now another type of legitimizing takes on greater urgency: Third World activism. As an oppressed Jew who ministers to the needy, Maimonides becomes a soul mate of the Latin American folk, marginalized both internally and internationally but ever more conscious of this status and determined to combat it.

The change from a passive to an active attitude is new, with an emphasis on questioning and changing society. There is also a willingness to leave behind the image of the Technicolor Promised Land. Aguinis now portrays a lame and hungry Latin American nation, downtrodden and seeking justice. These twin threads, battered republic and critical activism, would increase in the author's personal commitment and writing.

In 1985 Aguinis founded the National Program for the Democratization of Culture (PRONDEC), and his subsequent essays and novels deal with the fight against antidemocratic forces and the horrid 1994 AMIA Jewish Center bombing.[26] They include *La cruz invertida* (1970; The Inverted Cross), *Carta esperanzada a un general* (1983; Hopeful Letter to a General), *Un país de novela* (1988; Country Worthy of a Novel), *La matriz del infierno* (1997; Hell's Womb), about the Nazi influence in Argentina during World War II, and *Los iluminados* (2000; The Enlightened), about the dangers of fundamentalism and unchecked power. Aguinis's essay collection *El atroz encanto de ser argentinos* (2001; The Atrocious Enchantment of Being Argentines) carries his frontal criticism of a nation that has hit bottom into the new millennium, against the background of the financial default and pauperization of a large portion of Argentina's people after the rampant corruption of the Menem government. His book *¿Qué hacer?* (What to Do?) continues the search for a better Argentina.

The topic of an injured nation and Aguinis's political criticism, inaugurated by *Maimónides, sacerdote de los oprimidos* and sustained so forcefully through decades of imagining Argentina, mark the metaphorical sephardism of *La gesta del marrano*. The sephardism of this novel and its historical protagonist, Maldonado da Silva, must be understood within the context of Aguinis's bravery in denouncing totalitarianism. It is not incidental that an inquisitorial trial forms the novel's center. The allusions to secret jails and the loss of rights make it clear that Aguinis intends to unmask the inquisitorial mind, whose contemporary avatars have impeded the development of democracy in Latin America. Long before the Holocaust, he asserts, the Inquisition served as a local antecedent for dictatorship.

Maldonado da Silva is a native-born Latin American. Despite the family's nostalgia for Iberia, he has no doubt about his belonging to the New World and he refuses to lose his identity in a society that demands uniformity. If *Los gauchos judíos* symbolized hoped-for Jewish assimilation, *La gesta del marrano* represents the opposite: raised as a Christian in a family that has hidden its distinctiveness in the face of overwhelming pressure, Maldonado da Silva returns to Judaism and accepts circumcision, the most visceral identification mark of a Jew, and a virtual death sentence.

The novel gives narrative substance to Maldonado's fight against the Inquisition, which culminated with his death in the great auto-da-fé of 1639. (The pioneering Jewish Chilean historian Günther Böhm has published the minute and maniacal inquisitorial records of Maldonado's trials.)[27] Unlike his father, the martyr refuses to become "reconciled" with his torturers. The Portuguese-born senior da Silva, hounded by the Inquisition in the New World, accepted "reconciliation" with the Church and for the rest of his life wore a penitential vestment called a *sambenito*, the sartorial sign of a contradictory existence: Diego was at once a judaizer and a Catholic, a defender of his ancestral faith who, under societal pressure, still wanted acceptance from his surroundings. He was at peace neither with his Judaism nor with his society and continually told his son not to repeat his trajectory.

The relation between father and son can be read as a metaphor of the relation between the sephardism of the fathers and the sephardism of the son Aguinis. Like the elder da Silva, the literary patriarchs were immigrants tired of persecution in the Old World who never lost their foreignness in the New. They maintained their Judaic heritage but, in a milieu that demanded religious-cultural conformity, they constructed a version of Sepharad that tended to advocate sameness. Aguinis, Latin American–born like Maldonado da Silva, proposes a more painful but promising version of the metaphor of Sepharad. Only by confronting the perplexities of Sepharad, what destroyed Sepharad, can we build a future that precludes "reconciliation." Only by confronting the perplexities of Sepharad can its metaphor continue to nourish generations of committed intellectuals and culture makers.

Six The Life and Times of the Picaro-Converso from Spain to Latin America

Yael Halevi-Wise

> Many Spaniards have written about how we lived in America when they first came here. But very few Latin Americans have looked across the Atlantic, in the opposite direction, to examine Spanish society at the turn of the fifteenth century. We cannot fully understand what has happened in America during the past five hundred years if we lack an understanding of the Spain that conquered it.
>
> Homero Aridjis, public lecture on his novel *1492: The Life and Times of Juan Cabezón of Castile*

This chapter focuses on three contemporary Latin American historical novels that provocatively entangle the literary and political history of the picaresque genre. Written during the last quarter of the twentieth century, these novels use picaresque features to portray the experiences of Jews and conversos in Spain, Portugal, and colonial Latin America. In so doing, they foreground an ideological struggle that to some extent was already encoded in the original picaresque novels that had been invented in Spain during the sixteenth and seventeenth centuries.

Angelina Muñiz-Huberman's *Tierra adentro* (Inland, 1977), Moacyr Scliar's *A estranha nação de Rafael Mendes* (The Strange Nation of Rafael Mendes, 1983), and Homero Aridjis's *1492: Vida y tiempos de Juan Cabezón de Castilla* (1492: The Life and Times of Juan Cabezón of Castile, 1985) are just three prominent examples from a larger conglomeration of late twentieth-century Latin American novels that openly enlist the picaro as a converso to illuminate elements previously cast into the margins (and dungeons) of Ibero-America's cultural ethos.[1] Always keeping in mind that these are *historical novels* upon which picaresque elements have been grafted,[2] I compare them with seminal picaresque novels invented in Spain by Old and New Christians, who from the beginning had imagined the picaro as a converso.

Although the historical span covered by our contemporary Latin American novels playfully extends from antiquity until today, their main action takes place during the sixteenth and seventeenth centuries, when the picaresque genre emerged in Spain. Aridjis's *1492* opens with the forced baptisms of 1391, a year that marked a sharp decline in the fortunes of Spanish Jewry; and it ends with the simultaneous departures of Columbus's caravels and Spain's Jews in the famous year of the novel's title.[3] Muñiz-Huberman's *Tierra adentro* is set during the period in which Jews were officially barred from residing in Spain and the Inquisition cast its shadow everywhere.[4] Scliar's *The Strange Nation of Rafael Mendes* traces a much wider geographic and temporal path, from ancient Israel via Spain and Portugal to the New World, framed by a crisis in Scliar's own contemporary Brazil during a modern dictatorial regime.[5]

Spain's classical picaresque novels cover largely the same period and geographic scope as their Latin American counterparts: *The Life of Lazarillo* (1554)—considered Spain's first picaresque novel—spans half a century preceding its mid-sixteenth century date of publication and is set in the contemporary environment of its anonymous author. Mateo Alemán's paradigmatic *Guzmán of Alfarache* (published in two parts in 1599 and 1604), and Francisco de Quevedo's *Life of the Buscón* (1626)—a satire of Alemán's novel—are likewise set in their authors' lifetimes; and, significantly, both end with an unconvincingly reformed picaro traveling to the New World.

In the following pages, I will first define the picaro as a converso. I will then consider why this particular aspect of the picaro's identity appeals today to Latin American writers from completely different religious and national backgrounds. Throughout my analysis, I will toggle between Spain's classical picaresque narratives and their modern Latin American counterparts, focusing all the while on four features of the picaresque genre that are most relevant to the converso's experience: the picaro's lineage, delinquency, anti-idealism, and the fascinating question of the picaro's conversion. We will see that current Latin American historicizations of the picaresque generally participate in what Roberto Gonzales Echevarría articulated as a struggle between the legitimacy of the archive and the power of myth in modern Latin American literature and politics.[6] They seek to dispel the myth of a homogeneous empire in order to strengthen democratic and revisionistic platforms in their authors' contemporary Latin American environments.[7]

Defining the Picaro-Converso

A connection between the picaresque novel and the history of conversos will come as no surprise to anyone familiar with Américo Castro's work on the multicultural tension that simmered in Spain during the sixteenth and seventeenth centuries. Departing from a strictly philological approach to literature, Castro insisted that Spain's modern character had resulted from a suppression of its medieval multiculturalism, and that Spain's Golden Age genres could not be properly understood without acknowledging the presence and impact of conversos and Moriscos (descendants of Jews and Muslims converted to Catholicism prior to 1492).[8]

Castro maintained that the picaresque genre emerged in sixteenth-century Spain as a result of the converso's experience. He interpreted Spain's earliest picaresque narratives as a coded expression of a bitter ethnic struggle foisted upon the conversos. In particular, he noted that the typically orphaned picaro, who engages in a lifelong battle to redefine a lineage that renders all his goals and beliefs suspect, relates to his world and tells about it from the perspective of a half-outsider.[9]

A helpful clarification of Castro's views on the picaresque is Claudio Guillén's well-known summary of the ethnic parameters of this genre. There, Guillén underscores that Castro was of course aware that the original Spanish picaro was *not* actually a Jew, considered "a genuine outsider in the sixteenth century," but a converso:

> Castro believes that the author of *Lazarillo* was a *converso*. We know for a fact that a Jewish forefather of Mateo Alemán was burned alive by the Inquisition. Several heroes of picaresque novels (as in *La pícara Justina*, *El Buscón*) are of Semitic origin. The family background of the hero of *Guzmán de Alfarache* is willfully obscure and ambiguous; his father appears to have been a Levantine . . . and the plot is based on the young boy's attempt to . . . claim his inheritance. . . . The *picaro*, in other words, is an orphan and a self-made man in social and religious terms. Alemán, as a descendant—rejected by his environment—of

> converts from Judaism, was able to envisage not only the society of his day, but the values of Christianity itself both from within and from without. This was surely an important incitement to the picaresque author's discovery of the orphan and the type of the half-outsider.[10]

Guillén's summary pinpoints the principal sense in which the picaro's situation as a "half-outsider" functions as a plausible metaphor for the converso's differentiated position in Ibero-American societies. It also underscores the incontrovertible fact that several picaresque novels—whether composed by New Christian apologists such as Mateo Alemán or Old Christian purists such as Francisco de Quevedo—explicitly *do* define their picaros as conversos.[11] At the same time, Guillén corrects imprecisions arising from Castro's unfortunate tendency to exaggerate epithets, such as referring to the author of *La Celestina* (1499) as "that Jew Fernando de Rojas,"[12] even though Rojas belonged to a family of New Christians whose actual beliefs under the threat of the Inquisition will never be fully transparent to us.[13]

Despite these clarifications by Guillén and others, Castro's insights tend to be celebrated in some quarters yet are notoriously disparaged in others.[14] The result is cautious ambivalence surrounding the citations of his work. Specifically in relation to the picaresque genre, such ambivalence can be observed for example in Alexander Parker's initial reaction to what he called Castro's "rash speculations that really get us nowhere,"[15] followed just four years later by Parker's reluctant admission that,

> It did not occur to me then that a picaro's *converso* mother had any overt determining meaning, nor did I read his social aspirations as a satire against a new type of nobility achieved through money rather than pure lineage. Today this must be taken into consideration; more so, it must be accepted as the "literal sense," the apparent primary intention, of the author.[16]

Castro's arguments gained currency during the tide of historical revisionism that accompanied the quincentennial anniversary of 1492, the year that saw both Columbus's discovery of the New World and Spain's official homogenization of its population under Catholicism. Speaking in 1992 at Mexico City's *Plaza de las tres culturas*—thus named to celebrate Mexico's multicultural heritage—King Juan Carlos I of Spain acknowledged that his own country was also built from three cultures: Christian, Moorish, and Jewish. That a Spanish monarch should proudly evoke Spain's multicultural heritage, moreover in the framework of a dialogue with one of its former colonies, would have been inconceivable before the era of historical revisionism to which Américo Castro contributed.

The Ghosts of History

Spanish Republican intellectuals like José Ortega y Gasset, Claudio Sánchez-Albornoz, and Américo Castro—the latter two having escaped from Franco's fascism to the Americas—can be largely credited for spearheading this modern revisionist attitude toward Ibero-America's history.[17] A daughter of Republican refugees, the Spanish-Mexican writer Angelina Muñiz-Huberman first encountered Castro's work as a university student in Mexico City; and through it, she claims, the panorama of her own background became clearer. Muñiz-Huberman actually descends from conversos:

> One afternoon, on the balcony of our first house in Mexico . . . my mother confessed to me that she was of Jewish origins. . . . Her Judaism was by now quite diluted, and she mixed it with forms taken from Christianity, though also diluted. . . . Later I learned that my mother's last name, Sacristan, apparently so Christian, was nothing but the translation of the Hebrew Shamash, [a caretaker in the synagogue; to identify themselves, they signed the Hebrew letter shin ש with three fingers].[18]

Considering her personal heritage and graduate training in Spanish literature, it makes sense that the converso dimension of Spanish history, and its relationship to Spanish genres, came to occupy a prominent place in Muñiz-Huberman's work.[19]

But why did Homero Aridjis, a non-Jewish Mexican writer of Greek heritage, decide to draw on converso elements in Hispanic history to clarify a sense of *his* own identity as a modern Mexican? The harrowing experience of his father at the end of World War I awakened this writer's interest in Jewish history as a paradigm for a sudden loss of control over one's destiny. During the series of lectures that he delivered upon the publication of *1492*, Aridjis revealed that his father had been among the last Greeks to leave Turkey in 1922 after witnessing massacres of

Greeks and Armenians in Smyrna (now Izmir). As a result, his father immigrated to Mexico, where he married a villager from the state of Michoacán:

> I grew up aware of the nightmare that had been his life, his youth spent subject to constant persecution in a hostile territory. . . . But the people in my Mexican village didn't fully understand where my father came from or what nationality he had, because he would speak of Turkey, and Greece, and other countries in Europe as well, and they would refer to him sometimes as a Greek, sometimes as a Turk, and sometimes as a Jew (none of them had ever met anyone who was any of these three things). As a child I was confused about this myself. When I was writing *1492* I always had my father's past in mind, how he lived as part of a minority in an alien country, belonging to a different religion, and what it felt like to live among hostile people who might kill you at any time. My father, like Juan Cabezón [*1492*'s hero] relinquished his country and set out to seek his destiny in the unknown.[20]

In contrast to Homero Aridjis's and Muñiz-Huberman's rather unusual backgrounds among contemporary Latin Americans, the eastern European origins of the Brazilian Jewish author Moacyr Scliar are more common—at least among Jewish communities established in Latin America over the course of the twentieth century.[21] Yet despite his markedly Ashkenazi Russian background, Scliar's *The Strange Nation of Rafael Mendes* celebrates Brazil's Sephardic heritage through a protagonist who starts off being a nominally Catholic husband and father in Brazil of the 1970s, but who awakens one morning to discover that he is the last scion of an illustrious family of conversos going all the way back to ancient Israel, through medieval Spain and colonial Brazil.[22]

The Luso-Brazilian reception of this novel lost no time connecting Scliar's emphasis on the Judaic component of Brazil's history with Castro's "famous polemical theories."[23] Yet Scliar's revisionism goes beyond mere acknowledgment of the presence and impact of Jews and conversos in Brazilian history, to seek a full normalization of the Jew's image in contemporary Brazilian society. When asked to describe what type of education he would choose for his son, Scliar expressed the hope that knowledge of history and the mechanisms that move society might impart wisdom and tranquility to all the young, freeing them from the "ghosts of paranoia."[24]

Indeed, a deep preoccupation with the Jew's cultural image is intimately tied to the cultural endeavors of each of these authors—a Brazilian Jew of Russian origins, a Mexican intellectual of Greek heritage, and a Spanish refugee who moved to Mexico and discovered her crypto-Jewish background there—all of whom, by curious twists of fate, happen to have Jewish children, and thus perhaps an extra reason to be concerned with the status of Jews in the world. The misattribution of Jewish allegiances routinely leveled at Castro by some his detractors is hence an authentic allegation in this case, whatever it may be worth.

Historical Revisionism

To explain how and why these Latin American authors place a picaro-converso at the center of their historical novels, we must first understand the relevance of converso history within Ibero-American polities and identify how these authors accordingly wield or alter literary techniques associated with the picaresque genre.[25] Before turning to this historicized analysis of a genre, I will therefore round out our discussion of the cultural contexts of these twentieth-century Latin American novels by situating them more specifically within their authors' political environments.

The Strange Nation of Rafael Mendes appeared toward the bitter end of a twenty-year dictatorship in Brazil, which lasted from 1964 to 1985. This novel was written at a time when repression of free speech had not yet abated, although the military was already perceived as trying to withdraw from power.[26] From a literary-historical point of view, such transitional periods often produce a mixture of history and fiction that looks to the past for clues as to what went wrong in the present before even daring to imagine a better future. During such junctures, creative writing can function as a cathartic act, as well as a rectification of what the Brazilian cultural critic Roberto Reis calls an "absence of History" in narratives that had reinforced the ruling hierarchy.[27] As Seymour Menton has shown, an unprecedented amount of historical fiction was produced in Latin American republics as they emerged from various degrees of dictatorship toward the end of the twentieth century.[28] Many intellectuals in these nations began to reevaluate their foundational ethos and discourses, just as the writers examined here have done.

Mexican writers did not experience a climate of repression analogous to the dictatorships that oppressed Latin America's Southern Cone; still, Homero Aridjis and Muñiz-Huberman belong to a generation of Mexican intellectuals jolted into political awareness by what is known as the "Night of Tlatelolco" on October 2, 1968, when the government orchestrated an attack on university students who had staged a political demonstration in Mexico City's Tlatelolco Plaza. (This plaza, where dozens of protestors were shot in 1968, and where far more Aztecs fell during the conquest of Mexico in 1521, has since been renamed the *Plaza de las Tres Culturas*, where, as mentioned earlier, King Juan Carlos of Spain delivered his reconciliatory speech during the quincentennial anniversary of that first meeting between Old and New Worlds.)

Although, as in Brazil, liberal voices in Mexico have called for greater pluralism and democratization since colonial times, a strong impetus for Mexican historical revisionism came through the influence of Spanish Republican intellectuals who immigrated there in the 1940s; they founded the Colegio de México and influenced social studies and humanities curricula through the media and prestigious institutions of higher learning.[29] Like Américo Castro, who relocated to the United States, but whose books were often produced and disseminated by Mexican and Argentinian publishers, the Spanish Republicans who moved to Mexico subjected all traditional accounts of Ibero-American history to a systematic modernization. Yet, while Mexico's cultural critics tended to focus on the tension between Mexico's colonial ideology and its indigenous populations,[30] as in Octavio Paz's groundbreaking book of essays *The Labyrinth of Solitude* (1950), the authors examined here decided to rehabilitate "heterological" elements within the European legacy itself,[31] revising Ibero-American history through a Spanish genre. When Octavio Paz (Aridjis's early patron) discussed the connection between Mexico's modern character and its colonial and pre-Columbian past, he was not concerned with Spain itself in the sixteenth century; he was interested rather in a psychological fissure within Mexicans' self-image, which he viewed as resulting from a violent historical—as well as metaphorical—mixture between the male conqueror and a native woman.[32]

By contrast, the cultural history that interests Aridjis and Muñiz-Huberman is that of a rift within the European society that conquered

Mexico—a background to which they are perhaps particularly attuned on account of their own "half-outsiderhood" as immigrants and children of immigrants from Europe. Muñiz-Huberman claims that she never felt at home anywhere,[33] and indeed, the theme of exile has become the main focus of current scholarship on her work.[34] Even *Tierra adentro*'s picaro-converso laments that "leaving Spain hurts. It hurts to break something forever . . . for there is nothing I can keep from Spain except an image that perhaps never existed" (*Tierra adentro*, 128). To fashion this image of an ancestral Spain into new sustaining roots, Muñiz-Huberman launched a revision of Spanish history and genres.

Aridjis also turned to history as a means of appraising his national identity. As a young poet he championed the rights of indigenous people and in recent years he has been involved in high-profile ecological campaigns. In her study of *1492* and its sequel *Memorias del Nuevo Mundo* (*Memories of the New World*, 1988), Victoria Campos observes that Aridjis, "like many post-Tlatelolco intellectuals," regards official government documents as "agents of social abuses, but he also recognizes them as a rich cultural legacy. As such, Aridjis does not write against documents, but rather alongside them, incorporating, emulating, and re-ordering them."[35] Aridjis may distrust official documents, but he nonetheless weaves them into his novel, using actual Inquisitorial records to dramatize important aspects of Ibero-America's past in ways that challenge a complacent view of its cultural ethos. To flesh out Spain's converso history in picaresque form, Aridjis traveled to Spain to absorb its landscapes and consult Inquisitorial archives—literally rummaging through Spain's closets. In response to a Spanish publisher's complaint—"Why drag dead Jews out of closets?"—Aridjis has explained that "we cannot fully understand what has happened in America during the past five hundred years if we lack an understanding of the Spain that conquered it" (see this chapter's epigraph). In this revisionist enterprise, Aridjis follows Castro's lead, admitting, however, that Américo Castro's view is "extreme in attributing everything good in Spanish literature to the Jews. . . . He saw everybody as a Jew."[36]

From a literary historical point of view, the politicized picaresque novels featured in this essay expose their authors' multilayered cultural and historical contexts. They embrace the modernizing agenda of the historical novel, adding to it a picaresque dimension that colors our view of Ibero-America's political history and affects our understanding of the picaresque's seminal characteristics and subsequent influence on the development of the modern novel.

The Picaro-Converso's Lineage, Delinquency, Anti-idealism, and Conversion

What I find most intriguing about late twentieth-century Latin American historicizations of the picaresque is the way their representations of the converso's predicament reinforce, reshape, and even compromise some of the picaresque's original characteristics. In other words, they change the nature of the picaresque genre in the process of illuminating it. Whereas among Spain's first generation of conversos, the picaresque became an "agreed-on strategy for wryly comic acceptance of their fate," as Stephen Gilman famously put it, [37] Latin American historicizations of the picaresque *reject* this compromise, implicitly calling for serious and genuine rehabilitation of traditional Ibero-American attitudes toward minorities and dissenters.

Furthermore, if we accept that Spain's classical picaresque novels *encode* some sort of anxious response to the converso's status in early modern Spain, then our contemporary Latin American historicizations of the picaro-converso should merely *decode* an ethnic conflict already present in the original picaresque. One finds, however, that the genre's original characteristics are compromised through systematic and sympathetic emphasis on the converso's experience. This occurs not merely because we are actually dealing here with historical novels upon which a picaresque mode has been grafted: it is rather a consequence of a different *attitude* toward the converso and his environment. For when the Inquisition is targeted and condemned as the picaro's persecutor, then the genre that famously made comedy out of the converso's tragedy loses its slapstick tone, and instead of appearing as a pathetic delinquent whom nobody loves, the picaro-converso in our historicized picaresque novels becomes a tragic hero.

To investigate what happens to the picaresque novel when it is placed at the service of a historical account of the converso's plight, I shall isolate four aspects of the classical Spanish picaresque that seem most relevant to the converso's experience, namely, (1) overt descriptions of the picaro's lineage; (2) the nature of the picaro's delinquency; (3) the genre's anti-romantic stance and inherent rejection of idealism; and (4) the picaro's ambiguous "conversion."

When we compare these aspects of Spain's original picaresque with the same features in our contemporary Latin-American variations of the genre, it immediately becomes evident that Homero Aridjis and Muñiz-Huberman greatly compromise the comic nature of the original picaresque mode despite their careful rendition of the picaresque's characteristic first-person mode, retrospective narration, and episodic plot, while Scliar's parodic interplay with both history and genre paradoxically replicates the picaresque's original satirical atmosphere despite the liberties it takes with the picaresque's form. Moreover, *The Strange Nation of Rafael Mendes*'s rehabilitation of its picaro-converso (as a "Jew") brilliantly mirrors the classical picaro's ambiguous reformation (as a "Christian"). This provocative representation of the picaro as reformed (or deformed) by sudden conversion casts the traditionally vexing question of the picaro's ambiguous reformation—indeed the principal crux anchoring most interpretations of classical picaresque novels—in an entirely new light.

Inescapable Traces of Lineage

Following standard picaresque conventions, Aridjis's *1492* opens with a survey of the protagonist's background, including a discussion of the picaro's converso ancestry, as if this were but one more tainted element circumscribing the picaro's prospects. As a point of comparison, the first chapter of Mateo Alemán's paradigmatic *Guzmán of Alfarache* immediately flags the problem of who his father was, from what nation, and of what occupation ("nation" being a euphemism for conversos, as in *The Strange Nation of Rafael Mendes*). More satirically, the protagonist of Quevedo's *Buscón* confesses from the onset that his mother was suspected of not being an Old Christian—though she does her best to hide this by changing her names and becoming a prostitute, presumably a lesser dishonor. Unlike these classical picaresque narratives, though, Aridjis's survey of his picaro's background expands into a historical account of the raids unleashed upon Spain's Jewish communities in 1391 witnessed by the protagonist's grandparents. However, it soon becomes evident that the grandparents themselves are no longer Jewish, although they still dwell near the *judería* and are tied to their neighbors in subtle ways that become more significant as the narrative progresses.

Muñiz-Huberman's *Tierra adentro* opens in standard picaresque manner with an announcement of the protagonist's name and birthplace: "My name is Rafael. I was born in Toledo, one fall day in 1547" (9). Here we might note that Rafael, from the Hebrew "God will cure," was a favorite Judeo-Christian name that sounds Hispanic while retaining its Hebrew roots. Furthermore, as Márquez Villanueva observes regarding *Lazarillo*'s strategic references to Toledo, any allusion to this once prominently Jewish city in the context of a sixteenth-century Spanish narrative can be considered "tantamount to evoking the crudest social tension surrounding *conversos*."[38] Indeed, the crux of Muñiz-Huberman's novel is that her Rafael refuses to forsake his ancestral roots, despite the dangers involved, for which his parents pay with their lives.

Like *Tierra adentro* and *1492*, and indeed like most picaresque narratives, Moacyr Scliar's *The Strange Nation of Rafael Mendes* also opens with a first-person narration that flirts with lineage. Its narrator, however, is not the protagonist, but rather a professional genealogist who helps to trace the protagonist's converso heritage. This tongue-in-cheek acknowledgment of a problematic heritage then withholds the typical survey of the picaro's ancestry until a third of the novel has progressed, at which point Rafael Mendes's fantastically exaggerated genealogy—going all the way back to the prophet Jonah!—altogether parodies the picaresque convention of genealogical exposures. Moreover, what Francisco Rico calls the autobiographical "necessity" of the picaresque form is split here into two separate narratives: the father's autobiography and the framing narration of his genealogist friend, each linked to the protagonist's crisis and rehabilitation.[39] If we insist, however, on the importance of a retrospective first-person technique for the picaresque novel, we must also remember that its relevancy lies, as Guillén has pointed out, in the hero's "split between what was once traditionally called the 'inner man' and 'outer man.'"[40] And it is precisely this split between private feelings and social expectations that leads Rafael Mendes's father to search for his troublesome genealogy in the first place. (Note: to distinguish Scliar's Rafael from Muñiz-Huberman's, I shall refer to Scliar's protagonist by his full name.)

The younger Rafael Mendes learns about his lineage on the morning of November 17, 1975, to the tune of radio broadcasts announcing the imminent death of Spain's General Franco. This reference to a modern heir of Spain's medieval despots will constantly hover over Rafael Mendes's journey of self-discovery, contextualizing his realization that "He wasn't a Jew, but now he's a Jew" (Strange Nation, 287)—as if only now that fascism seems to be abating, can he claim his ancestry without suffering unduly for it. On the other hand, Rafael Mendes has no actual knowledge of Judaism: so what kind of Jewish identity can he actually claim? Regarding this question, Naomi Lindstrom observes that all of Scliar's fiction celebrates "the hardiness of Jewish tradition"; even characters who have a "scanty acquaintance with their legacy" find Judaism reasserting itself in their lives unexpectedly.[41] *The Strange Nation of Rafael Mendes* is an extreme example of this pattern in Scliar's work.

Rafael Mendes's inheritance encompasses all aspects of the converso's multivalanced allegiances. First of all, his perspective as "half-outsider" develops through a belated and vicarious acquaintance with a father of whom he previously had "an idealized and somewhat comforting image," but "now he knows that his father was an eccentric . . . bequeathing to his only son nothing save some old clothes, books and notebooks with stories about the nation" (Strange Nation, 288). His father's notebooks actually trace a transatlantic Sephardic experience that spans thirteen generations of Rafael Mendeses, with a genealogy harking back to Maimonides and the exposure of the fugitive prophet Jonah.[42] Moreover, the role played by the picaro's cruel masters in Spain's original picaresque novels—a role that Aridjis transposes into Juan Cabezón's blind mentor and Muñiz-Huberman into a magical muleteer who rescues conversos—acquires in Scliar's novel the shape of problematic companions attached to the Rafael Mendeses and enticing them into wild schemes and utopian dreams. Thus, even though Scliar does not follow picaresque conventions as deliberately as Aridjis and Muñiz-Huberman, the lineage of his protagonist extends the picaro-converso's predicament into one hyper-picaresque adventure that reenacts the classical picaresque's episodic pace and tragicomic atmosphere, as each Rafael Mendes takes another highway and flees to another country—until the last Rafael Mendes decides to halt this pattern.

However, at the moment when Rafael Mendes decides to stay put, he is in fact already sitting in jail: just the day before he "had a good position or at least it looked good; he had a high paying job, people looked up to him. Now he is unemployed and in prison" (Strange Nation, 287). Within the plot of Scliar's novel, this situation results from Rafael Mendes's financial embezzlements, yet the satirical contiguity of the protagonist's discovery of his roots and his exposure as a delinquent organically stems from the picaresque's fundamental linkage between these categories. Rafael Mendes's delinquent status immediately puts him in the position of a sudden outsider who can envision his society from both within and without, a capacity that Scliar historicizes through Rafael Mendes's ancestral background.

The Nature of the Picaro-Converso's Delinquency

Without connecting delinquency with lineage, Alexander Parker's *Literature and the Delinquent* describes the classical picaro's adventures as misdemeanors that rarely transcend petty theft and swindling. He attributes the genre's systematic *avoidance* of violent crime to the picaresque's comic nature and thematization of freedom.[43] But how is this equation affected when the picaro's delinquency is attributed directly to the social restrictions imposed upon conversos in Ibero-America? In other words, when the picaro's delinquency is portrayed primarily as the consequence of his lineage, what happens to the genre's comic stance, and especially to its thematization of the legal and moral boundaries of freedom?

Muñiz-Huberman's *Tierra adentro* establishes an extreme clash between the picaro's faith and freedom. Her Rafael belongs to a family of conversos that still practices a few remnants of Judaism. However, on the eve of Rafael's Jewish coming of age, the father announces: "I want to protect you from suffering, my son, and therefore we shall not celebrate your bar mitzvah. Within your heart, you may celebrate, but at home we shall have no feast. . . . I know this decision is painful, but it is a way of protecting you" (*Tierra adentro*, 14–15). This prudence backfires when the thirteen-year-old runs away from home in protest.

Rafael's passage into Jewish adulthood thus coincides with his debut on the picaresque road. However, once there, Muñiz-Huberman's picaro does not engage in the genre's conventional petty theft and swindling, and he even does his utmost to avoid lying. Instead, his delinquency takes the form of an association with teachers of illegal subjects such as Jewish texts and alchemy, thus turning into an intellectual and spiritual pursuit of forbidden interests. Only later on in the novel is the picaresque's fundamental link between delinquency and lineage articulated more explicitly and unsympathetically by pilgrims who travel alongside Rafael when he tries to escape to the Holy Land:

—They say that his past isn't clean.
—Has he murdered, has he stolen?
—Worse.
—What can be worse?
—They say that his past isn't clean, alluding to his lineage. (*Tierra adentro*, 131)

The historicization of the picaro as a converso requires that the classical picaresque's *minor* delinquency be recast into intangible "crimes" punishable even by death in Ibero-America's autos-da-fé. This occurs even when the picaro-converso himself does not profess any attachment to Judaism, as in the case of Homero Aridjis's Juan Cabezón, whose crime is that he harbors a judaizer sought by the Inquisition, as we will see in the next section. While the original picaro lies, steals, and swindles to get what he can from a cruel world, the historicized picaro-converso—living on the precarious outskirts of society, as the classical picaro does—survives through a network of fellow conversos whose transgressions range from actual Jewish practice to consorting with Marranos and other ambiguous characters.

The Picaro-Converso as a Lover Despite His Times

In addition to shifting the picaro's laughable delinquency to capital crimes of ethno-religious allegiance, some Latin American historicizations of the picaro-coverso romanticize their protagonists in a manner that further erodes the classical picaresque's fine line between comedy and tragedy. Their picaro-converso becomes an ardent lover in defiance of the callous anti-heroism of the original picaresque genre. This transformation is most evident in Aridjis's *1492*, where Juan Cabezón starts off as a reincarnated Lazarillo, but soon turns into a faithful and sensitive lover when he meets a beautiful conversa hiding from the Inquisition, with whom he eventually has a son.[44]

Given that the original picaresque novel systematically rejected romance's idealization of love and heroism,[45] Juan Cabezón's commitment to the fugitive Isabel strains *1492*'s reliance on the picaresque to the utmost. Classical picaresque novels actually mock *all* vows, as when Lazarillo "proves" his rehabilitation by sharing his wife with a bishop. Indeed, if romance appears at all in Spain's classical picaresque novels, it tends to function as one more adventure on the picaresque road. We must therefore ask, if romance's idealized wish fulfillment represents the ultimate antithesis to the picaresque's social pessimism, then how can romantic and picaresque elements coexist—and do they actually coexist—in modern novels that rely on picaresque features to historicize the Judeo-Spanish experience?

In this context, it is important to remember that the picaresque's greatest innovation was what Guillén calls an "entanglement" between a fictional protagonist and an author's contemporary environment.[46] This entanglement is adumbrated in the very titles of the first picaresque novels, which announce a life anchored in a historically recognizable location. Hence, *The Life of Lazarillo of Tormes* (or from Tormes), *The Life of the Rogue Guzmán of Alfarache* and, of course, the metafictional "Life of Ginés of Pasamonte" in Cervantes's *Quixote*. The compounded subtitle of Homero Aridjis's *1492: The Life and Times of Juan Cabezón of Castile* thus underscores from the onset that Juan Cabezón's life cannot be understood except in relation to both place *and* time. Indeed the momentous date of 1492 reinforces the reader's awareness of how a particular historical environment circumscribes love and life.

Although both the Old and New Christian authors of Spain's first picaresque novels satirized a social environment in which true piety and kindness had gone awry, the comic delinquency of their picaros was consistently portrayed as a negative condition soon to be checked and punished. By contrast, Aridjis's picaro-converso becomes a tragic champion of love and justice hunted down by villains. Here the classical parental figure that thwarts lovers is transformed into the long arm of the Inquisition and a political context that supported its mandate. Juan Cabezón's romance with Isabel de la Vega does come to fruition to some extent, but because she is a fugitive and Juan's own converso roots place him in a precarious position, their living happily ever after gets continuously deferred.

Aridjis's novel ends as Juan sails off to the New World with Columbus, while Isabel departs in the opposite direction with the exiled Jews. "Shall we ever see each other again?" Juan cries, as Isabel leaves with their son. This question, left tragically open in *1492*, is taken up again in its sequel, *Memorias del Nuevo Mundo*. But there, too, the hallucinatory atmosphere of Juan and Isabel's reunion on his deathbed suggests, at least to me, that stark realism asserts itself cruelly against romance's tantalizing promise.

In *1492*, the *times* in which the lovers live definitely curb an ideal extension of their relationship, reinstating the picaresque's pragmatism over romance's wish fulfillment. Yet even if the picaresque's pragmatic disillusionment is preserved, it is not accompanied here by satire as it had been in the original picaresque. Moreover, by allowing the reader to sympathize wholeheartedly with the novel's hero, *1492* challenges a conventional picaresque mode that made comedy out of the pícaro's plight. But here the shock effect of the picaro-converso's flight from the Inquisition, which would condemn him to the stake if it could catch him, nevertheless does reproduce to some extent the frisson evoked by the pícaro's original delinquent activities. Thus the anxious tension that pervades Aridjis's novel manages to revitalize the picaresque's topical relevance in a historicized context.

Muñiz-Huberman's picaro-converso is also a lover, but one whose multicultural sexual experiences serve to allegorize a sense of covert heterodoxy in seventeenth-century Spain. Rafael's relationship with Miriam functions as *Tierra adentro*'s main love plot even though she is neither his first nor sole love interest, as Isabel is for Juan Cabezón. In a pattern that echoes Castro's celebration of Spain's medieval multiculturalism, Muñiz-Huberman's picaro-converso samples a Muslim Almudena, a Greek Helena, and a Christian innkeeper before and after meeting the crypto-Jewess Miriam. Although it is she who redeems him when he is about to renounce his struggle for religious freedom, their love cannot be fully consummated until they escape from Spain to the Land of Israel, and even there, scarring memories of their family's autos-da-fé tarnish their romantic happily-ever-after.

The motif of a beloved who functions as a preserver of ethnic identity recurs in Scliar's *Strange Nation of Rafael Mendes*, where Rafael Mendes *père*'s attachment to a Jewish colleague leads to the discovery of his own Jewish roots. This epiphany results in tragedy when the father abandons his wife and son, and drowns at sea while recklessly following his flame; subsequently, his son's love life does not differ much from the damaged and episodic relationships that characterize classical picaresque's flirtations with romance. It must be said, however, that despite the picaresque's systematic devaluation of romance, even classical picaros can hardly be accused of failing to anchor their personalities to some "idea or ideal of conduct," as Stuart Miller argues, for after all, the classical picaro is *determined* to improve his lot even if he is unscrupulous about the means.[47] Still, it is true that such a self-centered quest can elicit neither romance's idealized blessings nor the reader's sympathy in the manner that the picaro-converso's plight does, especially when bolstered by romance.

The Picaro's "Conversion"

In every classical picaresque novel, the picaro's adventures unfold between the young protagonist's sudden awareness of his or her vulnerable position in society—due to indigence, orphanhood, and lineage—and his or her usually unconvincing social and moral rehabilitation as an adult. As the picaro ages, he more desperately tries to integrate himself into mainstream "honorable" society. This desire for social integration was portrayed quite differently by Spain's foremost New and Old Christian picaresque authors. Toward the end of *Guzmán de Alfarache*, Mateo Alemán seriously explores the possibility of the picaro's full social reintegration through an ambiguous reformation that critics refer to as Guzmán's conversion. By contrast, the reformation of Pablos in Francisco de Quevedo's *Life of the Buscón* is blocked "cynically and systematically."[48] "Where Alemán intends the punishment as corrective and finally beneficial to the self, Quevedo holds out little hope for anyone's reformation."[49]

I find it fascinating that critical discourse on the picaresque genre traditionally refers to the picaro's ambiguous rehabilitation in terms of a "conversion," without making any attempt to consider this conversion in its historical context. Indeed, among the four aspects of the picaresque novel that we have been tracing here in relation to the picaro-converso's historical experience—lineage, delinquency, anti-idealism, and conversion—the traditionally vexing question of the picaro's rehabilitation is illuminated most poignantly when we consider the historical impact of forced conversions and the laws over purity of blood that convulsed Spain and Portugal in the centuries that followed the mass baptisms of 1391.

A consideration of the picaro's conversion naturally acquires a special inflection when we look at its role in historical novels where the picaro's troubles clearly derive from an ambiguous religious status. In this case the picaro's conversion is not merely a problem arising out of the hermeneutic difficulty of reconciling a vital protagonist with an allegedly reformed narrator who confesses his past delinquencies: it marks a drastic switch in religious affiliation that tragically separated conversos from Jews and Old Christians alike, unwittingly creating a new and distinct "nation."

Derived from the picaresque's indebtedness to Augustinian confession and interpreted within the context of a Renaissance poetics that demanded moral edification as much as entertainment,[50] the classical picaro's abjuration of his delinquent ways normally occurs at the end of picaresque novels, though the concept of a conversion is sometimes applied as well to the picaro's early recognition of his disadvantageous position in a pitiless world.[51] Therefore, when José María Micó affirms that "the cornerstone of every interpretation of *Guzmán de Alfarache* is the protagonist's conversion," he merely refers to Guzmán's abjuration of his immoral ways at the end of his autobiographical narrative, without in the least considering the picaro's ethnic background.[52]

An analysis of the picaro's conversion naturally acquires special meaning when interpreted in the context of the massive religious conversions that engendered the New Christians' ambiguous status in the first place. In this context, an examination of the picaro's conversion transcends the usual difficulty of reconciling a zesty delinquent with his repentant confession. Instead, conversion becomes, first of all, the indelible marker of a lineage that had become a criminalized liability. Yet how can we interpret this weighty moment of change when it occurs in historical novels where a seminal act of religious conversion sets in motion the ambiguous status of the picaro-converso as a half-outsider for generation upon generation?

And yet, surprisingly, this all-important marker of identity in the picaro-converso's family background is merely implied or portrayed indirectly in our Latin American examples. In *Tierra adentro*, we see various members of the protagonist's family worrying about their persistent Jewishness, and we can only deduce that at some point they must have nominally converted to Catholicism either expediently or by force. Aridjis's novel opens with a dramatic description of the mass riots and baptisms that swept through Spain's Jewish neighborhoods in 1391 and the years following, but here, too, the actual conversion of Juan Cabezón's ancestors remains shrouded in ambiguity. Even the detailed family history of Scliar's *Strange Nation of Rafael Mendes* does not volunteer a precise account of how and when in their long history the Jewish Mendeses became New Christians.

It is most interesting to compare this lack of clarity regarding the actual religious affiliations of our Latin-American picaro-conversos, with the role of conversion in the classical picaresque's original narrative structure. Since the classical picaresque novel presented the retrospective autobiography of an allegedly reformed narrator, as Joan Arias persuasively argues, this implies that the actual moment of conversion in the picaro's story is "not the end point, but the beginning. It is essential that we become aware of the conversion from the start because it is the vantage point from which the narrator writes."[53] Yet as Arias's argument shows, this stance is counterintuitive because from the beginning, readers of classical picaresque novels are delightedly swept away by the picaro's transgressions—which are largely free of repentant discourse—so that his final avowal of an alleged reformation strikes us as unconvincing.

A similar type of ambiguously comic conversion occurs at the end of Scliar's novel, where the rehabilitation of Rafael Mendes (who up until that point believed that he descended from Old Christian stock) hinges on a sudden counterconversion that recasts Jewish stereotypes in a healing light. Unlike Muñiz-Huberman's *Tierra adentro* and Homero Aridjis's *1492*, which faithfully adhere to the picaresque's typical first-person retrospective narrative mode, *The Strange Nation of Rafael Mendes* oscillates between the picaresque's complicit and retrospective first-person mode and the historical novel's distanced third-person, thereby undermining the reader's confidence in either narrative perspective.[54] This paves the way for a defamiliarization of ethnic, national, and narrative stereotypes.[55]

Scliar's erosion of stereotypes reaches a crescendo when the last Rafael Mendes reconnects to his ancestors through a strident and indeed far-fetched acceptance of the Jewish lineage he has just discovered: "He wasn't a Jew, but now he's a Jew" (Strange Nation, 287). How can we interpret this affirmation of Judaism at the end of Scliar's novel in light of the classical picaro's claims of rehabilitation at the end of most picaresque narratives? First of all, Rafael Mendes's counterconversion to Judaism is tragicomic and perplexing, not only because he has no actual knowledge of Judaism, but also because his sudden Jewish allegiances coincide with his exposure as a financial delinquent. Yet beyond the picaresque's conventional link between delinquency and lineage, Rafael Mendes's crucial decision *not* to flee from legitimate charges against him—a decision he attributes to his newly discovered lineage—paradoxically marks a *break* with the very lineage he has just embraced, in that his decision *not* to flee halts the picaresque rollercoaster that ostensibly impelled his ancestors to move away every time they were in danger.

To properly judge a picaro's rehabilitation, Joan Arias has argued, we must first investigate the "reality of the conversion as well as its goal. If a conversion has taken place, to what new faith has the picaro been converted, and how has his life changed? We must examine his life to see if it reflects such a change."[56] In other words, if the picaro's rehabilitation is truly the vantage point from which he allegedly narrates, then we should be able to examine his narrative for evidence of this reformation. Having judged Guzmán of Alfarache in this manner, Joan Arias finds him wanting, that is, she remains unconvinced by his assertion of change. This persuasive line of reasoning does not apply to Scliar's novel, however, because it is not narrated as the retrospective autobiography of a picaro who claims to have changed. Yet in spite of this, and even despite the suddenness of his conversion/counterconversion at the end of the novel, Rafael Mendes's decision to acknowledge his historical roots represents a break, as much as a point of continuity, in that he decides to reconnect to Judaism itself rather than to the liminal identity of the converso. His reconnection to his ancestors is therefore a plea for a new beginning, a plea for rehabilitation and change that revisits in paradoxical ways the *endings* of the original picaresque novels written by Spanish conversos.

The ending of Scliar's novel promises a bittersweet road for Rafael Mendes as he chooses to tie his uncertain personal fate to his nation's fate. But *which* nation is that? Is it a Jewish nation, a clique of conversos, or a modern Brazilian nation? It is a Brazilian nation with a Jewish component that includes—and this is Scliar's point—"rebellious prophets as well as . . . pioneers; illustrious physicians as well as senile Indians; great financiers as well as swindlers" (Strange Nation, 188). As soon as it becomes clear that the Jewish component in Brazilian history contains a spectrum of social types, the Mendeses' ambiguous allegiances are transformed from a perilous secret affiliation into a celebration of Ibero-America's complex multicultural identity.[57]

Scliar's sensitivity toward stereotypes extends to his treatment of literary genres. For, after all, what are genres except habitual frameworks for the reader's interpretative expectations, which delight us by fulfilling conventions or impress us by subverting them? Fredric Jameson's exhortation to always historicize genre, his distrust of any smooth harmonization of "heterogeneous narrative paradigms which have their own specific and contradictory ideological meanings,"[58] is enacted in Scliar's postmodern refusal to harmonize the fantastic, historical, and picaresque components of his novel. Instead, he leaves them in dissonant contradiction so as to defamiliarize and deactivate long-standing ideological attitudes toward Jews and conversos in Brazilian culture.

The Strange Nation of Rafael Mendes leaves us perched on the threshold of a potential new life, yet it is a life that we perhaps cannot imagine except as a continuation of what we read before. As Stuart Miller says of the *Lazarillo*, its "unity might have been more inclusive had the ending been consistent with *all* that had gone before."[59] On one hand, Rafael Mendes's acceptance of the lineage he has just discovered breaks with that very ancestral chain of picaro-conversos, because, unlike them, he is not threatened with conversion or death as they had been: he can perhaps stop being a picaro and a converso. On the other hand, he and his Jewish boss participate and become the scapegoats of a national financial crisis. In this way, the ending of Scliar's novel enables tragedy to peek under comedy, as happens in the classical picaresque.

In classical picaresque fashion, the ambiguity of the picaro's conversion serves to destabilize all ideological positions, throwing the burden of conversion into the lap of a reader, who is gently exhorted to examine his or her own attitudes toward Jews, history, and Ibero-America's traditional half-outsiders.[60]

Functioning within the "fantastic and multiple . . . dialectical positions that disable stereotypes,"[61] Scliar's work is first and foremost concerned with the normalization of the Jew's image in the modern world. He therefore deliberately exaggerates stereotypes in order to diffuse them. In response to Regina Igel's question, "What feeds you most as a writer of Jewish themes?" he explained that "Jews are a homogeneous block only to the eyes of an anti-Semitic person, [but in actuality they] are as different from each other as everybody else. . . . Judaism has its controversial aspects, what makes it alive. My fiction discovers those aspects."[62] Elsewhere, he attributed this anti-stereotyping impulse to his own experiences as a youth, when he attempted to transform himself into the opposite of what he believed that his Catholic classmates expected from a Jew: "Did they think Jews were cheap? I would be generous. Avaricious? I would be careless with my money. . . . The Goyim looked at me in surprise, and they *distrusted* me."[63] As a result of this experience, Scliar decided to turn negative behaviors attributed to Jews into picaresque comedy.

As Jeffrey Lesser notes, in a land where "the imagined Jew, not the real one, was considered the danger"—where Jews could be simultaneously regarded as greedy capitalists *and* evil communists, immigrant riffraff *and* overly successful entrepreneurs—stereotypes persist as a last anti-Semitic frontier.[64] To conquer and neutralize this form of anti-Semitism, Scliar and other Latin American writers try to adjust the conventions of a familiar Spanish genre so as to offer a corrective history of conversos.

Whether they do so playfully, like Scliar, or with a sober dose of historical pessimism, like Aridjis and Muñiz-Huberman, these writers are essentially concerned with a reformation of the Jew's image in Latin American societies as one facet in a wider struggle for a modernization of civic rights and responsibilities in their respective milieus. By portraying the historical suppression of heterodox and pluralistic elements in Ibero-American societies, these writers essentially promote greater openness to reform, filtering current sociopolitical concerns through the prism of Judeo-Spanish history compounded by genre and colored by an accumulation of traumatic upheavals in their various distinct backgrounds. Significant participants in Latin America's ongoing struggle between the populist myth and the authoritarian archive,[65] the historicizations of the Spanish picaro examined here recast stereotypes of Jews and conversos in a healing light to clear new territory for an unambiguous rehabilitation of Ibero-America's traditional half-outsiders.

Part III *Between Israel and Spain*

Seven

Facing Sepharad, Facing Israel and Spain

Yehuda Burla and Antonio Gala's Janus Profiles of National Reconstitution

Stacy N. Beckwith

In her scholarship on the use and refraction of medieval Sepharad in modern Latin American literature, the Hispanist Edna Aizenberg has referred to a 1964 debate on the plausibility of a "neo-sephardism" among Jews who do not have an ancestral connection to Iberia, but who acquire an osmotic "memory" of medieval Spain through their modern Spanish-speaking environments.[1] Aizenberg has advocated a "possible neo-Sephardic literary genealogy traced in the work of Latin American Jewish writers not genetically Iberian," but who nonetheless link themselves to Sepharad creatively by portraying a range of modern national contexts in Latin America through the lens of Sephardic history.[2]

Tracing an "allure of Sepharad" in modern Latin American literature, Aizenberg has focused primarily on how Argentinian authors have presented their fictional Andalusian landscapes as allegories of scenes and stages in their own nation's modern history. These authors were drawn to Sepharad because they could make a statement about conditions in Argentina when they transported these conditions back to an ancient Iberian environment, and then expressed them in the guise of a Sephardic world that became a metaphor for the image of modern Argentina which they either critiqued or endorsed.[3] In 2004, following an international conference on sephardism in Germany, Aizenberg intuited that in wider international fiction, sephardism can also be conveyed through other literary devices. There may be a "kaleidoscope" of ways in which the "allure of Sepharad" can captivate authors, such as inspiring them to "rummage" in the repertoire of famous Sephardic historical figures in order to recast them allegorically.[4]

The ideological nature of such recasting has been highlighted by the French philologist Stephen Nichols in his discussion of the emergence of medieval studies as an academic discipline in the nineteenth century. As Nichols has explained, medievalists of that era were "armed with the tools for accurate chronological measurement superior to any age."[5] With these they developed a "historical timeline of medieval literature" and a "hierarchical view" of specific texts, often according to how each one established or enhanced the "origins" of a contemporary nation's founding narrative. In the makeup of nations that have stressed specific origins as central to their conceptual and teleological growth, Nichols also identified a dichotomous "historically-oriented" and "future-oriented" modernism.[6] The nationalist literary and theatrical projects of two mid-twentieth-century Sephardist authors in Israel and Spain illuminate the composition of such a bidirectional outlook. In these writers' works a simultaneous gaze toward one's national past and future does not necessarily imply that both vistas are equally apprehended through holistic cultural insight. To the contrary, collective origins may become visible in terms of how effectively they might enhance a contemporary projection of national reconstitution and progress.

In particular, one of the authors I examine aimed to reinforce Zionism's teleological depiction of Israeli history, while the other strove to critique Spanish history and point beyond fascism's exclusionary narration of it. Whether they were pro- or anti-establishment within their respective societies, in order to convey their ideological messages in indelible literary or theatrical images, Yehuda Burla, an Israeli author of Sephardic descent (1886–1969), and Antonio Gala, a Spanish dramaturge, novelist, and journalist (1936–), each looked back at Sepharad as an imagined space: this was an ancestral world whose popular recollection in contemporary Israel and Spain had less to do with historical precision than with fabricated images or legends based loosely on historical fact. In twentieth-century retrospect, both medieval Spain with its vibrant Jewish communities shifting within Iberia between the eighth and fifteenth centuries, and early modern Spain with its Jewish remnants amid converted but suspect "New Christians" (or conversos), were figurative coffers. Each preserved mythic and foil images that could underwrite modern Israeli or Spanish national trajectories with implied patrimonial endorsement. Like their nineteenth-century medievalist counterparts, Burla and Gala were able to select renowned figures and create composite characters from their societies' conceptual Sephardic pasts in ways that "perpetuate[d] historical decontextualization."

At the same time, however, their writing showed that contextual accuracy in historical narration was a nationalist imperative.[7] Engaging with Sepharad from a distance, each writer exhibited a politics of reading Spain's medieval past with a deliberate panorama of contemporary national reconstitution in mind. The result is that a Janus-faced dynamic emerges when we read Burla's commissioned historical novel *Eleh masaʿei Rabi Yehuda Halevi* (These Are the Travels of Rabbi Judah Halevi, 1959)[8] and Antonio Gala's political drama *Las cítaras colgadas de los árboles* (The Zithers Hanging from the Trees, 1974)[9] with an awareness of how nationalistic modernists have engaged with the Middle Ages in general, and with Sepharad in particular. Each work exhibits a doubling and reflection of the present in the past, which is analogous, in visual terms, to a double profile on a Roman coin or frieze: a face and its exact complement looking in opposite directions. In each case this Janus face characterizes both the author behind the scenes and the protagonist he specifically constructed from a blend of national myth and historic Spanish-Jewish material. This leading character animates a neo-Sephardic world that, whether Mediterranean in the twelfth century or Spanish in the sixteenth, presents a metaphoric tableau that signals a potential for significant change in modern Israeli or Spanish national life. Identifying such a catalyst in both Israeli and Spanish literature builds on Edna Aizenberg's scholarship on the allegorical use of Sepharad in Argentine and other Latin American fiction. It also affirms her intuition of diverse and expanding modes of engaging with Sepharad in the modern literary imagination.

For in Burla's novel and Gala's play, a landscape or scene in medieval or early modern Spain, North Africa, or Palestine is not initially metaphoric. It becomes so when each author's agent provocateur, crafted from collective memory surrounding an actual medieval Sephardic biography or an enduring Spanish stereotype of Jews and conversos, orchestrates the setting's historical nuances so that the scene mirrors national life in mid-twentieth-century Israel or Spain. In this way, allegory initiates in both the author and his fictional proxy's archaeological gaze toward Sepharad, and culminates in their simultaneous counterfixation on and beyond contemporary Israeli or Spanish malaises. Potential for future societal improvement is signaled by the medieval or sixteenth-century Spanish Jewish protagonist who, in animating his or her literary surroundings, evokes from their complementary Sephardic features the author's thematic message of ultimately achievable national repair and renewal.

Starting in late 1947, Israel's first decade as a state was fraught with many existential and internal challenges. In the late 1950s, Yehuda Burla was approached by a publishing firm seeking to capture the loyalty of older readers as it competed for market share.[10] Burla's commissioned historical novel was intended to shore up this audience's confidence in Zionism as the proven guarantor of modern Jewish statehood and as the best steward of the country's future development. Accordingly, the author based his catalytic character on a Sephardic luminary who had the authority of an early Zionist visionary in Israeli collective memory. This was the medieval Andalusian poet and philosopher Judah Halevi (ca. 1075–1141), whose truncated pilgrimage from Spain Burla refashioned into a model for a Jewish return to Zion and an end to life in Diaspora. Considerable inspiration for this transformation came from oral legend surrounding Halevi that was first printed in 1587, and from ideological interpretations of Halevi's poetry by the influential Israeli historian Ben-Zion Dinur, the architect of Israel's dominant historical narrative and civic education in the early 1950s.[11] Burla's novel exhibits little counterinfluence from the prestigious local publication, in the mid-1950s, of medieval epistolary confirmation that Halevi perished in a town near Cairo in 1141, having never reached the Land of Israel.[12]

Charting Antonio Gala's rise to preeminence in Spanish dramaturgy since the mid-1960s, the contemporary Spanish theater scholar Victoria Robertson has highlighted Gala's tendency to "identify himself with the numerous catalytic characters in his plays: those who renew a sense of raison d'être in the other players, and sustain hope in a dream's potential for eventual realization." Indeed, Gala repeatedly used the theater to suggest possible exits from the spiritual stagnation, both individual and national, that prevailed in Spain during Franco's dictatorship from 1939 through 1975. Stylistically eclectic, Gala drew from "serious" realist theater once this began to distinguish itself from the fascist conformism that draped Spanish drama following the Civil War in the 1930s. From 1943 through the production of Gala's first play two decades later, critical Spanish theatrical engagement with "suffocating" daily reality swung between "soft" allegories and more forthright denunciation.[13]

Would-be redeemers in many of Gala's plays in the 1960s and 1970s spread news of paradise options beyond the cast's—and audiences'—immediate physical and conceptual boundaries. However, these leading characters typically could not enable an exodus from prevailing national conditions. *Las cítaras colgadas de los árboles* is one in a series of plays from the 1970s that Gala set during critical junctures in Spanish history, when national development took a particular turn, amid other possibilities. In Gala's view, when his dramatic plots made national audiences focus on Spain's constitutive crossroads, they helped contemporary Spaniards to "live sincerely with their history," and thereby with one another, in their own modern era.[14] At times the dramaturge etched a convergence of distinct currents or mind-sets in Spanish history directly onto one of his characters, such as Olalla, the Jewish-descended protagonist of *Las cítaras colgadas de los árboles*. Her Janus face transmits Sephardic songs of freedom and tolerance from medieval Spain into the play's allegorically linked sixteenth- and twentieth-century milieux, while also registering the persistence of anti-Semitic stereotypes in the Spanish imaginary throughout these eras.

These Manichean opposites operating through Gala's construction of Olalla as the lone Jew by descent, who communicates via the play's sixteenth-century old Christian farmhands and townspeople with Gala's contemporary Spanish audiences, highlight the importance of investigating Olalla's pseudo-historical composition. For in Burla and Gala's literary sephardism, it is the pivotal main character who makes historic Jewish Spain "metonymically present" for twentieth-century readers or theatergoers, with ancestral resonance that magnifies the writer or dramaturge's modern nationalist message.[15]

In Yehuda Burla's case, a reconnaissance of the actual Andalusian philosopher and poet, Judah Halevi, including his early trajectory in medieval Spain and particularly his private motives for reaching Jerusalem, contrasts instructively with the creative recontextualization involved in bending his narrative to that of a proto-Zionist martyr for Jewish repatriation in Israel. Since she was modeled not on a real person from the Sephardic past but on a reductive Spanish concept of Jewish otherness, Antonio Gala's Olalla invites reverse inquiry into how entrenched cultural images combined to stage a seemingly real conversa, with Jewish instincts and actions rendered natural through their accordance with a national mental picture of the Judeo-Spanish ethos.

Facing Sepharad

Whether the starting point for designing their lead characters was a renowned Andalusian figure and his written legacy or a collection of stagnant Jewish traits in Spanish vocabulary, refrains, and legends,[16] looking back at Sepharad in search of an indigenous foundation, Burla and Gala would first have needed to determine which Iberian regions were considered part of Jewish Spain, and in which historical periods. The medievalist Jonathan Decter has discussed Sepharad's shifting referents within Jewish tradition itself in his study of Iberian Hebrew poetry during the Almoravid consolidation of 1091, which prompted Jewish emigration from Islamic al-Andalus to northern Christian territories. Decter noted that particularly during this first displacement, "Jewish Iberia was an imaginary construct. Sepharad underwent a physical transformation as al-Andalus became a memory." Indeed, the name Sepharad, popularly derived from the biblical Book of Obadiah, "functioned discursively in Hebrew as the equivalent of al-Andalus in Arabic."[17] As a result, "mapping the exact borders of Sepharad during the medieval period is tricky. Whereas kingdoms such as Seville, Granada, Castile, and Aragon had actual (albeit shifting) borders, Sepharad never had a political reality; it existed only in the minds of Jews . . . only after centuries did the whole of the Iberian peninsula come to be identified with Sepharad."[18]

In many ways, the fluidity in this picture is mirrored in the historic Judah Halevi's professional shifts between east central and southern Iberia before he embarked privately for the Holy Land. Following the publication of Burla's novel in 1959, reviewers in the popular Israeli press and literary journals wrestled with how convincingly the author recreated Halevi as the Sephardic forefather of Jewish repatriation in the Land of Israel. For some critics, Burla overcame the challenge of fleshing out his Judah Halevi with venerable appeal in the 1950s–1960s by blending information on his namesake's multifarious career with conducive interpretations of his poetry.[19] At the same time, a dissenting reviewer also noted the superficial nature of information gleaned from the medieval Halevi's vocational map, and the limiting fact that his poetic style typically did not include epic or narrative composition. According to this critic, these lyrical modes might have revealed more to Burla about Halevi's personal habits and physique, letting the author's contemporary Israeli readers feel as though they were engaging with a substantive novel about "a personality" and "an idea," not just about a concept alone.[20]

Recent studies of Judah Halevi's poetry have found that even in the absence of more expansive epic or narrative styles, his verse exhibits a range of personal attachments, passions, and motives for achieving different goals. Many of these have come to light through coordinated attention to physical, cultural, and personal circumstances that affected the poet. Scholars have discerned such influential conditions by reading entire (not truncated) poems from across Halevi's repertoire, often in conjunction with verse by the poet's Andalusian peers. Though unavailable to Burla when he was composing his novel in the late 1950s, such contextually attuned scholarship helps us understand the author's contrasting Sephardist adaptation of Halevi's biography and its representation in his poetry. Burla's approach was fragmentary and programmatic, since he isolated episodes from Halevi's life and pieced them together so that the travel mission undertaken by his fictional protagonist, Halevi, would seem rooted in authentic Andalusian Jewish fears and desires.

Appearing early in the novel as a nondescript departure point for Burla's Halevi, when it had, in fact, been a place of great emotional and artistic significance to the medieval poet, the city of Granada particularly illustrates how the novelist adapted key environments from the real Halevi's life to the needs of his Zionist allegory. Burla elided the Andalusian's early love of the city for its own sake, and the grief Halevi expressed when religious persecution forced him to relocate. In this way, the novelist narrowed and altered the contextual perspective his readers would have on Granada, reducing the city to an indistinct steppingstone along his protagonist's communally inspiring route to Jerusalem. In contrast, contemporary scholars have seen the historical Halevi's affection for Granada as an early indicator of how singularly he would later commune with Jerusalem for its own sake.

The literary historian Ann Brener has focused on the centrality of Granada in the first significant impressions Halevi made in his career as a poet. According to her more inclusive reading of his early works, if Halevi's wide-ranging talents suggested any programmatic coherence it was around the social and artistic charms of the Andalusian city. Halevi had forged an independent path there when, as an unknown youth and incipient poet, he had been drawn from "Eastern" Christian regions of Iberia to "Western" al-Andalus by the allure of Muslim-Jewish symbiosis in Granada.[21] He had been particularly captivated by the creative radiance of the renowned Hebrew poet Moses Ibn Ezra, deploying his own verse as business correspondence to parlay his way into this luminary's esteem and "circle of Granada poets," as a "dazzling . . . new star in the firmament of poetry."[22] As Brener has illustrated, the city first "function[ed] as a kind of mirror for the emotions" of Halevi and his colleagues. In their verse, Granada frequently appeared as a *rimon* (pomegranate), whose beauty and juice would be anticipated or missed like that of a beloved if one were nearing the urban gem or relocating to the comparative desert elsewhere.[23] Against this nuanced background Brener has helped us to understand how Halevi's eventual displacement from Granada, through a fundamentalist change in Muslim regime and increased Jewish persecution, inculcated a yearning that would later magnify in response to Jerusalem's overwhelming pull.

Indeed, where the poet's early "love-lament" for Granada inspired poetic schemes through which this city resounded,[24] the Hebrew literary scholar Sidra deKoven Ezrahi has foreground Halevi's erotic, devotional dialogue with Jerusalem symmetrically late in his life.[25] Both Brener and Ezrahi put into relief how Halevi was "mapping his world according to a different set of coordinates"[26] or "expectations"[27] when he undertook the personal pilgrimage that would bookend his early love of Granada with a latent bid to unite himself individually with Jerusalem: Judaism's long feminized, primary "geographic referent"[28] and "focus of piety."[29] For as Raymond Scheindlin has argued, Judah Halevi's poetic record evinces no *communal* "summoning voice" that urged the start of a Jewish return to Zion in order to hasten a divine halt to diasporic existence.[30] Eleventh- and twelfth-century Iberia did evince a "vigorous reaffirmation of messianic hope" among prominent Andalusian Jews, including Halevi.[31] Along with the poet and theologian's forced relocations within the peninsula, such hope also furnished him with a vast range of religious images and analogies with which to modulate the formal and more popular tones of address in his verse. As Jonathan Decter has shown, this often enabled Halevi to intone "Israel's collective consciousness or . . . predicament of exile and hope for redemption" like a public mourner when he opened his elegies for the comparatively inconsequential deaths of various individuals.[32] Though striking in Halevi's oratory, such an incongruity between the public and private scope of a funerary address was organic to a Sephardic environment in which, as Ross Brann has described, "liturgical poetry served as [an] important literary vehicle for inner Jewish resistance to the memory and condition of displacement, dispersion, and powerlessness."[33]

What scholars such as Ross Brann and Raymond Scheindlin have stressed, however, is that when influential poets in medieval Spain reflected on the Jewish historical condition, the concerns and possible individual responses they expressed were private, even in the form of alleviating fantasies about journeying east. Imagined trajectories from Iberia to Zion focused on the transformation of one's soul by coming to live in the land of Jewish prophecy as a servant of God. In his recent contextual reading of the correspondence and poetry that Judah Halevi composed during his pilgrimage, Scheindlin has consistently dismissed any supporting evidence for an early nationalist dimension. Instead, from reading Halevi's Zionist-sounding letters and poems in full, he has concluded that the Andalusian's "pilgrimage bespoke a definitive embrace of quietism on the national level, signifying that he had despaired of all attempts to force a resolution to the Jewish problem."[34] As Scheindlin has shown, these texts often bracket Zion as an imaginative option or as one beset by empirical delays through forces of nature and the social machinery of Egyptian Jewish aristocracy.[35]

Such an assessment accords with letters by merchants, influential Jewish hosts, rabbis, and other contemporaries who exchanged news of Judah Halevi as he traveled beyond Spain, and who also received some personal correspondence in Arabic from him. Introduced in Israel in the mid-1950s, letters of this type confirmed the poet's diasporic demise in 1141. They were found in the Cairo Genizah collection by the preeminent Jewish ethnographer and historian of medieval Jews in Islamic lands, Shelomo Dov Goitein.[36] His primary research into Halevi's five to ten months in Egypt challenged a persistent trend in Israeli nationalism of recasting Hebrew poetry from Jewish Spain as consonant with Zionist goals.[37] Goitein presented many of his revelations about Halevi's later biography in the Hebrew University's quarterly for Judaic Studies, *Tarbiz*.[38] Even though his articles coincided with the gestation of Burla's novel, as the Hebrew literary scholar Shmuel Werses has affirmed, "it is known that Burla ignored Goitein's findings."[39] The author gave his novel a "realistic dimension" of its own by seeding it with contrived, thematic testimony about his iconic Halevi's transition from delaying around Cairo and Alexandria to residing in Crusader Jerusalem. Burla minimized the "folk tale" origins of this Halevi postscript by infusing it with plausible, doubt-filled banter with and among his Sephardist protagonist's fictional travel companions and portions of Egyptian Jewish society.[40]

The Hebrew literary scholar Lev Hakak has established that "accurate period detail" in Burla's depictions of his medieval settings establishes *Eleh mas'e Rabi Yehuda ha-Levi* as a historical novel, since it elides a sense of temporal distance between the reader and narrator.[41] However, as indicated by a degree of skepticism amid initial acclaim for the book in Israel, for some contemporary readers such immediacy faltered in connection with Burla's tautological method of giving his protagonist physical and emotional dimensions. Having encountered the known dearth of personal information on Judah Halevi when Burla looked back at the medieval scion in his Sephardic Iberian and Mediterranean contexts, the novelist generated his protagonist's mood swings and their corporeal expression from within his own literary text. In the novel, Halevi appears to have a body only when he reacts mercurially to the inconstant fortunes that visibly assist or detain him and his entourage in their Zion-bound expedition. The allegorical hero's expressive repertoire is limited to what energy and productivity he shows through his professional activities, whether vigor and effectiveness, or lassitude and futility in journeying, mediating disputes, counseling, healing, or composing poetry.

In the sixteenth-century Spanish aristocratic estate where she has long catered to Christian appetites from the sexual to the gastronomical, Antonio Gala's conversa protagonist Olalla also has specific vocational skills through which her body reflects the dramaturge's selective and, in this case, culturally conflicted engagement with Spanish Jewish history. Unlike Burla, Gala did not imbue his Sephardist lead with abilities that would trigger and advance a consistently linear nationalist mission. Rather, in his portrayal of historical Spanish turning points, such as the demise of medieval pluralism due to the consolidation of state and colonial powers, Gala pointed to a circular route for sociopolitical redress in both sixteenth-century imperial and twentieth-century fascist Spain. We can infer that this route started with the instructive, liberating inclusiveness the dramaturge inferred from Sepharad, even though he pointedly excluded this from the opening of the drama. Onstage, following the Catholic expulsion of Jews and the defeat of the last Muslim dynasty in Granada in 1492, remaining religious hybrids such as Olalla suffocate in an atmosphere of puritanical fanaticism. This climate mirrors Franco's dictatorship in retrospect and as the regime neared its end in 1975, a little over a year after the drama debuted in Madrid in 1974.

Through her genetic Jewish memory Olalla is able to recall traces of her Sephardic ancestors' folk songs. These melodies become fleeting portals to an earlier multicultural Iberia whose loss is repeatedly invoked in a town elder's refrain, "Granada should never have been [re] conquered."[42] During Spain's fascist coda in the 1970s, Gala's theatrical realism precluded easy passage from national repression to reconstitution for his allegorical characters. In the 1500s, despite the visible wealth of its growing empire in the Americas, Spanish society was deeply divided according to caste and privilege. On returning to Spain from her colonies, Olalla's former Christian lover finds that the disadvantaged in their community lack the wherewithal to heed his gospel about pockets of human innocence in the New World that would lend themselves to an equilibrating Spanish national rebirth. Indeed, introducing a 1977 edition of Gala's "sixteenth-century populist fresco," his contemporary the writer and dramaturge Enrique Llovet highlighted the "fascinating choice of historical period" in *Las cítaras colgadas de los árboles*:

> Spain, ever stronger on the outside and more miserable within, seemed divided into heroes and rogues, inquisitors and victims, great Caesars and common folk. Cleansed of Jews and Muslim-Christians, a collective craze for ennoblement intensified the divisions Gala dramatizes—rich and poor, castle-owning conquerors and broken renegades, those who dealt in Amerindian gold and those who went hungry and were themselves dealt with: two Spains.[43]

For Olalla and her repatriated beloved, only elected death can overcome such fault lines, which in their case also include Christian aversion to miscegenation with a Jewess. When their self-sacrifice grants them unassailable union at the end of his drama, Gala moves beyond his occasional references to medieval Sephardic songs and reconnects with ancient Judaism in "a new gloss on the eternal Psalm of captives."[44] Harp chords close *Las cítaras colgadas de los árboles* invoking, as does Gala's title, those biblical exiles from Zion who were unable to make music in Babylonian detention. In their reflexive silence, the dramaturge saw a metaphor for the predicament of Spain's internal exiles, both the early modern disenfranchised and their equivalents under contemporary fascism. Neither could intone against a power differential that divided Spanish national character into two antithetical faces.

By the same token, even though Olalla is unable to sing her way out of prejudicial captivity with the tunes she half recalls from her Jewish ancestors, as she attempts to access their implied traditions of tolerance, she looks back at Jewish Spain with esteem. Through Olalla's philo-Sephardic countenance Gala displays his authorial process of engaging deferentially with Spanish, and even more ancient, pre-Sephardic Jewish history. Such veneration is tempered, however, by the fact that throughout *Las cítaras colgadas de los árboles*, Olalla's singularly appealing Sephardic songs are the *only* examples of a thematic link between an imagined liberal Iberia from which they emerged and the diverse yet integrated Spain that Gala projects for sixteenth- and twentieth-century national inspiration. That a more equitable society remains illusory for the drama's players and spectators alike is not solely due to deteriorating relations (onstage) between a reactionary squire, his conservative and disruptive guests, and his laborers, including Olalla, at his traditional Christmas pig slaughter in the 1500s. A lack of communal harmony also comes across through a skewed kinship that Gala establishes between Olalla and the pig. Neither one would have been perceived as fully Christian according to the medieval and early modern Spanish symbolism with which the dramaturge is engaging.

In her study of a manufactured affinity between Jews and pigs in European Christian discourse since the early Middle Ages, the anthropologist Claudine-Fabre Vassas has examined the religious symbolism surrounding the killing and precise butchering of pigs ahead of the

Christmas season in several northern Spanish locales. Since a pig's flesh and blood were popularly understood to be potentially Christian and to harbor a conceivable Christian soul, a Jewish convert to Catholicism could prove the thoroughness and integrity of his or her religious transformation by handling each step from slaughter to gastronomy in a public display of exemplary solo technique. A presumed affinity between Jewish and porcine flowing blood made the alchemic task particularly appropriate for a conversa, as illustrated by Olalla in her main professional role in Gala's play.[45]

In an initial show of Sephardic telepathy with a dying pig that Gala suspends "as if crucified" above the actors, Olalla alone perceives a kinsman's farewells in its last moans and hoof twitches.[46] At the same time, Catholic liturgy echoes intermittently in the form of her dialogue, particularly in a call-and-response paternoster with local women when the animal is first bound and suspended. When the conversa ascends a dais in order to handle and reach into the pig's carcass, Gala's native Christian characters are particularly attentive to her touchstone isolation with the animal, whose duplicitous religious character could highlight her own. Capitalizing on this seasonal opportunity to reassert her Catholic alignment, however, Olalla repels any insults. These include the squire's assumption that her Jewish genes will prevent her from eating holiday dishes made of the blood and meat with which she was just in communion. Her defiant reaction elicits a public warning against being duped by "these New Christians . . . who are all talk."[47] Indeed, the Luso-Hispanist Erin Graff Zivin has argued that the conversa's accession to Christian subjectivity is only partial in Gala's drama. Drawing on Emmanuel Levinas, Zivin investigated Olalla as a site of discursive tension wherein her uniquely suited deconstruction of the pig does not simultaneously erase her Jewish origins. The conversa seeks a traceless transformation into an unsuspicious Catholic woman. Her "textual conversion" in *Las cítaras colgadas de los árboles* merely puts in play the "multiple" Spanish cultural attitudes toward Sephardic Jews and their "spectral" peninsular remnants, to borrow a term from the medievalist Steven Kruger.

Through his penetrating analysis of Jewish dis/embodiment in "medieval Christian texts—theological, historical, polemical, autobiographical, [and] fictional," Kruger has argued that these writings were permeated by a generalized Jewish foil that became "spectral" through an ongoing recession of actual historical referents and the subsequent intercession of "fantasy constructs of Jews" from popular lore.[48] Gala's is a Sephardist script that contemporized this process in support of a Spanish national makeover. Onstage, the invoked Jewish captives in Babylon are patrimonial metaphors for Spaniards who were pinioned and negligible under sixteenth- and twentieth-century despotism, and collectively represent a foil to Spain in each era. Olalla particularly reveals how Spanish lore became Sephardic history for Gala. When after her physical immersion in the pig she offers her breasts to the squire's son for sexual tutelage, the conversa seems about to suckle the next fully Christian generation with milk from a beast that, like her, has only recently and tenuously transcended its Jewish origins.[49] So sequenced, Olalla's actions also raise the specter of a *Judensau* (Jews' Sow) an anti-Semitic motif common in medieval German architecture, and at times, also evoked in Spanish historical fiction.[50]

In 1974, the medieval historian Isaiah Sachar published a detailed study of *Judensau* carvings on private, public, and religious buildings in German-speaking territories between the thirteenth and sixteenth centuries. He described their thematic depictions of a sow suckling Jews, as well as nourishing and entertaining them with its excrement. Underlying the grotesque anti-Semitism of this "uninhibited" period image was a presumption of filial relations between Jews and pigs,[51] similar to the widespread Spanish practice of derisively referring to Jews as "Marranos," or suckling pigs. By incorporating such a stereotyped and unsubstantiated equation into his play, Gala highlighted his limited empirical engagement with Iberian Jews and conversos as he looked back at Sepharad for an indigenous foundation for his ideological drama. Similarly, in excising Judah Halevi's lyric intimacy with Andalusian locales such as Granada, Burla also gave his novel only a patina of Sephardic authenticity.

Facing Israel

The Israeli author had two extrapolative sources of inspiration for his account of Judah Halevi's travels, one popular and the other scholarly, but intended for popular historical education. The former was a fictional epilogue to the real Halevi's incomplete quest, in which the Sephardic pilgrim succeeds in reaching the Holy Land. Initiated in 1587 by a descendant of a prominent Portuguese Sephardic family, this legend spawned a series of increasingly elaborate denouements, including Burla's, in which Halevi is eventually killed by an Arab horseman while he prays at the Western Wall.[52] In Burla's version, the murderer is one of the Muslim pseudo-disciples who, near the end of the novel, frequent Halevi's Jerusalem home to hear him expound the rights, the imperative, and some of the bicultural benefits of increased Jewish immigration to the Land of Israel.

In the same vein, the architect of Israeli historical education by the early 1950s, Ben Zion Dinur, thematized the other end of Judah Halevi's life: his Iberian beginnings and his poetic conversation with Zion from Spain.[53] The sociologist Uri Ram has called Dinur less of a "researcher" than a "designer" of Jewish history with respect to streamlining the origins of Israeli identity for national curricula.[54] In 1935, Dinur published a study of Judah Halevi's writing related to his pilgrimage. Reprinted in 1964, this paper aimed to (re)introduce Halevi as a key ancestral catalyst for the emergence of the Jewish state. Dinur built a case for indications of incipient Zionism in Halevi's voice, first in his poetry and then in his main philosophical text, *The Kuzari*.

Though messianic in its instantiation of a human-divine cooperation, the ascent to Zion from exile resounds as propaganda particularly when Dinur discusses how the structure of Halevi's religious poems magnified the ideological message he inferred from their content. Dinur asserts that such a synergy occurs in places where Halevi, like generations of liturgical writers before him, added new motifs to the perennially familiar tones and structure of *piyyut* verse. As they read and prayed regularly, Jews would encounter these new stylistic elements "in the company of" traditional *nusach*, or form. Novel ideas were thus rendered more palatable and inspiring through contiguity with the staples of familiar liturgy.[55]

Indeed, such an integrated textual call to community members, or in Marxist terms, "interpellation,"[56] also issued from Dinur's ideological analysis of Halevi's homing poetry. In his essay, the historian briefly explored and then rejected what he indicated were merely traditional interpretations of Halevi meditating on the ups and downs of pilgrimage to Jerusalem as a solitary endeavor. In Dinur's view, if one only perceived private intimacy with Zion and the divine in these poems, they were hardly singular. Not finding a personal sin that would have required such extreme atonement, Dinur called Halevi's quest for the Holy Land during Crusader perils "superfluous and excessive."[57] All of this magnified his announcement of what *did* make Halevi's poetic lines distinct. It was the allure of Zion they projected, with intensifying implications that one *aliya* (ascent to the Land of Israel) would generate several more, until all Jews were redeemed from the Diaspora.

That Burla embraced such a Sephardist hagiography in 1959 was evident in the course he charted for his fictional Halevi between the allure of Sepharad, such as Edna Aizenberg conceived it, and the counter-allure of Zion in Dinur's national gloss on Halevi's journey. For his medieval catalyst of Jewish reconstitution in the Land of Israel, Burla simultaneously pursued a convincing historicity and an effective re/interpellation of twentieth-century readers grown variously weary of Zionism's collective focus. This double profile appealed to the Am Oved publishing firm in the late 1950s as it searched for a new market niche to transition from the heroic-realistic literature they published around the time of Israel's independence. Am Oved then looked to older readers, and what it perceived as their need for reassurance about the relevance and continuity of Zionism, as Hebrew literature entered an era of focusing on individual versus collective concerns, with more persistent existential questioning. The press commissioned a series of historical novels projecting a range of Zionist contributions to eventual Jewish statehood by authors widely recognized as the preeminent literary chroniclers of their diverse Jewish communities.[58]

As such a renowned veteran ethnographer, Burla was in a position to stage a campaign for Zionist-style redemption among medieval Sephardic and North African Jews in a way that might "harmonize" their rich cultural achievements with the Euro-dominant narrative of modern Jewish statehood.[59] Structurally, the Mediterranean arc through which Halevi travels in the novel is a metaphor for different façades of medieval Sepharad. From Spain through North Africa and Egypt, Andalusian-style Muslim-Jewish *convivencia* is on display, with inherent power plays and restrictions on Jews as subjugated citizens. Within the Land of Israel at the time of Halevi's journey, the occupying Frankish kingdom of the

First Crusade is a copy of pre- and post-1492 Inquisitorial Spain, with scant communities of Jews living in hiding and "underground," much like condemned Marranos. Revealing even more of its Zionist inspiration, the cloak-and-dagger world of the Promised Land becomes a landscape that synthesizes Sephardic and Ashkenazic fears of anti-Semitism in an environment that also recalls Europe during the Holocaust.

The normative allure of Zion is most apparent in the fictional Halevi's social networking and mediation as he progresses from one Jewish community to the next between Granada and Jerusalem. When fortune favors his journey the poet-physician reconciles neighbors as if their diasporic antagonisms need to be resolved before a collective Jewish return to the Land of Israel can occur. In a study honoring Burla's literary achievements, his contemporary Dov Kimhi observed that Burla "knew one content and one subject: one man's fate. What mainly interested him is how the individual struggles and how he applies his strengths to the forces, impulses, actions, and squabbles that rise up around him."[60] In *Eleh masa'ei Rabi Yehuda Halevi*, such struggles are parables that draw attention to actions, attitudes, and character virtues that complement Israel as a composite Jewish state. Such expression of unity through diversity grew out of Burla's familiar depictions of local and regional Middle Eastern communities. Noting that this novel marked an ideological phase between Burla's early and late focus on the tumults of small folk in Sephardic Jerusalem, Damascus, Aleppo, or Baghdad, the literary scholar Batya Shimoni has discussed a "double consciousness" in this author.[61] However, she undermines her recourse to the cultural theorist Homi Bhabha's articulation of hybridity by foregrounding Burla's "utopic" goal of "straddling two worlds" without elaborating on their inherent differences in power structure.[62]

For instance, the potential mission-derailing inferiority of Oriental Jews culminates in Burla's novel when Halevi is able to reach Jerusalem not only by means of favorable commercial, security, and weather conditions, but also because in Egypt he rejects the love and tether of a local Jewish woman. Suspended until the end of the novel, the agony Halevi experiences in her presence is finally revealed in a series of impassioned notes and poems from his sojourn near Alexandria. After his murder, these writings come to light and disclose an inner battle between emotions and discipline, which Burla may have bracketed for heightened intrigue and exotic appeal. That he clearly intended to reiterate Halevi's situational Western pragmatism in a textual appendage heightens the novel's didactic emphasis on the value of choosing progress over stagnation when distinct worldviews collide and the one seen as outdated is left behind. Indeed, if as Bhabha has indicated, hegemonic narration "continually puts under erasure" its Other, then here, as in Antonio Gala's play, authentic elements of Spanish and North African Jewish history recede and become "spectral," haunting their own "partial representation" in Sephardist literature that "faces two ways without being two-faced" about its primary source of ideological interpellation.[63]

Facing Spain

For Gala, the allure of a reconstituted, multi-accentual Spanish democracy after Franco's dictatorship may not have emanated so measurably from a paradigm-shattering source like Ben Zion Dinur's. Instead, activating a circular route through *Las cítaras colgadas de los árboles*'s imagined liberalism in medieval Sepharad to parallel authoritarianism in sixteenth- and twentieth-century Spain, the play extends a pattern of political and artistic sephardism initiated in Madrid in the 1900s. Similarly entranced by the heights of medieval Iberian Jewish achievement, but ultimately less impressed by contemporary Sephardic descendants in Diaspora, the influential senator Ángel Pulido Fernández envisioned a cadre of Jewish cultural and commercial satellites for Spain in the wake of her final loss of empire in 1898. Once their abiding Spanish loyalties were stirred, Sephardic Jews from Morocco to the Balkans would form a restorative, pseudo-imperial network for promoting Spanish trade and international influence.

Since the mid-1990s, a number of high-profile Spanish and Madrid-based Sephardic historians have discussed Pulido's campaign as a pecuniary bid to co-opt Spanish Jewish capital, allegedly accumulated through stereotypical Semitic ingenuity. The scholars José Antonio Lisbona, Gonzalo Álvarez Chillida, and Jacobo Israel Garzón have all described Pulido's anthropological interest in contemporary Sephardic Jews as superficial,[64] as did a young Spanish writer with some Sephardic ancestry who answered Pulido's first call for literary and journalistic support in Madrid.[65] In his first meeting with the senator at his residence, Rafael Cansinos-Asséns was struck by how Pulido's public pro-Sephardic effusiveness contrasted with his air of superior detachment in private. At his home, Pulido resembled more of a strategist, "inclining over" maps and documents on a "great table" as if over Spanish territory that had expanded through Sephardic colonization.[66]

In his own encyclopedic manner, Pulido also categorized Sephardic correspondents in these outlying regions who were intrigued by his project of Castilian rapprochement. The compendia he presented to the Spanish government and public cited all of his Jewish candidates for cultural and economic association with Spain, from the undesirable to the promising. Since Pulido included letters and photographic images of those he discredited, his "unwanted" categories of Mediterranean Sephardim literally remained on his pages as specters, foreshadowing a similar outcome for the archivist himself. After visiting many Spanish Jewish communities and "fraternizing" with their representatives, Pulido's ascent up Madrid's political ladder was stopped. His name was removed from candidate lists for promotions he merited through experience, integrity, and dedication to Spanish nationalism.[67] In essence, through his association with Sephardic individuals, Pulido's character was dismissed by the same folkloric, anti-Semitic criteria for Spanish integration that impede Olalla's social future in Gala's 1974 drama.

Indeed, a flight of stairs obstructed at the top is an apt analogy for how, at the height of his philo-Sephardic appeal in Madrid, Pulido introduced his Jewish contacts to the Spanish parliament and to the public. They enter his persuasive texts in ascending categories of resemblance to contemporary Spaniards, stopping short of parity. Sephardic Jews who showed little interest in replacing their unruly, polyphonic Judeo-Spanish jargon with pure Castilian ranked low in terms of Spanish national interest, while those who favored widespread training in the modern Spanish language and mores enjoyed a higher standing as "hispanophiles."[68] Over half a century after Pulido's campaign to re-Hispanicize regional Sephardic Jews, Antonio Gala's drama also promotes a stratified Spanish-Jewish relationship. His conversa protagonist compares to Pulido in that the upward, redeeming trajectories of both are curtailed by their involvement with Sephardic Jews as specters in the Spanish imaginary.

In connection with Judah Halevi's philosophical work, *The Kuzari*, Ben Zion Dinur highlights a tension between a fated Jewish existence within a perpetual circuit of Diaspora hardships (*goral*), and a break-through teleological destiny (*yi'ud*).[69] This dichotomy characterizes both Yehuda Burla's and Antonio Gala's Janus-faced literary sephard-ism. Both authors look back at medieval Jewish Spain but are fixated on assumptions and generalities configuring their modern nationalist visions. Sephardic specificities are therefore destined to recede. Focused on national reconstitution after two thousand or forty years of torment, respectively, each author issues a public textual summons to *yi'ud*. Burla and Gala build teleological narratives that draw inspiration and frag-mented material from ancestral Jewish Spain. As Sephardist writers, they recast the pseudo-medieval as modern allegory, but then also let us see their respective nations in double profile: one face looking back at an alluring source of historical legitimation, and the other focused on a captivating future.

Eight Sephardic Identity and Its Discontents

The Novels of A. B. Yehoshua

Bernard Horn

> "'Doctor Starkmann?' Molkho asks a wide-eyed little boy, who is apparently all alone in the apartment, 'Doctor Starkmann?'"
>
> A. B. Yehoshua, *Five Seasons*

Sephardism, as defined in in this book, reveals how gentile and Jewish novelists have used the history of Spain's Jews to fashion modern national identities of such countries as England, Germany, Spain, Brazil, Mexico, and even India. Such an approach to the experience of Sephardic Jews demonstrates how nations in the process of self-definition have used or accessed this historical experience as a repertoire for interactions between nation-states and what they regard as Others: dramatic historical interactions that assume the form of tolerance, assimilation, inquisition, conversion, expulsion, and even annihilation. The idea of sephardism in the literary works surveyed is hence not only a matter of how Sephardic writers represent Sephardic characters or how particular characters are shaped by Sephardic circumstances in the traditional approach of psychological or sociological analyses. The crux here is not the fact of Sephardic identity, but rather the use of the idea of sephardism as a lens for examining ideological questions regarding the formation of modern nationalism. It is a methodology or perspective that includes the identity of non-Sephardim rather than limiting itself to the identity of Sephardic Jews themselves or the ways in which Sephardic identity feeds into overall Jewish identity.

To understand this critical approach to Sepharad as a methodological platform even in the work of authors who possess an actual Sephardic background like A. B. Yehoshua, it would perhaps help to imagine sephardism as an action rather than a noun or adjective: הוא מספרד or הוא מסופרד ("he sephardizes" or "is sepharded")—a process that takes us beyond this writer's very real Sephardic background and the many specifically

Sephardic characters in his works toward an analysis that illuminates the Sephardic elements in this writer's fictional works from a perspective that is both wider and more nuanced than those that have been undertaken so far.

The literary implications of ethnic identity would not matter much if Israeli literature were an "art for art's sake" sort of literature in which society is either irrelevant or viewed exclusively as an impediment to the full realization of an individual's potential. But the contrary is the case for Israeli literature, which began and for the most part continues to be an engaged literature, a literature of allegory and advocacy in which the vicissitudes of Jewish identity in the Diaspora and Israel play an important role. Nevertheless, the literary potential of the Sephardic experience in the stew of national identities that participate in the development of Israeli identity has not been fully explored, creatively or critically. Therefore, I would like to explore in a nuanced way the boundaries and implications of a twentieth-century national Jewish identity that formed itself, like the various eighteenth- and nineteenth-century nationalisms of which Jews were both participants and victims, against a variety of Others, non-Jews as well as a *doubled* Jewish Other—that is, not only the Ashkenazi diasporic past supposedly left behind in Europe, but also the Sephardi Other that Ashkenazi newcomers encountered when arriving in Tiberias, Safed, or Jerusalem, where a Sephardi Jewish majority existed from the end of the eighteenth century. Although authors and critics of Hebrew literature have certainly not been blind to the relevance of these elements in the construction of modern Hebrew culture, they have approached the Sephardic dimension of Hebrew literature mostly through the lens of a binary ethnic determinism rather than in the broader context of the sort of national, historical, and literary developments I explore in this essay.

Sephardic Identity and Beyond

Among all contemporary Israeli writers, no one seems better suited for a Sephardic-oriented analysis than A. B. Yehoshua. He is a fifth-generation Sephardic Israeli who grew up in Jerusalem, whose mother immigrated to Israel from Morocco as a young girl, and whose father, an Orientalist and folklorist, left many volumes of research on the Sephardic neighborhoods of his native Jerusalem. For the past twenty years, Yehoshua's ethnic background has therefore functioned as a fertile field for critical discussions of Sephardic elements in his work, and he himself has been forthcoming in trying to understand and explain his complex relationship to this Sephardic heritage.

Since the publication of *Mr. Mani* in 1990, critical commentaries on Sephardic elements in Yehoshua's work have passed through two main stages. The first stage contrasted the virtual absence of Sephardic elements in his early fiction with their gradual emergence as a secondary theme in *The Lover* (1977) and *A Late Divorce* (1982). Scholars at this stage began to wrestle with representations of Sephardic characters and history in *Five Seasons* (Hebrew *Molkho*; 1987) and *Mr. Mani* by concentrating either on the construction of Sephardic characters in these texts or by arguing that an allegedly Sephardic point of view is a key theme of the novel.

For example, in 1991, Gila Ramras-Rauch traced the emergence of Yehoshua's Sephardic roots from *The Lover* through *Five Seasons* to *Mr. Mani*, arguing that Yehoshua is "bemoaning the marginality of the Sephardic community in the early days of European Jewish settlement."[1] Shortly afterward, Muhammad Siddiq described *Mr. Mani* as a Sephardic challenge to an Ashkenazi Zionist "hegemonic master-narrative . . . historically credited for the creation of the state of Israel."[2] Arnold Band stated that this novel's organizing theme is "its obsession with Sephardic identity,"[3] while other critics made similar assessments regarding the centrality of its Sephardic perspective—Gershon Shaked observing that "the Sephardic theme . . . is essential here,"[4] and Alan Mintz calling *Mr. Mani* "a Sephardic novel par excellence."[5] Nancy Berg observed that although "clearly not an ode to Sephardic identity," this novel nevertheless calls "for a radical rewriting of the Zionist narrative" by positing "an alternate narrative."[6]

Among these studies, Arnold Band's and Gila Ramras-Rauch's are especially grounded in a key essay that Yehoshua wrote while he was working on *Mr. Mani*. This essay—which Yehoshua titled "In Search of the Lost Sephardic Time," and which he published in 1988 as the introduction to a posthumous collection of essays by his father—had a great impact on Yehoshua scholars because it marks the first time that this author addressed his ethnic identity in a deliberate and discursive manner. Yet as Band notes, the crucial revelation here is not the Sephardic background itself, which was already known, but rather Yehoshua's unusual attitude toward it; in particular, Yehoshua's elusive statement about "My Sephardism, which began to enter a drawer, not too small and surely not locked, but a definite drawer, that you open from time to time, but mostly it is closed."[7]

Although scholars during this first stage of Sephardic interest agreed on the centrality of Sephardic elements in Yehoshua's identity and fiction, there was little agreement about what this means. While Band, like other critics of a psychological bent, regards the Manis' idiosyncratic ideas as instances of internal and external self-deception, Muhammad Siddiq and others who interpret the Manis' ideas from a national historical perspective view their idiosyncrasies as a serious critique of modern Zionism.

The second stage in the analysis of Yehoshua's Sephardic dimension began to question the centrality of Sephardic identity in Yehoshua's ethos altogether, disputing the notion that even *Mr. Mani*, as Gilead Morahg puts it, "provides a counternarrative to prevailing versions of Zionist discourse by engaging Jewish history from a Sephardic point of view."[8] Yael Feldman spearheaded this position early on, when she noted that although Yehoshua "offers a view of Zionism from the unlikely perspective of Sephardic experience," he likewise "offers an unconventional analysis of Sephardism from the point of view of Zionist ideology."[9] In my own 1998 analysis of the novel as a meditation on the Shoah, the ethnic identity of the Manis is not at issue:[10] what matters rather is their ideas, which, as they accumulate over the course of the novel, make a case for a territorial identity that Yehoshua recently articulated in terms of clearly defined national "borders" as a pragmatic solution to the vulnerability of diasporic rootlessness.[11] Gilad Morahg, too, has shown how *Mr. Mani* shifts the parameters of the relationship between Diaspora and Zion to a discussion of "territorial and communal bounds."[12] For the three of us, the broader issues of Jewish and Israeli identity trump the narrower question of Sephardi-Ashkenazi relations in Yehoshua's work.

What I now wish to propose, though, might be called a third stage in the investigation of Sephardic elements in Yehoshua's fiction. This approach applies questions raised by scholars of sephardism from other national contexts to an analysis of Yehoshua's fiction and ethos, highlighting concepts of national identity as a process that develops in relation to some Other. For Yehoshua, this Other is not a separate, threatening entity to be pushed away: on the contrary, the Other is expected to participate in a positive and ongoing process of constructive dialogue.

While modern national Jewish identity in relation to various Others is the theme of this essay, its understated motifs are the ideas about assimilation, conversion, and fear of extermination that play themselves out in profound and textured ways in Yehoshua's novels. One general conclusion I can draw at this point is that in opposition to a national identity based on racial and religious homogeneity, Yehoshua insists on a Jewish nation based on historical experience and multiple heterodox identities coexisting side by side. Sephardism functions for him as a way of promoting and expanding sensitivities—enlarging the national conversation—but within clearly defined sovereign borders.

Approaching Yehoshua's work in terms of oppositions or countermoves is of course not a new perspective within Yehoshua studies; for example, scholars observed early on that Veducha, the Sephardi grandmother in *The Lover*, was born in Jerusalem in 1882, the same year that witnessed another birth—in Russia, that of BILU, the first modern Zionist movement.[13] Indeed, the main collection of essays on *Mr. Mani* is titled *Bekivun hanegdi* (In the Opposite Direction), thus drawing full attention to the idea of countermoves as an organizational and ideological pattern in Yehoshua's masterpiece.[14] During the heady days of the mid-1990s, when the Oslo Accords seemed to carry the promise of a peace settlement between Israelis and Palestinians, Yehoshua even re-envisioned the main pillars of Israeli identity—war, immigration, and settlement—as counteridentities rooted in conflict and imperiled by peace.[15] What I wish to question, however, is whether these countermoves, which occur so prominently in Yehoshua's ethos, are simple polarities, or whether they function according to a multivalanced perspective that seeks to refine our understanding of personal and national identity.

I argue that Yehoshua's sephardism—his *supposed* position from the sidelines of Israeli culture, *his* supposed Otherness—functions primarily as a vehicle for transcending and bypassing *any* narrow ethnic allegiances (including Sephardic identity itself) in favor of a universal notion of morality that offers—and at the same time also demands—total empathy *for* and *from* the Other. The most obvious expression of this pattern occurs in *A Journey to the End of the Millennium* (1998), where Ben Attar—the proto-Sephardic protagonist who hails from Tangier in the year 999 CE, before the Sephardic diaspora was properly known as such—seems to be arguing in favor of serious multiplicity (in this case simplified down to a multiplicity of wives), while the Ashkenazi woman whom Ben Attar's nephew marries feels so threatened by this that she dissolves the business partnership between the uncle and her husband. By the end of the novel, however, an enlarged sense of sexual and social morality envelops all the principal characters, freeing them from the narrow sociological allegiances that initially determined their ideas of proper family relations. Yehoshua enlarges this sense of morality in a swerve in perspective so typical of his literary technique, in which the definitive spokesperson for this wider view turns out to be none other than the same Ashkenazi wife who seems so prudish and narrow minded when we encounter her in a first cursory reading of the novel.[16]

Sephardism, Cosmopolitanism, and *Mr. Mani*

Yehoshua's valorization of heterogeneity and multiplicity, which perhaps at some level derives from his own Sephardic heritage, resonates with the cosmopolitanism that Kwame Anthony Appiah has explained in terms of ongoing ethical conversation across boundaries of identity in a world full of strangers.[17] Such conversations, explains Appiah,

> begin with the sort of imaginative engagement you get when you read a novel or watch a movie or attend to a work of art that speaks from some place other than your own. So I'm using the word "conversation" here not only for literal talk but also as a metaphor for engagement with the experience and the ideas of others. And I stress the role of the imagination here because the encounters, properly conducted, are valuable in themselves. Conversation doesn't have to lead to consensus about anything, especially not values; it's enough that it helps people get used to one another.[18]

This statement by Appiah serves as an apt introduction to a closer examination of *Mr. Mani*—a quintessential novel of conversations—as the "Sephardist novel to end all Sephardist novels."[19]

To get at exactly what this claim means requires revisiting the first stage of criticism of this novel's Sephardic dimension, especially the positions taken by Arnold Band and Gila Ramras-Rauch. Whereas Band approaches Yehoshua's Sephardic identity from an almost essentialist point of view, Ramras-Rauch retraces Israeli literary history to include Yehoshua among "hitherto unacknowledged Sephardic literary forefathers,"[20] notably Yehuda Burla and Yitzhak Shami, before suggesting some political implications that emerge from positioning *Mr. Mani* within such a Sephardic constellation: "The Sephardic point of view, reflected in this fictional chronicle, points to a close proximity and amity between Arabs and Jews; it also points to the use of both the romantic and the political elements suggested by the more moderate thinkers among Jews."[21]

Band, by contrast, adopts a psychological approach to the relationship between Yehoshua's Sephardic identity and his creative work, singling out three main parameters: "Yehoshua's relationship to his father; his attitude to his Sephardism; and the types of fictions he produces. The ambivalences of the first and second inform the multivalences and polyphonies of the third."[22] Though Band argues that, ideologically, the novel offers "Sephardic Zionism" as a constructive alternative to the Ashkenazic variety, he at the same time points to the novel's critique of the dynastic notion of a "Sephardi Tahor"—a mythological "pure" Sephardic identity—which, according to Band, is so relentlessly undermined in this novel that it becomes paradigmatic of all the "self-deception" that, to Band, lies at *Mr. Mani*'s core.[23]

A case in point for Band is the second Joseph Mani, who Band argues "became a self-styled 'homo-politicus' as a result of his fear of sexuality and neglect by his father"[24]—so that the character's psychological condition obviates any discussion of his actual ideas as a contextualized historical choice, freely made. Succumbing to a newfangled version of the genetic fallacy, Band claims that Joseph Mani's "political theorizing is clearly portrayed by the author as a warped compensation for deep-seated psychological problems,"[25] in a way that is then generalized for all the Manis and their conversation partners: "Just as individuals often do not understand themselves and the motives for their behavior in personal relationships, they fashion group-identifications (Sephardism, Zionism, Pacifism, Universalism, Nazism, Religion) which, they delude themselves to believe, will solve their problems."[26]

Though Ramras-Rauch emphasizes matters of literary history, she too stresses the Manis' psychological tribulations, characterizing them as "idiosyncratic individuals in extreme reaction to their environment," who "maintain very strange relations to reality."[27] Indeed, most critics have adopted this approach to the Manis. Ted Solotaroff defines them as a "bizarrely fated family," from the first "unhinged" Joseph Mani onward.[28] For Robert Alter, ideology and Sephardic identity are secondary matters in a novel whose "real subject . . . is incest" by Manis inclined "to make politics a vehicle of self-destruction under another name."[29] The problem with this emphasis on the psychological problems of this strange, bizarre, unhinged, incestuous, and self-destructive family, however, is that it subverts a reader's desire to take the ideas of the Manis seriously; although these scholars cannot erase the Manis' ideas, for they keep bubbling to the surface of even the most psychologically oriented arguments, the ideas themselves have been pushed aside in favor of an analysis of the characters that espouse them.

To take the Manis' ideas seriously, on the other hand, entails reading the novel politically in relation to the statements that Yehoshua has issued over the years. Contemporary critics are of course not so naïve as to hang their arguments on an author's assessment of his purposes, yet neither can we blind ourselves to significant parallels between Yehoshua's positions and those of several Manis, including even Efrayim Mani's radical belief that Jewish identity is entirely a matter of choice that cannot to be determined by birth or society. Discussing the Holocaust in respect to Efrayim Mani, Yehoshua once told me that

> I wanted to oppose with all my heart the conception that you *cannot* run away from your Jewish fate, that Hitler decides who is a Jew and who is not a Jew because he . . . has the power to put me in the concentration camp, so he decides if I am a Jew or if I am not a Jew [?]. . . . I cannot bear this idea . . . and I wanted to oppose it . . . the Jew is always free to choose his Jewishness. Even in the Holocaust. If a Jew says I am not a Jew . . . he is not a Jew. And the fact that Hitler killed him did not make him a Jew. I respect *his* will and not Hitler's.[30]

The political ideas of the second Joseph Mani, as Gilead Morahg has argued convincingly, are also close to Yehoshua's own: not a rigid ideological position, but rather a flexible perspective that takes changing historical circumstances into account.[31] Therefore, to say, as Mintz does, that the Sephardic Manis have an idée fixe in contrast to the pragmatism of Ashkenazi Zionists, is to allow the retrospective cunning of history to triumph.[32] For what, as Yehoshua has tirelessly pointed out, has been more of an idée fixe than modern Zionism itself, which, when it was proposed, challenged all existing Jewish establishments, both secular and religious?[33] And, within the novel itself, the Manis' ideologies differ so radically from one another that, at the climax in the final conversation, the pragmatic complicity of Avraham Mani in the killing of his own son—an expression of Avraham Mani's own problematic convictions about Jewish identity—ensures that his son's convictions, which adulterate nationality and religion, would never become a pragmatic option.

An ethnocentric interpretation of *Mr. Mani* as proposed by Arnold Band, Gila Ramras-Rauch, and others—even if admitting that this novel's Sephardic dimension is unconventional and oppositional—still organizes its ideological components according to a simplified version of Yehoshua's ideology. In truth, there is no Sephardic point of view, no Sephardic ideology or even Sephardic anti-ideology in this novel. Instead there are multiple ethnic, political, and idiosyncratic ideologies in dialogue with one another, with each Mani proposing an identity and behavior that is not only a countermove to collective historical choices made by the Jewish people, but also—and this point is essential—a countermove to the visions of all the other Manis. Although Sephardi characters present these countermoves, their positions are not Sephardi per se: they are rather versions of Jewish identity that are not compatible one with another.

For what does the first Joseph Mani's Canaanite ideology have in common with his father's obsession with religion and seed; or with the first Efrayim Mani's insistence on Jewish identity as a personal choice that is consequently cancelable at will (the idea that Yehoshua defended to me so vehemently)? And what do any of these views share with Dr. Moses Mani's universalism; Judge Gabriel Mani's apolitical and nonreligious—if suicidal—normality; or the second Joseph Mani's politicized reaction to the changing historical realities of his life (the position closest to Yehoshua's own)? And, furthermore, what do all these Manian countermoves have in common with the teenage Israeli identity of Hagar Shiloh; or her mother's rigid kibbutznik synthesis of

Marx and Freud; or Efrayim Shapiro's and Ivor Horowitz's diasporic ambivalences; not to mention the ambivalences of the Nazi soldier Egon Brunner?

No uniform psychological motivation or sociological determinism binds the Manis or the novel's five conversations together; multiplicity and heterogeneity take over. Under these extreme conditions of ideological variability, the challenge for a reader is to find some sort of coherence within the tangle of ideas. But although Yehoshua may have posed "a grand riddle,"[34] he is not the sort of writer who relishes confusion; on the contrary, though he challenges readers to become more alert to nuance and indirection, he is eager to solve puzzles and answer riddles according to his interpretation of reality. Thus, if any homogeneity exists in Mr. Mani, it takes the abstract form of a grand seminar discussion between all the Manis, as well as those who speak and listen to the stories about them, all sitting together at a table abuzz in conversation:

> The most important thing to me . . . is to imagine Hagar Shiloh sitting right next to Rabbi Hananiah Haddaya, and it was very important to me to show the relationship even between this kibbutznik kid, Ashkenazi, sitting in the kibbutz in the desert in 1982, and this old Sephardic rabbi, sitting in Athens in the nineteenth century. They are related and I wanted to present this relationship."[35]

Related to them in this indirect conversational manner are also the Nazi soldier Egon Bruner and the British Colonel Michael Woodhouse, the gentile who becomes the only conversation partner to completely accept the arguments of his interlocutor, Lieutenant Ivor Horowitz, the diasporic Jewish lawyer stationed in Jerusalem with the British army. We begin to understand from this perspective that the "Canaanite" ideas of the first Joseph Mani open up a new type of conversation between Ishmaelite and "Isaackite," a conversation that symbolically deepens through the names of the speakers of the first and last conversations, Hagar and Abraham, the mother and father of the Biblical Ishmael.[36] Against static notions of identity, Yehoshua pits a heterogeneous and expansive conversation, what Appiah calls a "cosmopolitanism" that transcends conventional boundaries of ethnicity, religion, gender, and nationality.

In short, Yehoshua's Sephardist perspective—as opposed to a Sephardic perspective—is truly cosmopolitan in a dialogic sense, for it creates an interface rather than an opposition or confrontation between Sephardim, Ashkenazim, and non-Jews as well. Neither is Ashkenazi Zionism a homogeneous ideology in Yehoshua's eyes; it is only a useful "medicine for a certain Jewish disease called Diaspora"—medicine that for him boils down to a question of "borders" and "sovereignty."[37] Thus, Morahg's assessment of the second Joseph Mani—the Sephardic *homo politicus*—applies to his creator also, in the sense that each seeks "a practical wisdom derived from careful attentiveness to the multifaceted political realities of his time and distilled from the views resonating in the diverse communities that share his space."[38]

A pragmatic attentiveness to history—which Yehoshua contrasts with mythology—is no secondary matter for him.[39] For instance, in the 1990s, when a settlement between Israelis and Palestinians seemed possible, he reconsidered his well-known valorization of Israeli Zionism at the expense of Diaspora Jewishness, proposing that Israeli identity enter into a more creative dialogue with the Jewish Diaspora.[40] More recently, he expressed hope that "Diaspora Jewish culture . . . could also attempt to dissolve the trap of mythical thinking and identity to which Jews are attracted, and try to exchange it for historic thinking, which always sees the other person and believes in change."[41]

But if Yehoshua's Sephardic Manis and the Ashkenazi and gentile characters "related" to them are all different aspects of an ideal cosmopolitan conversation, then why choose Sephardim as the central characters in *Mr. Mani* since their ideas are not Sephardic in themselves and far from representative of the historical Sephardic communities in Jerusalem or Salonika? Perhaps because their Sephardic component, presented largely from the point of view of their non-Sephardic interlocutors, affords them an exotic status that makes them more plausible as carriers of unusual and even radical ideas. Their sephardism thus functions as a vehicle or outlook that affords the opportunity to reexamine historical identity from an expansive, cosmopolitan, and heterogeneous moral standard that transcends any narrow sense of sociological identification and is hence universal rather than ethnic. The ethnic dimension is just a means for promoting a wider conversation between normative and idiosyncratic ideologies that come from a multiplicity of sociohistorical backgrounds—whether Sephardi and Ashkenazi, Jewish and Gentile, male and female, aging and young, and so on.

If we nonetheless insist in defining Yehoshua as a Sephardic author, and locating a Sephardic ideology within his works, then we must investigate how this identity plays itself out across his works, not only those that exhibit an obvious Sephardic component such as *Mr. Mani* and *Five Seasons*, but also novels like *Friendly Fire*, which do not display any obvious Sephardic markers yet are nonetheless a product of the "Sephardic" novelist A. B. Yehoshua as much as his most deliberately "Sephardic" texts.[42]

First of all, Yehoshua has been interested in redefining Israel as more of a Mediterranean than a Middle Eastern nation. A propos of sephardism in a recent lecture in Spain on the identity of Sephardic Jews, Yehoshua asks, "What are the characteristics of Mediterranean identity?" and answers as follows:

> Since the Mediterranean Sea is a closed circle, it incorporates into one group all the countries and peoples living on its shores. As an inland sea, it is quite homogenous, in that its gulfs and coastlines are all quite similar. And therefore, despite the cultural pluralism, the ethnic, religious, and historical differences among the peoples living here, there is a unifying geographic matrix. The traveler from Beirut, or Antalya in Turkey, to the beaches of Greece or Sicily will not feel a great dissimilarity, despite wide differences in the religion, ethnicity, and history of the populations. Despite the enormous difference, for example, between Jewish religious civilization and the pagan civilization of Greece and Rome, they share a unifying physical landscape.[43]

Such a cultural geographic identification is again consonant with Kwame Appiah's call for "conversations across boundaries of identity," to which I referred earlier.[44] In Appiah's formulation,

> the points of entry to cross-cultural conversations are things that are shared by those who are in the conversation. They do not need to be universal; all they need to be is what these particular people have in common. . . . We can learn from each other; or we can simply be intrigued by alternative ways of thinking, feeling, and acting.[45]

A Sephardist interpretation of Yehoshua's ethos becomes an invitation, according to Appiah's formulations, "to get used to" one another, "be intrigued by" one another, and best of all, "learn from" one another. Yet for Yehoshua, cross-cultural learning is not the end of the story, but just the beginning of a path toward shared commitments to universal ethical values. His most incisive probe into the limits of any ethnic, religious, or psychological perspective occurs within a crucial conversation in *Friendly Fire*, a novel that, as mentioned, has no overt Sephardic elements at all.

Friendly Fire and the Limits of Empathy

The conversation in question, which is both the dramatic seed and the thematic core of *Friendly Fire*, takes place on a rooftop in Tulkarm in the West Bank, between Yirmi, the bereaved father of an Israeli soldier, and a pregnant Palestinian woman who studied at the Israeli Ruppin College until the Second Intifada erupted. Yirmi's son, Eyal, has been killed by "friendly" fire on the roof of this woman's house. After an all-night lookout for terrorists, he had slipped out to rinse a bucket that he had requested from one of the resident families to use as a chamber pot during the night. As he returns to the building, his comrades mistake him for a terrorist and shoot him. Eyal's death devastates his parents. His mother's sexual identity is completely shattered—she herself dies shortly afterward—while Yirmi becomes "shackled by the attempt to find meaning in the fire that killed his son."[46]

The conversation in which Yirmi learns some of the details surrounding his son's death is not relayed to the reader directly, but is narrated six years later by Yirmi (who by now has moved to Africa), to Daniela, his sister-in-law, when she visits him there. Indeed, as Daniela discovers, Yirmi is still reeling from this conversation with the Palestinian woman. Driven by a desire to find meaning in an accident that seems "no more than a random stupid absurdity" to others (360), he twice risks his life to visit the exact site of his son's death. Yet, as he later explains to Daniela, he fully understood his motive only when he confronted the Palestinian woman during the second visit:

> "I had this revelation, that it was in fact she who had drawn me to risk my life and return back here. Yes, it was her sympathy I was looking for. I wanted to hear from a well-educated young woman, in her gentle

> Hebrew, that even if, like the others, she sees us as enemies, she is still capable of sympathy for a naïve and stupid soldier, who risked his life so as not to leave filth for his enemies." (328)

The bereaved father cannot be content with just a superficial exchange in which he and this young woman merely get used to, are intrigued by, or even learn from one another. What he wants is sympathy—and sympathy, or the lack of it, becomes the crux of this novel—because for Yehoshua, morality based on sympathy is the highest form of morality.

In *The Terrible Power of a Minor Guilt*, a probing experiment in literary analysis from a moral point of view, Yehoshua distinguishes between moral behavior activated by guilt and duty and moral behavior that stems from identification and sympathy:

> The moral act that stems from guilt might be fine, but in the final analysis, because it aims at satisfying the needs of the giver rather than those of the receiver, the thread of its duration is short. Activity that stems from sympathy, that takes on the other as if he or she were a member of the giver's family, might be unruly and undisciplined, but in the end, the thread of its duration is longer and stronger, and its moral definition is also truer.[47]

This is not the moral or ideological behavior of a particular ethnicity, or any other narrow form of identity politics, but rather a position that approaches an absolute standard of universal ethics, though on the surface, what could be more inimical to an ethnic perspective than the idea of universal values?

Yehoshua's formulation of this principle bears a powerful affinity with the thinking of Martin Buber, an affinity Gilead Morahg identified as early as 1979.[48] In his well-known essay on "Distance and Relation," Buber writes that "The basis of man's life with man is twofold, and it is one—the wish of every man to be confirmed as what he is, even as what he can become, by men; and the innate capacity in man to confirm his fellow men in this way."[49] This principle leads Buber to the definition of authentic or "genuine" conversation: "Genuine conversation, and therefore every actual fulfillment of relation between men, means acceptance of otherness."[50]

According to these terms, the conversation on the roof was anything but "genuine." For Yirmi, his son "was a soldier who was ready to disobey explicit orders so he could say, I too am a human being, and I am giving you back a clean pail, I may have conquered you, but I did not contaminate you" (289). Under these particular circumstances, "indifference over his simple human gesture was unacceptable" (320). Yet the woman's response is deliberately unsympathetic:

> What do you want from me? That I'll offer you compassion for your soldier? Why should I feel sorry for a soldier who invades a space that does not belong to him, and doesn't care about us, who we are and what we are. Who takes over a family's roof in order to kill one of us, and thinks that if he does us a favor and leaves us a clean bucket, washing away the evidence of his fear, we'll forgive him for the insult and humiliation. But how can we forgive? Can we be bought with a clean bucket?" (329)

She sees only the context, her political and historical reality. Yirmi, like Antigone, sees, or at least believes he sees, the individual and the universal. She understands Eyal but refuses to confirm him "as what he is, even as what he can become," and Yirmi understands her, but cannot justify her perspective, because to confirm is to deny himself the consolation of finding some positive meaning in the end of his son. Instead, she deliberately disregards the terrorist attacks that brought Eyal to a stakeout on her rooftop in the first place, insisting only on the "clarity and logic" of her own ethnic perspective (329).

Yirmi's eventual response is to detach himself from any sense of collective identity, both Jewish and Israeli—"to wipe away," as his sister-in-law puts it, "his whole biography and identity and the world he grew up in, and the history that has been and the history that will be" (360). But, by extending this withdrawal to his wife as well, Yirmi commits an even greater moral failure—and this is the moral nub of the novel. Although Yehoshua, as is his practice, provides rich psychological texture for Yirmi's alienation from his wife (who dies soon afterward), neither the general narrator nor Daniela let him off the hook from a universal moral standpoint. From a moral point of view, Yirmi's failure is absolute, as emerges from Daniela's final judgment of his failed responsibility toward the woman who had been a living wife:

> Because even if Shuli suppressed her womanliness after the death of her son, his duty was to fight for it. . . . His duty was to fight for Shuli,

> for her sexuality and her desire. To console her instead of helping her extinguish herself. So she could live and not die. (360)

That is, whatever the psychological repercussions of his son's death and his wife's suffering, Yirmi has the moral responsibility, and the moral freedom, to act responsibly toward the woman who had been his beloved through their long life together, to fight for her so that *she* could live and not die. "Instead of hiding his wretched obsession with that roof from her sister, and instead of humiliating himself, and indirectly her too, in a fruitless attempt to win sympathy from a suicidal pregnant young woman just to give meaning to the friendly fire," Daniela tells him, "his obligation" was to Shuli and their bond. His destruction of their intimate relationship is his greatest moral failure, whatever the context or his private suffering (360).

This episode is one more instance in Yehoshua's work where a narrow psychological or sociological context stands in opposition to universal moral accountability. As I noted elsewhere, "In Yehoshua's novels, psychology is always at the service of morality," a principle that Yehoshua has expressed in many ways over the years.[51] "Modern literature is mostly too subservient to psychology," he wrote in 1998 in *The Terrible Power of a Minor Guilt*.[52] Seven years later, he explained to Donald Macintyre, "The clear straight moral judgment—'Is it right to do it?' This was lost a little bit by too much psychology. I don't always succeed but I myself try to bring morality more to the front stage of my writing."[53]

This belief in the importance of an individual's moral responsibility does not cancel an individual's human freedom. On the contrary, the one entails the other—which brings us back to my earlier observations about Efrayim Mani's insistence on his right to freely choose an identity in Mr. Mani's second conversation, and the passion with which Yehoshua defended Efrayim Mani's position to me—a countermove in which Jewish identity, and hence Jewish history, is understood as a matter of choice. This commitment to the right to choose an identity has been a permanent pillar of Yehoshua's thought. "A Jew is someone who identifies as a Jew," he wrote in his 2004 reflection on the last words of Daniel Pearl. "The determining factor is the act of identification, free will, and not the formal conversion." And he adds: "This element of freedom in the act of Jewish identification has of late been obscured, but it is an element of tremendous importance, for it brings with it responsibility. If I identify as a matter of free choice I assume certain responsibilities."[54]

Beyond Efrayim Mani's declaration of identity in the face of the Nazi onslaught, Yehoshua invites his reader to ascribe and demand moral choices from all his characters, because their behavior is weighed between the poles of psychology and morality, cause and motive, understanding and judgment. Thus, although Ephraim Mani finds himself in a desperate historical situation, he remains, after all, the most mentally stable of the lot! This then leads us back to a restatement of the question we asked earlier: How can the ideas of such an extreme, strange, bizarre, unhinged, incestuous, murderous, and self-destructive set of individuals be a deliberate product of their free wills? Are they, in Band's words, nothing more than a pack of "posturers, imposters, or self-deceivers"?[55] And is *Mr. Mani*'s final vision, as Anne Golomb Hoffman observes, one in which "beings are seen to be the creatures of their instincts, lacking control over their lives, despite all their efforts at control, narrative and otherwise"?[56]

The answer to these questions involves a small change in our critical perspective, a shift in our assessment of the connection between the Manis' psychological makeup and their radical ideas: Rather than accepting the conjecture that their psychological background necessarily determines their ideas, we must consider the alternative hypothesis that they *choose* their ideas despite their psychological background, or, to go a step further, that their idiosyncratic psychological dynamics—reinforced by their sociological status as Sephardim—liberate them enough from social convention to enable them—when confronted with a multicultural environment—to be intellectually and morally daring. In the case of the second Joseph Mani, for example, it is not, as Band argues, that Joseph's "political theorizing is clearly portrayed by the author as a warped compensation for deep-seated psychological problems,"[57] but rather that these deep-seated psychological "problems" engender a mind of such unconventional intellectual flexibility that it enables him to fashion, as Morahg argues, a creative response to the challenges of mutable historical circumstances.[58]

Perhaps the best test case for this interpretation of the Manis' ability to transcend their immediate psychological and sociological contexts is the behavior and narration of Avraham Mani, the only Mani who narrates his story directly. Though he is alive in 1848, he lives profoundly within the depths of a medieval Jewish and even biblical imagination in which the propagation of his seed is of paramount importance. Yehoshua represents him as living under the spell of a foundational myth—the myth of the *akeda* (the binding of Isaac)—yet caught at the same time in a personal psychological morass, confused by growing ambivalence toward his beloved Rabbi Hananiah, who married Doña Flora, the woman whom Avraham still desires. But Doña Flora is replicated in her niece, Tamara, the wife of Avraham's son, whose marriage is consummated posthumously by Avraham himself as he plants the seed that his murdered son had failed to deliver. Whether we approach Avraham's story as a psychoanalytical case history or as an intertextual dialogue with the biblical *akeda*, does any character seem less a candidate for the free exercise of his will than Avraham Mani?

And yet when viewed from the perspectives of his commitment to Judaism as a tribe and religion, Avraham Mani emerges in his narration as a daring, if guilt-ridden, individual willing to commit incest and even filicide in order—in Yehoshua's words—"to cancel the *akeda* by means of its realization."[59] In plain words, as Ted Solotaroff explains it: "Behind the deadly antics of these folies à deux that gives the novel much of its pace and spin lies a thesis: namely, that the Manis, like the Jews of Yehoshua's polemical essays, are responsible for their own fate."[60]

Ultimately, then, what Yehoshua offers is a strong and to some extent old-fashioned commitment, both in life and art, to universal moral values of individual responsibility and freedom of choice rooted in the capacity of all humans to sympathize and identify with one another. Yehoshua would extend Appiah's list of cross-cultural possibilities to an absolute and Buberian requirement: not only to get used to, but also to learn from; not only to learn from, but also to be intrigued by; not only to be intrigued by, but finally to confirm one another in genuine conversation, suffused with identification and sympathy.

It is worth reminding ourselves how often a belief in some universal moral standard can disguise or become a vehicle for tyranny that runs counter to the openness inherent in what we have been outlining here as Yehoshua's special trans-Sephardist or cosmopolitan approach to human interactions. His notion of universal morality entails a dialogic heterogeneity that counters any idea of nation based on racial or religious homogeneity. As Martin Buber put it, "Human life and humanity come into being in genuine meetings":

> There man learns not merely that he is limited by man, cast upon his own finitude, partialness, need of completion, but his own relation to truth is heightened by the other's different relation to the same truth—different in accordance with his individuation, and destined to take seed and grow differently. Men need, and it is granted to them, to confirm one another in their individual being by means of genuine meetings.[61]

The Boundless Empathy of Molkho

For most readers, Yehoshua's third novel, *Five Seasons*, seems to be his least ideological; nonetheless, it dramatizes the most radical countermove in the wrestling between Sephardi and Ashkenazi identity. Yehoshua has acknowledged that there is a symbolic element in the fact that its protagonist, Molkho, is Sephardic and not Ashkenazi, but he insists on the genesis of this novel in terms of a deliberate turn away from collective ideology to personal psychology. Having begun *Mr. Mani* but finding himself at an impasse with its enormous cultural and historical reach, he embarked on *Five Seasons* as a respite from the conflicts that take up so much of Israeli cultural life: "I picked a very personal subject," he told me, "a very intimate question of what happens to a man of fifty after the death of his wife. I tried to penetrate in the slowest and most detailed way his movement after her death."[62] Three years after the publication of the novel, he still felt the relief of having been able to say to himself, "I stop history. I'm not concerned with ideology. There is nothing political in it." He even mocked the critics who insisted on finding allegorical implications in this novel: "When I published it, immediately there were articles saying this is a symbol of this, this is a symbol of that, and I could not escape."[63]

What this suggests is that Yehoshua's conception upon embarking on this novel, at least in retrospect, was to subsume any collective ideological elements under the character's personal circumstances, so that, for example, the function of Molkho's *sepharadut*, his Sephardic identity, would be simply to give a special texture to his relationship with his assertive and beloved Ashkenazi wife. That this was Yehoshua's main preoccupation is implicit in a further exchange I had with him over the issue of Molkho's identity:

> "Molkho," I said, "wears his Israeli identity comfortably, like an old shoe."
>
> He approved of my analogy. "You put it very well—he wears his Israeli identity 'like an old shoe,' yes, like an ancient shoe," he added, laughing. "He has the most Israeli identity, the most comfortable, the simplest. He does not have to think about it; it comes from inside him."[64]

At stake for Yehoshua here is a distinction between a deliberately constructed *idea* of identity and a seemingly unmediated, "natural," unproblematic sense of identity. (And notice that Yehoshua emphasizes Israeli-ness rather than any form of Sephardic identity.) But nonetheless, it is no accident that it is a Sephardi character, not an Ashkenazi, who wears his Israeli identity "like an ancient shoe." Indeed, as Yehoshua immediately reminded me, "you shouldn't forget entirely that in *Five Seasons* it's also a question of East and West, Sephardi and Ashkenazi, the Arab countries and Europe."[65] This ideological, symbolic, and even allegorical dimension to Molkho's quest lies behind Yehoshua's passionate comparison of *Five Seasons* (*Molkho* in Hebrew) with *Mr. Mani*.[66]

> "Of course," he said, "*Molkho* is the anti-*Mani*, the total anti-*Mani*. No two books are so opposed to each other, by the characters, by the way they are structured. *Five Seasons* is a narrative, slow, present, ironic, without any of those dialogues, prologues, and epilogues, not historical, very limited in time and space. Nonetheless, the two novels are very much linked together. Elements that are not in *Five Seasons* are in *Mani*, and elements that are not in *Mani* are in *Five Seasons*."[67]

Yet even if we approach *Five Seasons* symbolically or allegorically, we still find that Molkho's relationship with his wife speaks to moral issues that are far more important to Yehoshua than ethnicity. "You killed her" recurs as a crucial refrain in this novel. At first this accusation of Molkho seems to indicate merely that he feels guilty and forlorn after his wife's death from a long fight with cancer. Yet on closer analysis it becomes evident that Molkho enjoyed taking care of his dying wife—in other words, that he would have liked to prolong her illness, so that he could continue to find a sense of identity in his devoted care for her, so that, if he had had his way, he would have gone on "killing her" forever. To explain this better, I would draw an analogy to Yehoshua's story "Early in the Summer of 1970." In that story it seems, at first, that the old Bible teacher reminisces about the moment he received news of his son's death because he is so grief-stricken by this news; yet it gradually becomes clear that he actually enjoys thinking about this moment because it was then that his life acquired more glorious meaning. What we have here is an obsession triggered by powerful moral ambivalence. "Am I good? Am I evil forever?" the old teacher might be asking himself. In *Five Seasons* Molkho's deepest desire is that his wife should go on dying so that he may continue to care for her, and elicit sympathy for doing so.

If we slip into simple allegory there could be danger of suggesting that the "dying" Ashkenazi culture that is European Zionism is nourishing and giving meaning to Molkho's life; for after all, his wife certainly embodies an Ashkenazi stereotype, clichés and all. But although Molkho certainly starts off as an outsider to his wife's Ashkenazi culture, which is indeed portrayed here as the normative one, after her death he launches into an "unconscious dialogue with his wife, in which he swallows her into himself."[68] But even this "swallowing" is actually multidimensional because, first of all, during his wife's lifetime, Molkho had assimilated, and even converted, we might say, into mainstream Ashkenazi Zionist culture, and so his "unconscious dialogue" with his wife after her death is a countermove. Yet even at the height of his allegiance to her, his assimilation appears as a comic sort of conversion: his looks are decidedly Sephardic, though he lives like a normative Ashkenazi Zionist while functioning, according to Yehoshua, as a passive, "mediocre" Sephardi.[69]

Nevertheless, the most revealing and powerful moment in this novel is also perhaps Yehoshua's most audacious invention along the Sephardic-Ashkenazi fault line: the most radical power shift of all. At the novel's climax—in the return of autumn, the season of his wife's death—Molkho travels to Berlin, the city of her birth and the city of her father's suicide, from which she had been driven by the Nazis as a child, and which she had refused to visit during her adulthood. Deeply ambivalent about his attraction to this city, he is nonetheless drawn toward what he imagines to be the house of her birth. Boundaries now dissolve, and this simple, solid, mediocre man almost dissolves into madness himself. On a psychological level "He loved his wife to such an extent that he wanted also to heal her wounds, the source of her cancer, that came in Germany. So he returns to the city of her birth and tries metaphorically to return her to the place from which she was brutally thrown away."[70] He even figuratively enters into her cancer, as he ascends in an elevator described as a "malignant cell."[71] But on an ideological level what we have is a Sephardic Jew undoing, if only in his imagination, the great traumatic destruction of Ashkenazi civilization, the Shoah itself.

This way of reading the end of *Five Seasons* complicates, reverses even, conventional interpretations of assimilation, in terms of power. Who is the Self here and who is the Other? Who is being assimilated into whom? Whereas, earlier, Molkho had been assimilated into the majority culture signified by his wife, here *he* is the one doing the assimilating. He redeems this other culture—if only in a fantastic flight of the imagination. In a liminal moment in which fifty years of time collapse, as he reverses not only the annihilation of his wife's father, but also, figuratively, the death of his wife: "'Doctor Starkmann?' Molkho asks a wide-eyed little boy, who is apparently all alone in the apartment, 'Doctor Starkmann?'"[72] For one mad moment, Starkmann, Molkho's father-in-law, is still a young doctor, untouched by horror—his life in Germany pristinely ahead of him, as is Molkho's now: a half-mad hero finally coming to possess his own life.

Imagine Molkho, not as a stand-in for either a conventional Sephardic identity or a "normal" post-1948 Israeli identity, but rather as the incarnation of a truly dialogic, empathetic approach to human identity that transcends any narrow position of identity politics—including, paradoxically, Sephardic identity, to say nothing of the infernal identities of those who have historically wished to assimilate, convert, expel, or annihilate Others: a Molkho vaccine or antidote against the cultural conflicts that have afflicted the world so demonically over the course of so many centuries.

Part IV *Postmodern Reimaginings of Sepharad in Francophone, Latina, and Other Transnational Literatures*

Nine "Le Juif Espagnol"

The Idea of Sepharad among Colonial and Postcolonial Francophone Jewish Writers

Judith Roumani

"Je suis le juif espagnol," I am the Spanish Jew, sings Enrico Macias, the popular French singer. Born in Algeria, where he began his musical career, "Enrico" (his real name being Gaston Ghrenassia) has lived in France since 1961. So in what sense is he Spanish?

This song actually expresses his identification with the "oppressed of the earth" as a universal phenomenon. Nevertheless, Enrico would surely maintain that the identity of the Spanish Jew is his own, for he considers himself Sephardic and possibly descended from Jews who left Spain in 1492. Thus the oppression, discrimination, and exile he sings of are historical facts, not just a sympathetic leap of the imagination. However, these hardships would have been inflicted on his ancestors five hundred years ago, rather than on Macias himself or even the immediate generations preceding him. A leap of the imagination to feel like a Spanish Jew is still required, not horizontally across cultures (as when, for example, enlightened Europeans identified with the plight of the colonized) but vertically, down into history.

While the generation of the Jews of 1492 and their immediate descendants undoubtedly suffered in their experiences of expulsion and exile—to the extent that some argue that the messianic Sabbatean movement grew out of their desperation and disorientation—later generations of Sephardim living in North Africa and the Ottoman Empire frequently became comfortable in their new homes, even with the *dhimmi* status accorded them by sharia law, and even under European colonialism. Moreover, many identifying themselves as Sephardim did not actually originate from Spain, though they were part of the same cultural universe. Could it be that the upheavals associated with the *end* of colonialism paradoxically renewed insecurity—despite the lapsing of their inferior status—for all Jews in Muslim lands? At the same time, could the birth of new nations (including Israel)—which in the mid-twentieth century once again necessitated the exile of most of those calling themselves Sephardim—have occasioned this sympathetic leap of imagination back to the expulsion from Spain?

The trauma of exile in their own lifetimes has aroused thoughts of Sepharad among a number of francophone Jewish novelists. This paper will therefore discuss a phenomenon which is similar to nationalism in that it blends ethnicity and history in the construction of an evolving modern Sephardic ideology where displaced nostalgia merges with the historical imagination and with history itself. To understand this ideology, I examine three generations of novelists from Algeria, Tunisia, Greece, and Morocco who have used the French language and the French cultural universe to allude to their relationship with Spain and their Sephardic heritage, thereby helping to create a new Sephardic identity in a modern French context.

The attitude toward Spain, the idea of Sepharad, and Sephardic identity—ideas held by Mediterranean Jewish writers over the course of the twentieth century—changed radically in response to historical circumstances affecting Sephardic communities. In the early years of the twentieth century, Jewish writers who lived under French colonialism reflected contemporary French attitudes toward Spain and were therefore averse to defining themselves as Sephardim. A transitional group, the generation of independence, cherished the best French intellectual traditions, though they themselves sometimes experienced French anti-Semitism. Some of these writers were intellectually and emotionally invested in the new nations coming into being in their places of birth, but as Jews they also found themselves marginalized in these newly emerging nationalist discourses. These multiple alienations, which often coincided with new involuntary migrations for Jews, found expression in a literature of irony and self-parody. A third, slightly younger generation of displaced writers has discovered a new cultural identity in pan-sephardism and a new tone of nostalgia for a lost, possibly mythical, wholeness, whether lost through exile from Spain, or from more recent ancestors' homes. The term Sepharad/Sefarad has both narrow and broad applications.[1] The answer to the question "Who are the Sephardim? is, "the people of Sepharad." Many francophone Jews, especially those from North Africa, have found, within the cultural universe of *la francophonie*, and against the backdrop of their similar relations with their countries of origin and their countries of destination (mostly Canada, France, and Israel) commonalities that have led to the creation of Sepharad. Thus, the Sepharad of these francophone Jews, in my view, represents not only the Iberian Peninsula but common traditions, religious practices, melodies, and a Mediterranean way of life, crystallizing through their now-shared French language into a reconstructed mythical homeland of the heart. The views of scholars as to who is really Sephardic and which origins count are less important for this construct than the intermittent yearning for a lost way of life. Even though the longing is tinged with pain, insofar as these francophone Jews were often discriminated against and were virtually expelled, many have been drawn back to visit their countries of birth, often to be disillusioned again. This coincides with the strong urge to commemorate in song, film, or literature what has been lost. Naïm Kattan, a francophone Jewish writer from Iraq, now Canadian, views the term Sepharad as a convenient one to describe an existing Sephardic reality in Israel, France, and Canada today: a Sephardic way of life, a way of being Jewish, of living Judaism in relation to tradition and in relation to the modern world. For him, sephardism is also a way of establishing a relationship with reality and with the Other.[2]

Francophone Jews have thus over the last generation embraced an idea of pan-sephardism, which in the early part of the twentieth century would have appeared unlikely and ill-advised. Sephardim whose ancestors actually originated in Spain had—over the centuries of slow decline and fragmentation of the Ottoman Empire coinciding with the economic decline among the Sephardim themselves—lost touch with one another and had become scattered among different diasporic communities. The persecutions and expulsion left deep wounds, and it was not until the nineteenth century (after 1868), as the Spanish authorities gradually began to ease restrictions on Jewish immigration, that a few Jews (mainly from Morocco) began to drift back to Spain.

From Fez to Tunis, and from Cairo to Constantinople and Salonika, efforts were made in the first generations to continue the religious and cultural life of the Iberian Peninsula, even in exile.[3] Traveling rabbis (e.g., Rabbi Shimon Labi, who came from Spain and Morocco intending to reach Jerusalem, but settled in Libya in the sixteenth century) attempted to raise the spiritual and educational level of these somnolent communities. Common traditions, such as knowledge of Kabbalah and especially the Zohar,[4] linked many Sephardim across the Mediterranean. But by the nineteenth century, especially in North Africa, where Ladino/Judeo-Spanish was seldom used, awareness of their historical connection to Spain had dissipated.

From 1830 onward, the French colonial enterprise began to bring new challenges and opportunities to the Sephardim of the Ottoman Empire, especially in North Africa. This was the year that France took Algeria from the Ottomans.[5] The descendants of Jews whose presence in North Africa predated the Muslim invasion, as well the exiles from Spain, found new economic opportunities in supplying the needs of the colonial armies and of the French civilians who followed them, acting as translators, intermediaries of all sorts, and suppliers of the material needs of the French. In giving up their humble but protected *dhimmi* status under an Islamic regime, the Sephardim of North Africa gained new ambitions and new privileges, but also a new precariousness within colonial society.

The extent of this precariousness was dramatically demonstrated with the Damascus Affair of 1840, instigated by Christian (French) charges of ritual murder, which unleashed anti-Jewish sentiment among Muslims in the Ottoman Empire. It was largely efforts by European Jews (Adolphe Crémieux and Moses Montefiore) and European Jewish organizations that secured the release of Jewish prisoners in Damascus,[6] by pleading with the occupier, the rebel Mohammed Ali of Egypt.[7] Such incidents were the impetus for the founding of international Jewish organizations to protect vulnerable Jews overseas, such as the Anglo-Jewish Society and the Alliance israélite universelle (AIU). Reflecting France's own sense of destiny, these institutions had a modernizing mission to improve the living conditions of Jews who, they believed, needed to achieve the same level of well-being and education as the Jews of the colonial metropolis. In improving the lot of these overseas Jews, French Jews also incidentally created grateful allies for France's colonial ambitions.[8] In both respects, the AIU was extraordinarily successful. The Sephardim of the French colonies distanced themselves more and more from their relations with Muslims and adopted the habits of Europeans. Adolphe Crémieux obtained French citizenship for the Jews of Algeria in 1870; the Alliance opened its first school in Morocco in 1862, and by 1909, it was running 149 schools around the Middle East and the Mediterranean, from Morocco to Persia. The French language was the cornerstone of the education provided in AIU schools, but religion, Hebrew, and another local language such as Ladino or Arabic were also taught.[9] The teachers were dedicated, well trained, and effective, and succeeded in communicating not only languages but modern scientific and philosophical modes of thought typical of the metropolis.

Thus, over the century or so during which they educated thousands of Sephardim, the Alliance schools achieved largely positive but also some inadvertently negative results. In causing Sephardim to identify with the colonizers, Alliance schools contributed to the demise of the age-old relationship between Jews and Muslims. At the same time, Sephardim, whose ancestors had languished in the Ottoman Empire,[10] became well equipped linguistically and mentally to enter or reenter the Western sphere. Aron Rodrigue recounts how the schools were so popular that mob scenes occurred annually on registration day, as parents fought for a better future for their children.[11]

All this explains why francophone Jewish writers and intellectuals, in North Africa especially, had little interest in a Sephardic identity in the early twentieth century. On the other hand, Spain itself had been building contacts with the Sephardim of the eastern Mediterranean. Senator Angel Pulido's discovery of a Jewish family speaking what he believed to be medieval Castilian on a ferry in European Turkey, and his subsequent contacts with Sephardic communities, caused a great sensation in Spain and reawakened Spain's aspirations to be an international power at a time of national crisis. With such an international climate and Sephardim unsure of France's real acceptance of them despite having been granted citizenship in Algeria, it would have been foolish to voice pro-Spanish sentiments, even if one wished to.

Transformed over a century from subject Ottoman *dhimmis* to full citizens of France, the Jews of Algeria were thus eager in most cases to express their French patriotism. The highest privilege to which a Jewish writer could aspire was membership in the Légion d'Honneur. Elissa Rhaïs, one of the first francophone Jewish novelists, almost achieved this distinction, and her autobiography is perhaps as interesting as her works. She wrote popular romantic novels and under her pseudonym was presented to the French public by her publishers as "a young Oriental girl" who had escaped from her Muslim husband's harem. In reality, much of her biography was fabricated—it was hinted that she used a ghostwriter and was not even literate in French, and a scandal eventually erupted. As a result, she was denied the ultimate honor. She had, however, been a popular best-selling novelist in her time.

Rhaïs's career may be contrasted with that of her contemporary Raphaël Lévy, director of the AIU schools of Tunis and author of stories and poetry in a realist and naturalist vein on the life of traditional Jews in the ghetto (or *hara*) of Tunis. Through different types of novels—one sentimental and popular, the other realist—Rhaïs and Ryvel (both pseudonyms) were looking back to an earlier, more traditional way of life, which they saw disappearing under the waves of change created by the colonial experience. Paradoxically, Alliance teachers in Tunis (e.g., Ryvel, Vitalis Danon) were aware of the price that was being paid for entering the modern world. In Tunis, it was the "Alliance School" of Jewish writers (all teachers, administrators, or students at the modernizing Alliance schools) that saw the need to preserve traditional Jewish culture in the face of impending change. Yet they wrote and encouraged Tunisian Jewish literature in French. From then on, the means of expression for Maghrebian Jews—and the means of evoking their cultural roots—would be the French language. They preferred the short story or novel, the most Western of genres.

Thus the idea of Spain, a hypothetical part of North African Jews' searching the past for their cultural roots, was expressed imaginatively, if at all, through the novel. Implicit in the writing of a novel is its audience: in this case, the audience probably consisted of Europeanized North African Jews and French-speaking Europeans themselves. Though she broke new ground by being the first North African woman novelist, Elissa Rhaïs's public personality was a construct of her publisher. Her first novels were tales in an Orientalist vein, popular because they catered to a French public hungry for Orientalism.[12] Her novel *L'Andalouse* (*The Andalusian Woman*, 1925) confirms that it was intended for a francophone audience through the stereotypical views it expresses about Spain and the Spaniards. Nevertheless, this novel differs from Rhaïs's previous ones, mainly in that the characters are not indigenous to North Africa, but are almost all either Spanish or French.

In the highly stratified and definitely nonegalitarian colonial society of Elissa Rhaïs's North Africa, ethnic allegiance and gender were the determinants of one's fate. Being Spanish (only one step better than being Jewish) and a woman, Dolorès in *L'Andalouse* is subject to prejudice too. Pedro, the Spanish fisherman to whom her father has betrothed her, has a low opinion of women, even though he loves her. "I trusted your father's word. As for yours . . . I didn't put much store in it! The word of a woman, and especially the word of an Andalusian woman. . . ."[13] His mistrust is well placed, because she has eloped with his best friend. In addition, she is frivolous, capricious, and selfish. The reader may have some flashes of sympathy for Dolorès in her act of betrayal, because her French companion Boissel is a workaholic who only relaxes because he considers it his duty to do so. But Dolorès is so immoral that she even abandons her own children, sending them back to the Frenchman with a change of clothes. The ethnic/national portraits of the French and Spanish characters thus admit few nuances.

Many of Rhaïs's descriptive passages resemble advertising copy, and the characters fashion plates of the time. The author expects the reader both to savor these descriptions and to perceive the shallowness of Dolorès's emotions and motivations. Here, for example, is how she sees Boissel, the Frenchman with whom she elopes:

> Louis Boissel seemed so elegant and so simple at the same time, he wore his grey suit with such ease, his boots with steel-grey buttons, his starched high collar and his tie knotted in such an impeccable way that he reminded her of one of those prints in the catalogues from Parisian department stores that Dolorès would often leaf through and that led her thoughts toward the luxury of capital cities. (35)

Though such characters do appear in Spanish literature (e.g., Pérez Galdós's bourgeois *madrileñas*, or ladies of Madrid, who will sacrifice all for a fashionable dress), Elissa Rhaïs seems to rely mainly on negative national stereotypes of the "other" in her portrayal of Dolorès. Her frivolity is matched only by her indifference and lack of even maternal feeling: "She answered him in that singsong, Spanish accent, with extreme indifference, 'Yes, they [her twin sons] are handsome, but they would have done better staying where they were'" (116).

Boissel would probably not have wanted Dolorès to read novels such as those of Elissa Rhaïs, unless he found the tragic ending sufficiently uplifting. It is somewhat incongruous that such a conscientious administrator would have resigned from his post in order to pursue Dolorès back to Tangiers, but the final scene when she sends her sons back to him and returns to her Spanish lover, while snowflakes fall over Tangiers, is so heartrending that it merits any amount of plot manipulation. Though the Frenchman contemplates killing her for her betrayal, he cannot stoop to "behaving like a Spaniard." Thus the novel comfortingly confirms the French reader's national prejudices.

Other ethnic groups receive passing references. The astonishingly naïve Frenchman acknowledges, for example, that his Jewish servant was more perceptive than he about Dolorès' true personality—a passing reference, perhaps, to the role of Jews as social and economic intermediaries in North Africa and reliable guides for the French colonizers (246). Dolorès does have a brief affair with one Cryba, a French-educated Jew who is a teacher and her husband's assistant, and who invites her to accompany him to a Muslim wedding (indicative of the Jews' intermediate position in colonial society), which she does not attend. Apart from this brief relationship, mainly included to demonstrate Dolorès's unstable and treacherous nature, Spaniards and Jews have no connection in this novel other than their similar subordinate positions in French colonial society. Rhaïs's novel shows little if any sympathy between North African Jewish and Spanish cultures. The curious reproduction of dialogue in Spanish shows little familiarity with the language or its dialects. If anything, Elissa Rhaïs's novel emphasizes the gulf and alienation engendered between Jews and Spaniards during the expulsion and the following centuries. The French, it perhaps implies, need not be greatly concerned about the existence of any residual Jewish loyalty to Spain in the francophone world.

Half a century later, French concern was no longer about competing colonial powers but with the burgeoning movements for national independence. The new generation of francophone Jewish writers thus might be called the "generation of independence." This generation in the mid-twentieth century experienced the trauma of voluntary or involuntary exile from the lands of their birth, their homes of many generations. Whether descended from indigenous Jews or exiles from Spain five hundred years before (the distinction often being blurred by the mists of time), many well-educated Jews sincerely identified with their homeland's struggle for independence.

Albert Memmi, for example, supported the Tunisian movement for independence in the early 1950s. He collaborated with the nationalists (corresponding with and later meeting the future Tunisian president Habib Bourguiba, who was then in exile), and after independence, he became an editor of *L'Action culturelle*, later known as *Jeune Afrique*. He also headed an institute of psychology in Tunis. Some other well-educated Tunisian Jews stayed on, a few becoming well-known lawyers and even occasionally government ministers, in the early years of the Tunisian state. Memmi himself had climbed from humble origins, through the benefit of an Alliance education,[14] leading him to the French lycée and on to university in Algiers and Paris. His sense of justice led him to support self-determination for the North African peoples, and he became one of the original theorists of colonialism and decolonization.[15] Settled in Paris since the 1950s,[16] Memmi was granted the high honor of membership in the Order of the Tunisian Republic, bestowed on him personally by President Bourguiba in 1984.

A modern, secular thinker, Memmi has devoted considerable intellectual energy to examining his cultural origins and that of the Jews of Tunisia.[17] His novels have largely emphasized the indigenous nature of Tunisian Jewry, the Judeo-Arabic that his family spoke, his mother's store of folk beliefs, his father's proverbs, stories of Djoha and the *khurafa* women's and men's tales shared with Tunisian Muslims. *Le scorpion ou la confession imaginaire* (*The Scorpion, or The Imaginary Confession*, 1969) and *Le désert ou la vie et les aventures de Jubaïr Ouali El-Mammi* (*The Desert, or The Life and Adventures of Jubaïr Ouali El-Mammi*, 1977) emphasize the ancient presence, since at least the first century, of Jews in the Maghreb, evoking the figure of La Kahéna, the semi-mythical Jewish-Berber queen who is said to have led the resistance against the Muslim invaders in the sixth century and was betrayed by her own sons. In *Le scorpion*, several different semi-fictional personae coexist in contemporary Tunis. The narrator posits various origins for his family, and includes a photograph of an ancient Punic coin, with the family name engraved on it, discovered near Tunis. The hypothesis of an indigenous origin is supported thus: "The first reliable reference to our presence here . . . is found in the Arab historian El-Milli who, in his *Arab-Berber Chronicles*, mentions that among the followers of the famous Jewish-Berber queen La Kahena there was a certain El-Mammi."[18] *Le désert* takes up the story of this early ancestor, making him however the deposed prince of a small Jewish-Berber kingdom, which may or may not have existed in southern Morocco until the fourteenth century when in Memmi's novel it is totally destroyed by Tamerlane. El-Mammi becomes a roving ambassador, representing the interests of other potentates of the Maghreb and Middle East.

El-Mammi travels the known Sephardic and Islamic civilized world of the fourteenth century, from Damascus to Spain, without overt reference to any Jewish origins. In fact his worldview and biography parallel those of Ibn Khaldun, the Muslim historian, who did go on a mission to Spain and met Tamerlane in Damascus in 1401. However, superficial resemblances to history are merely catalyzers for Memmi's imaginative constructions. El-Mammi's adventures in Spain are probably an overt reference to Elissa Rhaïs's novel just discussed, since he has his prince fall in love with a Castilian princess named, of course, Dolorès.

The deposed prince is on a mission to Castile for his friend and host, Bologuine, the ruler of Tunis, who is seeking allies against the Bougiotes, or Algerians. The mission is a delicate one, for the Castilians are known to be temperamental and touchy. El-Mammi enjoys the sea journey but is not mentally prepared for his encounter with these unpredictable people. At first he ridicules their customs—high heels, even for men, the incomprehensible *corrida de toros*, and strange religious processions with images of their dead god. He finds an exaggerated sense of personal and national pride combined with hypocrisy, cruelty, and treachery: "That touchy pride was shared by the whole nation . . . who would kill each other because of an insult, or an insolent stare at a woman. Taking away the lives of others, losing one's own for some trivial reason, are part of their idea of honor" (101). We thus have the same string of Spanish caricatures that we saw in Elissa Rhaïs's novel.

However, the Spanish episode in Memmi's novel and his portrayal of the Spaniards has a twist to it. It has the same purpose as that of all the chapters in this novel: by telling of his mistakes and gaffes, the protagonist is mainly making fun of himself. The whole of *Le désert*, in fact, is a retelling of his life story, ostensibly so that the great conqueror Tamerlane may draw knowledge from the lessons of a failed prince and never lose his own kingdom.

El-Mammi chronicles how his previously strictly utilitarian view of women crumbles in the face of a fifteen-year-old Spanish princess, with whom he has no language in common, but whose future children (who he hopes will also be his) he soon begins to imagine. El-Mammi thinks up scheme after scheme to persuade Pedro the Cruel to allow him to marry the princess, such as offering a share of his own future kingdom. Meanwhile, the customs of the Castilians suddenly begin to appear admirable to him. In this way, Memmi, the modern writer, satirizes the colonial propensity to ascribe positive or negative characteristics to nations, depending on one's own national strategic interests. El-Mammi's about-face shows how dangerously subjective judgments like the ones Elissa Rhaïs makes can be.

Of Dolorès herself we know little, as she does little but smile and pick flowers. El-Mammi is surprised at the freedom given to women in Spain to be alone and unchaperoned. However, no doubt the king had heard of the affair, since it is hinted to El-Mammi that it is time for him to end his mission. At this point he panics, having practically forgotten the reason why he came to Castile; abruptly asking for her hand, he is told that he must first convert to Christianity and become Castilian, raising echoes of the forced conversions that preceded the expulsion. This ultimatum brings El-Mammi to his senses, and he leaves abruptly. A few leagues into his journey, he realizes what danger he has escaped from and returns to his usual stance of self-deprecating criticism, "Oh! What a snare woman can be!" (112), concluding, "Worst of all, I had committed the sin of mixing my private concerns with public affairs; so that I had confused one set of affairs with the other, without achieving anything" (112–13). The story of the prince's affair with Dolorès is thus a lesson in how not to allow one's weakness for a woman to interfere with high affairs of state.

When El-Mammi is trying to understand the Castilians, however, his experienced North African adviser Younous, who generally plays the role of a spiritual guide whose advice is often ignored, gives him a

Maghrebian view of the Spanish people in tune with the ideas of Ibn Khaldun:

> Those eternal Christians, he explained to me, were recently Muslims, newly converted after the victory of the Christian armies. This race, so "pure," experienced such a long occupation that it cannot distinguish between the blood that it has acquired from the invader and what remains of its own. The Castilians pride themselves on losing all memory in order to better exorcise their origins, which always show through. As for the virtue of their women, it has been put to the test so often! Far from seeing all this as scandalous or pathetic, I excused everything, I understood everything, I loved everything about the Castilians. (*Le désert*, 107)

One must conclude that this description tells us much about El-Mammi's personality, but little about the Spaniards themselves. They are another colorful people in the face of whom El-Mammi ridiculously fails, to the likely amusement of his sophisticated listeners in Damascus, only to draw a lesson from experience expressed in worldly wisdom. Since El-Mammi oscillates in his views of the Spaniards from negative to positive and back again, based on purely subjective emotions, we are obviously not to take any of his generalizations seriously.

El-Mammi's tales can be linked to the North African oral tradition of men's *khurafa*, or serious tales with a moral purpose, and more humorous genres such as the tales of Joha, an ambiguous character who is crafty, wise in a practical way, socially marginal, and often ridiculous. These are closer sources than the Spanish picaresque genre, which one would have to trace through French literature before reaching Memmi's novel. Younous, in fact, often echoes the themes of men's *khurafa*: morals to be applied in community and public life, or worldly and practical wisdom. Self-sufficiency, loyalty to one's employer, and the maximum use of one's powers of practical intellect are some of the lessons of survival that El-Mammi gradually learns. The last image of his Spanish beloved is evoked by El-Mammi in his old age when he applies a favorite tagline of late medieval Spanish literature, "Ubi sunt qui ante nos fuerunt?" (Where are those who were before us?),[19] to Dolorès, among other figures from his past experience, wondering whether she, too, is now old and wrinkled. The "Ubi sunt . . . ?" motif fits in perfectly with

El-Mammi's nostalgic reflections, although it is unlikely that Memmi himself is directly referring to the Spanish tradition here. Wisdom comes at the cost of painful perception—*dolor*—and to express it symbolically, Memmi, like Luis Buñuel, uses the images of the wounded eye and the scorpion committing suicide in the ring of fire, but refers to it as a folk tradition of Tunisia.

Through their Dolorès figures, both Elissa Rhaïs and Albert Memmi portray a stereotyped view of Spain, taken up by popular literature in several European languages: the image of Spain as a beautiful, but unfeeling, treacherous woman (Carmen and Dolorès are one and the same), borne out in the Jewish experience through anti-Semitism, mass conversions, and expulsion. Though a facile portrait, this has been the archetype of Christian Spain in the Jewish historical consciousness, the opposite of Jerusalem, the true beloved. Love of Spain can thus be viewed as a betrayal of Jerusalem, in the traditional religious view. This view was facilitated by French colonial influence in the early years of the twentieth century, and possibly by the need to emphasize the indigenousness of Maghrebian Jewry in the period of independence. In the centuries since the expulsion, the memory of Spain had faded for many Sephardim—even for those who could trace their ancestry to Spain—and was replaced by a modern sense of alienation. Memmi's writing, however, always has a large dose of irony, and his confession that, culturally, he always felt torn between various allegiances, makes his writing typical of the transitional generation of independence.[20]

Another writer of roughly Memmi's generation who has had a contemporary influence on French thinking on the subject of sephardism is Albert Cohen. While the Alliance israélite had several schools in his native Greece, Cohen did not attend any of these but actually moved with his family at a young age from the island of Corfu to Marseilles. Cohen published his first novel, *Solal*, in 1930, but fell silent for virtually thirty years as he pursued a career in Geneva as an international civil servant, until the publication of his major novel *Belle du Seigneur* in 1968. He is viewed as a French writer, but his name has frequently been invoked as a Sephardic writer as well, since his novels oscillate between the colorful folkloric world of traditional Jewish life in Corfu and the alienation of the modern bureaucratic life in international organizations.[21] The humor, mixed with tenderness, in his portrayal of traditional Jewish mores, contrasts with the irony of his adventures among non-Jews, two worlds that cannot possibly comprehend each other. Like Memmi, Cohen feels uprooted and dispossessed, but he appreciates less than Memmi the intellectual and artistic tools he has acquired in the French language. Cohen is torn between cosmopolitanism and tradition, but his personal experiences of anti-Semitism lead him to present Jewish life in a comic yet sympathetic light. Like others of his generation, he found it necessary to assimilate to French culture, which offered him few options for expressing cultural difference.

Born in 1895, around the time of the Dreyfus Affair, Cohen moved to Marseilles with his parents in 1900, when Greek and Turkish nationalism in the eastern Mediterranean created difficulties for Jews, while Ottoman reformism and later Arab nationalism disrupted the traditional place of Jews within Maghrebian societies on the Mediterranean's southern shores.[22] Cohen's family therefore moved to Marseilles, where Albert grew up as a marginal and solitary child, encouraged by letters that his absent working mother left on the breakfast table each morning. The letters were stories—animal fables with happy, moral endings—and writing represented a way for his mother and himself to subvert the harsh discipline of her daily routine, a way to express love in a rigid environment that did not leave much room for it. Cohen loved these stories and, as a lonely child, an immigrant rejected by non-Jewish children, he would write his own thoughts in the air.[23] His life story is rife with contradictions. At the age of thirteen, he went back to Greece for a few weeks and was impressed by his patriarchal grandfather: "The mysterious majesty of the past impressed the young boy and took over his imagination. An idealized Jewish community, rich in miracles, strange powers, customs and eccentricities, came to haunt him."[24] Later, though, Cohen evinced no desire to visit either Greece or Israel, despite being a staunch Zionist. He was first and foremost a creator, his biographer Jean Blot opines, preferring dream to reality: an exile of the imagination. Though he wrote in French and lived much of his life in France, Cohen was initially a Greek and later a Swiss citizen. Displacement, loneliness, and cultural contradictions were the source of his inspiration.

Cohen's colorful Jewish characters populate all his books, apparently confirming anti-Semitic stereotypes but at the same time endearing themselves to us. Their comic antics are usually contrasted with the cool, rational, and calculating behavior of the non-Jews they admire and envy. They are an amalgam of what Cohen regards as universal Jewish traits and of individuals he encountered in Corfu (the novels transfer the story to Cephalonia, another of the Ionian islands). The "Valiant Ones" a group of cousins, each with his own picturesque traits, come to importune and embarrass their (obviously autobiographical) Westernized nephew, a high official at the League of Nations in Geneva. Their naïveté and innocence are refreshing in this world of cold calculation, portrayed in Cohen's characteristic tone of irony and sarcasm.[25] Only love relieves his cynicism, and in *Belle du Seigneur*, even that palls, as the former bureaucrat and his non-Jewish beloved, cut off from society, eventually commit suicide. The beloved non-Jewish women in Cohen's novels are naïve, rather than treacherous, while the Jews of Corfu represent for Cohen a Jewish life of a Mediterranean, Sephardic variety. We are again in the realm of cultural stereotypes.

Saltiel recounts to his nephew Solal the cousins' visit to the British House of Commons, one of the exploits organized by the most extravagant of the cousins, Mangeclous:

> I almost forgot to tell you that, thanks to a subterfuge that would take too long to explain on the part of that devilish Mangeclous [Nail Eater], we attended a session of the House of Commons, wearing long raincoats and accompanied by the Sephardic beadle, who knows English well, and translated the debates for us, partly in French and partly in Spanish and Hebrew, which he pronounces quite correctly.[26]

The Valeureux cousins put great emphasis on dress, concocting absurd combinations of fashion from various cultures and centuries, as they consider appropriate for the occasion. For a visit to the Jewish homeland, they dress in Alpine costumes, Boy Scout shorts, and their customary top hats. Their eighteenth-century dress for their visit to their important nephew in Geneva amuses the doormen and bellboys.

The cousins, not surprisingly in view of their high expectations of a land of milk and honey, are somewhat disillusioned by their visit to Palestine, renaming it "Pollakstein." Cohen uses every opportunity to exploit the contrasts, real or stereotypical, between North and South or East and West. Though he seldom uses the terms Sephardic or Sepharad, Cohen's "Oriental Jew" and his sunny Mediterranean environment, with his emotional effusions and petty yet endearing vices, is constantly contrasted with the cold, heartless, convention-bound, and conformist North, the breeding ground of Nazism and Hitler. There is no doubt that Albert Cohen's heart lies with Sepharad as later Sephardic writers, including Albert Bensoussan, have noticed.[27]

The source of Cohen's writing, though, lies not in the idyllic Mediterranean but in the suffering caused by his own state of exile. In any case, the Corfu from which his family had emigrated at the end of the nineteenth century was idyllic only in retrospect. It is the anti-Semitism he experiences that makes him a committed Zionist, the ridiculousness of his characters that makes them most endearing and sympathetic. Albert Cohen is one of the original modern novelists whose writing is exilic.[28] In this sense, not only is this Sephardic writer a precursor to many postmodern writers, but his work reminds us that Sephardic history can be viewed as an archetype of the modern condition.

Our third generation of writers—again, less in terms of chronological age than in terms of the extent to which they embrace the idea of sephardism—has been somewhat less in the thrall of French culture. These writers are, however, just as able to employ the French language as a supple instrument of expression; and most important (with a ready public of francophone readers who are not necessarily Jewish), they have benefited from the movement toward diversity that occurred after 1968.

Though uprooted and exiled from their homes, North African Jews have had a powerful linguistic/cultural tool—consisting of their mastery of the French language and their being at home within it—with which to express their feelings of uprootedness. This has obviously led North African Jewish writers to integrate more easily into both general French and international Jewish literary circles, encouraging their creativity—in contrast, for example, to that of American Sephardim, whose smaller numbers and relative unfamiliarity with either English or Yiddish initially discouraged them from literary production.[29] What has been termed "the politics of minority nationalism" encouraged in French culture the growth of groups such as Le Cercle Gaston Crémieux, the periodicals *Combat pour le Diaspora*, *Pardès*, *La Lettre Sépharade*, and many other Sephardic institutions, such as an annual Djoha festival celebrating Sephardic folklore.

The other major impetus for francophone Sephardic writing has been the flourishing of literature produced by Maghrebian (mainly Arab and Berber) writers from the 1950s onward. However, most of this writing has been nationalist in tone and did not admit a Jewish presence in its neo-Herderian concept of the ethnically based nation-state. Despite their millennial presence in the Maghreb, in Arab and Berber eyes, the Jews were tainted by associations with both the colonizer and with Zionism. The speed with which the exodus took place and the general prohibition against taking belongings meant that many Jews had to leave almost empty-handed. They became preoccupied with making a living and assimilating into the new cultures to which they had immigrated. It was not until about twenty years later that the individual and collective digesting of the past, weaving memories through storytelling, began to give rise to a minor cultural renaissance.[30] As modern, Westernized individuals who have mastered the intricacies of Western civilization, the younger writers evoke inherited cultures and see them as both traditional and modernizing in a hybrid and naïve fashion. Bridging the widening gap of age, of different geography, culture, and language, their novels evoke the landscape of the past with detachment, humor, irony, or sentimental nostalgia. These Westernized individuals are stating that they once partook of a different identity, collective and traditional. Without wishing in the least to compromise their present voices, they nevertheless assert that their identity has a unique dimension not shared by others in the East or in the West.

Today, North African Jewish philosophers and novelists write as if belonging to one contemporary Western, particularly French, tradition.[31] One may suggest, however, that their common experience of migration from traditional Jewish, North African culture to modern Western culture gives them a critical awareness of the gap between expectation and reality; between the wish to communicate meaning, on the one hand, and the acceptance of a lack of understanding from the recipient, on the other; between "signifier" and "signified." The concern with difference, which these writers have in common, makes it worthwhile to discuss their work within the same context. However, it must be noted that while North African writers emphasize displacement due to their own cross-cultural experiences, contemporary French and, lately, Anglo-American philosophers and literary theories have likewise emphasized such a concern, which they arrive at through the internal dynamics of Western thought.[32] Without wishing to reduce the import of Jacques Derrida's theories, certain qualities perhaps connect deconstruction to the novelists being discussed: the emphasis on the text, love of analysis, abhorrence of facile resolutions of the terms of dialectical thought, and the constant displacement of terms from one context to another.

North African francophone novelists reflect similar attitudes that grow out of their experiences of displacement, disruption of traditional relationships, and migration to wholly new environments.[33] Three novelists—Albert Bensoussan, Algerian in origin and now living in France; Ami Bouganim, Moroccan in origin and living in Israel; and Claude Kayat, born in Tunisia and now living in Sweden—express a personal sense of displacement, while asserting their identity as authentically modern voices. Bensoussan uses lyricism, nostalgia, and humor, Bouganim humor and satire in a tragicomic collective consciousness, and Kayat humor and wordplay. Bouganim sees contemporary novelists as heirs to traditional storytellers, while the other novelists write from an individual sense of disconnection from tradition. All three reflect the dilemmas of modernity. Their literature mirrors the cultural contradictions of migration by favoring humor and analysis over harmony and reconciliation.

Bensoussan's nostalgic autobiographical text *Frimaldjézar* (1976) describes the destiny of his "tribe" as "Hebraic identity, Moghrebi identity, and soon enough French identity" (126).[34] He refers to North Africa as a place of refuge, to which Jews fleeing Europe begin to arrive during the Nazi period, bringing rumors of boxcars and crematoria (55). The implication is that Jews have always been able to take refuge in the hinterland of the Maghreb, from the time of the revolts against the Romans in Cyrenaica in the first century to the absorption of exiles from Spain, until today. Bensoussan recalls connections to Spain with his mention of "Toledo, the Jerusalem of Sepharad" (126). But by the early 1960s, with the renewed violence of the Algerian revolution, the Jews found themselves expelled along with the French. Centuries spent in North Africa have thus become another chapter in the history of the exiles of the Sephardim, as Bensoussan might say, in their migration from one country to another around the Mediterranean basin: "Our passing through Isbilia was just a detour. After Toledo, after Spain, after our age-old rootedness in the Maghrebi lands, and our long loping from one side of the Mediterranean to the other, goodbye Frimaldjézar" (185). Bensoussan himself, as we saw from his comments on Albert Cohen, invokes and promotes both Maghrebian Jewish identity and Sephardic identity through his imaginative writing and essays. Both nostalgia and solidarity with other Mediterranean Jews in exile in the North contribute to his sephardism.[35]

Where Bensoussan expresses loss in measured tones of nostalgia, Ami Bouganim's characters in *Le cri de l'arbre* (*The Cry of the Tree*, 1983) lament in strident voices. The comic figure of Mzel, an elderly woman from Marrakesh, in her exaggeration epitomizes the illusions that had led the Moroccan Jews to uproot themselves:

> A villa for each and every family! After drifting around for two thousand years. . . . At last they were about to cast the anchor of their destiny in the land of their ancestors. For two thousand years, their dreams had led them constantly back to Jerusalem—and they fell into a *ma'bara* (transit camp). Mzel was demanding her villa in a loud voice, one with four or five rooms, a tropical garden, and a magic kitchen with one faucet running milk and another one honey. (*Le cri de l'arbre*, 10–12)[36]

Storytelling is an essential element in this culture, whether from a predominantly French, Arabic, Spanish or Ladino-speaking Moroccan background. A counterpoint to Mzel is the poetic and romantic figure of Zohra, a Spanish-speaking aristocratic lady who sings in Ladino about the many exiles in the long history of her people: "She sings of exile, with a nostalgic tone hovering in her voice, the exile of Jerusalem, the exile of Spain, the exile of Morocco" (12). It appears that a new layer of exile may have been added to the previous ones, even though, paradoxically, the Moroccan Jews have come home: "Their souls were still shadowed with vague nostalgia, nostalgia for exile, nostalgia for a certain mobilization" (51). Once having been remobilized by the experience of exile, the Moroccan Jews described here do not find it easy to settle down. They feel frustrated and directionless: "How shall we free ourselves from those shifting sands we are mixed up in and toward which shores should we point the vessel on which we have embarked our history?" (188). According to Bouganim's novel, Israel brings together Jews of very different walks of life, speaking Arabic, French, and some form of Spanish or Ladino, among other languages, and, in opposition to their common problems, makes them realize that they are Sephardim. The novel reflects a trenchant sense of humor, based, as often with these novels, on cultural contradictions (here between Sephardic and Ashkenazi Jews).

Another novelist who has described the forging of Sephardic identity, this time within Tunisia, is Nine Moati. Her *Les belles de Tunis* (*The Beauties of Tunis*, 1983) encompasses four generations of women from a Tunisian Jewish family over the course of a century and a half. In this novel, the Italian-educated Livornese (the *gorni*) and the indigenous Jews of Tunis (*touansa*) eventually come together as one group.[37] This novelistic fusion reflects the actual blurring of distinctions as they entered the modern period. Thus a Sephardic identity for Tunisian Jews is formed through the joining of bloodlines that go back to Spain via Livorno and to the indigenous lines of Judeo-Berber Jews.

The year 1992 inspired many historical novels on the period leading up to and following the expulsion of 1492. Didier Nebot, a French Jew, projects back to the land of his distant ancestors, Spain, through the fate of the fictional Benavista family during the difficult century that preceded the expulsion. Two brothers, one a faithful but persecuted Jew, the other a Marrano-converso, figure prominently in this novel. Their love of the Spanish landscape is a keynote, though the faithful Jew's descendants are forced to choose exile, taking refuge in Muslim lands of the Maghreb. In this novel there is an implicit alliance between Jews and Muslims, who suffered similar collective fates in Spain (a choice of forced conversion or exile) at roughly the same time in a way that enables Nebot to draw an implicit parallel between Spain of the fifteenth century and France of the late twentieth century.[38] A somewhat rose-tinted view of Jewish life and Jewish-Muslim *convivencia* puts the novel in alignment with Nine Moati; a "Jewish girl imprisoned in the harem" subplot is reminiscent of Elissa Rhaïs (or of the Book of Esther); and the cold, implacable hostility of Castilian Old Christians reminds us of Memmi's *Le Désert*. The frontier between the Christian and Muslim realms in Spain up to 1492, and the lives of Marranos and conversos as wealthy but despised social pariahs—paralleled by persecuted Jews and Muslims left behind as this frontier moved southward—point to today's social misfits in postcolonial France. The Sephardic author's clear sympathy for a Jewish-Muslim symbiosis is shown not only in the structure of this novel, but also in the different focus of two of his subsequent works, *La Kahéna: Reine d'Ifrikia* and a historical essay, *Les tribus oubliées d'Israël: L'Afrique judéo-berbère, des origins aux Almohades*.[39]

The strength of Sephardic identity in francophone culture derives from a fortuitous combination of factors. It functions in France in two main ways: first, through the preservation of folkways such as recipes from the cuisine of the old country, participation in what are known as pilgrimages (*hilloula*), either transposed to a French setting or through ethnic tourism to such destinations as the island of Djerba, and cultural events such as the Djoha festival or Ladino/Judeo-Spanish classes or concerts such as those of Enrico Macias; and, secondly, through religious observance in synagogues following Sephardic rites (emphasizing the continuance of Daniel Elazar's three criteria of halakha [religious law], *nusach* [prayer service and melodies], and *minhag* [customs] that determine Sephardic identity). France recently had a Sephardic rabbi as chief of its entire Jewish community for over twenty years, until 2008. A radical rejection of assimilation following 1968 and an assertion of diversity among initially secular French Jewish intellectuals was popularized by the large numbers of well-educated and better-off, but still traditional, Maghrebian Jews who had chosen France over Israel at the time of decolonization. In this sense, French Zionism and validation of a diasporic Jewish identity have aided and abetted each other, rather than being in conflict. Moreover, the ranks of the Consistoire (the central unifying institution of French Jewry) have been filled with rabbis and scholars who were conversant with the essential unity of traditional Sephardic religious practice across the Middle East and the Mediterranean, yet sophisticated enough to convey their traditional message to more assimilated Sephardim. Secular French-speaking Jews from the lands of the former Ottoman Empire have also found cultural expression and identity in the movement to revive and teach Ladino/Judeo-Spanish. Synagogues have encouraged events such as the Hilloula of Bar Yohai,[40] and folklore advocates have instituted the annual Djoha festival in France. Cultural institutions of all sorts have been promoting Sephardic culture in many spheres. The francophone concept of sephardism has even influenced Jewish writers in other languages, such as the Hebrew writer A. B. Yehoshua, who lived and studied in Paris,[41] and André Aciman, author of *Out of Egypt*, a Proustian memoir in English of Jewish life in Alexandria.[42] The distinctions among Sephardim have often been submerged in a perceived need for solidarity. Their disruptions, displacements, and cultural incongruities, experienced due to the new exile occasioned by the end of colonialism, have become the imaginative reenactment of the exile from Spain. If the homeland is portable, it can also be projected further back, all the way to medieval Spain; although as perennial exiles, experiencing the pain of expulsion from several homelands, Sephardim can also see themselves as archetypal postmodern individuals.

Novels are but one expression of sephardism in the francophone world, yet they offer a perfect medium for creating identity through examining the intimate nuances of an interaction between the self and its environment. Novelists address vital issues such as: What are my values? How do I behave in relation to people who do not share these values? What can give me the courage, the incentive to go on, to survive in a hostile and alienating cultural situation? Sephardic Jewish identity, whether spontaneous or constructed as an "ism," has offered the francophone world tools to deal with the displacements and incongruities of postmodern life. Whether this form of self-identification will persist, dissolve into smaller, more distinctive groups, or be subsumed in a broader Jewish identity, is a question only time will solve.

Ten Sephardism in Latina Literature

Dalia Kandiyoti

In recent years, authors known and self-identified primarily as Chicanas and/or other Latin American diasporans in the United States have discovered their Sephardic heritage and publicly discussed or written about Sephardic experiences in the Americas. Writers like Demetria Martínez, Denise Chávez, Kathleen Alcalá, and Achy Obejas, whose most visible and institutionalized identities have been Latina, Chicana, or Cuban, have drawn attention to Sephardic history and heritage as a part of the Latina/o communities they belong to and imagine in their works. Demetria Martínez, a highly acclaimed New Mexican poet, novelist, and journalist for the *Catholic Reporter*, has recently talked about discovering her crypto-Jewish roots, considering converting to Judaism, and reflecting on her "obligation to my Sephardic ancestors."[1] Denise Chávez, one of the most renowned of all contemporary Chicana authors, is working on a book about her Sephardic roots, having already touched on the topic of converso New Mexicans in her novel *Loving Pedro Infante* (2001).

Like Martínez and Chávez, the authors of the works I discuss in this chapter, Kathleen Alcalá and Achy Obejas also discovered Jewish roots and identity as adults, though they continue to be known and marketed primarily as Latina or Chicana writers and less as Jewish authors. In this essay, I consider sephardism in Alcalá's and Obejas's works, paying close attention to the implications of representing Jewish-Spanish experiences in Latina/o and Jewish literature today. My aim is less to provide a comprehensive examination of Sephardic history in Latina literature than to consider how sephardism works to bring together Jewish and Latina/o diaspora literature and criticism, which are seemingly disconnected but actually present in overlapping narrative imaginaries. Following a synthetic reading of sephardism in two novels, Alcalá's *Spirits of the Ordinary* (1997) and Obejas's *Days of Awe* (2001), I explore what it means to bring Latina/o and Jewish experiences together through sephardism in our current moment,[2] focusing on the crossroads created by the U.S. Latina/o and Jewish American literary and cultural projects.

What I call sephardism here is somewhat different from its previous use in discussions of Jewish literatures in the Americas, where the term has been used to indicate a strategic embracing of a Sephardic past by some Sephardic and non-Sephardic Jewish authors and communities. According to Edna Aizenberg, for example, sephardism in Argentina at the beginning of the twentieth century was a discursive strategy that facilitated the transition and incorporation of Jewish immigrants into Latin American host societies through the articulation of a Spanish heritage purportedly common to Jewish immigrants and Latin American Catholics. For immigrant authors, sephardism served as a "tool of assimilation" through emphasis on a common Iberian identity and language,[3] so that even a first generation of Ashkenazi immigrants could use sephardism to evoke a glorious Jewish past in Spain, though they and the immigrants that populated their narratives hailed from eastern Europe and claimed no genealogical identification with Spain. In a foundational text like the 1910 *Los gauchos judíos* by the Jewish Argentine author Alberto Gerchunoff, Jewishness is treated as an identity that does not differentiate between Sephardim and Ashkenazim in order to construct proximities, affinities, and identities between "the" Hispanic and "the" Jewish cultures and histories.

In this chapter, I use the term sephardism more expansively to discuss the analogic, corrective, and comparative foregrounding of Sephardic identities, histories, and practices in works by Latina authors writing in the United States today. If, in Latin America, the strategies to identify Hispanic-Jewish intersections served as tools (not necessarily effective ones) for Jews to integrate themselves into Spanish-speaking Catholic countries like Argentina, sephardism in contemporary Latina literature of the United States is not used to collapse or create supposedly stable formations—like "Jews" and "Hispanics"—but rather to posit Jewish, Sephardic, Latin American, and diaspora Latina/o identities as historically connected. In the works of Alcalá and Obejas, sephardism alters ideas dominant in the United States about Jewishness in the Americas, linking Latina/o and Latin American histories to Iberian Jewish experiences in ways few novelists have done. Alcalá's and Obejas's approach to sephardism positions these Jewish/Sephardic, Latina/o, and Latin American identities and histories as overlapping instead of only proximate, distinct, or comparable. I shall explain some of these overlaps, which have been historically obscured and removed from most narratives of Jewish or Latina/o collective memory, and discuss their implications for our understanding of Latina/o and Jewish identities and for Latino and Jewish Studies today.

In many ways, Latina/o writers are engaging in a recovery project that involves the reinsertion of Iberian Jewish history and heritage into the Latina/o imagination and identity construction. While the African and Native American components of Latina/o identities have received some, albeit insufficient, attention, their use of Sephardic history remains largely unknown. But the implications of sephardism in these authors' novels, short works, and testimonies go beyond recovery and the disclosure of hidden or taboo genealogies. The invocation and elaboration of Sephardic experiences (crypto-Jewish and other) in Latina writing serves to expand and transform Latina/o identities: I argue in this essay that in these new narratives, sephardism emerges as an emblem of cultural connectivity, forged under repressive as well as productive conditions. The representation of Sephardic culture in Latina/o literature as intersectional complements the existing paradigms of hybridity and *mestizaje* in Latina/o writing. Sephardism adds a different dimension, most interestingly one of secrecy and unknowability, to the terms under which both conventional and radical Latina/o identities have been formulated. And the dominant Jewish American imaginary—in which Latin America, Iberian Jewry, and the place of the Sephardim in the Americas are barely marked—is jolted out of its insularity and Euro/U.S.–centrism through Sephardist historical, cultural, ethnic, and intellectual connectivity.

Alcalá's *Spirits of the Ordinary* and Obejas's *Days of Awe* tell stories of crypto-Sephardic families in Mexico and Cuba, respectively, who are publicly Catholic but secretly identify as Jews and practice Jewish rites. They testify to a legacy in Iberia and the Americas of the Inquisition, which destroyed almost all Jewish life in its reach. Some families continued to identify with and practice Judaism in secret, escaping scrutiny through dissimulation, retaining a clandestine Jewish identity even after several hundred years, and performing some rites behind locked doors—like the "public secrets" of Belmonte's crypto-Jewish community in Portugal.[4] Others retained residual practices and ideas that were not known or named as Jewish, such as abstention from pork or Friday-night candle-lighting, now frequently considered clues to crypto-Jewish heritage, though these are questioned (see note 7). Both novels follow the authors' discovery of their own Sephardic roots, making them part of a phenomenon of the past three decades, when interest in previously obscured and hidden Sephardic identities surged all over the Americas and especially in New Mexico. The reasons for this recovery are many, including evidence of a continuous crypto-Jewish community in present-day Belmonte; the attention to Sephardic life generated by the events around the quincentennial of the expulsion of the Jews from Spain; the perception of decreased Judeophobia; the relaxation of Catholicism's hold on individuals and communities; contemporary experimentation with and interest in ancestry and identity; and, according to one scholar, the projection of the Holocaust onto the Inquisition to argue implicitly and explicitly for a transhistorical anti-Semitism and the "Orientalization" of Hispanic New Mexico.[5] Alcalá and Obejas have surmised their Sephardic past through ancestral names and records of practices, like knowledge of Hebrew, and have embraced their new identities, without relinquishing their previous belongings in the Mexican/Chicana and Cuban American communities.

Days of Awe followed a book of short stories, *We Came All the Way from Cuba So You Could Dress Like This?* (1994), and the novel *Memory Mambo* (1996), both of which garnered critical acclaim for their telling of the Cuban American exile story and earned Obejas a solid place in Latina and Cuban diaspora letters. Obejas belongs to a latter-day expatriate artistic and literary Cuban community that has made bridges with Cuba, breaking with the embargo culture of disengagement that characterized the initial decades of the post-Castro period. *Days of Awe* is another connective effort, one that again recasts the alternative worlds of the Americas that Obejas created in her previous works, which are populated with exiles from and rebels against political and gendered norms. The narrator of *Days of Awe*, who belongs to a Cuban crypto-Jewish family that emigrates to the United States in the aftermath of the

Cuban revolution, traces that family's origins in Cuba from the seventeenth to the twentieth century.

Spirits of the Ordinary, Alcalá's first novel, and the first in a trilogy of her rewriting and reimagining the history of her borderlands, is the fruit of the author's first-generation claiming of Sephardic ancestry for her immigrant Protestant Mexican family. The novel imagines the lives of the crypto-Jewish Caravals, descendants of the historical figure Luís de Carvajal, a converso who died in prison and whose family members were burned at the stake in sixteenth-century Mexico for the crime of "Judaizing."[6] The novel is set in nineteenth-century Saltillo in northern Mexico (where Alcalá's own ancestors lived), an area that experienced tremendous instability at the turn of the twentieth century under the regime of Porfirio Díaz, two hundred miles from the U.S. border and all too close to the Texas Rangers.

Although they are very different in style and historical context and setting, *Spirits of the Ordinary* and *Days of Awe* draw on common strategies to tell the crypto-Jewish story. Both novels boast large casts of characters linked by kinship or propinquity. In each, the chapters alternately focus on different characters. The omniscient narrator of *Spirits of the Ordinary* connects these individuals, while in *Days of Awe*, the narrator—heir to broken family narratives—pieces together a hidden, disparate history of Sephardic Cuban Jews in the first person. The novels are built on a gradual unraveling of what Sephardic identity means to the young generation that has inherited this hidden legacy, but the emphasis is less on individual interiorities than on the interpersonal and historical entanglements that this generation is able to make. In *Spirits of the Ordinary*, Zacarías brings together Native and Jewish worlds, and in *Days of Awe*, Alejandra comes to inhabit an openly Jewish identity through her attachment to Sephardic and other diasporic worlds, unlike her father Enrique, a tormented secret Jew. While Obejas's narrative oscillates between the present and the past, Alcalá's novel follows a linear chronology, fantastically blended with borrowings from Kabbalah, Native spirituality, and representations of miraculous cures and visionaries. In both novels, women play important roles in understanding and narrating *converso* Jewishness. In *Days of Awe*, the narrator is a 1.5-generation Cuban born on the day of the Cuban revolution and brought to the United States as a baby. She discovers, keeps, and tells the story of her family's secret. In *Spirits of the Ordinary*, Mariana Carabal, who is mute, understands spirituality and Judaism more profoundly than her husband, who reads sacred Jewish texts most of the day and experiments with alchemy. Both novels destigmatize secret Jewish identity and practice, usually seen as blind, abnormal, miraculous, or false, according to recent critics.[7]

These thematic and structural components reveal what I see as three major, interrelated strategies in telling Sephardic Latina stories: the connective, the corrective, and the comparative. The texts are connective because they suggest that Sephardic Jewish history and the history of the Americas are intertwined. This is obvious to those interested in the Sephardic world but obscured to most others, whether the reading public, most scholars, or creative writers. Obejas drives this point home in her narrator's story about conversos who arrived as exiles in Cuba with Columbus, and Alcalá through her construction of Mexican history and the Mexican–U.S. borderlands as a crossroads with a formative, not incidental, Jewish component, which adds to and shifts the terms of *mestizaje* represented in other narratives of the borderlands as culturally syncretic spaces, as discussed further below. Another connective aspect of sephardism that Latina authors have explored in their novels and in interviews is that of kinship: Obejas, Alcalá, Chávez, Martínez, and other authors suggest a genealogical relation between Latinos and Jewish people through shared, blurred pasts involving conversos and underscore the suppressed Jewish origins of Latin Americans. The Latino-Jewish band Hip Hop Hoodios has expressed this with rap lyrics in their song "1492": "Well, here's some words that will hit you with a thud: Millions of Latinos got Jewish blood."[8]

These plausible cultural and genealogical connectivities (whether or not they are fully accurate historically) are linked to the corrective way in which sephardism is produced in these texts, which involves claiming a generally occluded Jewish presence in the collective and individual Catholic Latino body, as well as asserting Sephardic difference in the face of Ashkenazi majoritarian discourses that make Sephardic history and culture invisible. In her book of essays, *The Desert Remembers My Name: On Family and Writing* (2007), Alcalá alludes to the arguments that reject the existence of crypto-Judaism in New Mexico and suggests that it is "the difference in standing between North African/Mediterranean/Latin Jews and the Northern European Ashkenazi Jews that seems to be the subtext to many of the current arguments against the continued existence of crypto-Jews."[9] While she does not elaborate, it is clear that she is thinking about the contestation of crypto-Jewish identities as part of a general marginalization of the significance of Sephardic Jewry.[10] Her own testimonies, essays, and fictional work counter this marginalization of Sephardim within dominant Jewish bodies of knowledge, as well as in the wider world. Obejas also affirms Sephardic and converso particularity in Judeo-Spanish language, culture, and ritual. Her narrator Alejandra finds herself in the company of Sephardic Jews, to whom she is closer, though connections with Ashkenazi Jews are also important to her and her family (*Days*, 264–65). In interviews, Obejas has pointedly declared that most Cuban Jewish history is Sephardic history, although this is frequently ignored by Ashkenazi Cubans in the United States and Ashkenazi Americans who do not favor the Cuban embargo.[11] Hence, like many Sephardic authors, Alcalá and Obejas are engaged in a corrective project of recovering and emphasizing the significance of Sephardic presence and history.

What I find to be the most suggestive aspect of Latina/o sephardism is its comparative dimension: the deployment of Sephardic and crypto-Jewish representations as metaphors and analogies for other constructs. This is not unique to the U.S. Latina/o imagination; many, if not most, recent fictional works that have recreated medieval and postexpulsion Sephardic history draw analogies to other catastrophes, including the Holocaust and the torments of Latin American repressions and dictatorships. The best-known examples of such works are the Spanish author Antonio Muñoz Molina's *Sefarad*, the Argentine Marcos Aguinis's *La gesta del marrano*, the Spanish-Mexican Angelina Muñoz Huberman's *Tierra adentro*, and the Brazilian Moacyr Scliar's *The Strange Nation of Rafael Mendez*. Obejas, whose comparative impulse is more explicit than that of these other authors or of Alcalá, creates an analogy between Cubans (particularly diaspora/exile Cubans) and Jews through many references to their common sensibilities and condition of exile: Alejandra avers that Cubans are "the Jews of the Caribbean" (*Days*, 104). Obejas also makes parallel stories of the martyrdom of Indians in the early days of the Spanish conquest with that of Jews at Masada under the Romans in the first century CE (*Days*, 104–5). She compares diachronically and transnationally, drawing on her current moment as well. For example, the narrator's Ashkenazi American lover Leni wishes to be invisible and unmarked as a modern American, but this desire is foiled by her physiognomy and dark complexion, which identifies her as Jewish to outsiders. Leni's need to be unmarked recalls the crypto-Jewish experience and identity-in-hiding that is the story of Alejandra's own family. Hence, we are led to think analogically about the desire for the integrated Jew in America to be undetectable, like a secular converso who needs to be invisible.[12]

Like Obejas who invites us to consider the parallels between Sephardic crypto-Judaism and assimilation under modernity, Alcalá also sets up comparisons, especially between the double lives of the crypto-Jews and those of the community around them. For instance, the Catholic family that Zacarías Caraval marries into has plenty of its own secrets and shame, including adultery and androgynous relatives, who must hide their identities or leave the community. One chapter is told from the perspective of a female photographer who takes on a male disguise, thus becoming a crypto-female, in order to be able to travel and photograph the Southwest. This chapter, like all others in *Spirits of the Ordinary*, adds a Jewish dimension to the experience of the borderlands and recalls other representations of female masquerades in iconic masculinist eras and "Western" spaces.[13] Alcalá connects Jewish and gendered fates through contact and conflict zones in the United States and Mexico so that sexual crimes and secret genders are analogous to secret religious crimes in the novel. These analogies are also corrective, of course, because they destigmatize crypto-Jewish experiences by likening them to secrets practiced under other oppressions.

Metaphorization of the so-called Jewish condition has been an object of recent critique by Sander Gilman in his *Multiculturalism and the Jews* (2006). Gilman studies what he calls "multicultural literature by non-Jews," which encompasses works by people of color or minorities in the U.S., South African, and British contexts to which he refers. Gilman sees a problem with images of Jews in the works he identifies, ranging from Gish Jen's *Mona in the Promised Land* (1996) to Achmat Dangor's *Kafka's Curse* (1999) and Zadie Smith's *White Teeth* (2000), along with many others. Global multicultural literature avails itself of Jewish identities and histories, Gilman argues, only to reduce them to stereotypical Jewish physiognomy and ahistorical notions of Jewish victimhood, primarily resulting from an ahistorical understanding of the Holocaust. For Gilman such representations serve the particular purpose of representing the Jewish condition as a metaphor for the assimilation anxieties of other minorities: "Jews seem to have become the touchstone for all of the pitfalls that present themselves to other cultural groups."[14] And he asserts further that "Jews on the brave new frontier of multiculturalism seem always to be the subject of comparison."[15] In other words, comparing ethnicities in fictional narratives or in Ethnic Studies is a tricky business, because instead of underlining the particularities of ethnicities, comparison can actually erase or obscure difference.

In the novels I have been discussing, comparison works differently. Obejas and Alcalá do use the converso experience as an analogy to other experiences of oppression and displacement and to other strategies of secrecy that counter sexual taboos, religious criminalizations, and racisms. Especially in Obejas's case, the analogy of transhistorical Jews to Cubans can sometimes seem forced and stereotypical. But these works do not obscure the crypto-Jewish experience by using it only as a metaphor or analogy to other ethnic groups; instead, they place Sephardic stories at the center of their texts. For Obejas, the Jew is not the "touchstone" for a Cuban exilic identity that is the main source of the analogy: in *Days of Awe*, Jews are at the foundations of Cuban history itself. Nor does the Sephardic experience become a stable ground for comparison. Indeed, even though sephardism is pivotal to these novels, it is not a stable comparable entity, because these novels relentlessly complicate crypto-Jewish identities. In *Days of Awe*, instead of relying on a figure of "the Jew" or "the Sephardim," Obejas creates a multiplicity of Jewish characters, who vary in relation to their Jewishness and other identities. Even among crypto-Jews, there is no fixed identity: Alejandra's great-grandfather Yitzhak becomes completely invested in his Jewish identity, while his children are ignorant and indifferent, going through the rituals mechanically. Yitzhak's grandson exhibits another, rather tormented kind of relationship to Judaism that overlaps with that of his grandfather's, but is even more secreted. Alejandra herself ends up with a different conception of Jewishness from her mother, her Ashkenazi friends, and her male relatives. Likewise, in *Spirits of the Ordinary*, forms of Jewishness vary considerably within the same family, so that we cannot conclude that Alcalá's novel deploys the figure of "the Jew" or even "the crypto-Jew" as a fixed entity reduced merely to a subject of comparison.

Although informed to a certain degree by an analogical impulse, the two novels reconfigure the terms of their comparisons and signal overlapping practices among the different identities they portray. As Janet R. Jakobsen's discussion of Jewish and queer identities and activism shows, analogies can be forceful in arguing for recognition, rights, and equality through a "logic of equivalence" between one struggle and another.[16] However, Jakobsen also asserts, relying on Tina Grillo and Stephanie Wildman's critique, that analogies are problematic in their separation of the analyzed terms and their privileging of the first term (the basis) of the analogy and neglect of the second. Like Gilman, Jakobsen suggests that analogies lead to a loss of specificity and differentiation between compared terms that are then generalized through discussions of marginalization and minoritization. Jakobsen argues, instead, for "relational complexity" and "complicity" between "Jews" and "queers" to emphasize the possibilities of intersection, which is precisely what I am underlining in reference to Alcalá's and Obejas's construction of Latina and Jewish histories and identities as overlapping or inseparable. As with her other works, Obejas, for example, is attentive in *Days of Awe* to the particularities of Cuban history and social formations at large—the revolution, postrevolutionary Havana, and Cuban exile politics shape the novel in equal measure to its Sephardic/crypto-Jewish dimension, so that Jewish and Cuban histories become inseparable. Two modes coexist in *Days of Awe*: the act of comparison that Obejas sometimes deploys where two objects remain seemingly separate and stable—"Cubans are the Jews of the Caribbean"—and the discourse of intersectionality in terms of common historical destiny, as well as kinship with Cuba.

Spirits of the Ordinary further complicates the representation of Sephardic identity when it stages an imagined, transformative encounter—or to use Jakobsen's term, "complicity"—between Zacarías Caraval and indigenous people of northern Mexico. In addition to pointing to a *mestizaje* created through intermarriage (Zacarías to Estela) and the reproduction of "mixed" heirs, Alcalá connects the story of the Caravals to that of the indigenous people. In his last attempt to strike gold, Zacarías Caraval leaves behind his crypto-Jewish parents and his marriage to Estela to pursue his conviction that he is destined to strike gold obsessively. During his final days as a prospector, he settles in Casas Grandes (or Paquimé), the actual site of a well-preserved town of adobe structures in Chihuahua, which reached its peak as a trading center from the thirteenth to the fifteenth centuries and is now a UNESCO World Heritage site. These remains are the locus of Zacarías's transformation into a shaman after his experience of "enlightenment" in what turns out to be, not the city of gold of his dreams, but a city of light that regenerates Zacarías's self and spirituality. This miraculous encounter with the self is interesting for the role that it plays in Zacarías's bond with the indigenous people as a consequence of his perceived powers as a healer, an accidental shaman. Because he is also known as a storyteller of (Kabbalistic) miracles, Zacarías acquires a status and a vocation he had not sought and of which he is unsure that he is worthy. Around him an indigenous community grows, drawn to his powers and ready to put aside their own differences. They move by droves into the abandoned Casas Grandes in the hopes of being healed by Zacarías, whom they name the *Tecolote* (owl), and reestablish this site as the crossroads of peoples that it once was as a trading center. With them, Zacarías abandons Spanish and speaks exclusively in *el llanero*, a regional trading language, as the narrator tells us. Even Apaches, enemies of many other northern Mexican tribes (including the Opata, subjects of Alcalá's novels, who helped the Mexican army forces fight them), seek help from Zacarías. The community is destroyed when the government deems it to be a threat to its project of the brutal suppression of the indigenous people, most infamously of the Yaquis, but also of many other groups, like the Opata. As a result, the Native peoples are martyred in Casas Grandes after they lead their *Tecolote* to safety.

Before he leaves the area in flight from the Mexican army, Zacarías returns to Saltillo briefly to bid goodbye to his family and circumcise his infant son with his own hands. He crosses the Rio Grande in search of sanctuary, like many before and after him. The journey, however, is punctuated by his discovery of a resting spot in a "new world garden," an oasis of Jewish life identical to his father's, belonging to a Jewish family that opens its home to him. Yet despite these acts by Zacarías, which signal a "return" to a Judaism he had previously taken little interest in, the Caravals do not adhere to their ancestral faith, but continue in the path of *mestizaje* that Zacarías established by marrying a Catholic woman, furthered also by contacts he established during his miraculous time in Casas Grandes. Zacarías's half-Catholic, half-crypto-Jewish son becomes a Protestant who marries Rosa, an Opata, and the novel ends with the words: "The time had come to begin again" (244). The connection with the indigenous community that regathered in Casas Grandes survives in Alcalá's imagination, as we see in Alcalá's subsequent novels, in which the intertwining of Opata and Sephardic destinies begun in *Spirits of the Ordinary* continues albeit in other guises and sites along the Mexican–U.S. borderlands.

In his discerning analysis of *Spirits of the Ordinary*, Jonathan Freedman points out that the Casas Grandes community's blending of Christian, Native, and Kabbalistic beliefs is an instantiation of a "generative remaking" emblematic of borderlands syncretism. According to Freedman, Alcalá draws on the figure of the Jew, particularly the crypto-Jew, as a trope for the syncretism and the indeterminacy of Mexican racial and religious identity in nation-making, serving as a "metonym for a wide variety of secret identities and hidden practices forbidden and feared by Church and state alike that lie roiling under the surface."[17] Freedman is not claiming that "the Jew" is deployed as a "mere" and inauthentic metaphor, as Gilman argues about the texts *he* analyzes. Instead, he suggests that the figure of the crypto-Jew is productive and axial to understanding other secret syncretisms. I agree with Freedman's assessment, but I also want to emphasize that crypto-Jewishness plays not only the comparative role Freedman suggests here, but also a *connective* one.

When Alcalá brings together the fate of the indigenous people with that of the Sephardic Jews, she helps us complicate Latina/o, Mexican, and Jewish identities by connecting them. She underlines indigenous (and not only Creole/mestizo) presence in the borderlands in ways that few Chicana/o novelists have done, thus addressing the need to treat indigenity in unromanticized ways that do not simply provide an idealized basis for Chicana/o identities. Moreover, she inserts a Sephardic presence into our borderlands imaginary, currently blessed with many rich histories, novels, and visual materials, which are, however, largely shorn of any crypto-Jewish or other Sephardic references. Through her sephardism, Alcalá compels readers to think about alternative histories to the ones that currently prevail in the telling of Jewish histories of the Americas, which primarily address the experiences of Ashkenazi immigrants. And most important, she goes beyond the use of the figure of the crypto-Jew as ground for understanding syncretism, because she links the fates of Natives and Sephardic crypto-Jews as two groups that have disappeared, to different extents and by different means, from the official Creole and Christian stories that dominate the continent. Through the imagined story of Zacarías's time with the indigenous people of the borderlands, Alcalá creates a moment marked by the massacre of both Indians and Sephardic Jews. This is prefigured in Zacarías's conversations at the beginning of the Casas Grandes venture, when the people hear his Kabbalistic creation story and tell him that they share the messianic vision of "the fourth world" and that, since the conquest, they too have prayed in secret and retained their devotion to secret sacred places.

The Sephardic Jews and the indigenous people are connected not only analogically, through the common experience of genocides and forced or voluntary syncretisms, but also as fellow subjects to the *same* genocidal project: racist national identity and colonialism formed around religion, which was pioneered in fifteenth-century Spain and disseminated through the Americas. This shared fate does not signal equivalent outcomes; when the Mexican soldiers arrive in Casas Grandes, Zacarías is moved by the Indians to safety and told to leave them to their struggle. Even when a pogrom against Jews and their associates breaks out at the instigation of the Mexican military, who accuse Zacarías of fomenting trouble among Indians, Zacarías and his parents escape separately, while the Indians are either murdered or made to return to their forced labor. Fellow victims of the turning point in 1492 ("discovery" and expulsion), the crypto-Jewish and Native destinies interrelate in Alcalá's borderlands, though they are by no means identical. Crypto-Jewish Sephardic experience can be seen as a ground of comparison for highlighting other hidden and syncretic identities, as Freedman argues. But Alcalá's move is not only analogical; she shows how the destinies of the borderlands people are overlapping, especially in her intertwining of Jewish and Native stories, rarely encountered in the literature of the Americas. In Alcalá's oeuvre, Sephardic/Crypto-Jewish, Mexican, and Native stories are compared as separate entities that are, moreover, tied together. *The Flower in the Skull* (1998), the second novel in her trilogy, for example, places the Opata at the center of a narrative that ends with the marriage of Zacarías and Estela's Protestant-turned son to a Tucsonian of

Opata and Mexican culture (who is also half Irish by parentage). Alcalá's novels, each a different facet of the prism she has constructed, recast the trans-American imaginary by emphasizing the occluded Native and Sephardic elements as essential to borderlands histories and identities.

*

If sephardism is a connective mode through which to retell stories of borderlands, diaspora, and the Americas, which bodies of criticism should we as scholars of literary and cultural studies draw upon to think about such works? Latina/o Studies or Jewish Studies, the two most obvious fields through which to conduct the inquiry, have few institutional or scholarly meeting points. Jewish Studies, once frequently incorporated into Near East programs and departments, is now often autonomous and isolated from other diaspora studies programs although it is, in theory at least, a global and transnational field. Latina/o Studies, including the study of Chicano, Puerto Rican, and other Latin American diasporas, is normally institutionalized in universities and in the publishing world within Ethnic Studies or American Studies and is concerned with U.S. Latina/o and trans-American issues. Jewish American literary studies, undertaken usually by scholars in English departments who are frequently also part of Jewish Studies programs, is not generally considered to be part of Ethnic Studies, and Jewish Studies scholars have noted and criticized the exclusion of Jewish issues from Ethnic Studies and multicultural curricula.[18] It is true that in U.S. Ethnic Studies the overlaps between, for example, Jewish, Italian, Chicano, and Caribbean contexts, such as immigration, diasporization, and racialization in North America are deemphasized, and what has become understood as white ethnic studies is separate and generally not institutionalized. While some in Jewish Studies and other fields see this separation as unjustified, it is important to keep in mind that Ethnic Studies grew out of the Civil Rights movement, emerging in part to redress the historical subjugation and marginalization specifically of people of color. Moreover, African American, Chicana/o, Latina/o, Puerto Rican, and Native American Studies in particular continue to address the ongoing subaltern status and racialization of the populations under study in neocolonial and neoliberal conditions of exploitation. Programs in Ethnic Studies also continue the effort to recruit and retain faculty of color.

Hence, there are major differences in the issues at the core of, for example, Puerto Rican or African American Studies and Jewish American Studies, as the latter is frequently concerned with Jewish distinctiveness, assimilation, anti-Semitism, religious identity, ambivalence regarding mainstream success, equivocal whiteness, the Holocaust, and relations with Israel. However, this does not mean that connections between Jewish Studies and fields institutionalized under Ethnic Studies are not, cannot, and should not be made if we are to address the construction of race and ethnicity in the United States fully as a relational process, where ethnoracial identities are formed vis-à-vis one another.

To address the Sephardic presence and past in the Americas, we need to draw on the widely influential vocabulary developed by Latina/o critical studies. Concepts such as *nepantla*—the experience of being "in-between"—and *mestizaje* can help us understand the ways in which both Obejas and Alcalá investigate "secretism" and find syncretism and multiplicity in a crypto-Sephardic past generated by intermarriage, migration, and forced or voluntary adaptation. Zacarías, for example, is an amalgam of the iconic "frontiersman" on a solitary quest for gold, a Jewish mystic and shamanistic healer. As Theresa Delgadillo explains regarding "spiritual mestizaje" in *Spirits of the Ordinary*, the inhabitants of Casas Grandes merge Kabbalistic and Native belief systems, with both the indigenous people and Zacarías changing irrevocably after their experience in the community they have created together at the site of an ancient junction of cultures and languages.[19] And in *Days of Awe*, to cite just one example from the frequently difficult and dangerous (and not refreshingly hybrid) crossings, contacts, and conflicts between people, we have Alejandra's father Enrique, a lifelong crypto-Jew, but simultaneously a genuine Catholic, who nevertheless asks for Jewish rites from his daughter at his deathbed.

The secret syncretism of traditions, cultures, and languages in these texts speaks to the concept of *mestizaje* in Chicana and Latina critical discourses. *Mestizaje* is a rarely used term in Jewish literary criticism or Sephardic Studies, but it characterizes the way in which Alcalá and Obejas position Jewishness in the Mexican–U.S. borderlands, in Cuba, and in the Cuban diaspora. Even though the tenacity of Jewish tradition and the resilience of Jewish people under conditions of terror are often emphasized in popular discourses and some scholarship on crypto-

Jewishness, and this tenacity can indeed be remarkable, what Obejas's and Alcalá's narratives underline is the mixing that occurred: whether the tormented dual loyalties and allegiances of Enrique, Alejandra's own negotiations of sephardism and contemporary American life, or Zacarías's blending of Native and Jewish worlds. The point is not for Jewish Studies to appropriate or decontextualize concepts like *mestizaje* or detach them from their colonial or postcolonial moorings. *Mestizaje* itself is a contested and charged term that has varying and problematic applications and histories in the Latino diaspora context and within different Latin American countries.[20] But to think about Sephardic cultural phenomena of the Americas in terms of *mestizaje* is to assert them as belonging to the histories and disciplinary studies of Latina/o diasporas and Latin America, in addition, of course, to global Jewish contexts. In her 2005 essay collection *Confessions of a Berlitz-Tape Chicana* (whose title, relevantly, points to a struggle with authenticity and mixture), the New Mexican Demetria Martínez offers a rare formulation that articulates a Sephardic presence in the Americas in terms of *mestizaje*. She writes of her ancestors, who include Spanish conquerors, Pueblo people, Navajos, and "'*conversos*' who practiced a mishmash of Jewish and Catholic rituals, mixing Ladino with their Spanish." Martínez explains: "these were a mestizo people creating themselves anew every generation in an unrelenting odyssey away from the Spanish ideal of 'limpia sangre,' or pure blood."[21] Unlike dominant articulations of *mestizaje*, such as the official Mexican one (races mixing harmoniously to produce the *mestizo* Mexican), the *mestizaje* articulated in Chicana/o critical discourses foregrounds the historical and ongoing overlaps and conflicts among peoples and histories whose narratives are buried by ruling interests.

As part of the civil-rights-era assertion of historical difference and visibility, the project of rewriting official stories is now well established in the Chicana/o-Latina/o world of ideas, but it is by no means finished. Emma Pérez's recent call for queering the borderlands and "excavating the invisible and unheard" is only one example of the impetus to continue to complicate Latina/o experiences.[22] I believe that the recent interest of Latina authors in exploring the Sephardic component of the history of the Americas is a natural consequence of the long-standing Latina/o practices of imagining *mestizaje* to recover, transform, and effectively continue to reimagine Latina/o identities and stories.

But sephardism is not only a way of adding to existing aspects of *mestizaje*; it plays a role in further complicating the very term. Because the continuity of the crypto-Jewish component is secret and unknown, and perhaps irrevocably lost from documented history, the idea of dissimulation and unknowability must be considered part of *mestizaje*, leaving our imaginations open to its barely visible traces, shards, and ruins. This is Marie Theresa Hernández's project in her brilliant ethnographic study *Delirio: The Fantastic, the Demonic and the Réel* (2002), an examination of the buried histories of the northern Mexican state of Nuevo León. Among other occulted experiences in the history of this region, considered socially and politically remote from the Mexican national imagination, is its Jewish past. Hernández shows that Nuevo León, established by Luís de Carvajal, the historical ancestor of Alcalá's fictional Caravals, is fascinatingly redolent of histories that are denied or absent from the state's official narratives: a Sephardic past (and presence?), Native origins (and continuity), and many other taboo subjects, including grisly murders of women and organized crime. In her creative ethnography of secrets and absences, Hernández places the anecdotal, the oral, and the trace at center-stage, drawing on, among other concepts, Michel de Certeau's understanding of "the story that slips away" only to reappear in fantastic and demonic forms in myths and legends, which Hernández collects. This accords well with the fantastic elements in *Spirits of the Ordinary* (i.e., the powers of Zacarías), which bridge the gap between what we know to be plausible (Sephardic–Native encounters) and yet do not know through public history. In such gaps, Hernández identifies narratives of "renunciation," namely, the relinquishing of inconvenient stories in official histories.[23] Like Hernández, the historian Emma Pérez writes of a lack of documents and "proper history" on the subject of "queer borderlands," sure to have existed but disappeared from official history. Alcalá's and Obejas's creative acts of tracing the buried Sephardic elements of Latin American and Latina/o history and *mestizaje* take place in the context of other such explorations of residual and fantastic knowledges. Their sephardism hence raises the question of what to do with the unverifiable, suppressed components of national, ethnic, and transnational narratives, urging us to think about them as an integral part of *mestizaje*.

Another concept that has not been explored in Jewish or Latina/o Studies with reference to Sephardic history is *nepantla*, which the influential Chicana author Gloria Anzaldúa borrowed from a sixteenth-century scribe who used it to describe himself as being in a "state of in-betweenness." As she explains in her book *Borderlands/La Frontera* (1987), "mental nepantilism [is] "an Aztec word meaning torn between ways,"[24] a very useful term when we consider the characters of Alcalá's and Obejas's novels. This idea of being "torn" differs from felicitous versions of hybridity, multiculturalism, and cosmopolitanism, or celebratory versions of *mestizaje*. At the same time, and despite the suggestion that the state of *nepantla* is a damaged condition of "being torn," it does not duplicate the stereotype of the tragically hybrid Jew that Sander Gilman has written about in *Jews and Multiculturalism*. *Nepantlismo* can facilitate discussions of sephardism in Alcalá and Obejas without leading us into stereotypes, because as Anzaldúa uses it, albeit in a different context, *nepantla* functions as a countertopos to the loss, tragedy, and suffering that in-betweenness and multiplicity bring. In discussing *Borderlands*, she refers to the "layering" and "stacking" of multiple identities and explains: "where these spaces overlap, is nepantla, the Borderlands."[25] Frances Aparicio, a scholar of Puerto Rican diaspora culture, signals the importance of the concept in non-Chicano contexts, despite its Mexican provenance, and explains, "Latino scholars have emphasized what is called *Nepantla* in Nahuatl: that experience of living between two cultures, not always as victims but never completely free as cultural agents or historical subjects."[26] In both Alcalá's and Obejas's texts, we see the difficult, unknowable, and secret presence of *mestizaje* and *nepantlismo* that the characters undergo. Every one of the major protagonists in their works is born of *mestizaje* and in a state of *nepantla*, with the valences of these conditions differing according to historical circumstance. For example, Enrique's in-betweenness in *Days of Awe* appears at times as mysterious, self-hating, and wretched, because of the strength of his faith and the oppression he had felt and was implicated in during the war years in Cuba (when he found himself saluting Hitler). His daughter Alejandra, on the other hand, reaches a new stage of being and thinking through solidarities with other people of color and queer engagements. In *Spirits of the Ordinary*, Zacarías's foray into shamanism is itself an act of nepantilism, because shamans are considered to be liminal figures who travel between worlds. His descendants (in Alcalá's subsequent novels) travel and struggle in the

Opata, crypto-Jewish, Mexican, and southwestern U.S. geographical and cultural spaces. Indeed, *nepantlismo* informs most of Alcalá's characters in her trilogy, since they are almost all displaced people negotiating different worlds in the borderlands.

The novels' foregrounding of Sephardic histories and identities as a point of contact, then, allows for an expanded vision of both Jewish Studies and Latino Studies. By affirming the relevance of Latina/o critique and theory to Sephardic phenomena in the Americas, scholars of Jewish-American literature, including of our two novels, can forge links with Latina/o Studies. And for Latina/o Studies, it is fruitful to consider Sephardic experiences as part of the investigation of the absences and repressed terms within the *mestizaje* of Latina/o identities. As Frances Aparicio and others have asserted, internal differences among Latina/os have to be integral to Latina/o Studies.[27] The difference that sephardism foregrounds also needs to be acknowledged, partly through the insights of Jewish Studies scholars and their historical studies of Sephardic traditions.[28] In Latina/o Studies too, there is no stable or unified subject, ethnically or otherwise, to analogize to the Jewish subject. Both Jewish and Latina/o subjectivities can be viewed differently in light of one another through sephardism and the related consideration of the buried and the absent in the making of the Americas.

In the Latina/o context, considering Sephardic connectivity also permits the exploration of a different relation to Spain. In oppositional Latina/o literature and criticism, Spanish heritage figures very little, since emphasis has been placed rather on the indigenous and African components of *mestizaje*, as well as on the past and ongoing subalternity of Latin American and Latino people and narratives. Spanishness is usually relegated to background information on the protagonists' parents or ancestors' migration as, for example, in the works of Oscar Hijuelos or Cristina García. In the case of Nash Candelaria's *Memories of the Alhambra* (1977), the protagonist's obsession with a New Mexican Spanishness is a deluded racialized identification with the white "winners" in the conquest of the Americas. The Spanish "fantasy heritage" (a term coined by Carey McWilliams) constructed around conquistadorial "civilized" white Spanish identity against the Natives has overshadowed the more complex permutations that conform neither to continuous, untainted Spanishness propagated by an early twentieth-century "Spanish Revival" nor to official *mestizajes* in North America.[29] The known but little-documented Sephardic constituent in the Americas complicates this relation to Spain: the Jewishness of the Spanish heritage destabilizes the privilege accrued to Spanish identity after the waning of the Black Legend and the institutionalization of "Spanish Revival" and Hispanophilia in New Mexico and California. Without discounting the ambiguity of the conversos' status—oppressed *and*, at least as far as some individuals are concerned, oppressing conquerors[30]—we need to consider that all converso life was terminated or hidden as Catholic and "Spanish." Examining the Spanish component of Latina/o and Sephardic identities in ways that do not center either on a strategic image of *convivencia* or a "fantasy heritage" can instead highlight transactional formations (Jewish, Catholic, mestizo, Creole) and destinies occluded under the sign of conquest.

I am not implying that sephardism is the sole connection between the categories and identities of Jews and Latinas/os. Latin American Jewish authors in North America, such as Marjorie Agosín, Ariel Dorfman, Ilan Stavans, Ruth Behar, and those who study their multilingual writings forge those connections; whether they want it or not, they frequently become known as Latinas/os. Creative connections are also forged through popular culture, from the Latin sound of the bagels-and-bongos era that Josh Kun has written about to musical work by the Hip Hop Hoodios, Roberto Rodríguez, and the "Odessa/Havana" collaboration of David Buchbinder and Hilario Durán.[31] In policy circles, new political narratives are also emerging that attempt to create Latino-Jewish coalitions, exemplified by the 150-page collection of essays *Latinos and Jews: Old Luggage, New Itineraries* published by the American Jewish Committee (AJC) in 2002.[32] Many of these efforts are based on models of analogy or creative new cross-breedings. But Sephardic experiences and sephardism are cultural phenomena already present and inscribed in Latina/o and Latin American and Jewish histories that simply lack visibility in contemporary Jewish and trans-Americas studies.

Sephardic-Latina/o and Latin American *mestizaje* has been forged in layers of experience, memory, and imagination, but it is so far off the centers of the American Jewish and Latina/o collective discourses that it is a history that has to be constantly reimagined and retold. The Sephardic-

Latina/o-Latin American thread provides alternatives to the mainstream idea that Latinas/os and Jews are separate populations that can connect only through the analogical perspective. According to the Latina/o and Jewish leaders and commentators who authored the AJC document, for example, Latinos and Jews are similar because of their status as immigrant populations, albeit currently at different temporal points on the path to success. This similarity is based on their alleged divergence from white Christians and African Americans through a tenacious hold on "discrete identity that draws its power and its character from communal experiences from times and places far distant from American shores."[33] In addition to glossing over African Americans' status as a diaspora group, such comparisons keep the status of the populations in question stable and undifferentiated (as "the Jews" and "the Latinos") with a static relation to one faraway homeland, which, for many Mexicans, is not necessarily so "distant from American shores." Certainly not all comparative perspectives and creative syncretisms (bagels and bongos, Odessa/Havana) are deployed instrumentally to reinforce existing racial and cultural politics. But thinking through *and* beyond comparison can help us reconstruct Latina/o and Jewish narratives by producing new elective and creative affinities informed by shared and overlapping Jewish and Latino destinies in the conflict zones of the Americas, rather than based on parallel-and-distinct participation in the American Dream (as in the AJC document). In the academic context, paying attention to sephardism as a connective phenomenon in the present can help Jewish Studies demarginalize contemporary Sephardic Studies of the Americas, as well as build explicit bridges with Latina/o Studies and Ethnic Studies. Within Latina/o studies, the Sephardic narrative can provide another generative dimension of the transnational thrust of Latina/o critique by connecting Latina/o criticism literature to global Sephardic history and culture. And, finally, although the Sephardic world is often pronounced to be moribund, the recent interest in and identity claims around crypto-Jewishness, coupled with new fictional and poetic narratives, initiate a new chapter in ongoing Sephardic history, as well as alternative ways of imagining our Americas.

Eleven Sir Salman Rushdie Sails for India and Rediscovers Spain

Postmodern Constructions of Sepharad

Efraim Sicher

> A neurosis had attacked the balance of the nation, its pathology identifying Judaism and Islam as the scars upon the body politic. By the standards of the fifteenth century this country could not hope for acceptance as truly European and Catholic until the two were removed.
>
> Barnet Litvinoff, *Fourteen Ninety-Two* (1991)

> Jews pass Columbus in long columns, but the tragedy of their expulsion makes no mark on him.
>
> Salman Rushdie, "Christopher Columbus and Queen Isabella of Spain Consummate Their Relationship (*Santa Fé, A.D. 1492*)," in *East, West* (1994)

> Our current multiculturalism, the blight of our universities and of our media, is a parody of the culture of Córdoba and Granada in their lost prime.
>
> Harold Bloom, "Foreword," in María Rosa Menocal, *The Ornament of the World: How Muslims, Jews, and Christians Created a Culture of Tolerance in Medieval Spain* (2002)

Romancing Sepharad

The discovery of America in 1492 has been engraved in our cultural knowledge as a turning point in the making of the modern world. But while the discovery of America led to Spain's emergence as a global power, 1492 also marks both a terminal point of Jewish and Muslim symbiosis in the Iberian peninsula and the unification of Spain as a Catholic nation. In *Fourteen Ninety-Two*, Barnet Litvinoff questions the centrality of Columbus in ushering in a modern era, suggesting that the watershed event was not the discovery of America (actually mistaken for India) but rather the consolidation of Spain as a Christian kingdom after the defeat of the Moors at Granada and the expulsion of the Jews.[1]

This chapter looks at postmodern and postcolonial configurations of Sepharad in order to trace a narrative that has always adapted itself to current ideological discourses regarding race and nation. We shall see that these revisions of Spanish Jewish history do not necessarily recover an authentic, rich heritage as much as they question epistemologies of history. Such counternarratives remap cultural history and redraw the geopolitical lines of a Sephardic world that encompasses the Iberian peninsula, North Africa, and India, thus reimagining history from a marginal, subaltern view and positing new transnational options for diaspora identities.[2]

In modern literary history, two narratives have circulated about Sepharad, by which I refer to the rhetorical construct of an imagined cultural past in Andalusia, or the Iberian peninsula (akin to "Yiddishland" in multicultural evocations of Ashkenaz), and both belong to the realm of historical myth, rather than fact or geographical location.[3] One is essential to the formation of a modern Spanish identity based on notions of homogeneous racial origins that excluded New Christians from full membership in the Spanish nation. Another myth gave rise to the notion of a proud Sephardic nobility of exotic, orientalized Wandering Jews.

For Spain, consolidating the nation meant not just imperialist conquest, but also conversion of all native and colonial populations to the "true" faith. Later ages have regarded Spain's claim to a monolithic Catholicism based on pure blood (*limpieza de sangre*) with some ambivalence, and the victims of forced conversion have been accorded sympathy, romanticized as possessing a nobility of spirit and of blood, as well as a culture of their own, that commands respect. As Michael Ragussis has shown, a "culture of conversion" developed in early nineteenth-century England through which crypto-Jews stood as figures for and against conversion in a debate over national identity.[4] The Inquisition came to symbolize the inefficacy and cruelty of forced conversion (see Ragussis's chapter in this volume), so that compared to Catholic Spain, English Protestantism could present itself as tolerant. However, in Ragussis's reading of Scott's *Ivanhoe*, Rebecca's announcement of her departure for Muslim Spain (anachronistically for Boabdil's Granada) dispels English delusions of tolerance in anticipation of the expulsion of the Jews in 1290 and in contrast to ideals of Merrie England. In the transformation of history into romance, the final defeat of the Moors in Granada and the expulsion of the Jews spelled out a lesson that contrasted with the successful fusion of Norman and Saxon blood in the English nation and warned against the consequences of xenophobic racial and religious homogeneity in the formation of a modern nation-state.

The expulsion from Spain has long been a stock in trade of Jewish historical fiction, particularly in post-Holocaust novels such as Noah Gordon's *The Last Jew* (2000), which imagines what it is like for Yonah Toledano to be on the run from the Inquisition, feigning a fake identity while clinging to secret Jewish rituals in a *minyan* of one; this invention of postmodern Jewish spirituality *avant la lettre*, independent of synagogue and community, in a parable of Judaism as survival, speaks to contemporary Jewish drifters and assimilationists. From Grace Aguilar's *The Vale of Cedars* (1850) to Naomi Ragen's *The Ghost of Hannah Mendes* (1998), the anglophone Jewish literary tradition has continued to engage with Spanish Jewish history in ways that often extol the idea of martyrdom. However, while Marie's death in *The Vale of Cedars* counters the nineteenth-century discourse of conversion and establishes the Sephardic heritage as something to be proud of, for Ragen, writing after the Holocaust, the description of torture of the female body (in largely pornographic detail) vindicates centuries of Jewish women's struggle for survival and gives meaning to a family tradition almost forgotten in postmodern America. Michelene Wandor, a British Jewish feminist playwright, on the other hand, fantasizes the suicide of a Marrano woman in a short story, "Song of the Jewish Princess," in order to express her own feelings about a Jewish destiny overdetermined by history, as well as to fantasize her desire for sexual freedom that transgresses boundaries in a postmodern fluidity of diasporic identities.[5]

Jewish writers who do not regard Israel as their home or as a center of their cultural identity sometimes evoke Sepharad to reflect a cosmopolitanism that nonetheless remains distinctly Jewish. Recalling recent European martyrdoms in a poem that explores the meaning of Jewish diaspora identity, significantly entitled "Scattering," the British poetess and novelist Elaine Feinstein invents for herself a genealogy that does not go back to real ancestors in Frankfurt or Białystok; instead, the poet is lured by the embrace of a Moroccan lover. In her poetic return to Toledo, where her people "settled after Jerusalem" and enjoyed a Golden Age, Feinstein imagines the fate of Sephardim who did not leave in 1492 and

> . . . turned to the Holy Cross,
> though some lit candles on a Friday night
> without remembering why,
>
> and cooked in oil rather than lard;
> others became fervent New Christians,
> and married into the best families;
> until the Inquisition began to inquire
>
> more urgently into their old habits
> —for instance, if they did not light a fire
> on Saturdays in a cold winter.
> Neighbours gave evidence against the rich.
>
> Most admitted their sins under torture, as
> people will, and some brought to blame
> fellow *conversos* for their practices.
> It did not help them to escape the flames.
>
> Nor did the ignorant suffer any less.
> Read how Elvira del Campo pleaded,
> as they broke her arms, only to understand:
> "*Tell me what I have done that I may confess.*"[6]

Alternatively, in "Muslim lands, the refugees were welcome," though "always second-class citizens," and flourished as merchants, unlike their plight in the cruel and murderous lands of Ashkenaz.[7] This contemporary discourse that idealizes a medieval al-Andalus, or that identifies with the covert crypto-Jews known as Marranos, refashions Jewish history as an unending saga of exile and martyrdom, but tends to ignore the Marranos' courageous struggle to regain their Judaism.[8] At times, following a pseudo-Kabbalistic brand of mysticism that emphasizes the suffering that binds together the oppressed of the earth (migrant conversos among Jews and Muslims in a transnational covenant), it subtly negotiates discomfort with Jewish particularity. In her post-Holocaust anxiety, Feinstein looks forward to a happy Diaspora for Israeli Jews settling in Beverly Hills or London's Belsize Park.

The novels and polemical narratives discussed in this chapter adopt a political and ideological agenda that appropriates Sepharad—sometimes encompassing also the "Orient" or the "Levant"—in order to envision a cultural space that interrogates assumptions about "native" identities and homelands, but also in order to locate a shared environment for Jews and Arabs in a mythical world that more often than not glosses selectively over the realities of violence and genocide. The objective of these discursive moves is "resistance" to Eurocentricism, including the Europeanized culture that came to dominate the State of Israel in its early years,[9] and to national "exclusivity," especially Zionism, in the name of cosmopolitan progressive liberalism.

Sepharad in India

In order to approach this politicized, extraterritorial "Sepharad" with some historical perspective, it is worth first traveling to the Indian subcontinent where, as Aamir Mufti has argued, the Europeans transformed their handling of the "Jewish Question" into colonial policy.[10] This provided a paradigm for the postcolonial situation:

> The history of Zionism and Indian Muslim separatism unfolded over almost precisely the same period of time, that is, the first half of the twentieth century, and of course the establishment of the (European) Jewish state and the creation of the (Indian) Muslim state occurred less than a year apart in its fifth decade, both through massive transfers of population and the partitioning of territories in the process of their abandonment by the British Empire. . . . They are both signs of a crisis in the nation-state system at a specific moment in its history. They mark the inability of the modern system of nation-states to complete the nationalization of society except through its violent reorganization: breakdown of communities, massacres and transfer of populations, in the one instance, and, in the other, dispersal and industrialized genocide followed by resettlement in a distant and violently appropriated land and the displacement of its own indigenous inhabitants.[11]

In this postcolonial context, the Muslim has displaced the figure of the "Jew" in the Western imaginary, that ambivalent signifier in the cultural discourse of nation and outsider, and has erased real, historical Jews.

Now the Indian is taking on the prototypical role of a diasporic cosmopolitan citizen. As Sander Gilman notes, "Where Jewish was, Indian is."[12]

Amitav Ghosh's *In an Antique Land* (1992), for instance, portrays Sepharad as a symbiotic landscape in which the Middle East mirrors not Europe but India. In this novel, an anthropology student from India travels to a small village in Egypt to search for information about a twelfth-century Jewish merchant whose correspondence (actually found in the Cairo Geniza) brings to life a network of cultural exchanges and migrations at the time of both the medieval Christian crusades against Jews and Muslims and the Almohadic campaigns against those who resisted conversion to Islam. In the present, however, Ghosh's Indian narrator finds himself crushed by a "dissolution of the centuries of dialogue that had linked us."[13] It is no longer possible, he concludes, to engage in the kind of cultural exchange evident from the letters of the medieval Jewish merchant from Mangalore in India by the name of Abraham ben-Yijû. These letters, along with many others discovered in the Cairo Geniza, attest to a thriving and widespread community of adventurous Jewish merchants who traded between Muslim Spain, the Middle East, and India.[14] The cultural symbiosis that Ghosh adduces from this material has been replaced by a language of confrontation and conflict. The turning point, the narrator claims, was the moment Vasco da Gama landed in India in 1498 and demanded the removal of Muslim traders as the price of continued trade. Subsequently, the Portuguese defeat of the Indo-Egyptian fleet put an end to an ancient trading culture based on cooperation and compromise, paving the way for five hundred years of European imposition.

What Ghosh does not acknowledge—among several other examples of selectivity and omission—is that this cultural bridge between India and the Middle East was facilitated by an Islamic colonialism and a slave trade that preceded the Europeans by some centuries. However, for Ella Shohat what is important in Ghosh's account of the "colonization" by Solomon Schechter and other European scholars of the Cairo Geniza, where Abraham ben-Yijû's letters were preserved, is the way in which the expropriation of this treasure created a "cultural divide" between Ashkenazim, acting under imperial protection, and Sephardim, who thus lost rights to their heritage.[15] This leads Shohat to posit a controversial relational model that conflates "Mizrahi" or "Levantine"

Sephardi Jews with "Arab-Jews" as a symbiotic part of the cultural landscape until they were alienated from it by what she calls a "Euro-Zionist" ideologized narrative that took no account of Sephardic identity vis-à-vis other ethnic groups across time and space. Sephardim, she contends, were subject to a Eurocentric historiography, which dominated the quincentennial celebrations of 1492, even though Columbus conquered America in a conscious extension of Spain's forced conversion of Jews and Moors and despite evidence of converso traditions surviving among Mexicans and Chicanos who have themselves been similarly marginalized. In a further diatribe against the Zionist redemptive narrative, Shohat again conscripts Ghosh's novel but regrets that his ethnographic fascination with Egyptian peasant families perpetuates the rupture between "Arab-Jews" and Muslims.[16] The Indian anthropologist's abrupt departure in Ghosh's novel, assisted by the local police, prevents him meeting any Jewish pilgrims to the tomb of the holy sage he barely recognizes as Rabbi Ya'a kov Abu-Hatzeira, the Moroccan mystic also known as the Avir Ya'akov (1805–80), grandfather of the Baba Sali, a missed rendezvous that only affirms the disappearance of Jews from Egypt's Muslim world and their erasure from Arab history.[17]

In contrast to such tendentious and partisan views of history, the British postmodernist novelist Salman Rushdie regards all stories of migrations and expulsions skeptically as the stuff of mythical nation building. History is the making of individual whims and private intimacies. In his brief historical fantasy "Christopher Columbus and Queen Isabella of Spain Consummate Their Relationship (*Santa Fé, A.D. 1492*)," Salman Rushdie imagines that Columbus's discovery of America came about through his seduction of the Spanish queen, who is not satisfied by her final defeat of the Moors at Granada or by the banishing of the Jews. The Jews remind Columbus, exhausted by the loss of patronage and his ships, of the Old World. Only conquering the unknown world will satisfy Isabella, and in his vision of her vision, she summons him to entrust him with the voyage beyond the end of the west, only to be met by spiteful refusal; fortunately, when he is really summoned he does not refuse.[18] This fantasy both provides a psychological or erotic explanation for one of the irrational, often absurd factors that make history happen and removes the East-West divide in

Eurocentric explanations of the need for Spain's reunification. Columbus's religious motivation and the fall of Granada, which completed the Reconquista and provided the funds for his venture, are cynically written off as self-interest.

In *The Moor's Last Sigh* (1995), Rushdie goes further and juxtaposes the histories of two subcontinents, Iberia and India, turning each into a counterfeit and complementary mirror image of the other.[19] Written after the fatwa against him, and in the shadow of the demolition of the disputed Babri Mosque in Ayodhya, India, which set off Muslim-Hindu sectarian violence in 1992, this postmodern satire undoes a binary history of Muslim-Hindu conflict on the Indian subcontinent by looking instead at Indian history through the perspective of a hybrid protagonist, Moraes "Moor" Zogoiby, product of the union between a Jew of Sephardic ancestry and the daughter of a Catholic family that had reached India from Portugal with Vasco da Gama in 1498. Unlike many postmodern and postcolonial narratives that conscript Sepharad into a discourse that redefines the Diaspora in ways that are problematic and decontextualized, Rushdie offers alternate histories that break down ethnic divides and resist fundamentalism.

Puzzling over why Rushdie or Ghosh feature Jews so centrally in their novels despite the relative paucity of actual Jews in India, Tudor Parfitt reminds us of the myth of the Lost Tribes ascribed to the ancient presence of Jews on this subcontinent.[20] An ancient Jewish presence indeed existed in Cochin in the south of India, which eventually became one of the points of refuge for Jews expelled from Spain.[21] The complex background of India's Jews thus offers Rushdie an opportunity to explore postcolonial theories of diasporic identity and hybridity across time and space in a tale of the narrator's ancestry that goes back to a tragicomic union between the last Muslim king of Granada, Boabdil, and a runaway Jewess who escapes with the king's jewels in her bag and his seed in her womb. On the face of it, the narrator's background celebrates cultural hybridity, yet Rushdie shows that hybridity is a slippery creature that rests on an imaginary construction of racial origins.

In Rushdie's novel, every master narrative is so suspect that history dissolves into meaninglessness. Its house of fiction becomes a deliberate "jamboree of creative confusion" built on shifting sands, "a compromised construction whose undoing is written into its being from the start."[22] The story of the Jewish Diaspora—the mother of all diasporas—becomes a paradigm here for the crumbling myths that hold all nations and families together. In turn, this deconstruction enables a creative revisioning of India as seen through the Western yet marginalized eyes of Spanish Jews and Portuguese Christians, but also a revision of Spanish Jewish history through Indian eyes.[23]

When Moor's father, Abraham Zogoiby, confronts his Jewish mother with a disturbing old manuscript he has found, he questions the doubtful story of his ancestry:

> "Who is the author?" he asked . . . —"What was she?—A Jew; who took shelter beneath the roof of the exiled Sultan; beneath his roof, and then between his sheets." . . . *My mother who insists on the purity of our race, what say you to your forefather the Moor?*[24]

Indeed, if he is descended from miscegenation between a Jewess and the legendary Moorish prince Boabdil el Zogoiby (which means "the unfortunate" in Arabic), then Abraham must disbelieve his mother's claim to purity of race. But the tale of racial hybridity tempts him, as it does the reader, to substitute fiction for history.

By mapping India onto Sepharad, Rushdie warns that a similar decline may befall India if it follows Spain's insistence on homogeneity and purity: "Correspondingly, the rise of Hindu fundamentalism, Rushdie suggests, may herald the artistic demise of an India in which fertile miscegenation is rejected. In such an India, hybridity might become nothing more than a sort of trendy, but empty nostalgia."[25] For this reason the Moor's mother, Aurora, daughter of a wealthy family of Portuguese merchants, paints murals of a pluralistic nation, crowds in fancy-dress balls of all ages and religions, a "patchwork quilt of man" (227). Her canvases on the dissolution of Andalusian multiculturalism emphasize the parallels that Rushdie traces between Moorish Spain and Mughal India,[26] yet they depict a Palimpstine, suggesting a palimpsest of historical narratives and identities, as well as a Mooristan, suggesting the Moor's own personal fantasy world.

However, the definition of hybridity in this novel shifts gradually from an ideal unity of opposites—with the Moor painted by Aurora as a standard-bearer of the pluralism that is India—into a Baudelairean flower of evil—with the Moor as a figure of decay, a motherless "creature of shadows, degraded in tableaux of debauchery and crime" (303). This transformation of hybridity through the Moor's character is expressed most obviously in his physical deformity, a magical realist version of a premature aging syndrome. His deformed fist is a source of light and miracle for Aurora's eroticized imagination, yet it is also a source of brute power and of his downfall, as when it fatally attracts Uma and murders Mainduck. Rushdie means this to represent the violence that is rife and hyperbolic in India, the violence that is "in us too."[27]

Rushdie's decision to locate his principal emblem of hybridity in the descendant of a Moor and a Jewess reconfigures an image of deceit and deception that has long been associated with the clandestine identity of Spain's conversos. The Marrano or Morisco who hides under various names and covers—secretly Jew or Muslim, publicly Christian, and in some ways neither—represents, as Peter Berek puts it, the quintessential "Renaissance Man."[28] The Marrano is the stranger on whom all anxieties about change and innovation can readily be projected. Especially in the context of changing notions of race and nation, the secret Jew becomes an ideal model for modern conceptions of identity as potentially unstable and capable of being freely determined by individuals. The fluidity of identity that emerged during the Renaissance, and that has become so characteristic of the postmodern imagination, traveled across seas and continents along with the movement of goods and people in ways that did not necessarily fit preexisting conceptions of race, color, religion, and nation. Certainly, in the England of the sixteenth and seventeenth centuries, which served as refuge and way station for many foreigners, and where accusations of Judaizing were rife, it became difficult to define who or what was a Jew.[29]

Homi Bhabha defines hybridity in colonial India as an ambivalent resistance to the originary claims of the English conquest and its Christian mission, which Indians mimicked in mottled camouflage, subverting the colonial power's attempt to elide cultural differences.[30] Bhabha speaks of Gibreel Farishta in Rushdie's *The Satanic Verses* as just such an example, not of patchwork hybridity, but of the mote in the eye of national history whose mimicry of the colonizers singularizes and marginalizes a totalizing culture.[31] Rushdie's hybrid of Moor and Jew is, moreover, modern and secular in its indifference to the transmission of an ancient legacy, yet it also is shown to be an unreliable and possibly suspect account of history and not a credible model of postcolonial identity. The union of Aurora and Abraham is never consecrated, for example, since neither the bishop of Cochin nor the Cochin Jews would countenance a wedding between Jew and Christian. The product of their union, the "Moor," is therefore raised as neither a Catholic nor a Jew: "I was both, and nothing: a jewholic-anonymous, a cathjew nut, a stewpot, a mongrel cur. I was—what's the word these days?—*atomised*. Yessir: a real Bombay mix" (104).

If the "Jew" is the globalized hybrid par excellence, this is a postmodern identity emptied of meaning, yet also available for the construction of politicized postcolonial identities and all too conscious (like the Jewish ad-woman Mimi Mamoulian in *The Satanic Verses*) of being a postmodern pastiche, the minority migrant who has become the borderline figure of a massive demographic and cultural displacement.[32]

A postcolonial condition of fake identities in a hybrid complexion of "passing" echoes and reenacts the mask of the Marrano in terms that suggestively extend Peter Berek's definition of the "Renaissance Man." "Sepharad" in *The Moor's Last Sigh* effectively deconstructs all stable identities through the subversive and provocative historical parallelisms that Rushdie establishes. Hybridity therefore becomes a mixture of identities borrowed from fiction and from myth, and as such, it can never be originary or original, but is always indebted and inventive. Moor is so called because his siblings are named in nursery-rhyme fashion: Ina, Minnie, Mynah—and "moo" is his first cry—but he is also Moor because there is always more to him than readily appears (a joke borrowed from Launcelot in *The Merchant of Venice*). He might well joke, "What's in a name?" (84)—excessively, insatiably more, and more than the sum of his inherited contradictions: arbitrariness is his birthright and fate. Moraes Zogoiby embodies a cultural mix that deconstructs historical stereotypes by exposing a composite heritage that goes back to Muslim Spain. Rushdie explains:

> Although the Muslim sultans were the rulers, there were Christians and Jews and Muslims living side by side for hundreds of years, and their cultures affected each other. So the Muslims were no longer completely Muslim and likewise the others. . . . Now it seemed to me that the world I come from, India, the world this book comes out of, is also a composite culture.[33]

This may not be an accurate rendering of history, and Anna Guttman has questioned whether al-Andalus can really offer a model of multicultural harmony, since Muslims and Jews lived in separate communities and the heyday of the Spanish Jewish Golden Age faded well before the Reconquista; besides, Muslims and Hindus in India would find it much harder to reconcile their theological differences.[34] Nevertheless, Rushdie's Moor embodies a "mélange," a *masala* brew of identities that melt into one another, threatened by single, and thus false truths, specifically by fundamentalism. The hybrid "Jew" thus becomes a necessary minority from whose perspective Rushdie can examine the India in which Partition turned Muslims into the largest official religious minority.

The figure of the "Jew" introduces the complex cosmopolitan history of the Spanish-Jewish exiles, but also represents the idea of their symbolic displacement by India's Muslims. "MUSLIMS ARE THE JEWS OF ASIA," reads one slogan painted on walls during the Partition riots in *Midnight's Children*.[35] In this respect, Aamir Mufti regards *The Moor's Last Sigh* as a "cosmopolitical" novel that ushers in a new approach to Indian and Anglo-Indian history.[36] Dora Ahmad interprets its handling of fundamentalism as an oppositional stance that pits hybridity against historiography so that each becomes a distorted mirror image of the other. According to this view, Indian Jews and Muslims share a common historical expulsion from Spain as the formative memory of their Indianness, and can thus be considered parallel ethnic minorities amid Bombay's teeming and conflicted multitudes. The problem with such a metaphorical interpretation of Indianness, however, is that it overlooks the historical realities of Bombay's Jews (who suffered little persecution and whose upper echelons of wealthy merchants hailed from Baghdad, not Spain).[37] Dora Ahmad seems to divide Islam from fundamentalism by portraying Indian Muslims as "Jews" who define Indianness by difference, in defiance of an authoritarian Hinduism.[38] Joined by Abrahamic monotheism, Jews and Muslims are further linked in this view by a narrative of migration and survival.

Apart from overlooking the demographic and sociocultural realities of Bombay, Partition, and the language riots of 1957, the main problem with this position is that it misses Rushdie's preoccupation *not* with defining Indian identity, but with conveying a sense of the corruptive decay of both the body itself and a body politic, a coming apart of ethnic and national ties, through an imaginative inhabiting of other lives across genders, religions, languages, and ethnic groups in order to explore what is truly human. What Saleem describes in *Midnight's Children* as the Indian disease of trying to encapsulate all of reality is in fact a universal failure to arrive at a coherent narrative of all the voices in the writer's head.[39]

The role of the "Jew" in *The Moor's Last Sigh* can therefore be seen more productively as a paradigm of the ideological and narrative failure to contain all of India, or all of Rushdie's autobiographical self, or ultimately, the failure of any one identity to contain all that is essentially human ("self" is never singular, but always multiple and protean for Rushdie). Hence Rushdie's representation of the "Jew" is less a metaphor than a metamorphosis. His treatment of identities teaches us that one cannot escape the postmodern nightmare of history, and it demonstrates how difficult it is to trace the course of one's own destruction. Paradoxically, in Rushdie's self-deconstructing "shaggy-dog yarns" of a "Moor's tale" (4), history is debunked as an unreliable narrative, but nevertheless lives out its myths in a self-reflective and self-questioning art form that defies its own determinism and eschews the certainties of cause and effect.[40]

When Moor is forced back upon his forgotten Jewish identity through a confrontation with his father, he goes back to Spain to try and imagine himself as a Jew, but Maimonides's ghost laughs at him. "I was a nobody from nowhere, like no-one, belonging to nothing. . . . I had reached an anti-Jerusalem: not a home, but an away. A place that did not bind, but dissolved" (388). Here we have a statement—which for Moor seems like a truth—that identity is founded, not on a yearning for a lost homeland, but on a sense of not belonging anywhere. And so, instead of a pilgrimage to a point of origin, Moor finds himself thrown into a vortex of compulsive historical repetitions. After a surreal plane journey from India, he lands in a room that resembles Cochin's synagogue but is located in a remote Spanish village whose name reminds the reader of Cervantes's parody of the society and literature of his times. In a reconstruction of the Alhambra, which proves to be a trap set by the mad painter Miranda Vasco—Aurora's former lover, who stole her painting *The Moor's Last Sigh*—the latter-day Moor finds himself imprisoned under threat of death with a Japanese woman who convinces him that though love might lead to betrayal and destruction, it is still worth seeking. This conclusion would be entirely banal if the reader were not being teased with the figure of Don Quixote lurking ironically on the Spanish landscape.

Yet even Don Quixote proves to be of small comfort when history insists on repeating itself. After the mad Vasco shoots his prisoner, Moor relives Boabdil's trauma. The dying painter repeats the words of Boabdil's mother after the loss of Granada (the loss that completed the Reconquista in the year 1492): "You do well to weep like a woman for what you could not defend like a man" (440). Indeed, the spot from which Boabdil looked upon Granada for the last time is known in Spain as "the last sigh of the Moor" (*el último suspiro del Moro*), a last sigh/*soupir*/supper deconstructed in punning jokes throughout Rushdie's novel and finally reenacted through the sigh of Rushdie's Moor as he awaits death, thus closing not with redemption or return, but with defeat.

The "Jew" for Salman Rushdie—like Leopold Bloom for James Joyce—becomes the emblem of an exilic figure who cannot belong to one place or nation, a Zogoiby (misfortunate) whose complicated cultural baggage reflects the author's own artistic striving for an "imaginary homeland."[41] For Rushdie, "voluntary exile from identity is the only means to redefine that identity as an unfixed constantly evolving notion," in the sense that "[e]xile is identity in Rushdie's world, but the most productive sort of identity . . . mental, intellectual exile from fixed and constraining truths."[42] Through a deconstruction of Sepharad, Rushdie unfolds a postmodern situation in which the writer's identity is situated between two continents, at home only in his imagination.[43] By proceeding from Spain and Portugal to Bombay and back to Spain, Rushdie seems to celebrate a diasporic model that suits the multilingual and multicultural society in Bombay before the Hindu takeover. But the abrupt end of this multiculturalism demonstrates that one cannot trust any cultural symbiosis, even one exemplified by Spain before the Reconquista. Just as in Rushdie's novel *Shalimar the Clown* (2005), where the violence in Kashmir puts an end both to coexistence between Muslims, Sikhs, and Jews and to the Pachigam *bhands*' performance (an emblem of the multicultural symbiosis that existed, for example, in Bombay's theater during the 1950s), multicultural coexistence also comes to an abrupt end in the India of *The Moor's Last Sigh*. The idea of Sepharad in *The Moor's Last Sigh* proves to be a deceitful trap, which imprisons the

Moor in his own narrative (as a Scheherazade breathing out tales to prolong life) and in history (when the Moor expires as Boabdil did). As if paraphrasing Oscar Wilde, the Moor molds life after art, at once a victim of his magical realist malady and the Frankenstein-like fate conceived by his mother in her painting called *The Moor's Last Sigh*. Ultimately, the expulsion from Spain at the end of eight centuries of Moorish culture in the Iberian Peninsula signals in this novel not the discovery of the New World in 1492, but the permanent migrancy of the human condition.

Postcolonial Sepharad

John Docker's *1492: The Poetics of Diaspora* (2001) reiterates that the expulsion from Spain in 1492 is an apt expression of postmodern identities of "mixed conception."[44] Docker's own identities as an Australian of Irish Jewish descent with possible links to Portugal lead him to search for meaning beyond master narratives that can no longer be trusted. Like the Moor's physical/metaphysical voyage in Rushdie's novel, Docker's journey becomes a family romance in both the Freudian and literal sense, for it questions the origins of his ethnicity, subjecthood, and "race" through a narrative about those quintessential Wandering Jews, the Marranos. In this hybrid merger of fiction, biography, chit-chat, culinary experiments, e-mails, current events, and cultural history, the pivotal moment of 1492 entwines Europe, the Middle East, and India in order to rewrite Rushdie's construction of a nomadic Sepharad into a symbiotic union between Sephardic Jews and Palestinian Arabs as brothers in oppression by Ashkenazic Zionists.[45]

Docker's rehearsal of a politically correct postcolonial discourse hardly pays attention, however, to luminaries of the Andalusian Golden Age such as Solomon ibn Gabirol, Yehuda Halevi, or Abraham Abulafia; there is neither mathematics nor astronomy, neither mysticism nor exegesis, because for Docker, 1492 marks a traumatic turn to disaster since, in his view, the expulsion of the Jews and the defeat of Boabdil at Granada led to the construction of the modern nation-state as a warring exclusivist entity.[46] For him, "1492 is a date with disaster for Europe, because it enforced a notion of the emergent modern nation-state as ideally unified in ethnicity, religion, culture and mores. Such a notion became an assumption and frequently led to the further notion that the nation-state should be based on ethnic superiority, separatedness and contempt or hatred for other nation states."[47] Sephardism becomes a link here in an equation that sets up a mental and discursive resistance to Zionist historiography, as well as a defense of the claim (which at best risks an imprecise generalization) that Sephardim lived comfortably and unmolested in Arab lands before and after the expulsion of 1492.

Under a protected yet inferior *dhimmi* status in Muslim lands, Jews were no doubt fairly pleased not to be tortured or burnt at stakes, but they prayed ardently three times a day for the return to Zion and sang "next year in Jerusalem" at their Passover feast. They would have been surprised to learn of Docker's appropriation of Sepharad for a post-colonial celebration of diasporic pluralism, exile, diversity, hybridity, and multiculturalism from a postmodern position that tolerates no ethnic or national borders. Indeed, Docker implicitly denies that Sephardic heritage has any living relevance to the Jewish people; he values Sephardic culture only as a diasporic myth. From this point of view, he reimagines Scott's Rebecca as a paragon of the refined, educated, empowered, cosmopolitan Jewish woman of the Levant, a product of an idealized multicultural Diaspora.

It is thus hardly surprising that Docker's reading (or misreading) of *The Moor's Last Sigh* overlooks its skeptical assessment of all constructions of identity and nation-building, thus reducing Rushdie's novel to an uncomplicated endorsement of hybridity and interracial exchange. Docker uses works of fiction like Rushdie's novel and Amitav Ghosh's *In an Antique Land* (discussed earlier in this chapter) as exemplary texts to issue a decontextualized and sometimes anachronistic warning to the contemporary Middle East. Along with Rushdie's and Ghosh's novels he also calls for support on Richard Zimler's *The Last Kabbalist of Lisbon* (1998), a historical novel and picaresque murder mystery that practices precisely the kind of diasporic poetics/politics Docker advocates. But while in Zimler's novel home is a diaspora of the mind freed from religious orthodoxy (and the affinity of Zimler's protagonist with Baruch Spinoza is not accidental), Docker validates Zimler's diasporism mainly because it eschews "Eurocentric" Zionism and endorses existential despair.

Daniel and Jonathan Boyarin advocate a type of creativity generated through statelessness and point to potential links among diasporas: "if a lost Jerusalem imagined through a lost Córdoba imagined through a lost Suriname is diaspora to the third power, so is a stolen Africa sung as a lost Zion in Jamaican rhythms on the sidewalks of Eastern Parkway."[48] Diasporas (in the plural) and diasporism are being posited not only as a general alternative to the nation-state, but also as an antidote to an ideology that has reclaimed the land of Israel as the home of the Jewish people. This is a multicultural vision of diaspora that emphasizes *Golah* (a dispersion of trading posts and cultural mediation dating from Hellenistic times) and displaces *Galut* (exile with all its negative theological and political implications that would come to an end with redemption in the Land of Israel).[49] It argues for the experience of the Jewish Diaspora as normative—"Zion longed for and imagined through Córdoba, Cairo, or Vilna"—in a way that comes closest to Rushdie's postmodern palimpsest of historical identities.[50] Yet although the Boyarins adopt an anti-teleological, anti-Zionist rhetoric that rejects any form of Jewish identity tied to a historic homeland, they are nevertheless at pains to rebut postcolonial discourses that would reduce the Jewish Diaspora to an allegory detached from actual historical experience and that would see sephardism as characteristic of the global dispersion of migrants who form a transnational community.[51]

In conclusion, even if Rushdie conceptualizes it as another imaginary homeland that can never be regained, we have seen how Sepharad has been constructed as an idealized diaspora that might restore a mythical symbiosis "between the ancestral Jew and the Christian and Arab 'others' who inhabit his psyche"—as Victor Perera puts it in *The Cross and the Pear Tree* (1996).[52] The political lens through which history is read frequently glosses over incidents that considerably complicate the picture, such as the mass killings of Jews in Granada in 1066 at the hands of the Almoravide Muslims or the fact that Jews were found on both sides of the Christian/Muslim divide throughout the Reconquista.[53] For example, María Rosa Menocal's *The Ornament of the World* (2002) raises a monument to the culture of tolerance of al-Andalus, seeing the abrogation of the terms of recapitulation at Granada and the expulsion of 1492 as a prelude to Christian intolerance culminating in the bombing of Sarjevo's library exactly five hundred years later in 1992. While unconvinced by Menocal's placing of the entire blame for the 1066 massacre on Berber fundamentalists, Harold Bloom joins his voice to the plaint for the lost Muslim Andalusia and, from a post-9/11 perspective, the repression of true multiculturalism.[54] The hidden identities of Marranos and Moriscos, however, have provided a blessing in disguise, for Menocal would have us see the practice of fake cultural identities by Marranos and Moriscos as a founding principle of the modern novel from Cervantes' *Don Quixote* to Rushdie's *The Moor's Last Sigh*.[55] Postcolonial and postmodern visions of Sepharad posit a universalized hybrid identity that finds meaning in the loss and deracination at the heart of the postmodern condition. Yet one may ask whether, paradoxically, in the process of its reinvention, the construct of Sepharad has demolished the idea of a Jewish nation by displacing it with virtual and tentative global identities or by turning history on its head with a false picture of Sephardim clutching the keys to their homes in Toledo as they pine (in Ladino) in their "Palestinian" exile.[56]

Postscript

Rebecca Goldstein's *Spinoza*

Yael Halevi-Wise

> A postscript that [c]ould have been a preface.
>
> Walter Scott

Our primary goal in this volume was to show that writers from a wide variety of ethnic and religious perspectives, at different times and places, have approached Sephardic history as a prism through which to express modern preoccupations with the status and images of minorities, mainly in relation to potential reconfigurations of national identity. To round out this overview of the role of Sepharad in the modern literary imagination, I would like to touch upon a recent manifestation of this phenomenon—a case that intrigues me because it comes from a democratic and pluralistic environment that ostensibly resolved its most serious challenges vis-à-vis national identity and the status of minorities, the central preoccupations underpinning the majority of examples surveyed in previous chapters. Rebecca Goldstein's *Betraying Spinoza* (2006) is an intellectual biography of the famous seventeenth-century Dutch philosopher, but at the same time it is a brazen autobiography of a Northeast American Jewish Ashkenazi female novelist and philosopher, who crosses over boundaries of time, space, ethnic identity, gender, and literary genre to ground her own modern secular ideology in Spinoza's reaction to the Sephardic experience.[1]

Asking, "How far back must we go to get a sense of the communal inner life that had informed the passive identity of Baruch Spinoza, shaping that singular self that his ethics demanded he resist?" (78), Goldstein launches into a history of Sepharad that occupies more than a third of her slim volume, commissioned by Schocken Books for their prestigious Jewish Encounters series. Goldstein's history of Sepharad concentrates on those Jews who resisted conversion in Spain during the long century of conversionist onslaughts from 1391 until 1492, when they finally chose expulsion over conversion. Spinoza's ancestors sought refuge in Portugal, but were eventually forced into baptism there, and so began to live outwardly as Catholics while trying to preserve a semblance of Judaism in their homes. In the 1590s Spinoza's parents and grandparents escaped to the Netherlands, where it had become possible to practice Judaism openly again in reconstituted Jewish communities.[2]

As Yirmiyahu Yovel argues in *Spinoza and Other Heretics*—a source that Goldstein cites and draws upon—the impact of several centuries of anti-Semitic rhetoric, threats to life and property, and the habit of living publicly as Christians and privately as Jews, left a mark on the worldview of these communities of former Marranos. Some among them began to feel as ill at ease within one religion as their parents had felt within another—and this malaise, this detachment from received tradition, engendered a skeptical individualism, which Yovel and others identify as a major catalyst for modernity.[3] The subtitle of Goldstein's book, *The Renegade Jew Who Gave us Modernity*, announces this point quite boldly.[4]

Yet it is neither this positioning of Spinoza as a harbinger of modernity nor the rooting of his ideology in the Marranos' historical experience that has rubbed some of Goldstein's reviewers the wrong way, but rather Goldstein's claim that despite his excommunication, Spinoza maintained a soft spot for Judaism in his heart until the end of his life.[5] In a scathing review of her book, Allan Nadler harps on Goldstein's deviations from standard scholarly interpretations of the Dutch philosopher's life and thought—pointing to instances where Goldstein even departs from hard data to substantiate her claims about Spinoza's allegiances.[6] It is precisely in these fascinating interstices between historical fact and imaginative interpretation, as well as in awareness of the distance between received tradition and its ongoing reinterpretations, that our understanding of sephardism as a politicized metaphor grounds itself.

Early on in her book, Goldstein depicts an autobiographical scene in which she and her classmates at an orthodox Jewish school in New York learn about Spinoza. For their teacher, Spinoza's excommunication serves as a warning "against the dangers of asking the wrong questions" (21). At stake in this classroom scene is not the *right* to ask questions—expected and encouraged in Jewish tradition—but rather the *type* of questions considered fruitful and proper. The classroom dynamics also enables Goldstein to construct a dramatic platform for her teacher's riveting account of the special conditions under which Sephardic Jews and conversos lived, which forced them to depart from their usual denominational box, so that discussions they did not normally encourage had to be undertaken as a means of survival in the face of conversionist onslaughts.

It is quite true that former Marranos who reconstituted themselves into open Jewish communities in the Netherlands came inoculated, as it were, with a strong dose of religious rationalism developed through a long established tradition of talmudic argumentation in Spain and elsewhere, and particularly honed by Spanish rabbis reacting to conversionist disputations staged by Catholic authorities against Judaism. The wide dissemination of such counterpropaganda devised by the rabbinic leaders of fifteenth-century Spain, as Miriam Bodian explains, "insured that many Jews who were eventually baptized—of particular importance among them the Spanish exiles who settled in Portugal—departed from organized Jewish life firmly indoctrinated with anti-Christian teaching." Within this framework, "elite, polemically sophisticated forms of crypto-Judaism were able to achieve a degree of invulnerability to Catholic attack by gravitating toward a straightforward, unambiguous, rationalistic interpretation of Scripture." As they reintegrated themselves into traditional Jewish life in the Netherlands, the members of Spinoza's community could draw upon yet another variety of Jewish counterrhetoric, which depicted Christians converting to Judaism: "Typically . . . a pious Old Christian who underwent a crisis as a result of reading the Gospels critically. The Gospels, the person discovered, were full of contradictions. He was forced to conclude that they were nothing but a set of fables of human origin," yet when he turns to the Hebrew Bible, he meets with a revelatory experience that leads him to determine that the Law of Moses is the "one eternal law of God."[7] These polemical approaches to the Gospels paved the way for individuals whose faith had already been contested to apply a similar rationalization to the Hebrew Bible itself, and hence to all organized forms of religion, as Spinoza did.

When Jewish communities of former Marranos are viewed from this perspective, it suddenly seems surprising that there were so few heretics, and that none challenged their community's beliefs as drastically as Spinoza did. To properly understand Spinoza's extraordinary position, however, we must consider both his community's deep preoccupation with questions of personal salvation through a *specific* religion, and the fact that every individual's life in Europe, at this time, took place almost entirely within a specific religious community. Outlining such a broad theological and sociological context would draw me too far afield from what I intend here only as a brief sketch of how *Betraying Spinoza* articulates Sephardic history. Suffice it to say that Goldstein rightly follows Yirmiyahu Yovel's grappling with Spinoza's uniqueness vis-à-vis "other heretics," but she further insists on bringing him back into a Jewish fold by emphasizing—or inventing, as Harold Bloom or Allan Nadler might argue—a persistent emotional allegiance to the community from which he was excommunicated.

Allan Nadler admits that Goldstein's desire to redeem Spinoza as a Jew is hardly a new phenomenon.[8] Indeed, as Jonathan Skolnik has forcefully asserted, "any inquiry into the meaning of Spinoza for Jewish modernity" must, first of all, take account of the "lost tradition of German-Jewish Spinozism."[9] Indeed, as Skolnik points out, the very first modern Jewish historical novel ever written took Spinoza as its subject. In *Spinoza: Ein historischer Roman* (1837), the German-Jewish novelist Bertold Auerbach constructed a "battered and awestruck Wandering Jew" in opposition to the enlightened philosopher, in order to show how the Wandering Jew perishes as soon as he recognizes a secular redeemer in Spinoza.[10] Thus Auerbach not only invites the excommunicated philosopher to posthumously lead the way out of nineteenth-century political quandaries, he does this, as did so many other nineteenth-century German-Jewish modernizers, through a Sephardic matrix: "the secular messianism imputed by Auerbach to Spinoza seemed but a step along the cultural continuum from Córdoba to Amsterdam," as Ismar Schorsch points out in his essay at the beginning of this volume. Within the Latin American variation of this phenomenon, Spinoza's image likewise functions as a beacon of modernization through a neo-Sephardic matrix. Edna Aizenberg mentions how in Argentina at the turn of the twentieth century, the Jewish writer Samuel Glusberg hispanized his name to Enrique Espinoza in honor of *two* renegade Jews from central Europe: "Enrique" Heine and Baruch Spinoza.

But although Nadler mocks Goldstein's romancing of Spinoza, the title of his own review acknowledges that such a romancing has become an interesting phenomenon in its own right. More self-consciously than any of the writers of historical romances that we discuss in this volume, Goldstein unabashedly constructs a romance not only between the excommunicated philosopher and the Jewish tradition he eschewed, but especially between what she calls her "lovable" subject and his biographer (47). Goldstein's biography of Spinoza cannot be considered a historical novel like Bertold Auerbach's, or many other instances of that genre explored in this volume, but her premises and arguments may be better appreciated if we read her from the perspective of the conventions of historical romance, rather than the requirements of a historiographic treatise.

Unlike a typical historical romance, *Betraying Spinoza* does not present a love affair set in the past, though it does establish a hobbling "love" triangle—quite explicitly and as a structural device—between Goldstein, Spinoza, and the persistent problem of Jewish particularism in modern life and institutions. This problem, as we have repeatedly seen, lies at the center of most cases of sephardism from the eighteenth century until the present. Through various rhetorical moves, Goldstein links and extends the famous fissure between Spinoza and his own religious community to fissures between Goldstein and her environment, as well as between Spinoza's philosophical path and her contrary way of writing about it. These are the intertwined fault lines already announced in the title of her biographical/autobiographical encounter with Spinoza. After all, Goldstein betrays a man who notoriously betrayed his own community's expectations—even if she is at pains to bridge these gaps by identifying some avenues of transcendental reconciliation. Goldstein's main point—which constitutes a betrayal of Spinoza—is that although *he* rejected a belief in religious particularism or chosenness of any kind, and therefore based his philosophical system on a radical objectivity that demands complete abstention from any discussion of identity politics or personal attachments, *she* nonetheless finds it expedient and necessary to delve into Spinoza's unique psychological and sociological makeup in order to explain the development of his extraordinary philosophical system. In other words, even if Spinoza was content to withdraw from Judaism, his loving biographer plunges "him" right back into Jewish history and identity politics to highlight how he created for himself—just as his community was doing, only in the opposite direction—an unadulterated worldview from which to counter the unsettling effects of a traumatic converso heritage.

It is not clear whether we ought to approach *Betraying Spinoza* as an authoritative historical biography, as the musings of a postmodern biographer, or even as a kind of philosophical romance where an intrusive first-person narrator debates with various authoritative figures from the past. In a move that is quite unusual and even shocking, Goldstein weaves intimate details from her own life into this treatise on Spinoza, offering information about her own family, orthodox Jewish upbringing, and academic training in philosophy as credentials for establishing a unique sociological and psychological affinity with this seventeenth-century philosopher. Goldstein constantly weaves intimate details from her own life—information about her family, her orthodox Jewish upbringing, and her academic training in philosophy—into her treatise on Spinoza to suggest a sociological and psychological affinity between them, a tactic that is unconventional and even startling.

Perhaps because she is writing in an age "whose distinctive literary voice is the memoir"—and thus at a time when readers are particularly "ill placed to grasp the vision of Spinoza" with its fundamental mistrust of subjectivity (69)—Goldstein admits that her own knowledge of Spinoza was indeed shaped by her personal emotions, upbringing, and intellectual formation, but suggests that she surmounted this narrow formation to gain a reliable measure of objectivity. This rhetorical maneuver, however, entails a series of betrayals, firstly of the community in which she was brought up: a community of orthodox American Jews whose parochialism she exposes and mocks in order to prove her intimacy with worldviews that continue to excommunicate Spinoza. Just as she delivers key aspects of Spinoza to us via the arguments of her Orthodox Jewish teacher, Mrs. Schoenfeld, Goldstein also betrays her teachers of philosophy at Princeton, since they, too, were uninterested in the kind of philosophy that Spinoza offers: "And so I can imagine . . . Peter Hempel, at that time one of the last of the original members of the legendary Vienna Circle, which had propounded . . . logical positivism—translating Mrs. Schoenfeld into the language of positivism" (54–55). Yet through all these tongue-in-cheek betrayals, undertaken partly for the sake of romancing Spinoza, Goldstein not only succeeds in conveying to the reader a vivid image of the extraordinary young man that

Spinoza was; she also sparks an interest in "what the facts really were, and how far the novelist has justly represented them," as Walter Scott once argued in defense of his seminal historical romances.[11]

Throughout this volume, we have repeatedly shown how sephardism has functioned as a politicized literary metaphor for a wide variety of authors in different ethnic, religious, and national contexts. This claim is reinforced once again by the dubious political connection that Goldstein insists on drawing between Spinoza's historical environment and her circumstances in the United States at the turn of the twenty-first century. Regarding political history, Goldstein declares that the key to Spinoza's political theory is that "the rationally constructed cannot fail to get along" (68), and in reference to threatening encroachments of politics into science and philosophy, she worries that "the sides are drawn up now much as they were in Spinoza's day" (11).[12]

In particular, Goldstein highlights the impact of Spinoza's ideas on pivotal figures of the enlightenment such as Leibnitz and Locke.[13] But she furthermore traces an indirect link from Spinoza, via Locke's endorsement of a separation between Church and state, to Thomas Jefferson's inclusion of this doctrine in the Constitution of the United States. That this Jeffersonian line of influence has yet to be proven[14]—and that Spinoza did not actually advocate a total separation between Church and state, but only a regulation of religious institutions by the state so that the powers of the clergy could be kept in check[15]—is less of an issue, to my mind, than the fissure that emerges in Goldstein's book between the pluralistic character of the United States and her advocacy of secularism for *all* people. Here Goldstein effects yet another betrayal, perhaps the most serious of them all, for while she leans on Spinoza to champion secularism as the only "true" and "right" ideology for all people, the Constitution of the United States safeguards secular institutions in the same breath as it enables individuals to exercise freedom of religion and communal autonomy, including the right to send one's children to parochial schools such as the one that provided Goldstein with such excellent material for her creative writing. This multiple betrayal of core values functions as the paradoxical and self-conscious structure on which Goldstein mounts her book.

Betraying Spinoza is an intriguing example of sephardism from the United States at the turn of the twenty-first century. It demonstrates, first of all, that the retelling of Sephardic history continues to be relevant to creative writers in our own day, and reveals once again how sephardism functions as a politicized metaphor that cannot be simplistically pegged onto the ostensible ethnic or religious identity of its practitioners. Like the writers of U.S. Latina sephardism that Dalia Kandiyoti examines—whose novels strategically transcend the ethnic and gender context that initially defined them as an expression of a Latina identity, which now becomes marketed also in a Jewish context—Goldstein's sephardism operates simultaneously on assimilationist and anti-assimilationist levels. She uses Sephardic history to celebrate the resilience of Jewish practice, yet this same resilience is also adduced as proof of the problematic nature of ethnic, religious, and national divisions, so that a literary work initially identified and marketed on an ethnic/religious basis—*Betraying Spinoza* forms part of the Jewish Encounters series—paradoxically undercuts the very relevance of its own identity politics. By contrast, Naomi Ragen's *The Ghost of Hannah Mendes* (1998) operates exclusively on an *anti*-assimilationist level. It is a popular historical novel addressed primarily to young Jewish American female readers, who are enjoined to follow the novel's teenage American characters as they learn to appreciate their current level of freedom and comfort in light of the obstacles faced by their Sephardic ancestors. Goldstein's sephardism makes this claim too—arguing *both* for the relevance of Jewish identity and history, and emphasizing the perils of taking modernity for granted—yet Judaism as a way of life is sacrificed in the process, it is rendered irrelevant, and hence Goldstein's position, like Spinoza's, threatens a Jewish particularism whose existence depends on demarcations of differences between, for example, Holy days and work days, Jew and Gentile, or foods considered permissible and those prohibited in deference to traditional markers of a historicized identity.

At the beginning of her treatise on Spinoza, Goldstein avows: "There was a moment long ago when I knew next to nothing about the magnificent reconfiguration of reality laid out in the system of Spinoza, and yet when I felt I knew something about what it was like to have been him, the former yeshiva student, Baruch Spinoza. I would like to know that feeling again, even though I know that the desire amounts to betraying Spinoza" (66). To understand why Spinoza "would most radically rethink the very notion of personal identity itself"—to imagine this man and his world—she therefore pries into his family background, uncovering a harrowing story of conversions and counterconversions that reveals an "atmosphere in which the question of personal identity throbbed with all the cumulative tragedy of the Sephardic experience" (164).

With these words I can conclude, as well, my own efforts to prove that Sephardic history has played a key role in shaping our world: that an awareness of the Sephardic experience has been pervasive, sometimes subconsciously, throughout the political and literary history of the modern era from the Enlightenment to our days. Especially since the quincentennial of 1992, a larger number of intellectuals have become fully awake to the importance of understanding Sephardic history not only for its own sake, but also for the sake of extricating ourselves from its traumas and perhaps learn something from its moments of creativity and *convivencia*.

Reference Matter

Notes

Introduction

1. For an analysis of the rise of modern nationalism as a competition between cultures, see Liah Greenfeld's magisterial study *Nationalism: Five Roads to Modernity* (Cambridge, MA: Harvard University Press, 1992). Among the five national models she examines—England, France, Russia, Germany, and the United States—Greenfeld discusses representation of Jews only in relation to Germany; however, Biblical attitudes towards national chosenness form part of her wider discussion.

2. Jane Gerber's *The Jews of Spain: A History of the Sephardic Experience* (New York: Free Press, 1992) and Zion Zohar's *Sephardic and Mizrahi Jewry: From the Golden Age of Spain to Modern Times* (New York: New York University Press, 2005) provide a good survey of the Sephardic experience. Among the many authoritative volumes concentrating on specific aspects of the history of the Jews of Iberia, see in particular Yitzhak Baer's *A History of the Jews in Christian Spain* (Philadelphia: Jewish Publications Society, 1961); Haim Beinart's *The Expulsion of the Jews from Spain* (Portland, OR: Littman Library of Jewish Civilization, 2002); Mark Cohen's *Under Crescent and Cross: The Jews in the Middle Ages* (Princeton, NJ: Princeton University Press, 1995); and Ray Jonathan's *The Sephardic Frontier: The Reconquista and the Jewish Community in Medieval Iberia* (Ithaca, NY: Cornell University Press, 2006). Interest in the multicultural nature of Al-Andalus has burgeoned in recent years, as attested by the publication of Maria Rosa Menocal's *The Ornament of the World: How Muslims, Jews, and Christians Created a Culture of Tolerance in Medieval Spain* (Boston: Little, Brown, 2002); Chris Lowney's *A Vanished World: Muslims, Christians, and Jews in Medieval Spain* (New York: Free Press, 2005); and Olivia Remie Constable's *Medieval Iberia: Readings from Christian, Muslim, and Jewish Sources* (Philadelphia: University of Pennsylvania Press, 1997).

3. In recent years, four collected volumes from Germany, Spain, France, and the United States have approached Sepharad as a topic of cultural representation: *Das schwierige Erbe von Sefarad: Juden und Mauren in der spanischen Literatur* (Frankfurt am Main: Vervuert, 2002) and *El legado de Sefarad* (Salamanca: Amarú, 2003), both edited by Norbert Rehrmann; *Renewing the Past, Reconfiguring Jewish Culture: From*

Al-Andalus to the Haskalah, edited by Ross Brann and Adam Sutcliffe (Philadelphia: University of Pennsylvania Press, 2004); and *Les Sépharades en littérature: Un parcours millénaire*, edited by Esther Benbassa (Paris: Presses de l'Université Paris-Sorbonne, 2005).

4. Ron Schechter's "The Jewish Question in Eighteenth-Century France," *Eighteenth-Century Studies* 32.1 (1998): 84–91, demonstrates how political discussions during the months immediately following the French Revolution centered disproportionately on the status of Jews, even after it was already clear that both the Sephardic and Ashkenazic Jews in France would be granted full citizenship.

5. For a wider account of the "Jewish Question" in the context of the Enlightenment, see Arthur Hertzberg's *The French Enlightenment and the Jews: The Origins of Modern Anti-Semitism* (New York: Columbia University Press, 1968) and, in a somewhat later context, Michael Ragussis's *Figures of Conversion: "The Jewish Question" and English National Identity* (Durham, NC: Duke University Press, 1995).

6. Jonathan Schorsch, "Disappearing Origins: Sephardic Autobiography Today," *Prooftexts* 27.1 (2007): 83.

7. *Sephardic Identity: Essays on a Vanishing Jewish Culture*, ed. George Zucker (Jefferson, NC: McFarland, 2005).

8. I am thinking, for example, of David Graizbord's *Souls in Dispute: Converso Identities in Iberia and the Jewish Diaspora* (Philadelphia: University of Pennsylvania Press, 2003); Jonathan Decter's *Iberian Jewish Literature: Between al-Andalus and Christian Europe* (Bloomington: Indiana University Press, 2007); and Aviva Ben-Ur's *Sephardic Jews in America: A Diasporic History* (New York: New York University Press, 2009); as well as earlier foundational works by Daniel Elazar, Tamar Alexander, and Margalit Bejarano in Israel; Aron Rodrigue and Norman Stillman in the United States; and Esther Benbassa and Jean-Christophe Attias in France.

9. Growing acknowledgment of the impact of the Sephardic experience can be seen, for instance, in *Sepharad in Ashkenaz: Medieval Knowledge and Eighteenth-Century Enlightened Jewish Discourse*, ed. Resianne Fontaine, Andrea Schatz, and Irene Zwiep (Amsterdam: Koninklijke Nederlandse Akademie van Wetenschappen, 2007).

10. See Ragussis's Chapter Two in this volume, and his extended discussion of Disraeli in *Figures of Conversion*, 174ff.

11. Elena Romero, "The Theme of Spain in the Sephardic Haskalah's Literature," in *The Jews of Spain and the Expulsion of 1492*, ed. Moshe Lazar and Stephen Halizer (Lancaster, CA: Labyrinthos, 1997), 25–26.

12. *Medievalism and the Modernist Temper*, ed. R. Howard Bloch and Stephen G. Nichols (Baltimore: Johns Hopkins University Press, 1996), 26, 31; and see Stacy Beckwith's extended discussion of Bloch and Nichols in Chapter Seven of this volume.

13. On the Gothic novel as an opposition to authority in the eighteenth and nineteenth centuries, see Maggie Kilgour's *The Rise of the Gothic Novel* (London: Routledge, 1995) and Eve Kosofsky Sedgwick's *The Coherence of Gothic Conventions*

(London: Methuen, 1986). Regarding Jews and the Gothic novel in England, see Ragussis, *Figures of Conversion,* 135–36.

14. Edward Said, *Orientalism* (New York: Vintage Books, 1979), 1, 204.

15. Efraim Sicher's analysis of *The Moor's Last Sigh* in Chapter Eleven in this volume shows how Rushdie, a postmodern British Indian of Muslim descent, attempts to *reverse* the orientalization of India by gazing at Moorish Spain from a secularized, diasporic, and postcolonial point of view. In *Orientalism and the Jews* (Waltham, MA: Brandeis University Press; Hanover, NH: University Press of New England, 2005), Ivan Kalmar and Derek Penslar have begun the project of tracing the many ways in which "the Western image of the Muslim Orient has been and continues to be formed in inextricable conjunction with Western perceptions of the Jewish people" (xiii). As Kalmar and Penslar point out, this is something Edward Said recognized in his seminal study, but later underplayed for political reasons (xv). See Said, *Orientalism*, 27–28.

16. Bernard Lewis, *History: Remembered, Recovered, Invented* (New York: Simon & Schuster, 1987), 73.

17. Ibid., 77.

18. In "Gerchunoff y la legitimación hispánica," in *La identidad judía en la literatura argentina* (Buenos Aires: Pardes, 1983), 39–57, Leonardo Senkman provides an overview of Argentina's rapprochement towards Spain during the centennial celebrations of its independence from the mother country; on this topic, see also *Bridging the Atlantic: Toward a Reassessment of Iberian and Latin American Cultural Ties*, ed. Marina Pérez de Mendiola (Albany: State University of New York Press, 1996); and for an extended analysis of Gerchunoff's sephardism, see Edna Aizenberg's Chapter Five in this volume.

19. On hispanism in France, see esp. Antonio Niño, *Cultura y diplomacia: Los hispanistas franceses y España de 1875–1931* (Madrid: Consejo Superior de Investigaciones Científicas, 1988); and for a survey of the origins of French hispanism, Philippe Loupés, "Aux origines de l'hispanisme français: Georges Cirot et *Le Bulletin hispanique*," in *Minorités juives, pouvoirs, littérature politique en péninsule Ibérique, France et Italie au Moyen âge: Études offertes à Béatrice Leroy*, ed. Jean-Pierre Barraqué and Véronique Lamazou-Duplan (Biaritz: Atlantica, 2006), 501–17.

20. James Russell Lowell, quoted by Richard L. Kagan in the latter's excellent collection of articles on hispanism, *Spain in America: The Origins of Hispanism in the United States* (Urbana: University of Illinois Press, 2002), 254 (my emphasis). Another solid collection of articles on hispanism is Mabel Moraña's *Ideologies of Hispanism* (Nashville, TN: Vanderbilt University Press, 2005).

21. Kagan, *Spain in America*, 2.

22. Zucker, *Sephardic Identity*, 1.

23. What Kagan calls " Prescott's Paradigm" functions as the linchpin of his approach to U.S. hispanism (*Spain in America*, 247–76). For a discussion of Prescott's hispanism specifically in relation to sephardism, see Ragussis, *Figures of Conversion*, 159–73.

24. Barbara Becker-Cantarino, "The Rediscovery of Spain in Enlightened and Romantic Germany," *Monatshefte* 72.2 (1980): 122–23.

25. Susanna Heschel, "Jewish Studies as Counterhistory" in *Insider/Outsider: American Jews and Multiculturalism*, ed. Michael Galchinsky, David Biale, and Susannah Heschel (Berkeley: University of California Press, 1998), 104–5.

26. Tamar Garb and Linda Nochlin's pioneering collection of articles on *The Jew in the Text: Modernity and the Construction of Identity* (London: Thames & Hudson, 1995) and Bryan Cheyette and Laura Marcus's *Modernity, Culture and 'the Jew'* (Stanford, CA.: Stanford University Press, 1998) seek to deconstruct modern stereotypes of Jews. Galchinsky et al. in *Insider/Outsider* (n. 25 above) and Sander L. Gilman in *Multiculturalism and the Jews* (New York: Routledge, 2006) assess the paradoxical position of Jewish Studies within contemporary multicultural discourse—the latter as an extension of Gilman's now classical studies on Jewish self-hatred, anti-Semitism, and representations of the Jew's body. I would also like to mention Michael Brenner's insightful overviews of Jewish communities, for instance, *Jewish Emancipation Reconsidered: The French and German Models,* ed. id., Vicki Caron, and Uri R. Kaufmann (Tübingen: Mohr Siebeck, 2003).

27. Heschel, *Insider/Outsider*, 112.

28. David Block, "Quincentennial Publishing: An Ocean of Print," *Latin American Research Review* 29.3 (1994): 101–28.

29. Aside from György Lukács's groundbreaking analysis of *The Historical Novel* (Lincoln: University of Nebraska Press, 1962), prominent studies of Scott's achievement and influence can be found in Harry E. Shaw's *The Forms of Historical Fiction: Sir Walter Scott and His Successors* (Ithaca, NY: Cornell University Press, 1983); J. H. Alexander and David Hewitt's *Scott and His Influence* (Aberdeen: Association for Scottish Literary Studies, 1983); and David Brown's *Walter Scott and the Historical Imagination* (London: Routledge & Kegan Paul, 1979).

30. The National Library of Scotland's database lists 609 translations of *Ivanhoe*, beginning with German and French translations immediately following its publication in 1820.

31. Doris Sommer makes this point forcefully in *Foundational Fictions: The National Romances of Latin America* (Berkeley: University of California Press, 1991).

32. Ragussis, *Figures of Conversion*, 126.

33. Quoted ibid., 126.

34. In England, full emancipation of the Jews occurred in 1856, roughly at the same time that Jews were emancipated elsewhere in Europe, whereas in France, as noted, formal emancipation had been granted in the throes of the French Revolution. However, emancipation is not necessarily the best indicator of how well integrated or accepted Jews were in each place, as Michael Brenner argues in *Jewish Emancipation Reconsidered*, ed. id. et al., 2.

35. Sir Walter Scott, *Ivanhoe: A Romance* (New York: Signet Classic, 2001), 370.

36. For studies on the nineteenth-century historical novel, see n. 29 above; and

on its postmodern manifestations, see esp. Linda Hutcheon's *A Poetics of Postmodernism: History, Theory, Fiction* (London: Routledge, 1988).

37. *The Merchant of Venice*'s influence has been examined by many of our contributors either in this volume or in their work elsewhere. Efraim Sicher notes Rushdie's allusions to Shakespeare in *The Moor's Last Sigh*, discussed in Chapter Eleven of this volume; in *Figures of Conversion*, Michael Ragussis conducted a detailed exposition of *Ivanhoe's* relationship to *The Merchant of Venice* (114–18); the overall topic of Jonathan Skolnik's "'Who learns history from Heine?' The German-Jewish Historical Novel as Cultural Memory and Minority Culture, 1824–1953" (Ph.D. diss., Columbia University, 1999) is actually an examination of "the history of Shylock in Germany" (8); and Diana Hallman likewise devotes considerable attention to this play's influence on Fromental Halévy and Eugène Scribe's opera *La Juive* both in her Chapter Three for this volume and in *Opera, Liberalism, and Antisemitism in Nineteenth-Century France: The Politics of Halévy's "La Juive"* (Cambridge: Cambridge University Press, 2002), 234–52.

38. Michael Shapiro argues for this position in "Lewisohn's *The Last Days of Shylock*," in *Countering Shylock*, ed. Edna Nachshon and Michael Shapiro (Cambridge: Cambridge University Press, 2012).

39. For a useful chronology comparing conventional and postmodern historical novels, see Seymour Menton's *Latin America's New Historical Novel* (Austin: University of Texas Press, 1993), 2–13.

40. On Yehuda Halevi's ideological and physical trajectory between Sepharad and Zion, see Ross Brann's "Entre sefarad et terre d'Israël" in *Les Sépharades en littérature*, ed. Benbassa, 11–43.

41. These elegies are discussed by Miriam Bodian in *Dying in the Law of Moses: Crypto-Jewish Martyrdom in the Iberian World* (Bloomington: Indiana University Press, 2007), 7–9.

42. One could further argue that a significant narrative source for sephardism, as well as for the wider Jewish maiden plot, needs to be located in the anti-Semitic legend about Alfonso VIII and a Jewess from Toledo, originally recorded as a homily by King Sancho IV of Castile in the thirteenth century and thereafter retold by many authors. Lope de Vega's "Las paces de los reyes y judía de Toledo" (1617) is considered the first literary rendition of this legend. Vicente García de la Huerta's 1778 dramatic version, *Raquel, tragedia española en tres jornadas*, became particularly influential in the nineteenth century; it is through this version, which conflates elements from the Jewess of Toledo with both the biblical Book of Esther and Shakespeare's *Merchant of Venice*, that French renditions such as Jacques Cazotte's novella *Rachel ou la belle juive* (1788 [?]) and P.-E. Chevalier's 1803 melodrama of the same title alternately include a father or uncle figure in a leading role. Some versions of the legend are discussed by Élie Lambert in "Alphonse de Castille et la Juive de Tolède," *Bulletin hispanique* 25.4 (1923): 371–94, as well as by Edna Aizenberg in "Una judía muy fermosa: The Jewess as Sex Object in Medieval Spanish Literature and Lore," *La Corónica* 12 (1984): 187–94; the legend's origins are illuminated in

David Nirenberg's "Deviant Politics and Jewish Love: Alfonso VIII and the Jewess of Toledo," *Jewish History* 21 (2007): 15–41.

43. For a sustained exploration of this contention, see Robert A. Logan's *Shakespeare's Marlowe: The Influence of Christopher Marlowe on Shakespeare's Artistry* (Burlington, VT: Ashgate, 2007).

44. Surveyed in Harm den Boer's "Le 'contre-discourse' des nouveaux juifs" in *Les Sépharades en littérature*, 47–65; regarding New Christians and the Spanish Baroque, see Chapter Six in this volume.

45. A brilliant contextualization of the Dutch Republic as a precursor to the Enlightenment can be found in Jonathan I. Israel, *Radical Enlightenment: Philosophy and the Making of Modernity 1650–1750* (Oxford: Oxford University Press, 2001).

46. An argument that Yirmiyahu Yovel put forth initially in *Spinoza and Other Heretics: The Marrano of Reason* (Princeton, NJ: Princeton University Press, 1989) and more recently in *The Other Within: The Marranos, Split Identity and Emerging Modernity* (Princeton, NJ: Princeton University Press, 2009).

47. The picaresque's subsequent impact on the development of the modern novel has been well documented in classical studies of this genre such as Walter L. Reed's *An Exemplary History of the Novel: The Quixotic Versus the Picaresque* (Chicago: Chicago University Press, 1981); Alexander A. Parker's *Literature and the Delinquent: The Picaresque Novel in Spain and Europe, 1599–1753* (Edinburgh: Edinburgh University Press, 1967); and Robert Alter's *Rogue's Progress: Studies in the Picaresque Novel* (Cambridge, MA: Harvard University Press, 1964).

48. Edward Peter's *Inquisition* (Berkeley: University of California Press, 1989) discusses general representations of the Inquisition among the philosophes (see esp. chapters 6 and 7). For a more specialized discussion of the philosophes' interest in Jews and the Inquisition, see Diana Hallman's Chapter Three in this volume, as well as Arthur Hertzberg's *French Enlightenment and the Jews*, 273–81, and Lori L. McMann's "The Figure of the Jew in French Texts of the Eighteenth Century" (Ph.D. diss., University of Michigan, 2004). For a broader analysis of Jews and the Catholic Church in the writings of French and German intellectuals of the eighteenth and nineteenth centuries, see Ari (Alexander) Joskowicz's "Anticlerical Alliances: Jews and the Church Question in Germany and France, 1783–1905" (Ph.D. diss., University of Chicago, 2008).

49. Hertzberg, *French Enlightenment and the Jews*, 180–83.

50. Jonathan Skolnik observes that at work here is "a complex pattern of cultural transfer and cross-influence between 'high' and 'low' cultures and between England and Germany. . . . German-Jewish historical novelists are inspired by Scott, Scott was inspired by Goethe's historical dramas, and Goethe's plays are indebted to the rediscovery of Shakespeare in the *Sturm und Drang* era" ("Who learns history from Heine?" 103). Another fascinating point of cross-cultural influence can be found in Gerchunoff's *Jewish Gauchos*, where Argentina's eastern European Jewish immigrants congregate to read a historical novel about Sepharad by Shomer, a popular Russian novelist and dramatist who wrote in Yiddish. Thus, Old World sephardism

is carried over and reshaped through Gerchunoff's crucible (see Aizenberg's Chapter Five in this volume).

51. Brenner, *Jewish Emancipation Reconsidered*, ed. id. et al., 2.

52. On the representation of Jews and the Catholic Church among eighteenth- and nineteenth-century intellectuals in France and Germany, see Ari Joskowicz's "Anticlerical Alliances," cited in n. 48 above.

53. Regarding the modern history of the Jews of France, see Jay Berkowitz's *Rites and Passages: The Beginning of Modern Jewish Culture in France, 1650–1860* (Philadelphia: University of Pennsylvania Press, 2004); Paula Hyman's *From Dreyfus to Vichy: The Remaking of French Jewry, 1906–1939* (New York: Columbia University Press, 1979); and Esther Benbassa's *Histoire des Juifs de France* (Paris: Seuil, 2000).

54. The discourses of medievalism, hispanism, and orientalism responded in a large measure to national images and rivalries. Bloch and Nichols stress that "the nationalistic rivalry between Germany and France" was the leading factor in the rise of a medieval doctrine across nineteenth-century Europe (13). Edward Said's *Orientalism* responds to negative stereotypes of Arabs and Muslims as one of the "Others" against which Western nations define themselves. As for hispanism, Richard Kagan ascribes its origins in the United States to a "juxtaposition of Spanish decadence and U.S. progress" (*Spain in America*, 248).

55. Nochlin and Garb's *Jew in the Text* contains several excellent essays on literary and pictorial representations of Jews in France.

56. These French translations of García de la Huerta's play are mentioned in n. 42 above.

57. See Lynn Weiss's introduction to Victor Séjour's *The Jew of Seville*, trans. Norman R. Shapiro (Urbana: University of Illinois Press, 2002), xv–xxxiii.

58. Maurice Samuels, "David Schornstein and the Rise of Jewish Historical Fiction in Nineteenth-Century France," *Jewish Social Studies: History, Culture, Society* 14.3 (2008): 50.

59. Aron Rodrigue, "Léon Halévy and Modern French Jewish Historiography," in *Jewish History and Jewish Memory: Essays in Honor of Yosef Hayim Yerushalmi*, ed. Elisheva Carlebach, John Efron, and David Myers (Hanover, NH: University Press of New England, 1998), 413–27.

60. See Hallman, *Opera, Liberalism, and Antisemitism*, p. 13, and Chapter Three in the present volume.

61. Elaine Marks defines Marranos much too broadly as "Jews who have to some degree been taken in by or assimilated to the other religious cultures in which they live (these may be Christian or Muslim) and who continue in spite of this inevitable acculturation to profess a belonging to Jewishness," in *Marrano as Metaphor: The Jewish Presence in French Writing* (New York: Columbia University Press, 1996), xviii. More helpful definitions of this construct can be found in Shmuel Trigano's *Le Juif caché: Marranisme et modernité* (Paris: Inpress, 2000) and in a number of relevant items in the *Sepharad/Francophone* issue of *Contemporary French and Franco-*

phone Studies 11.2 (2007), edited by Eliane DalMolin, Roger Célestin, and Johann Sadock.

62. Didier Nebot, *Le chemin de l'exil* (Paris: Presses de la Renaissance, 1992), 316.

63. Isaiah Berlin, *The Roots of Romanticism* (Princeton, NJ: Princeton University Press, 2001), 109.

64. Edna Aizenberg, *Parricide on the Pampa? A New Study and Translation of Alberto Gerchunoff's "Los gauchos judíos"* (Frankfurt am Main: Vervuert; Madrid: Iberoamericana, 2000), 43.

65. In a study of marranism in the work of the North American Yiddish poet Jacob Glatstein, Leah Garrett observes that "even in the freest countries . . . we are Marranos . . . the self as Marrano not only means a homelessness (or nationless) self, but also a self in which there is a permanent fissure between the public and the private. . . . Marrano is the meeting point of a constantly shifting relationship between one's private reality, and how one is defined as a Jew by the ever changing outside world" (Garrett, "The Self as Marrano," *Prooftexts* 19 [1998]: 208–9). I find this definition of the Marrano too broad and insufficiently grounded in actual history, but Yirmiyahu Yovel's research and some of the studies cited in n. 61 above provide a firmer starting point for a fuller consideration of the figure of the Marrano.

66. Ben-Ami Feingold, "Historical Dramas on the Inquisition and Expulsion," *Journal of Theater and Drama* 1.22 (1995): 10. This is an excellent survey of Hebrew plays from Israel in the 1940s and 1950s that exhibit some of the themes examined here.

67. Reyes Coll-Tellechea, "Remembering Sepharad," in *Memory, Oblivion and Jewish Culture in Latin America*, ed. Marjorie Agosín (Austin: University of Texas Press, 2005), 4–5.

68. In works such as *Tropics of Discourse* (Baltimore: Johns Hopkins University Press, 1978) and *The Content of Form* (Baltimore: Johns Hopkins University Press, 1987), Hayden White convincingly demonstrated that historiographers follow generic conventions associated with imaginative literature, especially when they use figurative language and teleological plots. But narrative fiction, including the historical novel, still enjoys far greater imaginative liberties, although it is constrained at the same time by a far more onerous and sophisticated network of generic conventions. Dorrit Cohn has been among the most persuasive scholars to make these points against White in *The Distinction of Fiction* (Baltimore: Johns Hopkins University Press, 1999). See also Lionel Grossman's impassioned arguments contra White in *Between History and Literature* (Cambridge, MA: Harvard University Press, 1990).

69. Yosef HaimYerushalmi, "Modern Dilemmas," in *Zakhor: Jewish History and Jewish Memory* (Seattle: University of Washington Press, 1996), 101.

70. Homero Aridjis, interview by author, July 12, 2000.

71. Isaac Silbershlag's Hebrew play *In the Days of Isabella* portrays Torquemada deciding to obliterate Jews "by fire! Eradicate their memory!" As Feingold observes, "the contemporary significance of the words was obvious to all" when this

play was staged between 1939 and 1941 in Tel Aviv ("Historical Dramas," 12). On the eve of the Holocaust similar warnings via the prism of Sepharad appeared throughout the Jewish world, especially in eastern Europe and Germany, where historical romances of the type that we have been following continued to be published even after Kristallnacht, as Jonathan Skolnik points out in Chapter Four of this volume and in his essay on "Dissimilation and the Historical Novel: Herman Sinsheimer's *Maria Nunnez*," *Year Book of the Leo Baeck Institute* 43 (1998): 225–35.

72. Before the *Haskalah* movement in the modern era, only a catastrophe of this magnitude could propel Jewish scholars into recording their diasporic history, so that in the decades following the expulsion, scriptural studies and traditional modes of commemoration temporarily made way for secular and mystical accounts of Jewish history by Sephardic writers such as Samuel Usque and Solomon Ibn Verga (Yerushalmi, "In the Wake of the Spanish Expulsion," in *Zakhor*, 58–59).

73. Yerushalmi, *Zakhor*, 98–100.

74. For instance, in Angelina Muñiz-Huberman's *Tierra adentro* (discussed here in Chapter Six), an anachronistic reference to the Holocaust turns this novel into what Seymour Menton calls a "new" historical novel as opposed to a conventional historical novel (*Latin America's New Historical Novel*, cited n. 39 above, 138–62).

75. "Every society importing the foreign idea of the nation inevitably focused on the source of importations . . . and reacted to it," Greenfeld observes. "Because the model was superior to the imitator in the latter's own perception . . . and the contact itself more often than not served to emphasize the latter's inferiority, the reaction commonly assumed the form of *ressentiment*. A term coined by Nietzsche and later defined and developed by Max Scheler, *ressentiment* refers to a psychological state resulting from suppressed feeling of envy and hatred (existential envy) and the impossibility of satisfying these feelings" (Greenfeld, *Nationalism*, 15).

Chapter One: The Myth of Sephardic Supremacy in Nineteenth-Century Germany

I am grateful to the Leo Baeck Institute for granting permission to reprint this essay, which originally appeared in the *Leo Baeck Institute Year Book* 34 (1989): 47–66; it was later also included in my book *From Text to Context: The Turn to History in Modern Judaism* (Hanover, NH: University Press of New England, 1994), 71–92.

1. Haim Hillel Ben-Sasson, *Hagut Ve-Hanhagah* (Jerusalem: Mosad Byalik, 1959), 13–16.

2. Philipp Bloch, "Der Streit um den Moreh des Maimonides in der Gemeinde Posen um die Mitte des 16. Jahrhunderts," *Monatsschrift für Geschichte und Wissenschaft des Judentums* 47 (1903): 154–55, 167, 346.

3. David ben Solomon Gans, *Zemah David: A Chronicle of Jewish and World History (Prague, 1592)*, ed. Mordechai Breuer (Jerusalem: Magnes Press, Hebrew University, 1983), 133, 136–37.

4. Aharon F. Kleinberger, *Ha-Mahashavah ha-pedagogit shel ha-Maharal mi-Prag* (Jerusalem: Magnes Press, Hebrew University, 1962), 90–192.

5. Shabbetai ben Joseph Bass, *Sefer Sifte yeshenim: Li-fene ne'arim u-zekenim* (Amsterdam: David Tartas, 1680), author's introduction. See also Simon Brisman, *Jewish Research Literature: A History and Guide to Judaic Bibliography* (Cincinnati: Hebrew Union College Press, 1977), 9–13. It is worth noting that both Bass and Naphtali Herz Wessely in 1782 employ the same piquant rabbinic dictum to advance their respective views: "Any scholar without breeding is worth less than a carcass" (Kol hakham she-ein bo daat, neveila tova himenu); see Mordecai Margulies, *Midrash va-yikra rabah* (Jerusalem: Keren Yehudah Leb u-Mini Epshtein, she-'al yad ha-Akademyah le-Mada'e ha-Yahadut be-Artsot-ha-Berit, 1953), 32–33. Bass chose to interpret the term *daat* to mean "scholarly method that one can master alone" (Bass, *Sefer Sifte yeshenim*, 4–5). For Wessely, *daat* connoted "secular knowledge that must be acquired by every Jew in addition to and prior to the knowledge of Torah incumbent upon him" (Naphtali Herz Wessely, *Sefer Divre shalom ve-emet 'al torat he-adam ve-torat ha-ḥinukh le-ne'are bene Yiśrael*... [Warsaw: Y. H. Zabelinski, 1886]), end of chap. 1. The changing social and political circumstances of Ashkenazic Jewry, and not the differences in interpretation, altered the import of the dictum and determined the different reactions.

6. Jacob Emden, *Megilat sefer: Toldot ve-zikhronot*, ed. David Kahana (New York: Y. Gelbman, 1956), 7–53, esp. 46.

7. Morris M. Faierstein, "The Liebes Brief. A Critique of Jewish Society in Germany (1749)," *Leo Baeck Institute Year Book* 27 (1982): 219–41.

8. Alfred Feilchenfeld, *Denkwürdigkeiten der Glückel von Hameln*, trans. Alfred Feilchenfeld (Berlin: Jüdischer Verlag, 1913), 116–18, 86–87, 90–91.

9. Heinrich Heine, *Heinrich Heine: Säkularausgabe: Werke, Briefwechsel, Lebenszeugnisse*, vol. 8 (Berlin: Akademie-Verlag, 1970), 8.185.

10. Aaron Wolfsohn, *Hame'asef*, 7 (1794–95), 54–67, 120–58, 203–27, 279–360. On the import of the bon mot, see James H. Lehmann, "Maimonides, Mendelssohn, and the Me'asfim—Philosophy and the Biographical Imagination in the Early Haskalah," *Leo Baeck Institute Yearbook* 20 (1975): 101–3.

11. Wolfsohn, *Hame'asef*, 7 (1794–95), 210; Isaac Abraham Euchel, *Toldot rabenu he-hakham Mosheh ben Menahem* (Berlin: Orientalische Buchdruckerei, 1788), 7.

12. Salomon Maimon, *Solomon Maimon: An Autobiography*, trans. John Clark Murray (London: A. Gardner, 1888), 205.

13. Max Freudenthal, *Aus der Heimat Mendelssohns. Moses Benjamin Wulff und seine Familie, die Nachkommen des Moses Isserles* (Berlin: F. E. Lederer, 1900), 218–21.

14. Isaac de Pinto, *Apologie pour la nation juive ou Reflexions critiques sur le premier chapitre du VII. tome des Oeuvres de monsieur de Voltaire, au sujet des juifs* (Amsterdam: J. Joubert, 1762).

15. Frances Malino, *The Sephardic Jews of Bordeaux: Assimilation and Emancipation in Revolutionary France* (Tuscaloosa: University of Alabama Press, 1978).

16. Jewish National and University Library, Jerusalem, 4° 792/B-10, 36.

17. I. M. Jost, *Geschichte der Israeliten seit der Zeit der Maccabäer bis auf unsre Tage*, vol. 9 (Berlin: Schlesinger, 1820), 309.

18. *Transactions of the Parisian Sanhedrim, or, Acts of the Assembly of Israelitish Depu-*

ties of France and Italy, Convoked at Paris by an Imperial and Royal Decree, Dated May 30, 1806 (Lanham, MD: University Press of America, 1985), 6–8. I do think that this modern distinction between the enduring religious and temporary political components of Judaism derives a tenuous plausibility from a somewhat analogous distinction made by Maimonides in his *Guide* between the divine laws of the Torah that order the physical life of man in society and those that advance his individual spiritual perfection.

> Know that as between these two aims, one is indubitably greater in nobility, namely, the welfare of the soul—I mean the procuring of correct opinions—while the second aim—I mean the welfare of the body—is prior in nature and time. The latter aim consists of the governance of the city and the well-being of the states of all its people according to their capacity. (Moses Maimonides, *The Guide of the Perplexed*, trans. and ed. Shlomo Pines [Chicago: University of Chicago Press, 1964], 510)

19. For subsequent applications and elaborations of this distinction in Judaism, see Malino, 92–93; *Protocolle der ersten Rabbiner-Versammlung abgehalten zu Braunschweig vom 12ten bis zum 19ten Juni, 1844* (Braunschweig: F. Vieweg & Sohn, 1844), 63–69; and Samuel Holdheim, *Über die Autonomie der Rabbinen und das Princip der jüdischen Ehe: Ein Beitrag zur Verständigung über einige das Judenthum betreffende Zeitfragen*, 2nd enlarged ed. (Schwerin: C. Kürschner: in Commission der Plahn'schen Buchhandlung, Berlin, 1847).

20. Simha Assaf, *Mekorot le-toldot ha-hinukh be-Yiśrael: (mi-tehilat yeme-ha-benayim ʾad tekufat ha-Haskalah)*, 4 vols. (Tel-Aviv: Devir, 1925–42), 1: 234.

21. Leopold Zunz, *Die gottesdienstlichen Vorträge der Juden*, ed. Nehemia Brüll, 2nd ed. (Frankfurt am Main: J. Kauffmann, 1892), 474.

22. Eliezer Liebermann, *Nogah ha-tsedek; Or nogah: Divre hokhmah u-musar be-inyan avodat ha-Shem* (Dessau: C. Schlieder, 1818), 27.

23. It should be noted that the close resemblance in pronunciation between the biblical Hebrew taught at German universities of the time and the Hebrew of the Sephardim no doubt made the latter seem correct. See Wilhelm Gesenius, *Hebräische Grammatik* (Halle: Renger, 1813), 6–13. In a most interesting letter dated October 4, 1827, J. J. Bellermann, a well-known theologian, scholar, and director of the prestigious Berlin Gymnasium zum grauen Kloster, advised Zunz to teach the Sephardic pronunciation of Hebrew from the very beginning in the Jewish communal school over which Zunz presided. Bellermann had been invited to observe a public examination of the children. While expressing his pleasure at the event, he did see fit to challenge the retention of the "Polish pronunciation of Hebrew," because it managed to offend both the vowels and accents of the language. And in conjunction with the vowels, he pointed out the historical superiority of Sephardic Hebrew.

> As you well know, the writings of learned Alexandrian Jews—in the Septuagint, Josephus, Philo, and Aquila—show that the Polish pronunciation is incorrect. . . . The learned Portuguese, Spanish, French, and Italian Jews have the correct

one. Why shouldn't the Jews of Berlin and in fact of Germany choose the better [of the two]? Especially Berlin Jewry, which has already adopted so much that is correct? It would indisputably accrue to their honor if they offered other communities an example in this. (Ludwig Geiger, "Aus L. Zunz' Nachlass," *Zeitschrift für die Geschichte der Juden in Deutschland* 5 (1892): 256–57)

24. Wolf Heidenheim, ed., *Sefer Kerovot hu machzor* (Rödelheim, 1800–1805).

25. *Seder ha-avôda: Gebetbuch für die öffentlichen und häusliche Andacht nach dem Gebrauch des neuen Israelitischen Tempels in Hamburg* (Hamburg: Berendsohn, 1841).

26. *Der Orient*, 1842: 64; *Literaturblatt des Orients*, 1842: cols. 366, 379–81.

27. Abraham Geiger, *Der Hamburger Tempelstreit: Eine Zeitfrage* (Breslau: Leuckart, 1842), 28.

28. Gotthold Salomon, *Sendschreiben an den Herrn Dr. Z. Frankel, Dresden: In Betreff seines im "Orient" mitgeteilten Gutachtens über das neue Gebetbuch der Tempelgemeinde zu Hamburg* (Hamburg: Bödecker, 1842), 35.

29. *Bikurei ha-itim* 8 (1827): 184. Salomon refers to this passage in his own defense, 33.

30. Leopold Dukes, *Zur Kenntnis der neuhebräischen religiösen Poesie* (Frankfort am Main: Bach, 1842), 16–29, 93, 133.The book is structured thematically, but most of the examples are taken from the Sephardic orbit.

31. Harold Hammer-Schenk, *Synagogen in Deutschland: Geschichte einer Baugattung im 19. und 20. Jahrhundert, (1780–1933)* (Hamburg: H. Christians, 1981), 251–301. Cf. Hannelore Künzl, *Islamische Stilelemente im Synagogenbau des 19. und Frühen 20. Jahrhunderts* (Frankfurt am Main: New York, 1984), 109–26.

32. Philipp F. Veit, "Heine: The Marrano Pose," *Monatschefte* 66.2 (1974).

33. Siegbert Salomon Prawer, *Heine's Jewish Comedy: A Study of His Portraits of Jews and Judaism* (Oxford: Clarendon Press, 1983), 59–69.

34. Heine, *Säkularausgabe*, 56–57. Cf. Prawer, *Heine's Jewish Comedy*, 85–96.

35. Phöbus Philippson, "Die Marannen," in *Saron*, ed. Phöbus and Ludwig Philippson, vol. 1 (Leipzig: L. Schnaus, 1855), 92.

36. Berthold Auerbach, *Spinoza: Ein Denkerleben* (Mannheim: F. Bassermann, 1855); Ludwig Philippson, *Jakob Tirado. Geschichtlicher Roman aus der zweiten Hälfte des Sechszehnten Jahrhunderts* (Leipzig: O. Leiner, 1867).

37. Auerbach, *Spinoza*, 94. On the Maimonidean source and the later controversy about it, see Lehmann, "Maimonides, Mendelssohn, and the Me'asfim," 92–93.

38. On Spinoza in the mind of German Jewry in the nineteenth and twentieth centuries, see Leo Strauss, *Spinoza's Critique of Religion* (New York: Schocken Books, 1965), 15–31. On Auerbach, see Jacob Katz, "Berthold Auerbach's Anticipation of the German-Jewish Tragedy," *Hebrew Union College Annual* 53 (1982): 215–40.

39. Both *Der Orient* and the *Literaturblatt des Orients* appeared under the editorship of Julius Fürst from 1840 to 1851 and carried the subtitle *Berichte, Studien und Kritiken für jüdische Geschichte und Literatur*.

40. An excellent if not exhaustive overview of nineteenth- and twentieth-century

German translations of medieval Jewish philosophical texts can be found in *Katalogue der Judaica und Hebraica*, Stadtbibliothek Frankfurt am Main, Band Judaica, ed. Aron Freimann (Graz: Akademische Druck-u. Verlagsanstalt, 1968), 335–40.

41. See the introduction of Simon Scheyer to his German translation of part three of Maimonides, *Guide of the Perplexed* entitled *Dalatat Haiirim* (Frankfurt am Main: n.p., 1838), where he intones the similarities between the era of Maimonides and his own. Religiously, Scheyer moved rapidly from a state of devout Orthodoxy to one of total alienation. See Abraham Geiger and Ludwig Geiger, *Abraham Geiger's Nachgelassene Schriften* (Berlin: L. Gerschel, 1875), 5: 17.

42. Salomon Munk, "Salomo Ibn Gebirol," *Literaturblatt des Orients: Berichte, Studien und Kritiken für jüdische Geschichte und Literatur*, 1846: cols. 721–27. Maimonides, *Le guide des égarés, traité de théologie et de philosophie, par Moïse ben Maïmoun dit Maïmonide*, ed. and trans. Salomon Munk, 3 vols. (Paris: A. Franck, 1856–66).

43. Salomon Munk, *Philosophie und philosophische Schriftsteller der Juden: Eine historische Skizze*, trans. Bernhard Beer (Leipzig: H. Hunger, 1852), 38.

44. Franz Delitzsch, *Zur Geschichte der Jüdischen Poësie vom Abschluss der heiligen Schriften Alten Bundes bis auf die neueste Zeit* (Leipzig: K. Tauchnitz, 1836); Johann Gottfried von Herder, *Vom Geist der ebräischen Poesie: Eine Anleitung für die Liebhaber derselben und der ältesten Geschichte des menschlichen Geistes*, ed. Justi Karl Wilhelm, 3rd ed., 2 vols. (Leipzig: J. A. Barth, 1825). Herder's great study of biblical poetry prompted a biographer to dub him the "Winkelmann of Hebrew poetry" (quoted by Albert Lewkowitz, *Das Judentum und die geistigen Strömungen der Neuzeit* [Breslau: T. Schatzky, 1935], 183).

45. Delitzsch, *Zur Geschichte der Jüdischen Poësie*, 44–45.

46. Ibid., 79–80. As we have already seen, Dukes fully shared Delitzsch's critical opinion of the liturgical legacy of Ashkenazic Jewry, despite a spirited defense of it by Samuel Luzzatto, one of the most vigorous critics of the Sephardic mystique, in a letter to him dated May 3, 1836. In terms of emotional intensity, literary imagination, and wealth of vocabulary, the Ashkenazim surpassed the Sephardim no less than Dante surpassed Tasso. Their faults were an excess of their virtues. See Samuel David Luzzatto, *Igrot Shadal*, ed. Eisig Gräber, 2 vols. (Jerusalem: Makor, 1966), 336–37.

47. Michael Sachs, *Die religiöse Poesie der Juden in Spanien* (Berlin: Veit, 1845), 3–29.

48. Luzzatto, *Igrot Shadal*, 779.

49. Thus Sachs omitted a splendid example of a messianic lament by Yehudah Halevi sent him by Luzzatto (ibid., 767–68).

50. Ignaz Blumenfeld, *Otsar nehmad: Kolel igrot yekarot me-et hakhme zemanenu be-inyene ha-emunah veha-hokhmah* (Jerusalem: Mitshaf, 1966), 27. See Luzzatto's poignant defense of his review to an irate Sachs in Luzzatto, *Igrot Shadal*, 977–80. Luzzatto was also aggrieved because Sachs had cavalierly dismissed his failure to punctuate the Hebrew text of the poems provided by Luzzatto as a mechanical matter of minor import. Luzzatto had originally stipulated such punctuation as a condition for his assistance. Luzzatto, *Igrot Shadal*, 767.

51. Heine's self-description is translated by Prawer, *Heine's Jewish Comedy*, 531.

52. *Heinrich Heine: Werke*, ed. Christoph Siegrist (Frankfurt am Main: Insel, 1968), 1: 203–4, 521.

53. Meyer Kayserling, *Sephardim. Romanische Poesien der Juden in Spanien. Ein Beitrag zur Literatur und Geschichte der Spanisch-Portugiesischen Juden* (Leipzig: H. Mendelssohn, 1859), 137.

54. Salomon Löwisohn (Shlomo Levisohn), *Vorlesungen über die neuere Geschichte der Juden* (Vienna: Karl Ferdinand Beck, 1820). Leopold Zunz, "Salomon Ben Isaac, genannt Raschi," *Zeitschrift für die Wissenschaft des Judenthums*, 1823: 279 (with allusion to Löwisohn, *Vorlesungen*, 82), 281 (with overt reference to Löwisohn, *Vorlesungen*, 80), 370 n.94.

55. Löwisohn (Levisohn), *Vorlesungen*, 73. On Löwisohn, see Reuven Michael, "The Contribution of *Sulamith* to Modern Jewish Historiography" (in Hebrew), *Zion* 39 (1974), 106–13.

56. Ludwig Philippson, *Die Entwickelung der religiösen Idee im Judenthume, Christenthume und Islam und die Religion der Gesellschaft* (Leipzig: O. Leiner, 1874), 132. Moritz Steinschneider, "Jüdische Literatur," in *Allgemeine Encyklopaedie der Wissenschaften und Kuenste*, ed. Ersch and Gruber (Leipzig: Brockhaus, 1850), 27: 358, 448, 453, 469. See also Kayserling, *Sephardim*, 131–45.

57. Steinschneider, *Jüdische Literatur*, 385.

58. Ibid., 385–93.

59. Ibid., 394.

60. Ibid., 385.

61. See also Leopold Zunz, *Zur Geschichte und Literatur* (Berlin: Veit, 1845), 25–28; Michael Sachs, *An die verehrlichen Mitglieder unserer Gemeinde* (Berlin, 1845), 159–61, 167–68, 180–95.

62. The growing romantic fascination with Spain in Europe and America in the first half of the nineteenth century ("Oh, lovely Spain! renown'd, romantic land!"—Byron, *Childe Harold's Pilgrimage* 1.35), was, to be sure, a parallel cultural development that reinforced the Jewish bias. Byron's poetry, Juan Antonio Llorente's history of the Spanish Inquisition, Washington Irving's evocative historical narratives, and Owen Jones's magnificent folio edition of the *Plans, Elevations, Sections, and Details of the Alhambra* (London: O. Jones, 1842) unfurled the drama, glory, and cruelty of medieval Spain. The Boston Brahmin William Hickling Prescott could claim in the preface to his *History of the Reign of Ferdinand and Isabella, the Catholic* (1837; 2nd ed., Boston: American Stationers' Co., 1838) that "English writers have done more for the illustration of Spanish history than for that of any other, except their own." Despite the language barrier, Prescott's two sympathetic chapters on the history and fate of the Jews in Spain did not escape the attention of Zacharias Frankel, who was moved to translate and reprint them in his scholarly journal, *Zeitschrift für die religiösen Interessen des Judentums* 2 (1845): 485–86. The intent of my argument is not to discount the likely influence of these broader currents, but rather to point to what I regard as a deeper, specifically Jewish reason for the German Jewish appropriation of the Sephardic legacy.

63. Luzzatto, *Igrot Shadal*, 1031.

64. E. M. Butler, *The Tyranny of Greece over Germany: A Study of the Influence Exercised by Greek Art and Poetry over the Great German Writers of the Eighteenth, Nineteenth, and Twentieth Centuries* (Boston: Beacon Press, 1958), 80–81.

65. Wilhelm von Humboldt, *Humanist without Portfolio: An Anthology of the Writings of Wilhelm von Humboldt*, ed. and trans. Marianne Cowan (Detroit: Wayne State University Press, 1963), 79.

66. Leopold Zunz, "Essay on the Geographical Literature of the Jews," in *The Itinerary of Rabbi Benjamin of Tudela*, ed. Abraham Asher (London: Asher, 1841), 2: 303. Translation slightly revised.

Chapter Two: Writing Spanish History in Nineteenth-Century Britain

This essay originally appeared in *Critical Inquiry* 20 (Spring 1994), ©1994 by The University of Chicago; reprinted with permission. Ther material was further developed in Michael Ragussis's book *Figures of Conversion: "The Jewish Question" and English National Identity* (Durham, NC: Duke University Press, 1995).

1. See William Hickling Prescott's 1837 preface to his *History of the Reign of Ferdinand and Isabella, the Catholic*, ed. John Foster Kirk, in *The Complete Works of William Hickling Prescott* (London: Gibbings, 1896), 1: vi.

2. William Hickling Prescott, "Chateaubriand's English Literature," in id., *Complete Works*, 12: 31–32.

3. The larger project of which this essay is a part includes a study of these conversionist novels that flourished in nineteenth-century England and typically announced the conversion of the Jewish daughter in such titles as Osborn W. Trenery Heighway's *Leila Ada, the Jewish Convert* (reissued at least nine times between 1852 and 1885) and Annie Peploe's *Julamerk; or, the Converted Jewess* (reissued several times between 1849 and 1878).

On the effort to convert the Jews, see Mel Scult, *Millennial Expectations and Jewish Liberties: A Study of the Efforts to Convert the Jews in Britain, up to the Mid Nineteenth Century* (Leiden: Brill, 1978).

4. Prescott, "Spanish Literature," in id., *Complete Works*, 12: 555–56.

5. John Joseph Stockdale and Caroline Lydia Rhodes, *The History of the Inquisitions, Including the Secret Transactions of Those Horrific Tribunals* (London: J. J. Stockdale, 1810), v, 118–24, xv.

6. Matthew Lewis, *The Monk, a Romance* (London: Oxford University Press, 1973), 396, 170. For a similar use of the Wandering Jew in a Gothic novel set during the Inquisition, see William Godwin, *St. Leon: A Tale of the Sixteenth Century*, 4 vols. (London: G. G. and J. Robinson, 1799).

7. Walter Scott, *Ivanhoe*, ed. A. N. Wilson (Harmondsworth, UK: Penguin Books, 1982), 82, 319.

8. Edward Bulwer-Lytton, *Leila; or, The Siege of Granada* (1838; Boston: D. Estes, 1892), 81.

9. Grace Aguilar, *The Vale of Cedars, & Other Tales* (London: J. M. Dent; Philadelphia: Jewish Publication Society of America, 1902), 173. While almost entirely neglected today, Aguilar's novel was issued in many editions in every decade of the last half of the nineteenth century and remained in print through the opening decades of the twentieth century.

10. According to Aguilar, the chief disability that English Jews "complain of is, being subjected to take an oath contrary to their religious feelings, when appointed to certain offices ("History of the Jews in England," in *Essays and Miscellanies* [Philadelphia: A. Hart, 1853], 272). Also see M. C. N. Salbstein, *The Emancipation of the Jews in Britain: The Question of the Admission of the Jews to Parliament, 1828–1860* (Rutherford, NJ: Fairleigh Dickinson University Press, 1982), who explains that there were "no less than fourteen attempts to remove parliamentary disabilities. One bill was presented in each of the years 1830, 1833, 1834, 1836, 1847–48, 1851, 1854 and 1856 and four further measures were considered in 1857 and 1858" (57).

11. Aguilar's consistent aim as a writer was to expose certain Christian prejudices that distorted and undermined the Jewish woman's place in Judaism, making her the easy target of Christian proselytism. For example, her book on *The Women of Israel: Or, Characters and Sketches from the Holy Scriptures, Illustrative of the Past History, Present Duties, and Future Destiny of Hebrew Females, as Based on the Word of God* (London: Groombridge, 1845) critiques a series of works by Christian women who had argued that "Christianity is the sole source of female excellence," and "that the value and dignity of woman's character would never have been known, but for the religion of Jesus" (1: 8).

12. George Eliot, *Daniel Deronda*, ed. Barbara Hardy (Harmondsworth, UK: Penguin Books, 1986), 411, 410.

13. Grace Aguilar, *Records of Israel* (London: John Wertheimer, 1844), v.

14. Diogo Annunciação Justiniano [Carlos Vero], *The Inquisition and Judaism. A Sermon Addressed to Jewish Martyrs, on the Occasion of an Auto da Fé at Lisbon, 1705*, trans. Moses Mocatta (Philadelphia: Barnard & Jones, 1860), vi. In a similar vein, E. H. Lindo, *The History of the Jews of Spain and Portugal, from the Earliest Times to Their Final Expulsion from Those Kingdoms, and Their Subsequent Dispersion* (1848; reprint, New York: Burt Franklin, 1970), explains the need for "an impartial history of the Jews of Spain and Portugal," especially since previous historians have "written more in the style of a conversionist than in that of an impartial historian" (iii, iv).

15. U. R. Q. Henriques, "The Jewish Emancipation Controversy in Nineteenth Century Britain," *Past and Present* 40.1 (1968): 138. Henriques goes on to explain that "their opponents said that, on the contrary, Popish ritual was descended from Jewish rabbinism, and the Jews and Papists together were plotting to overthrow pure New Testament Christianity" (ibid.). With the unhistorical, anti-Semitic name "Jew inquisitors," the obfuscation of the history of the persecution of the Jews during the Inquisition reaches its absurd limit in England.

16. Grace Aguilar, "The Fugitive" and "The Edict," in *Home Scenes and Heart Studies* (New York: D. Appelton, 1870), 113, 122.

17. *George Eliot's Life as Related in Her Letters and Journals*, ed. J. W. Cross, 3 vols. (New York: Harper & Bros., 1885), 3: 30.

18. George Eliot, *The Spanish Gypsy*, in *The Writings of George Eliot* (Boston: Houghton Mifflin, 1908), 18: 294, 310.

19. Eliot was familiar not only with English works that used this Spanish setting but also with such works as Heine's *Almansor* (1823), which she characterized in the following way: "The tragic collision lies in the conflict between natural affection and the deadly hatred of religion and of race—in the sacrifice of youthful lovers to the strife between Moor and Spaniard, Moslem and Christian" (George Eliot, "German Wit: Heinrich Heine" [1856], in *Essays of George Eliot*, ed. Thomas Pinney [New York: Columbia University Press, 1963], 229).

20. Robert Blake, *Disraeli* (New York: St. Martin's Press, 1967), 542.

21. Benjamin Disraeli, "On the Life and Writings of Mr. Disraeli by His Son," in *Curiosities of Literature* (New York: A. C. Armstrong and Son, 1880), 1: 4. Cecil Roth, *Benjamin Disraeli, Earl of Beaconsfield* (New York: Philosophical Library, 1952), has challenged the accuracy of Disraeli's memoir, and it remains uncertain how many, if any, of his ancestors could in fact claim to be descended from Iberian Jews.

22. Benjamin Disraeli, *Coningsby, or, the New Generation*, ed. Thom Braun (Harmondsworth, UK: Penguin Books, 1983), 237.

23. Matthew Arnold, "On the Study of Celtic Literature," in *Lectures and Essays in Criticism*, *The Complete Prose Works of Matthew Arnold* (Ann Arbor: University of Michigan Press, 1962), 3: 335.

24. Isaac Disraeli, *Vaurien: Or, Sketches of the Times: Exhibiting Views of the Philosophies, Religions, Politics, Literature, and Manners of the Age*, 2 vols. (London: [n.p.], 1797), 2: 249.

25. Benjamin Disraeli, *Tancred; or, the New Crusade* (Westport, CT: Greenwood Press, 1970), 265, 266.

26. For this account of the Eastern crisis, I am indebted to Blake, *Disraeli*, 570–628.

27. T. P. O'Connor, *Lord Beaconsfield, a Biography* (London: T. Fisher Unwin, 1905), xvii, xviii, 672, 610, 663, 660, 611. O'Connor's work began to appear in 1877 in the form of pamphlets, which were collected in book form later in the year. For an account similar to O'Connor's, see Edward Augustus Freeman, *The Ottoman Power in Europe, Its Nature, Its Growth, and Its Decline* (London: Macmillan, 1877), who argued that "we cannot have England or Europe governed by a Hebrew policy" (xix). On Freeman's anti-Semitic slurs against Disraeli during the Eastern crisis, see R. W. Seton-Watson, *Disraeli, Gladstone and the Eastern Question: A Study in Diplomacy and Party Politics* (London: F. Cass, 1971), 113, 281, 437.

28. John Morley, *The Life of William Ewart Gladstone* (London: Macmillan, 1903), 2: 551.

29. William Flavelle Monypenny and George Earle Buckle, *The Life of Benjamin Disraeli, Earl of Beaconsfield*, 6 vols. (New York: Macmillan, 1910), 6: 58–59, and Blake, *Disraeli*, 604–8.

30. Morley, *Life of William Ewart Gladstone*, 2: 552–53.

31. See Blake, *Disraeli*, 601.

32. See for example Disraeli's explanation in *Coningsby* that members of the Sidonia family had served as prelates, archbishops, and even Grand Inquisitor, though "this illustrious family during all this period, in common with two-thirds of the Arragonese nobility, secretly adhered to the ancient faith and ceremonies of their fathers" (232).

33. William Makepeace Thackeray, "Codlingsby," in *Burlesques*, *The Complete Works of William Makepeace Thackeray* (New York: P. F. Collier, 1902), 25, 15.

34. *The George Eliot Letters*, vol. 6: *1874–1877*, ed. Gordon S. Haight (New Haven, CT: Yale University Press, 1975): 75–76n8.

35. Anthony Trollope, *The Way We Live Now*, 2 vols. (Oxford: Oxford University Press, 1984), 2: 263.

36. Anthony Trollope, *The Prime Minister*, 2 vols. (Oxford: Oxford University Press, 1987), 2: 58.

37. See for example, Robert Tracy, *Trollope's Later Novels* (Berkeley: University of California Press, 1978), 55.

38. See Cecil Roth, *A History of the Jews in England* (Oxford: Clarendon Press, 1964), 140–44.

39. See John Halperin, *Trollope and Politics: A Study of the Pallisers and Others* (New York: Barnes & Noble Books, 1977), for an informed account of the way in which Disraeli enters Trollope's fiction. Halperin emphasizes the political novels, attributing Trollope's hatred of Disraeli to the latter's success at a parliamentary career, which Trollope himself had failed to achieve. Halperin also intermittently remarks on Trollope's anti-Semitism, but he does not discuss the idea of "the secret Jew," or Disraeli's role in such an ideological construction, in Trollope's fiction.

40. Gordon S. Haight, *George Eliot: A Biography* (New York: Oxford University Press, 1968), documents Eliot's reading of Prescott (378), and Milman (472).

41. Prescott, *History of the Reign of Ferdinand and Isabella*, 1: 517. Also see Henry Hart Milman, *The History of the Jews, from the Earliest Period Down to Modern Times*, 3 vols. (New York: A. C. Armstrong, 1881), 3: 318.

42. George Eliot, *Romola* (London: Penguin Books, 1980), 642. See, for example, Milman on the way in which "some [of the Jewish exiles] were thrown into the sea by the cupidity of the sailors" (*History of the Jews*, 3: 318), and Prescott, "on the cruelty and the avarice which they frequently experienced from the masters of the ships which transported them from Spain" (*History of the Reign of Ferdinand and Isabella*, 1: 517).

43. This phase describes the title character in Maria Edgeworth, *Harrington* (1817; London: Bohn, Simpkin, Marshall, 1874), 128. On the founding role of this novel in the tradition of the revisionary novel of Jewish identity, see Michael Ragussis, "Representation, Conversion, and Literary Form: *Harrington* and the Novel of Jewish Identity," *Critical Inquiry* 16.1 (1989): 113–43.

44. Eliot, *Romola*, 649.

45. See Haight, *George Eliot: A Biography*, 491n3.

46. The radical nature of Eliot's plot, which reverses the popular plot in which a Jew converts to Christianity (see n. 3 above), originates in Eliot's critique of *Adonijah: A Tale of the Jewish Dispersion*, a novel in which the Jewish hero is "converted to Christianity after the shortest and easiest method approved by the 'Society for Promoting the Conversion of the Jews'" (Eliot, "Silly Novels by Lady Novelists," in *Essays of George Eliot*, ed. Thomas Pinney [New York: Columbia University Press, 1963], 321.)

47. On the nature of Jewish self-hatred, see Sander L. Gilman, *Jewish Self-Hatred: Anti-Semitism and the Hidden Language of the Jews* (Baltimore: Johns Hopkins University Press, 1986). On the conversion and assimilation of English Jews, see Todd M. Endelman, *Radical Assimilation in English Jewish History, 1656–1945* (Bloomington: Indiana University Press, 1990).

48. Disraeli, "On the Life and Writings of Mr. Disraeli by His Son," in *Curiosities of Literature*, 1:7.

Chapter Three: "Rachel, ou l'Auto-da-fé"

1. Bibliothèque nationale de France, Département des Manuscrits, n.a.fr. 22584, vol. VIII, fol. 66[r].

2. Bibliothèque nationale de France, Département des Manuscrits, n.a.fr 22502, 1°: 2°. See Léon Halévy, *F. Halévy: Sa vie et ses oeuvres*, 2nd ed. (Paris: Heugel, 1863), 23; Édouard Monnais, *F. Halévy: Souvenirs d'un ami pour joindre à ceux d'un frère* (Paris: Imprimerie centrale des Chemins de Fer, 1863), 14. Despite these claims, a Goa setting has not been found in the earliest extant text sources.

3. See Michael Ragussis's chapter in this volume and his *Figures of Conversion: "The Jewish Question" and English National Identity* (Durham, NC: Duke University Press, 1995), 90.

4. Scribe refers to "Rebecca de Walter Scott" among his compilation of dramatic ideas (Bibliothèque nationale, Département des Manuscrits, n.a.fr. 22584, vol. VIII, fol. 14[r]). It is possible that he could have become familiar with Lessing's play through the 1827 Parisian publication of *Chefs-d'oeuvre des théâtres étrangers*.

5. *Rachel, ou la belle juive, mélo-drame, en trois actes et en prose, à grand spectacle, orné de chants, danses, pantomime, etc. par P.-E. Chevalier, artiste dramatique, musique de M. Dreuilh, ballets de M. Adam . . .* (Paris: Fages, 1803). An earlier French version of the Jewess of Toledo legend was Jacques Cazotte's novella of the same title, *Rachel ou la belle juive* (1788?), which may have been based on the French translation of Vicente Garcia de la Huerta's 1778 version of the legend. Its first literary treatment was Lope de Vega's *Las paces de los reyes y judía de Toledo* of 1617; in the 1962 critical edition of this work (Chapel Hill: University of North Carolina Press, 1962), the editor, James A. Casteñeda, suggested the possibility that Scribe used the legend as a source for *La Juive*, but without evidence or further exploration. In my previous study of the literary sources of *La Juive* as discussed in my book *Opera, Liberalism, and Antisemitism in Nineteenth-Century France: The Politics of "La Juive"* (Cambridge: Cambridge University Press, 2002), I had not considered this legend nor found clear references

to it among Scribe's papers; further research is needed to establish Scribe's sources. However, his fragmented use of the real-life tale of Leonora de Guzman, favored courtesan of the Castilian king Alphonse XI, for the libretto of Donizetti's grand opera *La Favorite* (1840) makes more probable his knowledge of the similar Jewess of Toledo legend. Discussions of this legend's literary treatments can be found in Élie Lambert, "Alphonse de Castille et la Juive de Tolède," *Bulletin hispanique* 25. 4 (1923): 371–94, and David Nirenberg, "Deviant Politics and Jewish Love: Alfonso VIII and the Jewess of Toledo," *Jewish History* 21.1 (2007): 15–41.

6. Ragussis, *Figures of Conversion*, 11. One of several editions of Shakespeare's complete works to appear in Paris was *Oeuvres complètes de Shakspeare* [sic], *traduites de l'anglais par Letourneur, nouvelle edition, revue et corrigée par F. Guizot et A.P. [Pichot], traducteur de Lord Byron précédée d'une notice biographique et littéraire, sur Shakspeare, par F. Guizot*, 13 vols. (Paris: L'advocat, 1821). An English publication of *The Merchant of Venice*, with French notes, is listed in the *Bibliographie de la France*, December 1827: *The Merchant of Venice: A Comedy in 5 Acts, by W. Shakspeare [sic], as Performed at the Theatres Royal in Drury-Lane and Covent-Garden, with Explanatory French Notes* (Paris: Goetschy, 1827). In one of Scribe's book lists, he includes the citation, "Théâtre étranger-Shakspeare-Goethe-Schiller" (F-Pn, Ms., n.a.fr. 22584, vol. I).

7. Martyn Lyons, *Le triomphe du livre: Une histoire sociologique de la lecture dans la France du XIXe siècle* (Paris: Promodis, 1987), 86–87.

8. For a fuller account of their collaboration, see Hallman, *Opera, Liberalism, and Antisemitism*, chapter 1, "The Collaboration and Rapprochement of the Authors of *La Juive*."

9. See Jean-Claude Yon, *Eugène Scribe: La fortune et la liberté* (Ph.D. diss., Université de Paris-Sorbonne, 1993), 2 vols. (Saint-Genouph: A.-G. Nizet, 2000), 1: 242; Neil Cole Arvin, *Eugène Scribe and the French Theatre, 1815–1860* (Cambridge, MA: Harvard University Press, 1924), 7; and William L. Crosten, *French Grand Opera: An Art and a Business* (New York: King's Crown Press, 1948), 73–74, 90.

10. Although both Halévys were tightly bound to the Saint-Simonian circle, Léon Halévy's participation was more overt: before formally leaving the group ca. 1827, he served as Saint-Simon's secretary and wrote the introduction to the Saint-Simonian *Opinions littéraires, philosophes et industrielles* (1825), among other writings reflecting Saint-Simonian philosophy. See Hallman, *Opera, Liberalism, and Antisemitism*, 47–50, and Ralph P. Locke, *Music, Musicians and the Saint-Simonians* (Chicago: University of Chicago Press, 1986), 94–95. The Sephardic Jews Olinde and Eugène Rodrigues, descendants of a merchant family from Bordeaux, were central figures among the Saint-Simonians.

11. See Hallman, *Opera, Liberalism, and Antisemitism*, 75–83.

12. Fromental Halévy wrote *Marche funèbre et de profundis en Hébreu* (Paris: Ignaz Pleyel et fils aîné, [1820]) to commemorate the duc de Berry, the younger son of the future King Charles X, who had been assassinated on February 13, 1820, at the Opéra. Léon Halévy published *Résumé de l'histoire des juifs anciens* (Paris: Lecointe & Durey, 1825) and *Résumé de l'histoire des juifs modernes* (Paris: Lecointe, 1828); in

the latter book, he denounces "the hidden scheming and the active pernicious influence" of the clerical party (317).

13. For fuller portraits of the "Generation of 1820," see Alan B. Spitzer, *The French Generation of 1820* (Princeton, NJ: Princeton University Press, 1987), and David H. Pinkney, *The French Revolution of 1830* (Princeton, NJ: Princeton University Press, 1972). For the ideological stances and rapprochement of Scribe and the Halévys, see Hallman, *Opera, Liberalism, and Antisemitism*, 38–72.

14. Louis Véron, *Mémoires d'un bourgeois de Paris comprenant la fin de l'empire, la restauration, la monarchie de juillet, la république, jusqu'au rétablissement de l'empire*, 6 vols. (Paris: Librairie Nouvelle, 1856–57), 3: 181.

15. Bibliothèque nationale de France, Département des Manuscrits, n.a.fr. 22584, vol. VIII, fol. 66^{r}.

16. Ragussis, *Figures of Conversion*, 93.

17. Excerpts from *The Merchant of Venice* are drawn from the edition by Louis B. Wright (New York: Washington Square Press, 1957).

18. Bibliothèque nationale de France, Département des Manuscrits, n.a.fr. 22502, vol. XXIII, I°: 2°, 23: "Ah, s'écrie Rachel éperdue et tombant à genoux, dieu des Chrétiens—reçois l'enfant égaré qui revient dans ton sein—hymne doux et religieux. Cantique solennel et celeste qui termine la pièce. [E]au sainte du baptême reçu purifie son front."

19. Ibid., 4° (a).

20. Ibid., 4° (b). The "(b)" in this reference and the "(a)" in the note above are my own designations, used to distinguish the two partial fair copies of the libretto, acts 5 and 5.

21. Ibid., 4° (a) and (b). These verses correspond with those sketched in act 5, scene 5, of Bibliothèque nationale de France, Département des Manuscrits., n.a.fr. 22562, 114–15. All translations are mine unless otherwise indicated.

22. Ibid.

23. Ibid., 4° (b). A final violent death is common in French melodramas, as well as many French grand operas. Scribe chose the method of death in a *chaudière*, or cauldron of boiling oil (or water), according to Véron, *Mémoires*, 3: 181. He may have borrowed this from Marlowe's *The Jew of Malta*. Ragussis, in *Figures of Conversion*, includes an illustration that parodies the final scene of *La Juive* in its 1836 English adaptation at Drury Lane and features the figure of David Salomons climbing to "The CAULDRON OF CHRISTIAN INTOLERANCE" (53, fig. 5).

24. (Jacques-François) Fromental Halévy and Eugène Scribe, *La Juive*, 2 vols., facsimile of the orchestral score published in Paris by Maurice Schlesinger in 183[5] (New York: Garland, 1980). This ending can also be found in most music and libretto sources that are linked to the premiere and subsequent performances of the 1835 Paris Opéra production of *La Juive*.

25. A sixty-four-measure passage of the duettino that places greater emphasis on Brogni as guardian father appears in the piano-vocal score published by Schlesinger and reprinted by Lemoine (Paris: Henri-Lemoine, n.d.), but it is omitted from the

Schlesinger orchestral score (mentioned above) and the archival score copied for the Paris Opéra, and crossed out in red crayon in Halévy's autograph. See my more extensive discussion of this passage, and other aspects of Rachel's religious duality, in Hallman, *Opera, Liberalism, and Antisemitism*, 193–209.

26. See draft verse of act 4, Bibliothèque nationale de France, Département des Manuscrits., n.a.fr. 22502, vol. XXIII, I°: 3°, as well as partbooks for the tenor Adolphe Nourrit, the first Eléazar, and his understudy Pierre-François Wartel, Bibliothèque nationale de France, Département-Musée de l'Opéra, Mat. 19e[315 (17) and (18).

27. Arthur Hertzberg, *The French Enlightenment and the Jews: The Origins of Modern Anti-Semitism* (New York: Columbia University Press, 1990), 268, 273.

28. Voltaire, "De l'Inquisition," in *Oeuvres complètes*, 11 vols. (Paris: Chez Th. Desoer Libraire, 1817), 4, pt. 1: 682.

29. Ibid., 682–83.

30. *Fromental Halévy, "La Juive": Dossier de presse parisienne (1835)*, ed. Karl Leich-Galland (Saarbrücken: Musik-Edition Lucie Galland, 1987), 50.

31. Charles-Louis de Secondat de Montesquieu, *De l'esprit des loix ou du rapport que les loix doivent avoir avec la constitution de chaque gouvernement, les moeurs, le climat, la religion, le commerce, etc.* (Geneva: Barrillot et fils, 1748), 60–62.

32. See the discussions of Restoration repressions in Alan B. Spitzer, *The French Generation of 1820* (Princeton, NJ: Princeton University Press, 1987), and David H. Pinkney, *The French Revolution of 1830* (Princeton, NJ: Princeton University Press, 1972).

33. É.-L. de Lamothe-Langon, *Histoire de l'Inquisition en France, depuis son établissement au XIIIe siècle, à la suite de la croisade contre les Albigeois, jusqu'en 1772, époque définitive de sa suppression* (Paris: J.-G. Dentu, 1829), x.

34. Ibid., ii, iii, x.

35. *Archives parlementaires de 1787 à 1860: Recueil complet des débats législatifs et politiques des chambres françaises, seconde série*, ed. J. Mavidal and E. Laurent (Paris: Paul Dupont, 1887), 65: 317.

36. Unsigned, "Intolérance religieuse," *Le Réformateur* 2, no. 129 (February 15, 1835): 1; my translation.

37. *L'Univers religieux* 3, no. 428 (March 25, 1835): col. 1447.

38. Ibid., cols. 1447–48; no. 423 (March 19, 1835): col. 1389.

39. Bibliothèque nationale de France, Département des Manuscrits, n.a.fr. 22584, vol. 2, "Voyage dans le Mydi de la France, 1er Avril-1827," fols. 19v–20r.

40. Ibid., vol. 1, fols. 14^{v}–15^{r}.

41. See Ragussis, *Figures of Conversion*, chapter 3, "Writing English History: Nationalism and 'National Guilt,'" 89–90.

42. As pointed out in the introduction to this volume by Yael Halevi-Wise, she would not define Hugo's use of the Inquisition as an instance of sephardism.

43. Perhaps in coordination with a Goa placement, an early set depicting extensive canopies for an outdoor Inquisition with numerous seated clerics was sketched by the Opéra's chief painter, Pierre-Luc-Charles Cicéri (perhaps in 1834), but aban-

doned (Bibliothèque nationale de France, Département-Musée de l'Opéra, [Esq. Cicéri 13–14).

44. Archives nationales, $F^{21}960$, dossier V; my translation.

45. Ibid., $AJ^{13}202$.

46. Ibid.

47. Although Scribe passionately believed in authorial freedom and opposed governmental intervention in the theater, he argued, during his presidency of the Société des auteurs dramatiques, that preventive censorship was preferable to arbitrary repressive censorship, such as that represented by the 1832 banning of Victor Hugo's *Le Roi s'amuse*. In adapting to censors' ideas and demands during the Restoration, and perhaps to Commission concerns in the early 1830s, Scribe likely developed and used methods of self-censorship, as he implied in a 1836 speech given as the newly elected member of the Académie française, in which he states that "it is in what [the theatre] does not say that one must look for or guess at what actually goes on [in a society]." See Hallman, *Opera, Liberalism, and Antisemitism*, 6, 60–64.

48. Fromental Halévy, *Derniers souvenirs et portraits, précédés d'une notice par P.-A. Fiorentino* (Paris: Michel Lévy frères, 1863), 168. See, e.g., the *Gazette de France* review reprinted in *"La Juive": Dossier de presse parisienne*, ed. Leich-Galland, 51. See connections between Eléazar's depiction and eighteenth- and nineteenth-century views of Jewish fanaticism in Hallman, *Opera, Liberalism, and Antisemitism*, 285–96.

49. This scene drawn from *Ivanhoe* appears in the first published libretto of *La Juive* of February 23, 1835 (Paris: Maurice Schlesinger, 1835), and in previous manuscript libretti, but not in the libretto's second edition (Paris: Jonas & Barba, 1835). See a discussion of this scene in Hallman, *Opera, Liberalism, and Antisemitism,* 165–69.

50. See Ismar Schorsch, Chapter One in this volume, "The Myth of Sephardic Supremacy in Nineteenth-Century Germany."

51. Edgar Rosenberg, *From Shylock to Svengali: Jewish Stereotypes in English Fiction* (Stanford, CA: Stanford University Press, 1960), 34.

52. Lucette Czyba, "Misogynie et gynophobie dans *La Fille aux yeux d'or*," in *La Femme au XIXe siècle: Littérature et idéologie*, ed. Jean-François Tetu et al. (Lyon: Presses universitaires de Lyon, 1978), 141.

53. See n. 5 above.

54. "Chargé du soin de l'enfance de Rachel" (*Rachel, ou la belle juive*, act 1, scene 1).

55. In act 1, scene 1, as Ruben relates to Mathan the stages of their influence at court, which include Rachel's becoming the king's "favorite" and his becoming the king's confidant, the banishing of the king's wife Ermangère, and the replacing of the king's courtesans with "Hebrews," he states that all these developments have served his "designs" or "plans." In scene 2, Fernand speaks of Ruben's "hidden manoeuvres." In act 2, scene 1, when Rachel becomes enraged after she learns that the king has decreed her banishment, Ruben cautions her to restrain her emotions, but she lashes out with reminders of "the vast plans that you created" and a demand to avenge her or give back her former "days of innocence." After Rachel angrily tears

up the decree brought by Alvare and Fernand (act 2, scene 5), refusing to believe that she is no longer mistress in command, Ruben again chides her for her fury and says, "in an instant you can lose the fruit of all my politics" (act 2, scene 6).

56. See David Nirenberg's analysis of the Spanish sources, and subsequent versions of the Jewess of Toledo legend, cited in n. 5 above.

57. See the printed libretto of February 23, 1835, act 3, scenes 2 and 3; the duo, no. 14, mm. 11–13, 132–34, in the piano-vocal score published by Schlesinger and reprinted by Lemoine; and the autograph manuscript, Bibliothèque nationale de France, Département-Musée de l'Opéra, A. 509a, vol. II, 39, 52. The abandoned performing parts can be found in Bibliothèque nationale de France, Département-Musée de l'Opéra, Mat. 19e [315 (7), "retiré de la juive."

58. See Lormier's costume designs for the 1835 production of *La Juive* in Bibliothèque nationale de France, Département-Musée de l'Opéra, [D. 216 (10)-11, fols. 70–111, and as illustrated in watercolor by Eugène du Faget, in Bibliothèque nationale de France, Département-Musée de l'Opéra, [D. 216 (O^2).

59. See Marie-Jacques Hoog, "Ces femmes en turban," in *Women in French Literature*, ed. Michel Guggenheim (Saratoga, CA: ANMA Libri, 1988), 117–23, and Marian E. Smith, "Music for the Ballet-Pantomime at the Paris-Opéra, 1825–1850" (Ph.D. diss., Yale University, 1988), 38ff.

60. Delacroix painted his Jewess in Tangier, during a journey to Morocco and Algeria, when he accompanied the French delegation of the comte de Mornay, a diplomatic envoy of King Louis-Philippe to the sultan Moulay Abd el-Rahman—only two years after the French invasion of Algeria.

61. The watercolor by du Faget, Bibliothèque nationale de France, Département-Musée de l'Opéra, [D. 216 (O^2), fol. 82, cuts off her dress or skirt above the ankles (suggesting youth and perhaps innocence), whereas a lithograph by Devéria (Bibliothèque nationale de France, Département-Musée de l'Opéra) depicts a floor-length dress.

62. Another watercolor for the first production, Bibliothèque nationale de France, Département-Musée de l'Opéra, [D. 216 (O^2), fol. 84, illustrates the same costume, but without the blue and white bodice and overdress; without a turban, youthful braids hang from the back of Rachel's head. Other depictions of Falcon wearing this costume were rendered by Maleuve (1835) and by H. Robinson (Paris: Soulié, 1840) (see in Gallica, online catalog, Bibliothèque nationale de France).

63. Archives nationales, AJ^{13} 202, inventories of costumes used in 1835 production at the Paris Opéra.

64. During his journey to Algeria in 1832, Delacroix was permitted to visit the harem of a Turkish corsair, which inspired this painting that was presented at the Salon of 1834.

65. This sketch is reproduced in Catherine Join-Diéterle, *Les décors de scène de l'Opéra de Paris à l'époque romantique* (Paris: Picard, 1988), 191. I have not seen an illustration for the stage set or maquette for the fully realized set of act 2, and thus do not know whether this imagery was retained in the opera's production.

66. Archives nationales, AJ[13] 202, "Mémoire des peintures faites pour l'opéra de la Juive" (act 3), 1835.

67. See Marian Smith, *Ballet and Opera in the Age of Giselle* (Princeton, NJ: Princeton University Press, 2000), 47, table 2.5; id., "Music for the Ballet-Pantomime at the Paris Opéra," 91–93; and *"La Juive": Dossier de presse parisienne*, ed. Leich-Galland, 46.

Chapter Four: The Strange Career of the Abarbanels from Heine to the Holocaust

1. There are variations in the spelling of Abarbanel's name. In the text of this article, Heine's spelling "Isaak Abarbanel" is used. Other variations appear in the notes. On the 1937 Berlin exhibition, see Hermann Simon, *Das Berliner Jüdische Museum in der Oranienburger Strasse: Geschichte einer zerstörten Kulturstätte* (Berlin: Union, 1988), 63–71. On its curator, see Katharina Sabine Feil, "A Scholar's Life: Rachel Wischnitzer and the Development of Jewish Art Scholarship in the 20th Century" (D.H.L. thesis, Jewish Theological Seminary of America, 1994).

2. Rahel Wischnitzer-Bernstein and Josef Fried, *Gedenkausstellung Don Jizchaq Abrabanel: Seine Welt, sein Werk* (Berlin: M. Lessmann, 1937).

3. See Jean-Christophe Attias, *Isaac Abravanel: La mémoire et l'espérance* (Paris: Cerf, 1992). On Abravanel, see Benzion Netanyahu, *Don Isaac Abravanel, Statesman and Philosopher* (Philadelphia: Jewish Publication Society of America, 1972).

4. For a discussion of contemporary studies and bibliographic works in French, English, German and Hebrew, see Jean-Christophe Attias, "Isaac Abravanel: Between Ethnic Memory and National Memory," *Jewish Social Studies* 2.3 (Spring–Summer 1996).

5. Abraham Joshua Heschel, *Don Jizchak Abravanel* (Berlin: E. Reiss, 1937), 29f.

6. On the relevant passages in Heine's works and letters, see Siegbert Salomon Prawer, *Heine's Jewish Comedy: A Study of His Portraits of Jews and Judaism* (Oxford: Clarendon Press, 1983), 297–309. On the Damascus affair, see Jonathan Frankel, *The Damascus Affair: "Ritual Murder," Politics, and the Jews in 1840* (Cambridge: Cambridge University Press, 1997).

7. See, e.g., Irmgard Schüler, "Die Welt der Abarbanel," *Jüdisches Gemeindeblatt*, June 20, 1937, 3, and Olga Bloch, "Abarbanel-Austellung in Berlin," *Central Verein-Zeitung*, June 17, 1937, 8.

8. Sigmund Seeligmann, unpublished letter to Rahel Wischnitzer, June 17, 1937, Rahel Wischnitzer archives in possession of the late Rachel Bernstein Wischnitzer's son, Leonard Winchester, of Terrace Park, Ohio, whom the author thanks for making this material available. It is not apparent in this letter whether Seeligman considered "interest in A.'s works even in the present" to include Heine and other fictional works.

9. Abarbanel was also a popular subject in the Judeo-Spanish literature, but only after 1880. See Elena Romero, *Teatro de los Sefardíes orientales*, 3 vols. (Madrid: Arias Montano, 1979), 1: 495, cited in Attias, *Isaac Abravanel*, 151. Translations of

Phillipson's (1837) and Reckendorf's (1856) works into Yiddish, Hebrew, and Russian were available after 1859 (Phillipson) and 1865 (Reckendorf).

10. Feuchtwanger's comments are interesting in light of his later career: "At the present time, medieval Judaism has still not found an author who has the capacity to convey its complete emotional spectrum. Most efforts in this area have been artistically worthless story literature for Jewish newspapers," Lion Feuchtwanger, *Heinrich Heines Fragment: "Der Rabbi von Bacherach": Eine kritische Studie* (Munich: Kastner & Callwey, 1907), 113n307.

11. On the origins of modern Jewish historiography, see Yosef Hayim Yerushalmi, *Zakhor: Jewish History and Jewish Memory* (Seattle: University of Washington Press, 1982), 77–103; Ismar Schorsch, *From Text to Context: The Turn to History in Modern Judaism* (Hanover, NH: Brandeis University Press, 1994); and Kurt Wilhelm, *Wissenschaft des Judentums im Deutschen Sprachbereich. Ein Querschnitt* (Tübingen: Mohr, 1967).

12. On the ideology of these early Jewish historians, see Schorsch, *From Text to Context*, esp. 71–92, 177–232.

13. Among others, Hans Otto Horch, *Auf der Suche nach der jüdischen Erzählliteratur: Die Literaturkritik der "Allgemeinen Zeitung des Judentums" (1837–1922)* (Frankfurt am Main: P. Lang, 1985), 139. Manfred Windfuhr delivers a solid and objective introduction to the relevant issues in *Heinrich Heine: Historisch-kritische Gesamtausgabe der Werke, Düsseldorfer Ausgabe* (Hamburg: Hoffmann & Campe, 1994), 5: 498–624 (hereafter cited parenthetically as DHA).

14. Windfuhr emphasizes the parallels between Heine's Don Isaak Abarbanel and Cervantes's "knight of the rueful countenance" (DHA, 5: 705), and also refers to Heine's sensibility for "the satirical signification" of Don Quixote (DHA, 10: 263).

15. Windfuhr notices correctly that the "neutrality" of Heine's position as narrator is a consequence of his Walter Scott reception and as such forms the conception of his historical novel, cited in Gerhard Höhn, *Heinrich Heine: Ästhetisch-Politische Profile* (Frankfurt am Main: Suhrkamp, 1991), 276ff.

16. Phöbus Phillipson, "Die Marannen," in *Saron*, ed. id. and Ludwig Phillipson (Leipzig: L. Schnaus, 1855), 3–124.

17. Ibid., 28.

18. Ibid., 92, 99. For the entire speech, see 89–94.

19. Hermann Reckendorf, *Die Geheimnisse der Juden*, 5 vols. (Leipzig: Wolfgang Gerhard, 1856), vol. 5.

20. Ibid., 174.

21. Walter Benjamin, "Über den Begriff der Geschichte," in *Gesammelte Schriften*, ed. Rolf Tiedemann and Hermann Schweppenhäuser (Frankfurt am Main: Suhrkamp, 1974), 1: 701.

22. Reckendorf, *Geheimnisse*, 1.

23. Shmuel Feiner, "The Pseudo-Enlightenment and the Question of Jewish Modernization," *Jewish Social Studies* 3.1 (Fall 1996): 62–88.

24. Alfred Nossig, *Abarbanel: Das Drama eines Volkes* (Berlin: H. Steinitz,

1906). On Nossig's biography, see Shmuel Almog, "Alfred Nossig: A Reappraisal," *Studies in Zionism* 7 (Spring 1983): 1–29.

25. Nossig, *Abarbanel: Das Drama eines Volkes*, 8.

26. Ibid., 6.

27. Hermann Kesten, *Sieg der Dämonen: Ferdinand und Isabella* (Munich: K. Desch, 1953), 266.

28. Leo Perutz, *Nachts unter der steinernen Brücke*, ed. Hans-Harald Müller (Munich: Knaur, 1994); trans. Eric Mosbacher as *By Night Under the Stone Bridge* (London: Collins Harvill, 1989).

29. Since 1945, the Abarbanels occasionally make an appearance in works by Jewish authors in other languages. These novels are either inseparable from the problem of Jewish writing after the Holocaust (as in Philip Roth's *The Ghost Writer*, 1979) or they take up the romantic Abarbanel image again (e.g., Didier Nebot's *Le chemin de l'exil*, 1992). Robert Menasse's novel, *Die Vertreibung aus der Hölle* (Amsterdam: De Arbeiderspers, 2002), may signal a new German-language dimension of the Abarbanel saga in ways that go beyond the scope of this essay.

Chapter Five: Sephardim and Neo-Sephardim in Latin American Literature

A previous version of this essay appeared in Edna Aizenberg, *Books and Bombs in Buenos Aires: Borges, Gerchunoff and Argentine-Jewish Writing* (Hanover, NH: University Press of New England, 2002), © University Press of New England, Hanover, NH. Reprinted with permission. It appeared in Spanish originally as "Las peripecias de una metáfora: El sefaradismo literario judeoargentino," *Noaj* 7–8 (1992): 54–59.

1. Regarding Carvajal, see Martin Cohen, *The Martyr: The Story of a Secret Jew and the Mexican Inquisition in the Sixteenth Century* (Philadelphia: Jewish Publication Society, 1973), and Seymour B. Liebman, *The Enlightened: The Writings of Luis de Carvajal, el Mozo* (Coral Gables, FL: University of Miami Press, 1967).

2. On López Penha, see Itic Croitoru Rotbaum, *De sefarad al neosefardismo: Contribución a la historia de Colombia*, vol. 2. (Bogotá: Kelly, 1967), 174–75; on Curiel, see Edna Aizenberg, "Elías David Curiel: Influencias y temas," *Revista nacional de cultura* 32 (1971): 94–103.

3. On Dominican Jews, see Enrique Ucko, "La fusión de los sefardis [*sic*] con los dominicanos," *Cuadernos dominicanos de cultura* 2 (1944): 55–82; for Isaac Chocrón, *Three Plays by Isaac Chocrón*, ed. Barbara Younoszai and Rossi Irauquin-Johnson (New York: Peter Lang, 1995).

4. On Nissán, see Yael Halevi-Wise, "Puente entre naciones: Idioma e identidad sefardí en *Novia que te vea* e *Hisho que te nazca* de Rosa Nissán," *Hispania* 81 (1998): 269–77, and Darrell B. Lockhart, "Growing Up Jewish in Mexico: Sabina Berman's *La bobe* and Rosa Nissán's *Novia qua te vea*," in *The Other Mirror: Women's Narrative in Mexico, 1980–1995*, ed. Kristine L. Ibsen (Westport, CT: Greenwood Press, 1997), 159–74.

5. On Barnatán, see Naomi Lindstrom "*El laberinto de Sión*: Nueva Narrativa as Access to Kabbalah," *Discurso literario* 2.1 (1984): 175–91, and Edna Aizenberg, "*El laberinto de Sión*: Marcos Ricardo Barnatán's Borgesian Quest for Sephardic Identity," *Books and Bombs in Buenos Aires* (Hanover, NH: University Press of New England, 2002), 94–101.

6. See León Pérez, "El area de sefardización secundaria: América Latina," in *Actas del primer simposio de estudios sefardíes 1964*, ed. Iacob Hassán (Madrid: Instituto Arias Montano, 1970), 141–48.

7. Isaac Chocrón, *Rómpase en caso de incendio* (Caracas: Monte Avila, 1975), 229–230.

8. Alberto Gerchunoff, *Los gauchos judíos* (La Plata: J. Sesé, 1910).

9. Leonardo Senkman. "*Los gauchos judíos*: Una lectura desde Israel," *Estudios interdisciplinarios de America Latina* 10.1 (1999): 151.

10. Carlos M. Grünberg, "A Alberto Gerchunoff." In Manuel Kantor, *Alberto Gerchunoff* (Buenos Aires: Ejecutivo Sudamericano del Congreso Judío Mundial, 1969), 17; my translation.

11. Jorge Luis Borges, introduction to *Mester de judería*, by Carlos M Grünberg (Buenos Aires: Agirópolis, 1940), xi–xvi.

12. Grünberg's essay has been reprinted in *Un diferente y su diferencia: Vida y obra de Carlos M. Grünberg*, ed. Eliahu Toker (Buenos Aires: Taller de Mario Muchnik, 1999).

13. Borges, cited n. 11 above, xvi, xii. For a wider discussion of Borges in relation to Judaic subjects, see Edna Aizenberg, *The Aleph Weaver: Biblical, Kabbalistic and Judaic Elements in Borges* (Potomac, MD: Scripta Humanistica, 1984).

14. Henry Besso "Decadencia del judeo-español: Perspectivas para el futuro," in *Actas del primer simposio de estudios sefardíes 1964*, ed. Iacob Hassán (Madrid: Instituto Arias Montano, 1970), 259, 410.

15. Judith Laikin Elkin, "Centaur on the Roof: Neo-Sephardism in Latin America," *Proceedings of the Eleventh World Congress of Jewish Studies* 3 (1994): 353–60, acknowledges her debt to my concept of literary neo-sephardism, and the problematic nature of the term "neo-Sephardim," but still applies the terms to all Latin American Jewish writers, irrespective of background or literary themes.

16. On Gelman, see Monique Rodrigues Balbuena, "Diasporic Sepharadic Identities: A Transnational Poetics of Jewish Languages" (Ph.D. diss., University of California, 2003).

17. On Scliar, see Lois Baer Barr, "The Jonah Experience: The Jews of Brazil According to Scliar," in *The Jewish Diaspora in Latin America*, ed. David Sheinin and Lois Baer Barr (New York: Garland, 1996), 33–52; Nelson H. Vieira, *Jewish Voices in Brazilian Literature: A Prophetic Discourse of Alterity* (Gainesville: University Press of Florida, 1995); and Yael Halevi-Wise's Chapter Six in this volume.

18. On undermining fixed national identities, see Leonardo Senkman, "La nación imaginaria de los escritores judíos latinoamericanos," *Revista iberoamericana* 66:191 (2000): 279–98.

19. *Actas del primer simposio de estudios sefardíes 1964*, ed. Iacob Hassán (Madrid: Instituto Arias Montano, 1970), 411.

20. Ibid., 410.

21. Perez, "El area de sefardización secundaria," 144.

22. Edna Aizenberg, *Parricide on the Pampa? A New Study and Translation of Alberto Gerchunoff's "Los gauchos judíos"* (Madrid: Iberoamericana, 2000), 22.

23. Marcos Aguinis, "De la legitimación apologética a la critica reparadora," *Hispamérica* 42 (1985): 3–4.

24. Marcos Aguinis, *La gesta del marrano* (Buenos Aires: Planeta, 1991), 226–27.

25. Aguinis, "De la legitimación," 5–6.

26. On the PRONDEC, see Aguinis's *Memorias de una siembra: Utopía y práctica del PRONDEC. Programa Nacional de Democratización de la Cultura* (Buenos Aires: Planeta, 1990). Juana Alacira Arancibia has edited a collection of essays on Aguinis's activism and literature, *La gesta literaria de Marcos Aguinis* (San José, Costa Rica: Instituto Literario y Cultural Hispánico, 1998).

27. Günther Böhm, *Historia de los judíos en Chile. Período colonial. Judíos y judeoconversos en Chile colonial durante los siglos XVI y XVII, el Bachiller Francisco Maldonado de Silva 1592–1639* (Santiago, Chile: Andrés Bello, 1984).

Chapter Six: The Life and Times of the Picaro-Converso from Spain to Latin America

I thank Leor Halevi, Hadji Bakara, the Department of Hispanic Studies at McGill University, and the organizers and participants of the Manchester conference on "Jewish Culture in the Age of Globalization" for their valuable comments in relation to this chapter.

1. Among other relevant examples, one might cite Pedro Orgambide's *Adventures of Edmund Ziller in the New World* (1977), Antonio Brailovsky's *Isaac Halevy, King of the Jews* (1980), Baccino Ponce de León's *Maluco* (1990) and Angelina Muñiz-Huberman's *The Romantic Sephardi: The Luckless Life of Mateo Alemán II* (2005).

2. The way in which these novels narrate the actual history of Ibero-America's conversos is a separate question, which already has been studied to some extent (see n. 25 below). Since we are dealing with a multidimensional issue, I wish to focus here specifically on the picaresque nature of these texts, and in discussing this genre, I assume a basic familiarity with its general characteristics. For a basic definition and literary history of the picaresque, I recommend especially Walter L. Reed, *An Exemplary History of the Novel: The Quixotic Versus the Picaresque* (Chicago: University of Chicago Press, 1981), Robert Alter, *Rogue's Progress: Studies in the Picaresque Novel* (Cambridge, MA: Harvard University Press, 1964), and Peter N. Dunn, *Spanish Picaresque Fiction: A New Literary History* (Ithaca, NY: Cornell UP, 1993).

3. Homero Aridjis, *1492: Vida y tiempos de Juan Cabezón de Castilla* (Mexico, D.F.: Fondo de Cultura Económica, 1985), trans. Betty Ferber as *1492: The Life and Times of Juan Cabezón of Castile* (New York: Summit Books, 1991).

4. Angelina Muñiz-Huberman, *Tierra adentro* (Mexico, D.F.: Joaquín Mortíz,

1977). Translations from this novel are my own. While this volume was in press, Seymour Menton published an official translation under the title of *Mystical Journey* (Santa Fe, NM: Gaon Books), 2011.

5. Moacyr Scliar, *A estranha nação de Rafael Mendes* (Porto Alegre, Rio Grande do Sul: L & PM Editores, 1983), trans. Eloah F. Giacomelli as *The Strange Nation of Rafael Mendes* (New York: Harmony Books, 1986). Hereafter cited parenthetically in the text as *Strange Nation*.

6. Roberto González Echevarría, *Myth and Archive: A Theory of Latin American Narrative* (Cambridge: Cambridge University Press, 1990).

7. Strategic representations of Sephardic history have played a prominent role in Latin American Jewish literature. The most succinct exploration of this phenomenon is Edna Aizenberg's "Las peripecias de una metáfora: El sefaradismo literario judeoargentino," *Noaj* 7–8 (1992): 54–9 (included in this volume as "Sephardim and Neo-Sephardim in Latin American Literature"). In addition to Leonardo Senkman's seminal analysis of "Gerchunoff y la legitimación hispánica," in *La identidad judía en la literatura argentina* (Buenos Aires: Pardes, 1983), 39–57, notable studies of Latin American literature with Sephardic themes include Darrell Lockhart's "Narrative Assertion of Cultural Identity in Three Latin American Jewish Novels," *Romance Languages Annual* 5 (1993): 451–54; Seymour Menton's "Over Two Thousand Years of Exile and Marginality" in id., *Latin America's New Historical Novel* (Austin: University of Texas Press, 1993), 138–62; and Monique R. Balbuena's "Sepharad in Brazil: Between the Metaphorical and the Literal in *Entre Moisés y Macunaíma*," *Modern Jewish Studies* 15.1–2 (2007): 31–44. See also *Contemporary Sephardic Identity in the Americas*, ed. Edna Aizenberg and Margalit Bejarano (Syracuse, NY: Syracuse University Press, 2012).

8. Under Muslim rule (711–1492), Christians and Jews in Iberia were permitted to live as *dhimmis* in a multicultural environment. Yet after the Catholic monarchs extended their rule to the entire Iberian Peninsula, Jews and Muslims were faced with either conversion or expulsion. This essay centers on the period of Catholic hegemony in Spain, Portugal, and their American colonies. On the history of conversos in colonial Latin America, see Seymour Liebman, *The Jews in New Spain: Faith, Flame, and the Inquisition* (Coral Gables, FL: University of Miami Press, 1970), and Anita Novinsky, *Inquisicão: Prisioneiros do Brasil séculas XVI–XIX* (Rio de Janeiro: Editora Expressão e Cultura, 2002); as well as several items in *The Jewish Presence in Latin America*, ed. Judith Elkin and Gilbert W. Merkx (Boston: Allen and Unwin, 1987), and *Sephardim in the Americas: Studies in Culture and History*, ed. Martin A. Cohen and Abraham J. Peck (Tuscaloosa: University of Alabama Press, 1993).

9. Américo Castro's comments on the origins of the picaresque were interspersed throughout his writings, which he revised and augmented as his thinking on the subject evolved. Thus, while relatively little on this topic appears in first editions of his publications, subsequent editions enabled him to emphasize converso issues through prefaces and footnotes. See, in particular, the sections on "Perspectiva de la novela picaresca" and *El Lazarillo de Tormes* in the 1967 edition of *Hacia*

Cervantes (Madrid: Taurus, 1967), 118–42, 143–66, and *La Celestina como contienda literaria* (Madrid: Revista de Occidente, 1965).

10. Claudio Guillén, "Toward a Definition of the Picaresque," in *Literature as System: Essays Toward the Theory of Literary History* (Princeton, NJ: Princeton University Press, 1971), 101–3.

11. A general survey of converso elements in the Spanish picaresque is given by Yirmiyahu Yovel in *The Other Within: The Marranos, Split Identity and Emerging Modernity* (Princeton, NJ: Princeton University Press, 2009), 263–83. A more extensive and detailed survey can be found in Deborah S. Rosenberg's "Family Ties: The *Converso* in the Spanish Picaresque Novel" (Ph.D. diss., University of Chicago, 2004). Among earlier studies, see, e.g., Manuel Ferrer-Chivite's "Sustratos conversos en la creación de Lázaro de Tormes," *Nueva Revista de Filología Hispánica* 33 (1984): 352–79, and Victorio G. Aguera's "Salvación del Cristiano Nuevo en el *Guzmán de Alfarache*," *Hispania* 57–51 (1974): 23–30.

12. Américo Castro, *España en su historia: Cristianos, moros y judíos* (Buenos Aires: Losada, 1948), 575.

13. Stephen Gilman's study of *The Spain of Fernando de Rojas: The Intellectual and Social Landscape of* La Celestina (Princeton, NJ: Princeton University Press, 1972) presents evidence regarding Rojas's background and the social and emotional status of conversos in Spain shortly after the expulsion of its Jews.

14. In *La España imaginada de Américo Castro*, Eugenio Asensio refutes Castro's approach to Spain's history and identity (Barcelona: El Albir, 1976), as does Claudio Sánchez-Albornoz in *España, un enigma historico* (Buenos Aires: Sudamericana, 1956). Castro's principal champions have been, on the other hand, Guillermo Araya, Joseph Silverman, and Stephen Gilman; see esp. Araya, *Evolución del pensamiento historico de Américo Castro* (Madrid: Taurus, 1969) and Gilman, *Spain of Fernando de Rojas*. In addition, a very useful overview of Castro's opus can be found in Guillermo Araya's "The Evolution of Castro's Theories," in *Américo Castro and the Meaning of Spanish Civilization*, ed. José Rubia Barcia (Berkeley: University of California Press, 1976), 41–66. See also A. A. Sicroff, "Américo Castro and His Critics: Eugenio Asensio," *Hispanic Review* 40.1 (1972): 1–30.

15. Alexander A. Parker, *Literature and the Delinquent: The Picaresque Novel in Spain and Europe, 1599–1753* (Edinburgh: Edinburgh University Press, 1967), 13–14.

16. Parker's reconsideration appears in the preface to the Spanish translation of his *Literature and the Delinquent*, which was retitled *Los pícaros en la literatura: La novela picaresca en España y Europa (1599–1753)*, trans. Rodolfo Arévalo Mackry (Madrid: Gredos, 1971), 22. Translations from the Spanish are mine unless otherwise noted.

17. This is not to say that Spanish Republicans held a uniform opinion on Spain's character and heritage, attested by the fascinating polemic between Américo Castro and the medievalist Claudio Sánchez-Albornoz, president of the Spanish Republican government in exile. Regarding the reception of Américo Castro on both sides of the Atlantic, see *Américo Castro and the Impact of His Thought*, ed. Ronald E. Surtz, Jaime Ferrán, and Daniel P. Testa (Madison, WI: Hispanic Sem-

inary of Medieval Studies, 1988), and *Homenaje a Américo Castro*, ed. José Jesús Bustos Tovar and Joseph Silverman (Madrid: Universidad Complutense, 1987), in addition to the works cited in n. 14 above.

18. Angelina Muñiz-Huberman, "Death, Exile, Inheritance," in *King David's Harp: Autobiographical Essays by Jewish Latin American Authors*, ed. Stephen Sadow (Albuquerque: University of New Mexico Press, 1999), 51.

19. In one of her earliest novels, *Morada Interior* (1972), Muñiz-Huberman explored the converso background of Saint Teresa of Avila; and in a recent playful experiment, *El sefardí romántico: La azarosa vida de Mateo Alemán II* (2005), she imagines an incarnation of Mateo Alemán in sixteenth- *and* twentieth-century Mexico.

20. Homero Aridjis, public lecture transcript, Vancouver, 1993.

21. For a history of Jewish settlement in Latin America, see Judith Elkin's *The Jews of Latin America* (New York: Holmes & Meier, 1998).

22. On the paradoxical Sephardic dimension of Scliar's *The Strange Nation of Rafael Mendes*, see Balbuena, "Sepharad in Brazil" (cited n. 7 above), and Judith L. Elkin's "Centaur on the Roof: Can a Neo-Sephardic Culture Emerge in Latin America?" *Shofar* 13.2 (1995): 1–15.

23. See, e.g., Alfredo Margarido, "Um romance histórico: A explicação judaica da história do Brasil," *Jornal de letras, artes e ideias* 5.141 (March 1985): 4–5.

24. Moacyr Scliar, "Sohno de pai," Comunidade Israelita de Lisboa, www.cilisboa.org/sections/tikva_04/bu_4_36_reflx.htm (accessed July 12, 2011).

25. Some work has already been done in this direction, especially by Kimberle S. López, who laid out in clear terms the converso and picaresque dimensions of Aridjis's work in "Ambivalence Toward Converso Self and Conquered Other in Homero Aridjis's *1492* and *Memorias del Nuevo Mundo*," in her outstanding study of *Latin American Novels of the Conquest: Reinventing the New World* (Columbia: University of Missouri Press, 2002), 138–74. Also in relation to *1492*, Jane Mushabac has fruitfully compared Aridjis's masterpiece to the *Lazarillo of Tormes* in "Homero Aridjis's Picaresque Novel," *Midstream* 52.4 (July–August 2006): 33–36; Joseph James Lopez more generally mentions the "neo-picaresque modality" of Aridjis's "historically-engaged" work in "Eden in the Age of the Fifth Sun: The Narrative Work of Homero Aridjis" (Ph.D. diss., Florida International University, 2000), 212–28. Similarly, Edward H. Friedman comments on the picaresque elements of *Tierra Adentro* in "Angelina Muñiz's *Inland*: (Re)creating the Subject," in *Tradition and Innovation: Reflections on Latin American Jewish Writing*, ed. Roberto DiAntonio and Nora Glickman (New York: State University of New York Press, 1993), 179–92; and Menton's "Over Two Thousand Years of Exile and Marginality" assesses whether the Latin American novels analyzed here qualify as new historical novels that explicitly extend the past into the present, but he does not discuss their picaresque dimension.

26. Nancy T. Baden, *The Muffled Cries: The Writer and Literature in Authoritarian Brazil, 1964–1985* (Lanham, MD: University Press of America, 1999), xv.

27. On Brazilian writing in times of political transition, see Roberto Reis, *The Pearl Necklace: Toward an Archaeology of Brazilian Transition Discourse*, trans. A. de Godoy Johnson (Gainesville, FL: University Press of Florida, 1992), 39; and on creative writing as a cathartic act, Roberto E. DiAntonio, *Brazilian Fiction: Aspects and Evolution of the Contemporary Narrative* (Fayetteville: University of Arkansas Press, 1989), 203.

28. Menton, *Latin America's New Historical Novel*, 2–13.

29. Clara Lida conducted a series of studies on the impact of the Spanish Republicans on Mexico; see esp. *Inmigración y exilio: Reflexiones sobre el caso español* (Mexico City: Siglo Veintiuno, 1997); and also Patricia W. Fagen, *Exiles and Citizens: Spanish Republicans in Mexico* (Austin: University of Texas Press, 1973).

30. Carlos Fuentes's Iberian-oriented historical novels, especially *Terra Nostra* (1975), *El naranjo* (1993), and several of his outstanding collections of essays, such as *El espejo enterrado* (1992) are notable exceptions to this pre-Columbian and colonial focus among Mexico's cultural critics.

31. Beatriz Susana Cella discusses this aspect of Aridjis's work in "Una heterología por plenitud: Acerca de *El entenado* de Juan José Saer y *1492: Vida y Tiempos de Juan Cabezón de Castilla* de Homero Aridjis," *Literatura Mexicana* 2.2 (1991): 455–61.

32. Regarding Octavio Paz's cultural archaeology, see esp. "Los Hijos de la Malinche," in *El laberinto de la soledad* (México, D.F.: Cuadernos Americanos, 1950).

33. Muñiz-Huberman, "Death, Exile, Inheritance," 46.

34. On the theme of exile in Muñiz-Huberman's work, see Daniella Schuvaks, "Esther Seligson and Angelina Muñiz-Huberman: Jewish Mexican Memory and the Exile to the Darkest Tunnels of the Past," in *The Jewish Diaspora in Latin America: New Studies on History and Literature*, ed. David Sheinin and Lois Baer Barr (New York: Garland, 1996), 75–89; Judith Payne, "Writing and Reconciling Exile: The Novels of Angelina Muñiz-Huberman," *Bulletin of Hispanic Studies* 74.4 (1997); 431–59; and Leonardo Senkman, "Sefarad, exilio latinoamericano e intertextualidad cultural: Una aproximación a Angelina Muñiz-Huberman y Juan Gelman," in *El Legado de Sefarad*, ed. Norbert Rehrmann (Salamanca: Amarú, 2003), 85–98.

35. Victoria Eugenia Campos, "Twentieth-Century Debates on Mexican History and the Juan Cabezón Novels of Homero Aridjis" (Ph.D. diss., Princeton University, 1996), 21.

36. Homero Aridjis, public lecture transcript, Sephardic Temple of Los Angeles, 1991.

37. Stephen Gilman, "A Generation of *Conversos*," *Romance Philology* 33.1 (1979): 98.

38. Francisco Márquez Villanueva, *Espiritualidad y literatura en el siglo XVI* (Madrid: Alfaguara 1968), 107.

39. Francisco Rico, *The Spanish Picaresque Novel and the Point of View* (Cambridge: Cambridge University Press, 1984), 82.

40. Claudio Guillén, "Toward a Definition of the Picaresque," 81.

41. Naomi Lindstrom, "Oracular Jewish Tradition in Two Works by Moacyr Scliar," *Luso-Brazilian Review* 12.2 (1984): 22.

42. Lois Baer Barr's "The Jonah Experience: The Jews of Brazil According to Scliar," in *Jewish Diaspora in Latin America*, 33–52, interprets *The Strange Nation of Rafael Mendes* and Scliar's entire opus through the figure of the biblical Jonah. One could say that apart from studies centering specifically on the Sephardic dimension of this novel (such as Balbuena's and Elkin's, cited nn. 7 and 22 above), critical approaches to *The Strange Nation of Rafael Mendes* can be generally divided between, on one hand, examinations of its internal thematics (such as Barr's essay on patterns of exposure and expulsion; Nelson Vieira on instability, in id., *Jewish Voices in Brazilian Literature: A Prophetic Discourse of Alterity* [Gainesville: University Press of Florida, 1995], 182–87; Lockhart and Senkman on memory in Darrel Lockhart, "The Narrative Assertion of Cultural Identity"; and Leonardo Senkman, "Jewish Latin American Writers and Collective Memory," in *Tradition and Innovation*, ed. DiAntonio and Glickman, 33–43); and on the other hand, examinations of its status as a historical novel that challenges conventional boundaries between documented events and the artistic imagination (Carlos Alexandre Baumgarten, "O novo romance histórico brasileiro: O caso gaúcho," *Letras de Hoje* 37.2 [June 2001]: 75–82; Bella Josef, "El dialogo literatura/historia: Moacyr Scliar y Marcos Aguinis," in *500 años después*, ed. Jaime B. Rosa [Valencia: Jaime B. Rosa, 1993], 105–18; Luiz Fernando Valente, "Reflexões sobre o novo romance histórico brasileiro," in *Proceedings of the Brazilian Studies Association*, 1994: 77–96; David Schidlowsky, *Historischer Roman und jüdische Geschichte: Der Weg der Neuchristen in Brasilien bei Moacyr Scliar* [Berlin: Wissenschaftlicher Verlag, 1996]; and esp. Menton, "Over Two Thousand Years of Exile and Marginality," in id., *Latin America's New Historical Novel*, 149–55). My approach tries to bridge between these thematic and structural approaches.

43. Parker, *Literature and the Delinquent*, 19.

44. Jane Mushabac observes that the *Lazarillo* functions in Aridjis's novel as a prototype for a "primary social dismemberment," which Aridjis brings back to the period in which Jews were still present in Spain. He then shifts the style "from spare and unadorned to baroque and ornate, and the focus away from male interactions, to a male-female romance" (33–36).

45. Regarding the picaresque's fundamental rejection of romance, see Walter Reed, *Exemplary History*, 30.

46. Guillén, "Toward a Definition of the Picaresque," 77.

47. Stuart Miller, *The Picaresque Novel* (Cleveland: Case Western Reserve University, 1967), 131.

48. Benito Brancaforte, *Guzmán de Alfarache: ¿Conversión o proceso de degradación?* (Madison: Hispanic Seminary of Medieval Studies, 1980), 10.

49. Reed, *Exemplary History*, 67.

50. Regarding the picaresque's indebtedness to Augustinian confession, see, e.g., C. A. Longhurst, "The Problems of Conversion and Repentance in *Guzmán de Alfarache*," in *A Face Not Turned to the Wall* (Leeds: University of Leeds Press, 1987), 92–101, and David A. Boruchoff, "La malograda invención de la picaresca," in *Dejar*

hablar a los textos: Homenaje a Francisco Márquez Villanueva, ed. Pedro M. Piñero Ramírez (Sevilla: Universidad de Sevilla, 2005), 506–11.

51. See, e.g., Reed, *Exemplary History*, 52.

52. José María Mico, introduction to *Guzmán de Alfarache* (Madrid: Catedra, 1987), 47.

53. Joan Arias, *Guzmán de Alfarache: The Unrepentant Narrator* (London: Tamesis, 1977), 1–2.

54. Baumgarten, "O novo romance histórico brasileiro," 76.

55. Antithetical stereotypes are associated even with Rafael Mendes's very name, so that, while it is true that both the surname and profession of the novel's first Rafael Mendes refer to "an important family of Spanish mapmakers who played . . . a key role in the Age of Exploration" (Barr, "Jonah Experience," 44), the name also recalls "one Rafael Mendez who goes and comes solely to report to Holland on what is going on and what ought to be done" against Portugal in Brazil to promote a more liberal Dutch dominion (Cyrus Adler, "A Contemporary Memorial," in *The Jewish Experience in Latin America*, ed. Martin A Cohen [New York: Ktav, 1971], 183). Such revolutionary Rafael Mendeses appear in Scliar's novel alongside those who are eager to maintain the status quo or blend surreptitiously into the general population. Scliar has explained that this rummaging through Brazil's history subdues his own sense of social anguish by helping him define his Jewishness as a Brazilian identity, which together nourish his literary inspiration (Scliar, "Judíos en Brasil, de la inquisición a la pregunta por el futuro," in *Pluralismo e identidad: Lo judío en la literatura latinoamericana* [Buenos Aires: Milá, 1986], 177–78).

56. Arias, *Guzmán de Alfarache*, 7.

57. On the Jew as a complex multicultural figure in Latin American culture, see Erin Graff Zivin's excellent study of *The Wandering Signifier: Rhetoric of Jewishness in the Latin American Imaginary* (Durham, NC: Duke University Press, 2008) and Saul Sosnowsky's paradigm-changing essay "Latin American-Jewish Writers: Protecting the Hyphen," in *Jewish Presence in Latin America*, ed. Elkin and Merkx, 297–308.

58. Fredric Jameson, *The Political Unconscious: Narrative as a Socially Symbolic Act* (Ithaca, NY: Cornell University Press, 1981), 130.

59. Miller, *Picaresque Novel*, 102.

60. This appeal to the reader has been analyzed in relation to the original picaresque by Helen Reed in *The Reader in the Picaresque Novel* (London: Tamesis, 1984) and by David Boruchoff in "La malograda invención de la picaresca," in *Dejar hablar a los textos*, ed. Piñero Ramírez, 117–18.

61. Vieira, *Jewish Voices in Brazilian Literature*, 155.

62. Regina Igel, "Jewish Component in Brazilian Literature: Moacyr Scliar," *Folio* 17 (1987): 113.

63. Scliar, "A Centaur in the Garden," in *King David's Harp*, ed. Sadow, 69 (my italics).

64. Jeffrey Lesser, *Welcoming the Undesirables: Brazil and the Jewish Question* (Berkeley: University of California Press, 1995), 3. See also his "(Re)Creating Jew-

ish Ethnicities on the Brazilian Frontier," in *Jewries at the Frontier: Accommodation, Identity, Conflict*, ed. Sander L. Gilman and Milton Shein (Urbana: University of Illinois Press, 1999), 209–23.

65. Gonzáles Echevarría, *Myth and Archive*, 39.

Chapter Seven: Facing Sepharad, Facing Israel and Spain

I thank Yael Halevi-Wise for all our enthusiastic discussions about shaping this essay, for her vision of this volume, and for our friendship.

1. Edna Aizenberg, *Books and Bombs in Buenos Aires: Borges, Gerchunoff, and Argentine-Jewish Writing* (Hanover, NH: University Press of New England, 2002), 55–57, and "The Allure of Sepharad," in *Sephardic Identity: Essays on a Vanishing Jewish Culture*, ed. George K. Zucker (Jefferson, NC: McFarland, 2005), 157–63. At the first conference on Sephardic Studies in Madrid and Toledo in 1964, Leon Pérez, a physician and psychology professor from Buenos Aires, articulated a process of "secondary Sephardization" of Ashkenazim in Latin America. He outlined an eastern European Jew's entrée into multicultural Hispanic surroundings through Spanish language acquisition and inherent "reconnection" with the history and manifold legacy of medieval Jewish Spain. What Aizenberg frequently cites is Pérez's view of the "neo-Sephardi," not as a "fixed [or] completed label," but as a properly hyphenated term for a hybrid subject who evolves through diverse Ashkenazic, Sephardic, and Latin American cultural "fronts" coming into contact. While one discussant at the 1964 conference resisted such a vicarious, environmentally accrued Sephardic lineage, Pérez argued that the concept of "neo-sephardism" involved thinking beyond an identity conferred by genetic origins to identity emerging from "history as a process of becoming." Such "amplified criteria" suit sephardism in modern literary creativity particularly aptly. See León S. Pérez, "El area de sefardización secundaria: America Latina," in *Actas del primer simposio de estudios sefardíes*, ed. Iacob M. Hassán (Madrid: Instituto Arias Montano, 1970), esp. 142–44, 411 and the surrounding discussion on pp. 410–11.

2. Aizenberg, "Allure of Sepharad," 158

3. Aizenberg, *Books and Bombs*, 57; "Allure of Sepharad," 157.

4. Aizenberg, "Allure of Sepharad," 160.

5. Stephen G. Nichols, "Modernism and the Politics of Medieval Studies," in *Medievalism and the Modernist Temper*, ed. R. Howard Bloch and Stephen G. Nichols (Baltimore: Johns Hopkins University Press, 1996), 30.

6. Nichols, "Modernism and the Politics of Medieval Studies," 29, 33.

7. Ibid., 28–30.

8. Yehuda Burla, *Eleh masa'ei Rabi Yehuda Halevi* (These Are the Travels of Rabbi Judah Halevi) (Tel Aviv: Am Oved, 1959).

9. Antonio Gala, "Las cítaras colgadas de los árboles" (The Zithers Hanging from the Trees), in *Biblioteca Antonio Gala: El teatro de la historia* (Madrid: Espasa-Calpe, 2001), 49–119 (originally written and performed in Madrid in 1974).

10. The Israeli press was Am Oved.

11. Gedalia Ibn Yahya, *Shalshelet ha-Qabbalah* (The Chain of Tradition) (Venice, 1587). On Ben Zion Dinur, Israeli minister of education and culture, 1952–55, see n. 35 below.

12. S. D. Goitein, "Haparasha ha'aharona bhayei rabeinu yehuda haleivi" (The Last Episode in the Life of Our Rabbi Yehuda Halevi), *Tarbiz* 24 (1954–55): 21–47.

13. Victoria Robertson, *El teatro de Antonio Gala: Un retrato de España* (Madrid: Pliegos, 1990), 41, 28–32.

14. Antonio Gala, "Preliminary Words on *Las cítaras colgadas de los árboles*," in id., *Teatro de la historia* (Madrid: Espasa Calpe, 2001), 53.

15. This is Hans Ulrich Gumbrecht's phrase in "Narrating the Past as If It Were Your Own Time: An Essay on the Anthropology of Historiography," in *Making Sense of Life and Literature* (Minneapolis: University of Minnesota Press, 1992), 61.

16. See, e.g., Gonzalo Álvarez Chillida, *El antisemitismo en España: La imagen del judío, 1812–2002* (Madrid: Marcial Pons, 2002), 61–73, and José Manuel Pedrosa, "Los judíos en la literatura tradicional española," in *Los judíos en la literatura española*, ed. Iacob M. Hassan and Ricardo Izquierdo Benito (Cuenca: Ediciones de la Universidad de Castilla–La Mancha, 2001), 403–36.

17. Jonathan P. Decter, *Iberian Jewish Literature Between Al-Andalus and Christian Europe* (Bloomington: Indiana University Press, 2007), 211.

18. Ibid., 5.

19. See, e.g., Shai Panueli, "Two Options on *These are the Travels of Rabbi Judah Halevi*, a Historical Story in Past or Present Language," *Mozna'im* (Shevat 1959): 252–54, and Adir Cohen, "A Rich and Instructive Work," *Mozna'im* (Shevat 1959): 254–56.

20. Y. Zmora, "On *These are the Travels of Rabbi Judah Halevi*," *Dvar*, August 15, 1959.

21. Ann Brener, *Judah Halevi and His Circle of Hebrew Poets in Granada* (Leiden: Brill, 2005), 6.

22. Ibid., 20.

23. Ibid., 132–35.

24. Ibid., 134.

25. Sidra DeKoven Ezrahi, *Booking Passage: Exile and Homecoming in the Modern Jewish Imagination* (Berkeley: University of California Press, 2000), 39.

26. Brener, *Judah Halevi and His Circle*, 139.

27. Ezrahi, *Booking Passage*, 45.

28. Ibid., 34.

29. Ross Brann discusses Halevi's relationship to Sepharad and Zion in "Competing Tropes of Eleventh-Century Andalusi Jewish Culture," in *Sasson Somekh Festschrift*, ed. D. Wasserstein (forthcoming), 8.

30. Raymond P. Scheindlin, *The Song of the Distant Dove: Judah Halevi's Pilgrimage* (Oxford: Oxford University Press, 2008), 58.

31. Gerson D. Cohen, "The Typology of the Rabbinate," an analysis of Abraham Ibn Daud's *The Book of Tradition*, which Ibn Daud completed in Mantua in 1161, in

The Book of Tradition (Sefer ha-Qabbalah) by Abraham Ibn Daud (Oxford: Litman Library of Jewish Civilization, 2005), 288.

32. Decter, *Iberian Jewish Literature*, 53.

33. Brann, "Competing Tropes," 12.

34. Scheindlin, *Song of the Distant Dove*, 62.

35. Scheindlin, ibid., credits Ben-Zion Dinur (Dinaburg) with starting a trend of detecting the opposite in Judah Halevi's poetry: a call for Jewish repatriation in Zion that preempts divine redemption. I discuss the content and import of Dinur's work shortly. Here it is striking to note the contrast between Dinur's method of interpreting Halevi's verse and Scheindlin's. Scheindlin corroborates his argument for the private nature of Halevi's poetry about his pilgrimage to Zion by presenting significant poems he discusses in full, in their own visual space at the bottom of his pages. Dinur, on the other hand, inculcates his reductive message by interspersing one to two lines from disparate poems by Halevi and other contemporaries with his own interjections. Similarly, although he reprints what he sees as Halevi's most endorsing poem, "Song of a Distant Dove," in full, Dinur interrupts it several times with assiduous parsing that gives the impression of excessive guidance of reader response. See Scheindlin, *Song of the Distant Dove*, 64–65, and Ben-Zion Dinaburg [Dinur], "Rabbi Judah Halevi's Aliya to Eretz Israel and the Messianic Fermentation of His Time" (in Hebrew), in *Rabbi Judah Halevi: Volume of Research and Tributes*, ed. Zmora Israel (Tel Aviv: Mahbarot lesifrut, 1964), 47–83, 64–65, in particular (reprinted in *David Yellin Festschrift*, ed. S. Assaf [Jerusalem: Mass, 1935], 157–82).

36. S. D. Goitein indicates the length of Judah Halevi's time in Egypt in "Autographs in Rabbi Judah Halevi's Hand," *Tarbiz* 26 (1956): 393–413, 393. In my interpretation, "autographs" in the title of this article includes the personal letters Goitein discusses here, which Halevi wrote to colleagues and contacts in Egypt.

37. Shmuel Werses discusses this trend of Zionist "actualization" of medieval Sephardic poetry in "The Poet Yehuda Halevi in the World of Modern Hebrew Literature" (in Hebrew), *Pe'amim* 53 (1993): 18–74, 38.

38. See also S. D. Goitein, "The Final Episode in the Life of Our Rabbi Judah Halevi," *Tarbiz* 24 (1954–55): 21–47, and "Rabbi Judah Halevi in Spain in Light of the Genizah Manuscripts," ibid., 134–467.

39. Werses, "Yehuda Halevi in Modern Hebrew Literature," 39.

40. Ibid.

41. Lev Hakak, "To Tomorrow via Yesterday: On Judah Halevi's Travels by Yehuda Burla" (in Hebrew), *Pe'amim* 53 (1993): 61.

42. Gala, *Las cítaras*, 98.

43. Enrique Llovet, "Prologue," in *Las cítaras colgadas de los arboles y ¿Porqué corres, Ulises?* (Madrid: Espasa-Calpe, 1981), 27.

44. Ibid., 26.

45. Claudine Fabre-Vassas, *The Singular Beast: Jews, Christians, and the Pig*, trans. Carol Volk (New York: Columbia University Press, 1997), 285–91.

46. When *Las cítaras colgadas de los árboles* opened in Madrid's Teatro de la Comedia in September 1974, a pig was slaughtered onstage before Olalla set to work, and spectators could barely tolerate this "exacerbated realism." Gala, *Ahora hablaré de mí* (Barcelona: Planeta, 2000), 80.

47. Gala, *Las cítaras*, 74.

48. Steven F. Kruger, *The Spectral Jew: Conversion and Embodiment in Medieval Europe* (Minneapolis: University of Minnesota Press, 2005), xx.

49. Fabre-Vassas, *Singular Beast*, 72–74.

50. Carme Riera, *En el último azul* (Madrid: Santillana, 1996), 346. In this novel, the Inquisitor who pronounces this insult attributes it to a Lutheran outlook, indicating that it may have been an early import from northern European sources into Spanish Catholic discourse.

51. Isaiah Shachar, *The Judensau: A Medieval Anti-Jewish Motif and Its History* (London: Warburg Institute, University of London, 1974), 1.

52. Gedalia Ibn Yahya, *Shalshelet ha-Qabbalah* (Venice, 1587).

53. After Dinur became Israel's minister of education and culture in 1953, the Knesset enacted a law proposed by him that made the government responsible for uniformly educating the "young generation" on the "cultural heritage of the nation." The basis for this instruction was Dinur's own "historical paradigm" of Israel's emergence and development, according to Uri Ram, "Zionist Historiography and the Invention of Modern Jewish Nationhood: The Case of Ben Zion Dinur," *History and Memory* 7.1 (1995), 107.

54. Ibid., 93, 95.

55. Dinur, "Rabbi Yehuda Halevi's Aliya," 53–65.

56. Louis Althusser, "Ideology and Ideological State Apparatuses (Notes Towards an Investigation)," in id., *Lenin and Philosophy and Other Essays* (New York: Monthly Review Press, 1971), 127–86.

57. Dinur, "Rabbi Yehuda Halevi's Aliya," 51, 52.

58. Nurit Gertz, *Generation Shift in Literary History: Hebrew Narrative Fiction in the Sixties* (Tel Aviv: Porter Institute for Poetics and Semiotics at Tel Aviv University, 1983), 64–65.

59. Batya Shimoni, "Identity Under Trial—Yehuda Burla Between Sephardic Manners and Zionistic Being" (in Hebrew), *Mikan* 8/*El Presente: Studies in Sephardic Culture* 1 (2007): 55.

60. Dov Kimhi, "Y. Burla," in *Yehuda Burla: A Selection of Critical Essays on his Literary Prose*, ed. Avinoam Barshai (Tel Aviv: Am Oved, 1975), 38.

61. Shimoni, "Identity under Trial," 51.

62. Ibid., 57.

63. Homi Bhabha, *The Location of Culture* (London: Routledge, 2004), 126, 138; Kruger, *Spectral Jew*, xx.

64. José Antonio Lisbona explains early twentieth-century philo-sephardism in Spain by repeatedly noting that Pulido paid no attention to the small contemporary Jewish communities that were by then already established in Madrid,

Barcelona, and Seville. In 1912, King Alfonso XIII indicated to Sephardic Jews in Spanish Northern Morocco that he expected them to "help with the colonization and economic enrichment" of this zone. When the monarch later received Pulido, he encouraged his "very useful" Sephardic rapprochement campaign. By 1920, Moroccan commerce with Spain was 70 percent Jewish, and even though, according to Lisbona, Madrid did not value this commerce highly enough as an opening to greater "Spanish commercial penetration" in the region, there was always a "commercial motive" in Pulido's overall campaign. See José Antonio Lisbona Martín, *Retorno a Sefarad: La política de España hacia sus judíos en el siglo XX* (Barcelona: Riopiedras, 1993), 23, 25. Pulido was convinced that his campaign to "reconquer the Spanish Jews" would enrich Spain economically and politically, according to Álvarez Chillida (*El antisemitismo en España*, 262–63). Pulido's interest in the proximate Sephardic Diaspora developed into a larger courting campaign partly because by 1898 it registered in Spain as a type of "recompense for the loss of America," Jacobo Israel Garzón, a present-day Jewish historian, editor, and head of the Jewish Community Federations in Spain, notes in *Escrito en Sefarad* (Madrid: Hebraica ediciones, 2005), 20.

65. Rafael Cansinos-Asséns, *La novela de un literato*, vol.1 (Madrid: Alianza, 1996), 208.

66. Ibid., 208.

67. Ángel Pulido Martín, *El doctor Pulido y su época* (Madrid: F. Domenech, 1945), 212.

68. Ángel Pulido Fernández, *Españoles sin patria y la raza sefardí* (1905; Granada: Universidad de Granada facsimile, 1993), 208.

69. Dinur, "Rabbi Yehuda Halevi's Aliya," 72, 73.

Chapter Eight: Sephardic Identity and Its Discontents

Chapter epigraph: A. B. Yehoshua, *Five Seasons*, trans. Hillel Halkin (New York: Doubleday, 1989), 346.

1. Gila Ramras-Rauch, "A. B. Yehoshua and the Sephardic Experience," *World Literature Today* 65.1 (1991): 10.

2. Muhammed Siddiq, "The Making of a Counter-Narrative: Two Examples from Contemporary Arabic and Hebrew Fiction," *Michigan Quarterly Review* 31.4 (1992): 656, 651.

3. Arnold J. Band, "*Mar Mani*: The Archeology of Self-Deception," *Prooftexts* 12 (1992): 232, 239.

4. Gershon Shaked, "A Puzzle Greater than All Its Solutions," *Modern Hebrew Literature* 6 (1991): 44.

5. Mintz, "The Counterlives," *New Republic,* June 29, 1992, 41.

6. Nancy E. Berg, "Sephardi Writing: From the Margins to the Mainstream," in *The Boom in Contemporary Israeli Fiction*, ed. Alan Mintz (Hanover, NH: Brandeis University Press, 1997), 132.

7. A. B. Yehoshua, "Behipus ahar hazman hasfaradi haavud," reprinted in

Yehoshua's *Haqir vehahar* (Tel-Aviv: Zamora-Beitan, 1989), 228–41; trans. Gilad Morahg as "Finding My Father in Sephardic Time," *Moment* 22:5 (October 1997): 54–57, 85–92. For analysis, see Band, "*Mar Mani*," 232ff.

8. Gilead Morahg, "Borderline Cases: National Identity and Territorial Affinity in A. B. Yehoshua's *Mr. Mani*," *AJS Review* 30.1 (April 2006): 173n12.

9. Yael S. Feldman, "Identity and Counter-Identity: *Mr. Mani* and the Sephardi Heritage in Israeli Literature," in *The Jewish Communities of Southeastern Europe from the Fifteenth Century to the End of World War II*, ed. I. K. Hassiotis (Thessaloníki: Institute for Balkan Studies, 1997), 120.

10. Bernard Horn, "The Shoah, the Akedah, and the Conversations in *Mr. Mani*," *Symposium* 53 (Fall 1999): 136–50.

11. A. B. Yehoshua, "For a Jewish Border," *Jerusalem Post Magazine*, July 19, 2002.

12. Morahg, "Borderline Cases," 168.

13. See, e.g., Siddiq, "Making of a Counter-Narrative," 656; and Feldman, "Identity," 118.

14. See *Bekivun hanegdi* (In the Opposite Direction), articles on *Mr. Mani*, ed. Nitza Ben Dov (Tel-Aviv: Hakibbutz Hameuchad, 1994); esp. Yael Feldman's articulation there of the "countermove" motif in "Hazara le'bereshit: el ha'mudchak u'me'ever lo be'zehut ha'israelit" (Back to Genesis: Toward the Repressed and Beyond It in Israeli Identity)," 204–22.

15. A. B. Yehoshua, "Israeli Identity in a Time of Peace: Prospects and Perils," *Tikkun* 11 (January–February 1996): 34–40, 94; and see my discussion of this issue in *Facing the Fires: Conversations with A. B. Yehoshua* (Syracuse, NY: Syracuse University Press: 1997), 142–44.

16. See my essay, "Is There One Jewish People? Morality and Form in A. B. Yehoshua's *A Journey to the End of the Millennium*" (in Hebrew), in *Mabatim Mitztalvim* (Intersecting Perspectives: Essays on A. B. Yehoshua's Oeuvre), ed. Nitza Ben Dov, Amir Banjabi, and Ziva Shamir (Tel Aviv: Ha-Kibbutz ha-Meuchad, 2010), 527–40.

17. Kwame Anthony Appiah, *Cosmopolitanism: Ethics in a World of Strangers* (New York: Norton, 2006), xx.

18. Ibid., 85.

19. This was Gilead Morahg's response—his actual term was "Sephardistic"—to a version of this essay that I read at the 2008 NAPH conference in Montreal within Yael Halevi-Wise's panel on sephardism as a conceptual methodology in Hebrew literature.

20. Ramras-Rauch, "A. B. Yehoshua and the Sephardic Experience," 11.

21. Ibid., 12. Nancy Berg presents a similar view when she notes that "the cross-culturalism of the Sephardim, and the idea of the Sephardim as the link between Jews and Arabs [in *Mr. Mani*], are further developed in the works of Shimon Ballas" ("Sephardi Writing," 133).

22. Band, "*Mar Mani*," 235.

23. Ibid., 239, 241.

24. Ibid.

25. Ibid., 242.

26. Ibid., 241.

27. Ramras-Rauch, "A. B. Yehoshua and the Sephardic Experience," 11.

28. Ted Solotaroff, "Strange Jews," *The Nation*, June 15, 1992, 826–27.

29. Robert Alter, "Mr. Mani's Sweet Temptations," *The Forward*, March 20, 1992, 9, 14.

30. Horn, *Facing the Fires*, 113; my emphasis.

31. Morahg, "Borderline," 179.

32. Mintz, "Counterlives," 44.

33. See, e.g., A. B. Yehoshua, "Ha'mehapecha ha'tzionit—ha'im yesh la hemshech?" (The Zionist Revolution: Will It Continue?), in id., *Achizat moledet* (Homeland Grasp) (Tel-Aviv: Hakibbutz Hameuchad, 2008). For further discussion of Zionism in relation to *Mr. Mani*, see Feldman, "Identity and Counter-Identity," 116ff.

34. Shaked, "Puzzle Greater than All Its Solutions," 47; also see Dan Miron, "Me'ahorei kol mahshavah mistateret Mahshavah Nosefet" (Behind Every Thought Another Thought Hides: Reflections on Mr. Mani), in *Bakivun hanegdi*, ed. Nitza Ben-Dov (Tel-Aviv: Hakibbutz Hameuchad, 1994), 153–77; Miron's article originally appeared in *Siman qri'ah* 21 (December 1990): 61–80.

35. Horn, *Facing the Fires*, 125.

36. Regarding the symbolic role of Ishmael in this novel, see Mordechai Shalev, "Chotam ha'akeda be"Shlosha yamim va'yeled,' be' 'te'chilat kayitz 1970,' ube' *Mar Mani*" (The Stamp of the *Akedah* in "Three Days and a Child," "Early in the Summer of 1970," and *Mr. Mani*), in *Bekivun hanegdi*, ed. Ben-Dov, 445–47.

37. "Different and contradictory philosophies were combined in Zionism, such as the socialist and even Marxist doctrines of the Hashomer Hatzair movement, the Orthodox doctrines of Agudat Yisrael, and religious nationalist, bourgeois liberal, social democratic, general nationalist, and even fascist nationalist doctrines," Yehoshua points out in "Zionist Revolution" (cited n. 33 above), 47. And see A. B. Yehoshua, "For a Jewish Border," *Jerusalem Post Magazine*, July 19, 2002, passim.

38. Morahg, "Borderline Cases," 177.

39. Regarding the opposition between mythology and history, see, e.g., "From Myth to History," *AJS Review* 28.1 (2004): 205–12.

40. See also Yehoshua, "Israeli Identity in a Time of Peace," 34.

41. A. B. Yehoshua, "Israeli Culture, Jewish Culture, and the Future," public address at the Koret Jewish Book Awards ceremony, Harvard Club of New York, April 7, 2003.

42. A. B. Yehoshua has since published his ninth novel, titled *Hesed Sefaradi* (Spanish Kindness) (Bnei Brak: HaSifriyah Hahadasha, 2011). An English translation is in press (2012).

43. A. B. Yehoshua, "Beyond Folklore: The Identity of the Sephardic Jew," *Quaderns de la Mediterrània* 11 (2008), 129.

44. Appiah, *Cosmopolitanism*, 97.

45. Ibid.

46. A. B. Yehoshua, *Friendly Fire: A Duet*, trans. Stuart Schoffman (New York: Harcourt, 2008), 356. Subsequent citations will be given parenthetically in the text.

47. *The Terrible Power of a Minor Guilt: Literary Essays*, trans. Ora Cummings (Syracuse, NY: Syracuse University Press, 2000), 72.

48. See Gilad Morahg, "Outraged Humanism: The Fiction of A. B. Yehoshua." *Hebrew Annual Review* 3 (1979): 141–55.

49. Martin Buber, *The Knowledge of Man* (New York: Harper & Row, 1965), 67–68. The essay "Distance and Relation" originally appeared in *Hibbert Journal* 49 (1951): 105–13.

50. Buber, *Knowledge of Man*, 69.

51. Bernard Horn, review of *Friendly Fire* by A. B. Yehoshua, *Jewish Quarterly* 211 (Autumn 1999): 71.

52. Yehoshua, *Terrible Power of a Minor Guilt*, 84–85. This is a central theme of this book as a whole. See also A. B. Yehoshua, "Ha'roman veha'demokratia ha'modernit" (The Novel and Modern Democracy) and "Ezor ha'sahar ha'hofshi ben ha'sifrut l'psichologia" (The Free-Trade Zone Between Psychology and Literature), in id., *Achizat moledet* (Homeland Grasp),141–54 and 155–63, respectively.

53. Donald Macintyre, "A. B. Yehoshua: A Road Map to Righteousness," *The Independent*, Arts and Entertainment, May 20, 2005, http://enjoyment.independent.co.uk/books/interviews/article222142.ece (accessed July 13, 2011).

54. A. B. Yehoshua in *I Am Jewish: Personal Reflections Inspired by the Last Words of Daniel Pearl*, ed. Judea and Ruth Pearl (Woodstock, VT: Jewish Lights, 2004), 21.

55. Band, "*Mar Mani*," 242.

56. Anne Golomb Hoffman, "Fictions of Identity and Their Undoing in Yehoshua's *Mr. Mani*," *Prooftexts* 12 (1992): 249.

57. Band, "*Mar Mani*," 242.

58. Morahg, "Borderline Cases," passim.

59. Yehoshua, "Levatel et ha'akeda," 394–98.

60. Solotaroff, "Strange Jews," 829.

61. Buber, *Knowledge of Man*, 69.

62. Horn, *Facing the Fires*, 22.

63. Ibid., 68.

64. Ibid., 85.

65. Ibid.

66. On the close relationship between *Mr. Mani* and *Five Seasons*, see, of course, Abraham Balaban's aptly named *Mar Molkho* (Mr. Molho) (Tel-Aviv: Hakibbutz Hameuchad, 1992).

67. Horn, *Facing the Fires*, 70.

68. Ibid., 94.

69. Ibid., 91.

70. Ibid., 83.

71. Yehoshua, *Five Seasons*, trans. Halkin, 346.
72. Ibid.

Chapter Nine: "Le Juif Espagnol"

Sections of this chapter appeared in an earlier version as "'Le Juif Espagnol': Sephardism and the Idea of Sepharad in Jewish Francophone Writers of Colonial and Post-Colonial Times" in the *International Sephardic Journal* 2.1 (Spring 2005): 108–31.

1. Various scholars attribute differing meanings to these terms. Spanish scholars are generally concerned with the fate of the Jews who left the Iberian Peninsula around 1492. For example, Paloma Díaz-Mas refers to "the Jews from Spain" and, when referring to non-Ashkenazim in Israel, distinguishes between the "true Sephardim" and those Sephardim who cannot trace a bloodline back to the Iberian Peninsula. See Paloma Díaz-Mas, *Sephardim: The Jews from Spain*, 2nd ed., trans. George Zucker (Chicago: University of Chicago Press, 1992), 187. Some North American, French, and Israeli scholars adhere to this view, while others accept a broader definition of Sephardic identity, usually depending on their particular field of research. For a more detailed discussion, see the earlier version of this article in the *International Sephardic Journal* cited above.

2. Naïm Kattan, chapter on "Le Sépharadisme," in id., *L'écrivain migrant: Essais sur des citées et des hommes* (Montréal: Hurtubise, 2001), 93–100.

3. On the amazing persistence and achievements of scribes and printers, even before they had settled in new homes and despite the deliberate destruction of Jewish books in Spain and by accident in exile, see Menahem Schmelzer, "Hebrew Manuscripts and Printed Books Among the Sephardim Before and After the Expulsion," in *Crisis and Creativity in the Sephardic World, 1391–1648*, ed. Benjamin Gampel (New York: Columbia University Press, 1970), 257–66. The parallel Ladino language expressions immediately following the expulsion can be found in Moshe Lazar, *Sefarad in my Heart: A Ladino Reader* (Lancaster, CA: Labyrinthos, 1999). See also Haïm Zafrani, *Littératures dialectales et populaires juives en Occident musulman* (Paris: Geuthner, 1980, 2nd ed., 2003) on Spanish and Ladino-speaking Jews in Morocco, and, more generally, Eleazar Gutwirth, "On the Hispanicity of Sephardi Jewry," *Revue des études juives* 145.3–4 (1986): 347–57, on the persistence of Spanish influence among the exiles, e.g., Judeo-Spanish transcriptions of sixteenth-century Spanish works, found in the Cairo Geniza.

4. Bernard Lewis, *The Jews of Islam* (Princeton, NJ: Princeton University Press, 1984).

5. Although Morocco was not part of the Ottoman Empire, the rest of North Africa consisted of semi-autonomous provinces or principalities ruled by deys or beys. The Ottoman rule was so loose that even after the French takeovers in Algeria (1830—as a department) and Tunisia (1886—as a protectorate), Turkey still made a theoretical claim to sovereignty. Syria was also often ruled by semi-autonomous pashas, though the 'Azms did not question imperial central power, and by the mid-

nineteenth century, the Ottoman Tanzimat reforms were attempting to introduce some centralization in the parts of the empire still under control. However reform also destabilized relations between the religions. Though France had interests in Syria and sought to protect Christians there, it did not have official rule until 1916. See Mehran Kamrava, *The Modern Middle East: A Political History Since the First World War* (Berkeley: University of California Press, 2005), and esp. Mehmed Şükrü Hanioğlu, *A Brief History of the Late Ottoman Empire* (Princeton, NJ: Princeton University Press, 2008).

6. Michel Abitbol, *Le passé d'une discorde: Juifs et arabes du VIIe siècle à nos jours* (Paris: Perrin, 1999), 212–216.

7. On the wide repercussions of the Damascus Affair, see Esther Benbassa and Aron Rodrigue, *The Jews of the Balkans: The Judeo-Spanish Community, 15th to 20th Centuries* (Oxford: Blackwell, 1993, 1995), 73.

8. Aron Rodrigue's *Images of Sephardi and Eastern Jewries in Transition: The Teachers of the Alliance israélite universelle, 1860–1939* (Seattle: University of Washington Press, 1993), details the aims and activities of the AIU:

> This new Jewish ethnicity in France, already in evidence in the first decade after the Revolution, eventually found its natural home in the Third Republic, creating what can be called a 'republican Judaism' that pervaded all aspects of French life until Vichy. It became the duty of the Alliance to ensure that the rest of world Jewry followed in the footsteps of French Jewry to enter the new age. . . . The Alliance was not founded to serve and aid French influence. Nevertheless, the primacy given by the organization to the teaching of French and its missionary zeal to westernize, which in this case often meant to Gallicize, led inevitably to a convergence with the aims of French foreign policy, especially that of spreading the use of the French language to gain adherents to its cause. . . . the Alliance schools eventually became, intentionally or not, allies of French interests abroad. (11–12)

9. Ibid., 15, 25–33.

10. On some causes and effects of this decline, see Gerber, *Jews of Spain*, 221–24. "Family connections enabled the Sephardim to continue to play a part in the new economic configuration, even though they, too, gradually became isolated, losing their economic power in the Empire to Christian groups who were more closely linked to the West" (Benbassa and Rodrigue, *Jews of the Balkans*, 15).

11. Rodrigue, *Images*, 32–33.

12. "Whoever the author might be, the novels of Elissa Rhaïs now exist. She was the first Algerian woman to stand out in this way, with the opportunity of being launched and supported by a publisher in order to produce precisely the kind of Oriental literature that the public of the 1920s and 1930s demanded," Jean Déjeux writes in "Elissa Rhaïs, conteuse algérienne (1876–1940)," *Revue de l'Occident musulman et de la Méditerranée* 1 (1984): 47–79. See also Déjeux's *La littérature feminine de langue française au Maghreb* (Paris: Karthala, 1994), 10–11, and Mireille Rosello,

"Elissa Rhaïs: Scandals, Impostures, Who Owns the Story?" *Research in African Literatures* 37.1 (Spring 2006): 1–15.

13. Elissa Rhaïs, *L'Andalouse* (Paris: Fayard, 1925), 216.

14. In his first, semi-autobiographical novel, Memmi describes the anxiety of a child about to attend school in a language of which he knows nothing: "I faced an abyss, without any means of communicating with the far side of it. The instructor spoke only French and I only spoke dialect: how would we ever be able to meet?" *La statue de sel* (1953, rev. ed., Paris: Gallimard, 1966), 39–40; trans. Edouard Roditi as *The Pillar of Salt* (1955; Boston: Beacon Press, 1992), 31.

15. For an overview of Memmi's biography and writings, see my *Albert Memmi* (Philadelphia: CELFAN Edition Monographs, 1987). Memmi explicitly rejected comparisons with Fanon, since Fanon believed in the necessity of violence for the decolonization process. Also see Memmi's "La vie impossible de Frantz Fanon," *Esprit* 9 (1971): 248–73. On Tunisian Jewish literature in general, see *CELAAN Review* 7.1–2 (Spring 2009), the *Juifs de Tunisie/Jews of Tunisia* issue.

16. In an interview, Memmi shed some light on his departure: "My role was over; the country was on its way to independence. . . . Tunisia was going to become a young nation and I knew that it would be an Arab and Muslim one: members of minorities, like myself, would have no place in it." Catherine Simon, "Albert Memmi, marabout sans tribu," *Le Monde*, June 15, 2004.

17. On the porous border between the novel and autobiography, see Jonathan Schorsch, "Disappearing Origins: Sephardic Autobiography Today," *Prooftexts* 27:1 (Winter 2007): 82–150.

18. Albert Memmi, *Le désert ou La vie et les aventures de Jubaïr Ouali El-Mammi* (Paris: Gallimard, 1977), 25.

19. "Ubi sunt . . . ?" has been a frequent elegiac motif in Latin and English literature over the centuries.

20. See, e.g., Memmi's novel *La statue de sel*, trans. Roditi as *The Pillar of Salt*, 93–96, where he discusses his three cultural allegiances (European, Jewish, African) through the fictional character Alexandre Mordekhai Benillouche. Memmi's support of the idea of self-determination as a self-proclaimed *juif-arabe* led him eventually to be a *sioniste de gauche*. His views on this subject are expressed in his *Les Juifs et les Arabes* (Paris: Gallimard, 1974), trans. Eleanor Levieux as *Jews and Arabs* (Chicago: J. P. O'Hara, 1975), 11, 19–29.

21. "Inevitably, in the work of Cohen there is a defense of Sephardic identity, as we would call it now, which he simply called the Jewish Orient," Albert Bensoussan writes in "Aude, Adrienne, Rebecca, Rachel: L'image de la femme dans l'oeuvre d'Albert Cohen," *Nouveaux cahiers* 91 (Winter, 1987–88): 58.

22. Gerber, *Jews of Spain*, chap. 9, "Encounter with Modernity: Ottoman Decline and the Ascendance of the West," 213–52; Hanioğlu, *Brief History*, passim. See also Benbassa and Rodrigue, *Jews of the Balkans*.

23. Albert Cohen, *Carnets 1978* (Paris: Gallimard, 1979), 17–18, 29.

24. Jean Blot, *Albert Cohen* (Paris: Ballard, 1986), 24.

25. See Albert Cohen, *Belle du Seigneur* (1968; Paris: Gallimard, 1986), trans. David Coward as *Belle du Seigneur* (New York: Viking Press, 1995), esp. chaps. 12 and 13.

26. Albert Cohen, *Les valeureux* (Paris: Gallimard, 1969), 291.

27. For further discussion of Cohen's inherent sephardism, see Clara Lévy, "L'identité sépharade d'Albert Cohen," in *Les Sépharades en littérature: Un parcours millénaire*, ed. Esther Benbassa (Paris: Presses de l'Université Paris-Sorbonne, 2005), 139–57, and Véronique Maiser, "Sépharades et ashkenazes dans l'oeuvre romanesque d'Albert Cohen," *LittéRealité* 16.1 (2004): 23–30.

28. The theory of exilic literature and the exilic imagination has been developed by Michael Seidel, applying the concept to such writers as Conrad, Joyce, James, Proust and Nabokov. "It is precisely the metaphoric lines that exile plots along both a temporal and a spatial axis that make it so dominant a condition and so prominent an emblem for the narrative imagination," he writes in *Exile and the Narrative Imagination* (New Haven, CT: Yale University Press, 1986), 198. In other words, a broad interpretation of exile sees it as existing in both space (a geographical removal from home or a longing for an elsewhere) and time (nostalgia for the past or longing for a more perfect future). See also *Renewing the Past, Reconfiguring Jewish Culture: From al-Andalus to the Haskalah*, ed. Ross Brann and Adam Sutcliffe (Philadelphia: University of Pennsylvania Press, 2004), esp. Esperanza Alfonso, "The Uses of Exile in Poetic Discourse: Some Examples from Medieval Hebrew Literature," 31–49, which likewise suggests that exile has a dimension of time as well as space.

29. See Diane Matza's "Introduction" to *Sephardic-American Voices: Two Hundred Years of a Literary Legacy* (Hanover, NH: Brandeis University Press, 1997).

30. See Lucette Valensi, "From Sacred History to Historical Memory and Back: The Jewish Past," *History and Anthropology* 2 (1986): 283–305, esp. 294–303. Also Guy Dugas, *La littérature judéo-maghrebine d'expression française* (Philadelphia: CELFAN Editions, 1988).

31. Shmuel Trigano, "The Memory of the Lost People," *Contemporary French and Francophone Studies* 11.2 (2007): 177–88; and Solange M. Guenoun, "Accueils et écueils identitaires-communautaires en France post-coloniale: Ils disent que je suis sépharade," ibid., 217–30.

32. Or *différance*, as the Algerian-born philosopher Jacques Derrida would put it. Derrida's term (think of the English word "deferral") refers to the lag inherent in any signifying act (between speech or writing and meaning). See Barbara Johnson, introduction to Derrida, *Dissemination* (Chicago: University of Chicago Press, 1981), ix. On "displacement," see esp. a 1972 interview entitled "Positions," discussed in the introduction to *Displacement: Derrida and After*, ed. Mark Krupnick (Bloomington: Indiana University Press, 1983), 5, 12–16, and Shira Wolosky, "Derrida, Jabès, Lévinas: Sign-Theory as Ethical Discourse," *Prooftexts* 2 (1982): 283–302. See also Nathalie Debrauwere-Miller, "Hélène Cixous: A Sojourn Without Place," *Contemporary French and Francophone Studies* 11.2 (2007): 253–63.

33. See Judith Roumani, "Migration in the Novels of North African Jews: Bensoussan, Bouganim, Kayat" (in Hebrew) *Peamim* 35 (August 1988): 130–40.

34. Albert Bensoussan, *Frimaldjézar* (Paris: Calmann Lévy, 1976).

35. See Elisabeth Schousboë, *Albert Bensoussan* (Paris: L'Harmattan, 1991), 34–39. For Bensoussan, Schousboë explains, "Sepharad is . . . the lost land, nostalgic, ahistoric, and mythical, reuniting today, in the context of a French language, all those who have lost their native shores and participate in a Sephardic reawakening that finds a collective project in sephardism" (38–39, Yael Halevi-Wise's translation).

36. Ami Bouganim, *Le cri de l'arbre* (Tel Aviv: Stavit, 1983).

37. Nine Moati, *Les belles de Tunis* (Paris: Seuil, 1983).

38. Didier Nebot, *Le chemin de l'exil* (Paris: Presses de la Renaissance, 1992). For an in-depth analysis, see Louise Larlee's "Représentations littéraires de l'histoire sépharade dans *Le chemin de l'exil* de Didier Nebot" (M.A. thesis, McGill University, 2009).

39. Didier Nebot, *La Kahéna: Reine d'Ifrikia* (Paris: Carrière, 1998) and *Les tribus oubliées d'Israël: L'Afrique judéo-berbère, des origines aux Almohades* (Paris: Romillat, 1999). Regarding Nebot's *Chemin de l'exil*, see n. 38 above. Other historical studies support the ancient presence of Jewish-Berber tribes in the Sahara, e.g., Jacob Oliel, *Les Juifs au Sahara: Une présence millénaire* (Montréal: Elysée, 2007).

40. The Hilloula is a celebration marking the life of a well-known rabbi, sage, or "saint" on the anniversary of his death. It often consists of a pilgrimage to the gravesite and/or the sharing of a meal and lighting of candles. It is a Sephardic custom practiced especially in North Africa, and the most famous is probably the Hilloula of Bar-Yohai, the reputed author of the mystical *Zohar*. For an interesting description of how another Hilloula is celebrated today in France, see Laurence Podselver, "Le pélerinage du Maarabi à Sarcelles: Un pélerinage transposé du judaïsme tunisien," in *La mémoire sépharade: Entre l'oubli et l'avenir*, ed. Hélène Trigano and Shmuel Trigano, *Pardès 28* (2000): 205–18.

41. Yehoshua lived in France for four years, from 1963 to 1967, and is fluent in French. Though his father's family has lived in Jerusalem for many generations, his mother's family, Rosilio, was from Morocco, and much of the family eventually emigrated to France rather than Israel (my interview with A. B. Yehoshua, 22 August, 1987, and information provided by Jeanette Rosilio). See also Bernard Horn, *Facing the Fires: Conversations with A. B. Yehoshua* (Syracuse, NY: Syracuse University Press, 1997), 3, on Yehoshua's relation to the French language, and Pierre Assouline, "Conversation animé avec A. B. Yehoshua," June 25, 2007, http://passouline.blog.lemonde.fr/2007/06/25 (accessed July 13, 2011). See especially his novels *Mr. Mani*, trans. Hillel Halkin (New York: Doubleday, 1992), and *A Journey to the End of the Millennium*, trans. Nicholas de Lange (New York: Doubleday, 1999). *Mr. Mani*, especially, might be seen as the prototypical Sephardi novel, covering two hundred years in the life of a Sephardi family, ranging over much of the eastern Mediterranean and Middle East. For a wider discussion of Yehoshua's sephardism, see Bernard Horn's Chapter Eight in this volume.

42. André Aciman, *Out of Egypt: A Memoir* (New York: Farrar, Straus and Giroux, 1994). Aciman describes the lingering goodbyes and subsequent homesickness

of a Jewish family leaving Alexandria, some of whom speak Judeo-Spanish as they came from Turkey. The one Ashkenazi intermarried with this family describes their emotional effusions as "pathologically Sephardi" (48). In Proustian manner, they anticipate their homesickness before they have even left and are bitterly disillusioned by their experiences in Paris. The poignant chapter on the family's celebration of Passover on the eve of their own departure from Egypt is tragicomic in its reversal of the terms of the traditional seder and Haggadah: Aciman's new Haggadah, or story, does not celebrate but mourns the forced second departure from Egypt. In a lecture entitled "Francophonie des juifs d'Egypte" at Netanya Academic College in Israel, in March 2008, David Sultan asserted that the majority of the students in French-language schools in Egypt at the end of the nineteenth century were Jews.

Chapter Ten: Sephardism in Latina Literature

I acknowledge a research award from the Professional Staff Congress of the City University of New York held while I worked on this chapter and the help of the colleagues who offered comments and encouragement when I presented versions at the Association for Jewish Studies conference, McGill University, and the University of Toronto. I thank Eva-Lynn Jagoe for inviting me to present at the Latin American Studies Centre at the University of Toronto and Yael Halevi-Wise both for her invitation to McGill for a special seminar and for asking me to contribute to this ground-breaking volume and sharing her own work and ideas.

1. Demetria Martínez quoted in Gabriela Gutiérrez y Muhs, *Communal Feminisms: Chicanas, Chilenas, and Cultural Exile: Theorizing the Space of Exile, Class, and Identity* (Lanham, MD: Lexington Books, 2006), 66.

2. For an analysis of these novels' place within U.S. literature, specifically vis-à-vis the construction of U.S. ethnicity and race, see Jonathan Freedman's *Klezmer America: Jewishness, Ethnicity, Modernity* (New York: Columbia University Press, 2008). Freedman examines their representation of crypto-Jewishness as emblematic of the syncretic nature of ethnicity in the United States. While we share an interest in their syncretic dimension, my primary purpose is less to explore crypto-Jewishness as an instance of ethnic hybridity in the United States than to signal the alloying of sephardism with Latina/o narratives and identities.

3. Edna Aizenberg, *Books and Bombs in Buenos Aires: Borges, Gerchunoff, and Argentine-Jewish Writing* (Hanover, NH: University Press of New England, 2002), 51. See her Chapter Five in this volume.

4. I borrow the term "public secrets" from Michael T. Taussig's *Defacement: Public Secrecy and the Labor of the Negative* (Stanford, CA: Stanford University Press, 1999).

5. Michael P. Carroll, "The Debate over a Crypto-Jewish Presence in New Mexico: The Role of Ethnographic Allegory and Orientalism," *Sociology of Religion* 63.1 (2002): 1–19.

6. Martin A. Cohen, *The Martyr: The Story of a Secret Jew and the Mexican Inquisition in the Sixteenth Century* (Philadelphia: Jewish Publication Society of America, 1973).

7. I am referring to debates surrounding the claims of Jewishness by Latina/os in the United States (especially in New Mexico) and Latin America. While some scholars like Stanley Hordes have backed new explorations and assertions of Jewish ancestry and crypto-Jewish continuity, others have dismissed these claims as having little evidence or basis (e.g., Judith Neulander; Wesley Sutton et al.) or serving dominant racializations (Michael P. Carroll). And yet memoir publications and newspaper reporting on discoveries of Jewish identity and re-Judaization (e.g., Simon Romero) continue, as does networking through the annual conferences of the Society for Crypto-Jewish Studies and internet groups like Anusim and others. See Stanley Hordes, *To the End of the Earth: A History of the Crypto-Jews of New Mexico* (New York: Columbia University Press, 2005); Judith Neulander, "The New Mexican Crypto-Jewish Canon: Choosing to be 'Chosen' in Millennial Tradition," *Jewish Folklore and Ethnology Review* 18 (1996): 19–58; Simon Romero, "Hispanics Uncovering Roots as Inquisition's 'Hidden' Jews," *New York Times*, October 29, 2005, www.nytimes.com/2005/10/29/national/29religion.html (accessed July 13, 2011); and Wesley K. Sutton, Alec Knight, Peter A. Underhill, Judith S. Neulander, Todd R. Disotell and Joanna L. Mountain, "Toward Resolution of the Debate Regarding Purported Crypto-Jews in a Spanish-American Population: Evidence from the Y-chromosome," *Annals of Human Biology* 33 (2006): 100–111.

8. Hip Hop Hoodios, *Agua Pa' la Gente*, compact disc (Jazzhead Records, 2005). The group's song "1492" points to buried connectivities through Sephardic histories, frequently occluded from popular knowledge and academic scholarship, which tend to focus on a putatively undifferentiated Jewish Latin American population. This almost always refers, however, to the history and culture of the eastern European "majority" of Jews in Latin America. This erasure, often carried out through majoritarian discourses, and (note the irony) in the name of non-divisiveness, ignores the historical and current Sephardic-Ashkenazi divisions within Latin America (see, e.g., Adriana Brodsky, "The Contours of Identity: Sephardic Jews and the Construction of Jewish Communities in Argentina, 1880 to the Present" [Ph.D. diss., Duke University, 2004]). Hip Hop Hoodios' wide-ranging interests and inclusive outlook on Jewish culture have also led to their remixing of the neo-Ladino song "Ocho Kandelikas" (in *Agua Pa' la gente*), which positions this Sephardic language as another bridge between the Latina/o and Jewish worlds. Cultural productions like "1492" work to address erasures of Jewish heterogeneity and assert overlapping Jewish-Latina/o histories through a specific and Sephardic historical moment that resonates and is relevant today.

9. Kathleen Alcalá, *The Desert Remembers My Name: On Family and Writing* (Tucson: University of Arizona Press, 2007), 95.

10. Freedman opens his chapter on crypto-Jews with a telling anecdote: at a meeting about hiring a junior professor in Jewish American studies, a senior colleague dismisses the author's suggestion that a position in Sephardic Studies of the Americas be created with the words "the Sephardim are of no importance in the U.S. None. At best—they're a footnote" (*Klezmer America*, 209). This comment

is typical, not exceptional, in non-Sephardic Jewish academic, media, and political contexts in the United States.

11. Laura Sheppard-Brick, interview with Achy Obejas, July 2002, www.yiddishbookcenter.org/node/327 (accessed July 13, 2011).

12. On the irony of Alejandra's passing as a white Christian American on account of her lighter skin and "despite" her Latina and Sephardic heritage, see Freedman, *Klezmer America*, 243.

13. I am thinking, e.g., of *The Ballad of Little Jo*, Maggie Greenwald's memorable film about a cross-dressing woman passing as a man in the nineteenth-century U.S. West, a "wild" space of gender and racial crossings.

14. Sander Gilman, *Multiculturalism and the Jews* (New York: Routledge, 2006), 151.

15. Ibid.

16. Janet R. Jakobsen, "Queers Are Like Jews, Aren't They? Analogy and Alliance Politics," in *Queer Theory and the Jewish Question*, ed. Daniel Boyarin, Daniel Itzkovitz, and Ann Pellegrini (New York: Columbia University Press, 2003), 66.

17. Freedman, *Klezmer America*, 233, 237.

18. See, in this context, Evelyn Torton Beck's "Jews and the Multicultural University Curriculum," in *The Narrow Bridge: Jewish Views on Multiculturalism*, ed. Marla Brettschneider (New Brunswick, NJ: Rutgers University Press, 1996), 163–77; and Andrew Furman's *Contemporary Jewish American Writers and the Multicultural Dilemma: Return of the Exiled* (Syracuse, NY: Syracuse University Press, 2000).

19. Theresa Delgadillo, *Spiritual Mestizaje: Religion, Gender, Race, and Nation in Contemporary Chicana Narrative* (Durham, NC: Duke University Press, 2011).

20. For a nuanced discussion of this concept, see e.g., Josefina Saldaña-Portillo, "Who's the Indian in Aztlán? Rewriting Mestizaje, Indianism, and the Chicano from the Lacandón," in *The Latin American Subaltern Studies Reader*, ed. Ileana Rodríguez (Durham, NC: Duke University Press, 2001), 402–23; Jorge Klor de Alva, "The Postcolonization of the (Latin) American Experience: A Reconsideration of 'Colonialism,' 'Postcolonialism,' and 'Mestizaje,'" in *After Colonialism: Imperial Histories and Postcolonial Displacements*, ed. Gyan Prakash (Princeton, NJ: Princeton University Press, 1995), 241–75; and Ana María Alonso, "Conforming Disconformity: 'Mestizaje,' Hybridity and the Aesthetics of Mexican Nationalism," *Cultural Anthropology* 19.4 (2004): 459–90.

21. Demetria Martínez, *Confessions of a Berlitz-Tape Chicana* (Tulsa: University of Oklahoma Press, 2005), 8.

22. Emma Pérez, "Queering the Borderlands: Excavating the Invisible and Unheard," *Frontiers: A Journal of Women Studies* 24.2–3 (2003): 122–31.

23. Marie Teresa Hernández, *Delirio: The Fantastic, the Demonic, and the Réel: The Buried History of Nuevo Léon* (Austin: University of Texas Press, 2002), 189.

24. Gloria Anzaldúa, *Borderlands/La Frontera* (San Francisco: Aunt Lute, 1987), 87.

25. Anzaldúa, *Interviews/Entrevistas*, ed. Ana Louise Keating (New York: Routledge, 2000), 239.

26. Frances Aparicio, "Latino Cultural Studies," in *Critical Latino and Latin American Studies*, ed. Juan Poblete (Minneapolis: University of Minnesota Press, 2003), 20.

27. Ibid., 22.

28. See, e.g., Delgadillo, *Spiritual Mestizaje*, which provides a groundbreaking discussion of Alcalá's trilogy.

29. Nash Candelaria, *Memories of the Alhambra* (Palo Alto, CA: Cibola Press, 1977); Carey McWilliams, *North From Mexico* (New York: Monthly Review Press, 1961). See also Charles Montgomery, *The Spanish Redemption: Heritage, Power, and Loss on New Mexico's Upper Rio Grande* (Berkeley: University of California Press, 2002), and John M. Nieto-Phillips, *The Language of Blood: The Making of Spanish-American Identity in New Mexico, 1880s–1930s* (Albuquerque: University of New Mexico Press, 2004).

30. Luís de Carvajal, e.g., was given the task of "pacifying" Northern Mexican Indians.

31. "Bagels, Bongos, and Yiddishe Mambos, or The Other History of Jews in America," *Shofar: An Interdisciplinary Journal of Jewish Studies* 23.4 (2005): 50–68.

32. Robert Suro, "Two Peoples on a Journey," in *Latinos and Jews: Old Luggage, New Itineraries*, ed. David A. Harris(New York: American Jewish Committee, 2002).

33. Ibid., 13.

Chapter Eleven: Sir Salman Rushdie Sails for India and Rediscovers Spain

The research for this essay was funded by Israel Science Foundation Grant #233/06 and by the Vidal Sassoon Center for the Study of Anti-Semitism at the Hebrew University of Jerusalem.

1. Barnet Litvinoff, *Fourteen Ninety-Two: The Decline of Medievalism and the Rise of the Modern Age* (New York: Scribner, 1991), 60–61.

2. At one stage of his thinking about sephardism, in his novel *Mas'a el tom ha-elef* (1997), trans. Nicholas de Lange as *A Journey to the End of the Millennium* (1999), A. B. Yehoshua reconstituted a medieval past in which the wealthy Tangiers merchant Ben Attar has a Muslim business partner, enjoys two wives, as well as the services of black slaves, and is unafraid of the fanatic Christians. See Bernard Horn's essay on Yehoshua, in Chapter Eight of this volume, which argues that Yehoshua developed a new perspective on sephardism in this novel.

3. Gil Anidjar has contemplated the rhetorical location of the Andalusia from which Maimonides' *Guide for the Perplexed* and the *Zohar* emerged in the eschatological discourse of 1492 in *"Our Place in Andalus": Kabbalah, Philosophy, Literature in Arab-Jewish Letters* (Stanford, CA: Stanford University Press, 2002), 6–7, 57–65. On the actual chronology, changing politics, and instability of Muslim-Jewish re-

lations in Andalusia, see Esperanza Alfonso, *Islamic Culture through Jewish Eyes: Al-Andalus from the Tenth to Twelfth Century* (London: Routledge, 2008).

4. Michael Ragussis, *Figures of Conversion: "The Jewish Question" and English National Identity* (Durham, NC: Duke University Press, 1995), 36.

5. Michelene Wandor, "Song of the Jewish Princess," in *Voices of the Diaspora: Jewish Women Writing in Contemporary Europe*, ed. Thomas Nolden and Frances Malino (Evanston, IL: Northwestern University Press, 2005), 135–45.

6. Elaine Feinstein, *Talking to the Dead* (Manchester: Carcanet, 2007), 50–51. The excerpt is used with the kind permission of the author. Elvira del Campo was arrested in Toledo in 1567 on suspicion of Judaizing because she refused to eat pork; her story is related in Henry Charles Lea, *A History of the Inquisition of Spain*, vol. 3 (New York: Macmillan, 1922), 24–26.

7. Feinstein, *Talking to the Dead*, 51. Heine had also idealized the Spanish Jewish past of the Golden Age, but that was because it was more amenable than unemancipated German Jewry; it had dignity and offered a different exploration of the dilemma of the diaspora Jew. See Siegbert Salomon Prawer, *Heine's Jewish Comedy: A Study of His Portraits of Jews and Judaism* (Oxford: Clarendon Press, 1983), 598–99.

8. See Y. H. Yerushalmi, *The Re-education of Marranos in the Seventeenth Century* (Cincinnati: Judaic Studies Program, University of Cincinnati, 1980); *Zakhor: Jewish History and Jewish Memory* (Seattle: University of Washington Press, 1982). On the changing view of Sepharad in historical discourse, see *Renewing the Past, Reconfiguring Jewish Culture: From Al-Andalus to the Haskalah*, ed. Ross Brann and Adam Sutcliffe (Philadelphia: University of Pennsylvania Press, 2004).

9. See, e.g., Ammiel Alcalay's *After Jews and Arabs: Remaking Levantine Culture* (Minneapolis: University of Minnesota Press, 1993).

10. Aamir Mufti, *Enlightenment in the Colony: The Jewish Question and the Crisis of Postcolonial Culture* (Princeton, NJ: Princeton University Press, 2007).

11. Ibid., 175.

12. Sander Gilman, *Multiculturalism and the Jews* (New York: Routledge, 2006), 165.

13. Amitav Ghosh, *In an Antique Land: History in the Guise of a Traveler's Tale* (New York: Knopf, 1993), 236.

14. See S. D. Goiten, *Jews and Arabs: Their Contacts Through the Ages* (New York: Schocken Books, 1964), 101–20.

15. Ella Shohat, "Taboo Memories and Diasporic Visions: Columbus, Palestine, and Arab-Jews," in id., *Taboo Memories, Diasporic Voices* (Durham, NC: Duke University, 2006), 201–32.

16. Ella Shohat, "Rupture and Return: Zionist Discourse and the Study of Arab-Jews," ibid., 351–52.

17. Shohat, "Taboo Memories and Diasporic Visions," 228.

18. Salman Rushdie, *East, West* (London: Vintage Books, 1995), 105–19. Rushdie may have been inspired by the idea of a secret connection between Columbus's voyage and the expulsion of the Jews explored in Simon Wiesenthal, *Sails of Hope: The*

Secret Mission of Christopher Columbus, trans. Richard Winston and Clara Winston (New York: Macmillan, 1973).

19. On the parallels between India and Iberia in this novel, see Mona Narain, "Re-Imagined Histories: Rewriting the Early Modern in Rushdie's *The Moor's Last Sigh*," *Journal for Early Modern Cultural Studies* 6.2 (2006): 55–68.

20. Tudor Parfitt, "The Land of Hard Bondage: The Lost Tribes in India," *Journal of Indo-Judaic Studies* 5 (March 2002): 55–68.

21. On Cochin Jewry, see Nathan Katz and Ellen S. Goldberg, *The Last Jews of Cochin: Jewish Identity in Hindu India* (Columbia, SC: University of South Carolina Press, 1993).

22. Madelena Gonzalez, *Fiction after the Fatwa: Salman Rushdie and the Charm of Catastrophe* (Amsterdam: Rodopi, 2005), 114.

23. See Efraim Sicher and Linda Weinhouse, "The Passage of the 'jew' to India: Desai, Rushdie, and Globalized Culture," *European Review of History/Revue européenne d'histoire* 18.1 (January 2011): 111–21. The following discussion of Rushdie draws on some passages from this article. Carlo Ginzburg has argued that the comparison of Jews and Indians characterized Enlightenment discourse in his "Provincializing the World: Europeans, Indians, Jews (1704)," *Postcolonial Studies* 14.2 (2011): 135–150, a response to Dipesh Chakrabarty's *Provincializing Europe: Postcolonial Thought and Historical Difference* (2000). See also Jonathan Boyarin, *The Unconverted Self: Jews, Indians, and the Identity of Christian Europe* (Chicago: University of Chicago Press, 2009).

24. Salman Rushdie, *The Moor's Last Sigh* (London: Vintage Books, 1996), 82. Italics in original. All further references to this edition are given in parentheses.

25. Anna Guttman, *The Nation of India in Contemporary Indian Literature* (New York Palgrave Macmillan, 2007), 72.

26. On this aspect of Aurora's paintings, see Paul A. Cantor, "Tales of the Alhambra: Rushdie's Use of Spanish History in *The Moor's Last Sigh*," *Studies in the Novel* 29.3 (1997): 323–41.

27. Rushdie quoted in Gonzalez, *Fiction after the Fatwa*, 108n8.

28. Peter Berek, "The Jew as Renaissance Man," *Renaissance Quarterly* 51.1 (1998): 128–62.

29. James Shapiro, *Shakespeare and the Jews* (New York: Columbia University Press, 1996), 13–43.

30. Homi Bhabha, *The Location of Culture* (London: Routledge, 1994), 102–23.

31. Ibid., 168–69.

32. Ibid., 223–24.

33. Rushdie, quoted in Gonzalez, *Fiction after the Fatwa*, 102–103n3.

34. Guttman, *Nation of India*, 74–75.

35. Rushdie, *Midnight's Children* (London: Vintage Books, 1995), 72.

36. Mufti, *Enlightenment in the Colony*, 247.

37. On Rushdie's use of the complex history of the Cochin and Bombay Jewish communities, see Bindu Milieckal, "Shakespeare's Shylock, Rushdie's Abraham

Zogoiby, and the Jewish Pepper Merchants of Precolonial India," *Upstart Crow* 21 (2001): 154–69. Milieckal points out that in India, anti-Semitism began only with the coming of the Portuguese, whose encounter with Indian Jews colored (literally and metaphorically) the orientalized image of the "Jew" in Europe.

38. Dohra Ahmad, "'This fundo stuff is really something new': Fundamentalism and Hybridity in *The Moor's Last Sigh*," *Yale Journal of Criticism* 18.1 (Spring 2005): 5.

39. See Michael Gorra, *After Empire: Scott, Naipaul, Rushdie* (Chicago: University of Chicago Press, 1997), 113.

40. Gonzalez, *Fiction after the Fatwa*, 110.

41. Jonathan Greenberg, "The Base Indian or the Base Judean? Othello and the Metaphor of the Palimpsest in Salman Rushdie's *The Moor's Last Sigh*," *Modern Language Studies* 29.2 (1999): 94–95.

42. Gonzalez, *Fiction after the Fatwa*, 97.

43. Salman Rushdie, "Imaginary Homelands," in id., *Imaginary Homelands: Essays and Criticism, 1981–1991* (London: Granta Books, 1991), 9–21.

44. John Docker, *1492: The Poetics of Diaspora* (New York: Continuum, 2001), ix.

45. Regarding this post-Zionist position on the Sephardim's cultural status vis-à-vis Ashkenazim in Israel, see Amnon Raz-Krakotzkin, "The Zionist Return to the West and the Mizrahi Jewish Perspective," in *Orientalism and the Jews*, ed. Ivan Davidson Kalmar and Derek J. Penslar (Waltham, MA: Brandeis University Press; Hanover, NH: University Press of New England, 2005), 162–81.

46. Growing awareness of the Andalusian contribution to modern science has not always acknowledged the participation of Jews alongside Muslims—Sir Ben Kingsley's *1001 Inventions and the Library of Secrets*, a film produced for London's Science Museum in 2010, refers to "other faiths," but mentions not a single Jewish physician or astronomer of Spain's Golden Age.

47. Docker, *1492*, 210–11.

48. Daniel and Jonathan Boyarin, *Powers of Diaspora: Two Essays on the Relevance of Jewish Culture* (Minneapolis: University of Minnesota Press, 2002), ix. See also Daniel Boyarin and Jonathan Boyarin's seminal statement, "Diaspora: Generation and the Ground of Jewish Identity," *Critical Inquiry* 19.4 (1993): 693–725.

49. For a critique of postcolonial discourses on diaspora in comparison with the Jewish historical understanding of the term, see Michael Galchinsky, "Scattered Seeds: A Dialogue of Diasporas," in *Insider/Outsider: American Jews and Multiculturalism*, ed. David Biale, Michael Galchinsky, and Susan Heschel (Berkeley: University of California Press, 1998), 185–211. See also for a post-Zionist perspective, Jon Stratton, "Historicising the Idea of Diaspora," in id., *Coming Out Jewish: Constructing Ambivalent Identities* (London: Routledge, 2000), 145–63.

50. Boyarin and Boyarin, *Powers of Diaspora*, 11.

51. Ibid., 13.

52. Victor Perera, *The Cross and the Pear Tree: A Sephardic Journey* (Berkeley: University of California Press, 1996), 42.

53. See Mark Cohen, "Islam and the Jews: Myth, Counter-Myth, History,"

in *Jews Among Muslims: Communities in the Precolonial Middle East*, ed. Shlomo Deshen and Walter P. Zenner (New York: New York University Press, 1996), 50–63; Dario Fernández-Morera, "The Myth of the Andalusian Paradise," *Intercollegiate Review*, Fall 2006: 23–31.

54. Harold Bloom, "Foreword," in María Rosa Menocal, *The Ornament of the World: How Muslims, Jews, and Christians Created a Culture of Tolerance in Medieval Spain* (Boston: Little, Brown, 2002), xiv.

55. Menocal, *Ornament of the World*, 265.

56. Ibid., 249–50.

Postscript

1. Rebecca Goldstein, *Betraying Spinoza: The Renegade Jew Who Gave Us Modernity* (New York: Schocken Books, 2006); page numbers are given parenthetically in the text. The literary history of sephardism that I chart in the Introduction to this volume indicates that in the United States a significant cluster of historical novels about the Sephardic experience appeared around the time of the quincentennial commemorations of the expulsion of the Jews from Spain. One can cite Noah Gordon's *The Last Jew* (2002), Jacqueline Park's *The Secret Book of Grazia dei Rossi* (1998), Naomi Ragen's *The Ghost of Hanna Mendes* (2001), David Raphael's *The Alhambra Decree* (1988), Richard Zimmler's *The Last Kabbalist of Lisbon* (1998), as well as from Canada, Matt Cohen's *The Spanish Doctor* (1985) and Caroline Roe's medieval mystery series, *Chronicles of Isaac of Girona*, published from 1998 to 2004, in addition to the Latina novels that Dalia Kandiyoti discusses in detail in this volume. The degree of sephardism in these works depends on whether they are genuinely engaged with Sephardic history or merely use it as costume drama to drape a generic story, as Harry Shaw notes regarding "the different ways in which history has been employed in standard historical fiction" (Shaw, *The Forms of Historical Fiction: Sir Walter Scott and His Successors* [Ithaca, NY: Cornell University Press, 1983], 52ff.).

2. So far, reviewers of Goldstein's book have dwelled only cursorily on its Sephardic dimension despite the fact that the author has insisted on it, both within her book and in every interview she has given since its publication. For example, in her interview with Paul Comstock, Goldstein spells out that "Spinoza was brought up in a family, and a larger community, of former Marranos and it's one of the claims of my book that Spinoza's preoccupation with personal identity and salvation—the way that he interwove these two issues—was influenced by the preoccupations of his community. . . . The answer to who the Marranos were lies in the history of the Jews of Spain," "An Interview with Rebecca Goldstein," *California Literary Review*, March 30, 2007, http://calitreview.com/55, accessed July 14, 2011.

3. Yirmiyahu Yovel in *Spinoza and Other Heretics: The Marrano of Reason* (Princeton, NJ: Princeton University Press, 1989) argues that Spinoza went beyond even this "daring heterodox minority," and "with such a gulf separating him from his contemporaries, he could not sufficiently mask his thoughts without compromising his intellectual identity and goals beyond what he deemed tolerable." He thus

became "his own kind of Marrano, a Marrano of Reason whose esoteric truth . . . is not Judaism in opposition to Christianity but the immanent religion of reason in opposition to all historical religions" (143). See also Yovel's *The Other Within: The Marranos, Split Identity and Emerging Modernity* (Princeton, NJ: Princeton University Press, 2009).

4. For a wider discussion of the relationship between Enlightenment thought and Spinoza's legacy, see Jonathan I. Israel's magisterial analysis of the *Radical Enlightenment: Philosophy and the Making of Modernity, 1650–1750* (Oxford: Oxford University Press, 2001); and Arthur Hertzberg's *The French Enlightenment and the Jews: Origins of Modern Anti-Semitism* (New York: Columbia University Press, 1968), chap. 3, which details Spinoza's influence on Voltaire and other figures of the French Enlightenment.

5. Goldstein's infusion of human warmth into Spinoza's philosophy strikes Harold Bloom as endearing, but he maintains that Spinoza's work is "greatly cold, and coldly great . . . it will illuminate you, but through light without heat." He moreover rejects Goldstein's argument that Spinoza's "detachment and loftiness were defenses against the sufferings of Jewish history" (Bloom, "The Heretic Jew," *New York Times*, June 18, 2006).

6. Allan Nadler finds that *Betraying Spinoza* is "pickled with errors" including misconstruction of a date on a key piece of correspondence; confusion of liturgical practice; and mistranslations that expose a gap between Goldstein's view of the world and Spinoza's historical context (Nadler, "Romancing Spinoza," *Commentary* 122.5 [December 2006], 29).

7. Miriam Bodian, *Dying in the Law of Moses: Crypto-Jewish Martyrdom in the Iberian World* (Bloomington: Indiana University Press, 2007), 10–11, 177, 179–80. Regarding the impact of these anti-Christian polemics on the Sephardic community in the Netherlands, see Carsten Wilke, "Conversion ou retour? La metamorphose du nouveau chrétien en juif portugais dans l'imaginaire sépharade du XVIIe siècle," in *Mémoires juives d'Espagne et du Portugal*, ed. Esther Benbassa (Paris: Publisud, 1996): 53–67, as well as Daniel L. Lasker, "Jewish Anti-Christian Polemics in the Early Modern Period: Change or Continuity?" in *Tradition, Heterodoxy and Religious Culture: Judaism and Christianity in the Early Modern Period*, ed. Chanita Goodblatt and Howard Kreisel (Beer-Sheva: Ben-Gurion University of the Negev, 2006), 469–88.

8. Nadler, "Romancing Spinoza," 25, 27–28.

9. Jonathan Skolnik, "Kaddish for Spinoza: Memory and Modernity in Celan and Heine," *New German Critique* 77 (1999): 172. Regarding the impact of Spinoza on German Jewish thought, see also Willi Goetschel, *Spinoza's Modernity: Mendelssohn, Lessing, and Heine* (Madison: University of Wisconsin Press, 2004) and Leo Strauss's well-known analysis of this topic in *Spinoza's Critique of Religion* (New York: Schocken Books, 1965), 15–31.

10. Skolnik, "Kadish" 169–70; also see his "Writing Jewish History Between Gutzkow and Goethe: Auerbach's *Spinoza* and the Birth of Modern Jewish Historical Fiction," *Prooftexts* 19 (1999): 101–25.

11. Walter Scott, Introduction to *Peveril of the Peak* (Chicago: Belford and Clarke, n.d.), 3.

12. Goldstein emphasizes the connection between Spinoza's community in Amsterdam and the first Jews who settled in North America in the seventeenth century. These Jews—former Marranos like Spinoza's family—came from Recife in Brazil, which briefly became a Dutch colony, enabling crypto-Jews to practice their Judaism openly. When this territory reverted to Portugal, a small group sought refuge from the Inquisition in New Amsterdam (today New York). Isaac Aboab, their rabbi, did not accompany them, but sailed directly to Amsterdam, where shortly afterward he participated in Spinoza's excommunication (157). On the early Sephardic history of American Jewry, see Jonathan Sarna, *American Judaism: A History* (New Haven, CT: Yale University Press, 2004), chap. 1, and Aviva Ben-Ur's *Sephardic Jews in America: A Diasporic History* (New York: New York University Press, 2009).

13. Regarding Spinoza's impact on proponents of the Enlightenment and on Locke in particular, see John Marshall, *John Locke, Toleration and Early Enlightenment Culture* (New York: Cambridge University Press, 2006), 14, 560ff, as well as the books by Arthur Hertzberg and Jonathan Israel cited in n. 4 above. Locke lived in Holland after Spinoza's death, and his library did contain Spinoza's works. Yet as my colleague Carlos Fraenkel observed to me, Goldstein's Spinoza-Locke connection still stands "at odds with Jonathan Israel's portrait of Spinoza as the embodiment of the radical Enlightenment and Locke as the embodiment of the moderate Enlightenment."

14. As Goldstein explained in an interview, "I play around with . . . a possible path from Spinoza's influence in Amsterdam to the founding fathers of America, by way of John Locke, who spent time in Amsterdam a few years after Spinoza's death and fraternized with people of the same liberal persuasion as those in whom Spinoza had confided his ideas. No matter if Jefferson and Madison really did read Spinoza (Spinoza was in Jefferson's library) they often sound just like him in their letters" (see note 2 above). Significantly, the chronology at the back of Goldstein's book begins with the Muslim conquest of Spain in the year 711 and ends with the publication of John Locke's "Letter of Tolerance" in defense of religious liberties in 1689.

15. Nadler argues that "far from anticipating the Bill of Rights with its landmark protection of religious liberties, Spinoza would almost certainly have preferred France's more militantly secular approach to religion. . . . In the *Tractatus* he rejects the notion of special rights in the exercise of religion as a 'seditious idea,' and the very phrase 'religious liberties' would have likely struck him as an oxymoron. For anyone seriously attached to the First Amendment, Spinoza is no ally" ("Romancing Spinoza," 30).

Selected Bibliography

Primary Works

Aguilar, Grace. *The Vale of Cedars; or, The Martyr*. London: R. E. King, 1850.

Aguinis, Marcos. *La gesta del marrano*. Buenos Aires: Planeta, 1991.

Alcalá, Kathleen. *Spirits of the Ordinary: A Tale of Casas Grandes*. San Francisco: Chronicle Books, 1997. New York: Harcourt Brace, 1998.

Aridjis, Homero. *1492: Vida y tiempos de Juan Cabezón de Castilla*. Mexico, D.F.: Fondo de Cultura Económica, 1985. Translated by Betty Ferber as *1492: The Life and Times of Juan Cabezón of Castile* (Albuquerque: University of New Mexico Press, 1985).

———. *Memorias del nuevo mundo*. Mexico, D.F.: Fondo de Cultura Económica, 1998.

Auerbach, Berthold. *Spinoza: Ein historischer Roman*. Stuttgart, 1837.

Barnatán, Marcos Ricardo. *El laberinto de Sión*. Barcelona: Barral, 1971.

Bensoussan, Albert. *Frimaldjezar*. Paris: Calmann Lévy, 1976.

Bouganim, Ami. *Le cri de l'arbre*. Tel Aviv: Stavit, 1983.

Brailovsky, Antonio Elio. *Identidad*. Buenos Aires: Sudamericana, 1980. Reissued as *Isaac Halevy, rey de los judíos* (Buenos Aires: Tusquets, 1997).

Bulwer-Lytton, Edward. *Leila; or, The Siege of Granada*. London: Longman, Orme, Brown, Green & Longmans, 1838. Boston: D. Estes, 1892.

Burla, Yehuda. *Eleh masa'ei Rabi Yehuda Halevi* (These are the Travels of Rabbi Yehuda Halevi). Tel Aviv: Am Oved, 1959.

Canetti, Elias. *Die Blendung*. Vienna: Herbert Reichner, 1935. Translated by C. V. Wedgwood as *Auto da fé* (London: Jonathan Cape, 1946).

Cohen, Albert. *Belle du Seigneur*. 1968. Paris: Gallimard, 1986. Translated by David Coward under the same title (New York: Viking Press, 1995).

———. *Les valeureux*. Paris: Gallimard, 1969.

Chocrón, Isaac. *Escrito y sellado*. Caracas: Ex Libris, 1993.

———. *Rómpase en caso de incendio*. Caracas: Monte Avila, 1975.

Eliot, George. *The Spanish Gypsy*. London: William Blackwood and Sons, 1868.

Gala, Antonio. *Las cítaras colgadas de los árboles*. In *Biblioteca Antonio Gala: Teatro de la historia*, 49–119. Madrid: Espasa-Calpe, 2001. Originally written in 1974.

Gelman, Juan. *Com/posiciones*. Barcelona: Edicions del Mall, 1986.

——. *Dibaxu*. Buenos Aires: Seix Barral, 1994.

Gerchunoff, Alberto. *Los gauchos judíos*. La Plata: J. Sesé, 1910. Translated by Edna Aizenberg as *Parricide on the Pampa? A New Study and Translation of Alberto Gerchunoff's "Los gauchos judíos"* (Frankfurt am Main: Vervuert; Madrid: Iberoamericana, 2000).

Goldstein, Rebecca. *Betraying Spinoza: The Renegade Jew Who Gave Us Modernity*. New York: Schocken Books, 2006.

Grünberg, Carlos M. *Mester de juderia*. Introduction by Jorge Luis Borges. Buenos Aires: Argirópolis, 1940.

Halévy, Fromental. *La Juive: Opéra en cinq actes, paroles de Mr E. Scribe, musique de F. Halévy . . . représenté pour la première fois à Paris, sur le théâtre de l'Académie royale de musique le 23 février 1835*. Paris: Maurice Schlesinger, 1835. Musical score. MS 2000.

Heine, Heinrich. "Der Rabbi von Bacherach." In *Historisch-kritische Gesamtausgabe der Werke, Düsseldorfer Ausgabe*, ed. Manfred Windfuhr. 16 vols. Hamburg: Hoffmann & Campe, 1994. Originally written in 1824–40.

Lytton, Edward Bulwer. See under Bulwer-Lytton above.

Memmi, Albert. *Le désert ou La vie et les aventures de Jubaïr Ouali El-Mammi*. Paris: Gallimard, 1977.

Muñiz-Huberman, Angelina. *El sefardí romántico: La azarosa vida de Mateo Alemán II*. Mexico City: Plaza Janés, 2005.

——. *Tierra adentro*. Mexico, D.F.: Joaquín Mortíz, 1977. Translated by Seymour Menton as *A Mystical Journey* (Santa Fe, NM: Gaon Books, 2011).

Muñoz Molina, Antonio. *Sefarad: Una novela de novelas*. Madrid: Alfaguara, 2001.

Nebot, Didier. *Le chemin de l'exil*. Paris: Presses de la Renaissance, 1992.

Nissán, Rosa. *Hisho que te nazca*. Mexico City: Plaza y Janés, 1996. Translated by Dick Gerdes as *Like a Mother* (Albuquerque: University of New Mexico Press, 2002).

——. *Novia que te vea*. México, D.F.: Planeta, 1992. Translated by Dick Gerdes as *Like a Bride* (Albuquerque: University of New Mexico Press, 2002).

Nossig, Alfred. *Abarbanel: Das Drama eines Volkes*. Berlin: H. Steinitz, 1906.

Obejas, Achy. *Days of Awe*. New York: Ballantine, 2001.

Perera, Victor. *The Cross and the Pear Tree: A Sephardic Journey*. Berkeley: University of California Press, 1996.

Perutz, Leo. *Nachts unter der steinernen Brücke*. 1953. Edited by Hans-Harald Müller. Munich: Knaur, 1994. Translated by Eric Mosbacher as *By Night Under the Stone Bridge* (London: Collins Harvill, 1989).

Philippson, Ludwig. *Jakob Tirado. Geschichtlicher Roman aus der zweiten Hälfte des Sechszehnten Jahrhunderts*. Leipzig: O. Leiner, 1867.

Philippson, Phöbus. "Die Marannen." In *Saron*, ed. Phöbus and Ludwig Philippson. Leipzig: L. Schnaus, 1855. Originally published in 1837.

Reckendorf, Hermann. *Die Geheimnisse der Juden*. 5 vols. Leipzig: Wolfgang Gerhard, 1856.

Rhaïs, Elissa. *L'Andalouse*. Paris: Fayard, 1925.

Roe, Caroline. *Remedy for Treason* and other titles in the Chronicles of Isaac of Girona series. New York: Berkley, 1998–2004.

Rushdie, Salman. *The Moor's Last Sigh*. New York: Pantheon Books, 1995; London: Vintage Books, 1996.

Schornstein, David. "Les Marannos, chronique espagnol." *La Vérité Israélite* 6 (1862).

Scliar, Moacyr. *A estranha nação de Rafael Mendes*. Porto Alegre, Rio Grande do Sul: L & PM Editores, 1983. Translated by Eloah F. Giacomelli as *The Strange Nation of Rafael Mendes* (New York: Harmony Books, 1987).

Scott, Walter. *Ivanhoe: A Romance*. Edinburgh: Archibald Constable, 1820.

Scribe, Eugène. *La Juive: Opéra en cinq actes, paroles de Mr E. Scribe, musique de F. Halévy, divertissemens de M. Taglioni, représenté, pour la première fois, sur le théâtre de l'Académie royale de musique, le 23 février 1835*. 2nd ed. Paris: Jonas and Barba, 1835. Libretto.

Séjour, Victor. *The Jew of Seville (Diégarias)*. Edited by Lynn Weiss; translated by Norman R. Shapiro. Urbana: University of Illinois Press, 2002. Originally performed in 1844.

Yehoshua, A. B. "Behipus ahar hazman hasfaradi ha'avud." In *Hakir vehahar*, 228–41. Tel Aviv: Zmorah Beitan, 1989. Translated by Gilead Morahg as "Finding My Father in Sephardic Time." *Moment* 22.5 (October 1997): 54–57, 85–92.

———. *Hameahev*. Jerusalem: Schocken, 1977. Translated by Philip Simpson as *The Lover* (Garden City, NY: Doubleday, 1978).

———. *Hesed Sefaradi* (Spanish Kindness). Bnei Brak: HaSifriyah Hahadasha, 2011.

———. *Mar Mani. Tel Aviv: Hakibbutz Hameuchad*, 1990. Translated by Hillel Halkin as *Mr. Mani* (New York: Harcourt Brace, 1992).

———. *Mas'a el tom ha-elef*. Tel Aviv: Hakibbutz Hameuchad, 1997. Translated by Nicholas de Lange as *A Journey to the End of the Millennium* (New York: Doubleday, 1999).

———. *Molho*. Tel Aviv: Hakibbutz Hameuchad, 1987. Translated by Hillel Halkin as *Five Seasons* (New York: Doubleday, 1989).

Sephardic Studies, Spanish Jewish History, Sephardism

Aizenberg, Edna. "Una judía muy fermosa: The Jewess as Sex Object in Medieval Spanish Literature and Lore." *La Corónica* 12 (1984): 187–94.

———. "Las peripecias de una metáfora: El sefaradismo literario judeoargentino." *Noaj* 7–8 (December 1992): 54–59.

———. "*Nuevos mundos halló Colón*, or, What's Different About Sephardic Literature in the Americas?" In *Contemporary Sephardic Identity in the Americas: An*

Interdisciplinary Approach, ed. id. and Margalit Bejarano. Syracuse, NY: Syracuse University Press, 2012.

Baer, Yitzhak. *A History of the Jews in Christian Spain*. Philadelphia: Jewish Publications Society, 1961.

Balbuena, Monique Rodrigues. *Homeless Tongues: Poetry and Languages of the Sephardi Diaspora*. Stanford, CA: Stanford University Press, 2012.

Becker-Cantarino, Barbara. "The Rediscovery of Spain in Enlightened and Romantic Germany." *Monatshefte* 72.2 (1980): 121–34.

Beinart, Haim. *The Expulsion of the Jews from Spain*. Oxford: Littman Library of Jewish Civilization, 2002.

Benardete, Maír José. *Hispanic Culture and Character of the Sephardic Jews*. New York: Hispanic Institute, 1953. 2nd ed., revised and expanded by Marc D. Angel. New York: Sepher Hermon, 1982.

Benbassa, Esther, ed. *Mémoires juives d'Espagne et du Portugal*. Paris: Publisud, 1996.

——, ed. *Les Sépharades en* littérature*: Un parcours millénaire*. Paris: Presses de l'Université Paris-Sorbonne, 2005.

Ben-Ur, Aviva. *Sephardic Jews in America: A Diasporic History*. New York: New York University Press, 2009.

Berek, Peter. "The Jew as Renaissance Man." *Renaissance Quarterly* 51.1 (1998): 128–62.

Berg, Nancy E. "Sephardi Writing: From the Margins to the Mainstream." In *The Boom in Contemporary Israeli Literature*, ed. Alan Mintz, 114–42. Hanover, NH: Brandeis University Press, 1997.

Bloch, R. Howard, and Stephen G. Nichols, eds. *Medievalism and the Modernist Temper*. Baltimore: Johns Hopkins University Press, 1996.

Block, David. "Quincentennial Publishing: An Ocean of Print." *Latin American Research Review* 29.3 (1994): 101–28.

Bodian, Miriam. *Dying in the Law of Moses: Crypto-Jewish Martyrdom in the Iberian World*. Bloomington: Indiana University Press, 2007.

Boer, Harm den. "Le 'contre-discours' des nouveaux juifs." In *Les Sépharades en littérature: Un parcours millénaire*, ed. Esther Benbassa, 47–65. Paris: Presses de l'Université Paris-Sorbonne, 2005.

Brann, Ross. "Competing Tropes of Eleventh-Century Andalusi Jewish Culture." In *Sasson Somekh Festschrift*, ed. D. Wasserstein, forthcoming. Originally published as "Entre sefarad et terre d'Israël." In *Les Sépharades en littérature: Un parcours millénaire*, ed. Esther Benbassa, 11–43. Paris: Presses de l'Université Paris-Sorbonne, 2005.

Brann, Ross, and Adam Sutcliffe, eds. *Renewing the Past, Reconfiguring Jewish Culture: From Al-Andalus to the Haskalah*. Philadelphia: University of Pennsylvania Press, 2004.

Cheyette, Bryan, and Laura Marcus, eds. *Modernity, Culture and 'the Jew.'* Stanford, CA: Stanford University Press, 1998.

Cohen, Mark. *Under Crescent and Cross: The Jews in the Middle Ages*. Princeton, NJ: Princeton University Press, 1995.

Cohen, Martin A., and Abraham J. Peck, eds. *Sephardim in the Americas: Studies in Culture and History*. Tuscaloosa: University of Alabama Press, 1993.

Coll-Tellechea, Reyes. "Remembering Sepharad." In *Memory, Oblivion and Jewish Culture in Latin America*, ed. Marjorie Agosín, 3–14. Austin: University of Texas Press, 2005.

Constable, Olivia Remie. *Medieval Iberia: Readings from Christian, Muslim, and Jewish Sources*. Philadelphia: University of Pennsylvania Press, 1997.

Decter, Jonathan. *Iberian Jewish Literature: Between al-Andalus and Christian Europe*. Bloomington: Indiana University Press, 2007.

Díaz-Mas, Paloma. *Sephardim: The Jews from Spain*. Translated by George Zucker. 2nd ed. Chicago: University of Chicago Press, 1992.

Elazar, Daniel. *The Other Jews: The Sephardim Today*. New York: Basic Books, 1989.

Feingold, Ben-Ami. "Historical Dramas on the Inquisition and Expulsion." *Journal of Theater and Drama* 1.22 (1995): 9–30.

Feldman, Yael S. "Identity and Counter-Identity: *Mr. Mani* and the Sephardi Heritage in Israeli Literature." In *The Jewish Communities of Southeastern Europe from the Fifteenth Century to the End of World War II*, ed. I. K. Hassiotis, 115–22. Thessaloníki: Institute for Balkan Studies, 1997.

Garb, Tamar, and Linda Nochlin. *The Jew in the Text: Modernity and the Construction of Identity*. London: Thames & Hudson, 1995.

Gerber, Jane. *The Jews of Spain: A History of the Sephardic Experience*. New York: Free Press, 2005.

Gilman, Sander L. *Jewish Self-Hatred: Anti-Semitism and the Hidden Language of the Jews*. Baltimore: Johns Hopkins University Press, 1986.

———. *Multiculturalism and the Jews*. New York: Routledge, 2006.

Graizbord, David. *Souls in Dispute: Converso Identities in Iberia and the Jewish Diaspora*. Philadelphia: University of Pennsylvania Press, 2003.

Greenfeld, Liah. *Nationalism: Five Roads to Modernity*. Cambridge, MA: Harvard University Press, 1992.

Gubbay, Lucien, and Abraham Levy. *The Sephardim: Their Glorious Tradition from the Bablylonian Exile to the Present Day*. London: Carnell, 1992.

Hallman, Diana R. *Opera, Liberalism, and Antisemitism in Nineteenth-Century France: The Politics of Halévy's "La Juive."* Cambridge: Cambridge University Press, 2002.

Hassán, Iacob M., ed. *Actas del primer simposio de estudios sefardíes*. Madrid: Instituto Arias Montano, 1970.

Hertzberg, Arthur. *The French Enlightenment and the Jews: The Origins of Modern Anti-Semitism*. New York: Columbia University Press, 1968.

Heschel, Susanna. "Jewish Studies as Counterhistory." In *Insider/Outsider: American Jews and Multiculturalism*, ed. Michael Galchinsky, David Biale, and Susannah Heschel, 101–15. Berkeley: University of California Press, 1998.

Kagan, Richard L. *Spain in America: The Origins of Hispanism in the United States*. Urbana: University of Illinois Press, 2002.

Kalmar, Ivan Davidson, and Derek J. Penslar. *Orientalism and the Jews*. Waltham, MA: Brandeis University Press; Hanover, NH: University Press of New England, 2005.

Lambert, Élie. "Alphonse de Castille et la Juive de Tolède." *Bulletin hispanique* 25.4 (1923): 371–94.

Lea, Henry Charles. *A History of the Inquisition of Spain*. 3 vols. New York: Macmillan, 1922.

Lewis, Bernard. *History: Remembered, Recovered, Invented*. New York: Simon & Schuster, 1987.

Liebman, Seymour B. *The Jews in New Spain: Faith, Flame, and the Inquisition*. Coral Gables, FL: University of Miami Press, 1970.

Litvinoff, Barnet. *Fourteen Ninety-Two: The Decline of Medievalism and the Rise of the Modern Age*. New York: Scribner, 1991.

Lowney, Chris. *A Vanished World: Muslims, Christians, and Jews in Medieval Spain*. New York: Free Press, 2005.

Marks, Elaine. *Marrano as Metaphor: The Jewish Presence in French Writing*. New York: Columbia University Press, 1996.

Matza, Diane, ed. *Sephardic-American Voices: Two Hundred Years of a Literary Legacy*. Hanover, NH: Brandeis University Press, 1997.

Menocal, María Rosa. *The Ornament of the World: How Muslims, Jews, and Christians Created a Culture of Tolerance in Medieval Spain*. Boston: Little, Brown, 2002.

Moraña, Mabel. *Ideologies of Hispanism*. Nashville, TN: Vanderbilt University Press, 2005.

Netanyahu, Benzion. *The Origins of the Inquisition in Fifteenth-Century Spain*. New York: Random House, 1995.

Nirenberg, David. "Deviant Politics and Jewish Love: Alfonso VIII and the Jewess of Toledo." *Jewish History* 21 (2007): 15–41.

Peters, Edward. *Inquisition*. Berkeley: University of California Press, 1989.

Pulido Fernández, Ángel. *Españoles sin patria y la raza sefardí*. 1905. Granada: University of Granada facsimile, 1993.

Ragussis, Michael. *Figures of Conversion: "The Jewish Question" and English National Identity*. Durham, NC: Duke University Press, 1995.

Ray, Jonathan. *The Sephardic Frontier: The* Reconquista *and the Jewish Community in Medieval Iberia*. Ithaca, NY: Cornell University Press, 2006.

Rehrmann, Norbert, ed. *El legado de Sefarad*. Salamanca: Amarú, 2003.

———, ed. *Das schwierige Erbe von Sefarad: Juden und Mauren in der spanischen Literatur*. Frankfurt am Main: Vervuert, 2002.

Rodrigue, Aron. *Images of Sephardi and Eastern Jewries in Transition*. Seattle: University of Washington Press, 1993.

———. "Léon Halévy and Modern French Jewish Historiography." In *Jewish History and Jewish Memory: Essays in Honor of Yosef Hayim Yerushalmi*, ed. Elisheva Carlebach, John Efron, and David Myers, 413–27. Hanover, NH: University Press of New England, 1998.

Romero, Elena. "The Theme of Spain in the Sephardic *Haskalah*'s Literature." In *The Jews of Spain and the Expulsion of 1492*, ed. Moshe Lazar and Stephen Halizer, 311–27. Lancaster, CA: Labyrinthos, 1997.

Roth, Cecil. *A History of the Marranos*. New York: Harper & Row, 1966.

Said, Edward. *Orientalism*. New York: Pantheon Books, 1978.

Schapkow, Carsten. *Vorbild und Gegenbild Das iberische Judentumin der deutsch-jüdischen Erinnerungskultur 1779–1939*. Köln: Böhlau verlag, 2011.

Schorsch, Ismar. *From Text to Context: The Turn to History in Modern Judaism*. Hanover, NH: Brandeis University Press, 1994.

Schorsch, Jonathan. "Disappearing Origins: Sephardic Autobiography Today." *Prooftexts* 27.1 (2007): 82–150.

Senkman, Leonardo. "Gerchunoff y la legitimación hispánica." In id., *La identidad judía en la literatura argentina*, 39–57. Buenos Aires: Pardes, 1988.

Shaw, Harry E. *The Forms of Historical Fiction: Sir Walter Scott and His Successors*. Ithaca, NY: Cornell University Press, 1983.

Skolnik, Jonathan. "Dissimilation and the Historical Novel: Herman Sinsheimer's *Maria Nunnez*." *Year Book of the Leo Baeck Institute* 43 (1998): 225–35.

——. "'Who learns history from Heine?' The German-Jewish Historical Novel as Cultural Memory and Minority Culture, 1824–1953." Ph.D. diss., Columbia University, 1999.

Stavans, Ilan. *Imagining Columbus: The Literary Voyage*. New York: Twayne, 1993.

——, ed. *The Scroll and the Cross: 1,000 Years of Jewish-Hispanic Literature*. New York: Routledge, 2003.

Stillman, Norman A., and Yedida K. Stillman, eds. *From Iberia to Diaspora: Studies in Sephardic History and Culture*. Leiden: Brill, 1999.

Trigano, Shmuel. *Le Juif caché: Marranisme et modernité*. Paris: In Press, 2000.

Yerushalmi, Yosef Haim. *Zakhor: Jewish History and Jewish Memory*. Seattle: University of Washington Press, 1982, 1996.

Yovel, Yirmiyahu. *The Other Within: The Marranos, Split Identity and Emerging Modernity*. Princeton, NJ: Princeton University Press, 2009.

——. *Spinoza and Other Heretics: The Marrano of Reason*. Princeton, NJ: Princeton University Press, 1989.

Zohar, Zion, ed. *Sephardic and Mizrahi Jewry: From the Golden Age of Spain to Modern Times*. New York: New York University Press, 2005.

Zucker, George, ed. *Sephardic Identity: Essays on a Vanishing Jewish Culture*. Jefferson, NC: McFarland, 2005.

Index